D0471618

A Fresh Taste of Italy

You may have the universe
if I may have Italy.

Giuseppe Verdi

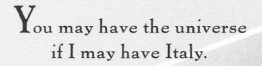

A Fresh Taste of ITALY

250 Authentic Recipes, Undiscovered

Dishes, and New Flavors

for Every Day

MICHELE SCICOLONE

BROADWAY BOOKS

BROADWAY

A FRESH TASTE OF ITALY. Copyright © 1997 by Michele Scicolone. Photographs copyright © 1997 by Ellen Silverman. All rights reserved. Printed in the United States of America. No part of this book may be reproduced or transmitted in any form or by any means, electronic or mechanical, including photocopying, recording, or by any information storage and retrieval system, without written permission from the publisher. For information, address Broadway Books, a division of Bantam Doubleday Dell Publishing Group, Inc., 1540 Broadway, New York, NY 10036.

Broadway Books titles may be purchased for business or promotional use or for special sales. For information, please write to: Special Markets Department, Bantam Doubleday Dell Publishing Group, Inc., 1540 Broadway, New York, NY 10036.

BROADWAY BOOKS and its logo, a letter B bisected on the diagonal, are trademarks of Broadway Books, a division of Bantam Doubleday Dell Publishing Group, Inc.

Library of Congress Cataloging-in-Publication Data

Scicolone, Michele.
A fresh taste of Italy : 250 authentic recipes, undiscovered
dishes, and new flavors for every day / Michele Scicolone. — 1st ed.
p.   cm.
Includes bibliographical references and index.
ISBN 0-553-06729-X
1. Cookery, Italian.   I. Title.
TX723.S366   1997
641.5945—dc20   96-9408
                                                      CIP8

Designed by Richard Oriolo
Photographs by Ellen Silverman

Some of the recipes in this book appeared in different form in *Gourmet*, the *New York Times*, *Food & Wine*, *Eating Well*, and *The Wine Enthusiast*.

97 98 99 00 10 9 8 7 6 5 4 3 2 1

FIRST EDITION

Contents

Acknowledgments

Saluti da Procida

M ANY OF THE PEOPLE *I meet both here and in Italy contribute to my knowledge and shape my thinking about Italian food and cooking. Some of the recipes and information comes from people and places whose names I never knew or may have forgotten though I am grateful to them nonetheless.*

My husband, Charles, is my traveling companion, resident wine expert, historical reference, all-around guide, editor, and, as always, the best taste tester.

My mother, Louise Tumminia, has been my teacher and inspiration as is the memory of my father, Michael Scotto, and other family members who shared their cooking secrets with me.

Thank you to the many friends and colleagues who have patiently answered my questions and aided me in translating Italian cooking to the American table, especially Nicola Marzovilla, Dora Marzovilla; Anna Tasca Lanza; Carlo and Kelle Mastroberardino; Augusto Marchini, Dr. Giorgio Lulli and the staff of the Italian Trade Commission; Alfredo and Luciana Currado, the Furlan Family; Lucio and Franca Landini; Livio and Andrea Felluga, and Pauline and the late Sheldon Wasserman.

A collection of experiences, recipes, and stories is just the beginning of the making of a cookbook. On the practical side, my friend and editor, Harriet Bell, has kept me focused, and I thank her for her commitment and belief in me and all that I have learned from her through the course of the five books and many years that we have worked together. Susan Derecskey has been invaluable for her careful and insightful reading of the manuscript and many helpful suggestions. Special thanks to the incomparable team of photographer Ellen Silverman and stylists Anne Disrude and Betty Alfenito for their understanding of the recipes and the gorgeous photos that are the result. Richard Oriolo captured the warm look of Italy with his elegant design.

My deepest appreciation to everyone at Broadway Books for their enthusiasm, especially Roberto de Vicq de Cumptich for his sensitive art direction and Daisy Alpert who did a fine job of keeping track of everything. Finally, thanks to Judith Weber who is an extraordinary agent and good friend.

A Fresh Taste of Italy

Introduction

⸻

I came from a country where food is the topic of all conversation:
while seated at lunch we seriously discuss what we will have for dinner that
night. Una bella mangiata, il giornale, un espresso, sigarette, una discussione politica,
una bella donna accanto. (A good meal, the newspaper, an espresso, cigarettes, a political
discussion, and a beautiful woman at my side.) This is an old Italian philosophical
saying that still holds after many centuries of change."

Alfredo Viazzi's *Cucina e nostalgia*
(New York: Random House, 1979)

A FAMOUS AUTHOR WAS asked where she likes to go when she travels. She replied, "Italy. I often think, 'While there is Italy, why go anywhere else?' "

I know just what she meant because for the last twenty-five years I, too, have found myself repeatedly drawn to Italy. I love the various regions of Italy, each one different from the others.

I love the Italian people, too. Although they are a disparate lot, descended from the Romans, Greeks, Arabs, French, Spanish, Normans, Germans, and others who came, saw, conquered, and remained in this beautiful land, Italians are proud of their country, its history and traditions. They are unfailingly warm and friendly, even kind and patient with visitors who fracture their melodic and colorful language.

I love Italian architecture and art, from the ruins of ancient Rome to the moving sculptures and paintings of Michelangelo and Leonardo da Vinci. I never tire of hearing the operas of Verdi, Puccini, Rossini, and other Italian composers, especially when performed in the great opera houses of Milan or Naples, or in the outdoor arenas of Verona and Rome.

Most of all, I love Italian food.

My love affair with Italy began in 1970 when my husband and I got married and honeymooned in Italy. Our first stop was Rome. Charles was studying for his doctorate degree in sixth-century Byzantine-Sicilian relations and wanted to visit every church, library, ruin, museum, and monument. While I, too, found them fascinating, my attention span was shorter. I would wander off to check out the menu posted in the window of a promising-looking trattoria or browse in the market stalls and food shops, photographing the mushrooms and gazing longingly at the fresh seafood recently plucked from the Mediterranean.

Somehow Charles and I managed to compromise. It was not long before he was skipping some of the historic landmarks to help me seek out authentic restaurants serving home-style food, the best bakeries, the renowned winemakers, and off-the-beaten-track cheese factories. He developed a particular interest in Italian wines and has since become an expert in the different varieties, styles, and vintages. This, of course, complemented my interest in food, and together, we set out to expand further our gastronomic research. We spent the time between our vacations learning to speak Italian, planning our next trips, and cooking and sharing great Italian meals accompanied by the finest Italian wines we could afford. Our friends and families thought our passion for Italy and all things Italian would eventually pass, or at least fade, but it never has. We try to visit Italy at least twice a year, and with each of our visits, we find out something new and fascinating about Italy's people, their food, wine, history, and culture.

Much of our time in Italy is spent searching out the best of contemporary Italian food. Armed with guidebooks, maps, and friends' recommendations, Charles and I travel from the North to the South, from the Adriatic to the Mediterranean seeking out restaurants known for their special pasta or excellent seafood. I talk to cooks and winemakers wherever we go to learn about old and new dishes that I have never heard of or eaten before. The more I discover, I realize the more there is to learn about Italian food and wine, so ours is happily an endless search.

With this book I have reproduced as closely as possible the fresh tastes and simple flavors of contemporary Italian food from all over Italy. Some recipes, such as Grandmother's Pot Roast with Pasta and Onion Sauce, are personal family favorites that originated in the region around Naples where my grandparents were born. Others are classics I have eaten in my travels, such as the Crispy Pasta with Chick Peas from Puglia in southeastern Italy, or The Soup of the Grain Threshing from Piedmont in the northwest.

Since cooking styles and tastes are constantly changing and evolving, I have also included some exciting "new" recipes that typify Italian cooking today. Smoked Salmon with Oranges and Fennel features a non-Mediterranean fish from northern Europe teamed with traditional Italian ingredients oranges and fennel.

When I first began work on this book, my plan was to organize the recipes by the regions where they originated. Although Italy became a unified nation in 1860, up until World War II and immediately after, its twenty or so regions were only loosely connected. Italian was the official language, but most people still spoke local dialects and could not even read Italian. Transportation was poor and products from the North did not reach the South, and vice versa. Cultural differences were vast, given the legacy of countless foreign invaders who settled in different parts of the country. In addition, there was a huge disparity between the economic and living conditions of the wealthy, industrial North and the poor, agricultural South. Not surprisingly, culinary traditions, based on local ingredients, varied from region to region as people managed to make do with what they had.

Today, the homogenizing effects of televisions, airplanes, supermarkets, and a national education system have unified Italy somewhat. Spaghetti with tomato sauce, once considered a foreign food in the North, is now eaten by all Italians, while southerners dine on veal milanese and fettuccine bolognese. People everywhere have added salmon, hamburgers, and even breakfast cereal to their diet, but fortunately, for the sake of diversity, regional differences persist and continue to thrive in Italy, particularly food and wine.

Despite this, I have concluded that it is impossible to duplicate Italian regional cooking styles outside of Italy. Even with an abundance of some ingredients similar to what is available to Italian cooks, we Americans definitely do not have a good or steady supply of others.

Visit an outdoor Italian fish market, and you will find the odd-looking, grayish white *canocchie,* a type of prawn; six to eight varieties of *vongole,* or clams; and *totani,* a kind of large squid, none of which, though common throughout Italy, can be found in the United States. Grown in volcanic soil under the blazing sun of southern Italy, Neapolitan tomatoes are incomparable. Only the best farm-fresh, vine-ripened tomatoes can even begin to approach the Neapolitan version. While an American friend of mine living in Naples complained that she could not find long, white potatoes for baking in Italy, I was marveling at how flavorful the ordinary boiled potatoes were that we were eating.

White truffles are native to Piedmont and are essential to authentic Piedmontese cooking, but their price here is prohibitive. Besides, since they do not sell well, they are often too old, dried out, and faded in flavor. If you can find them at all, chances are they are not worth the exorbitant price you're asked to pay.

Meats, cheeses, game, beans, and grains, all staples of the Italian diet, are not the same as comparable foods found here. Animals are bred, fed, raised, and butchered differently. While some things are better in Italy, other foods, such as meat, are not.

Even a basic food product like dried pasta is different. According to United States law, all pasta sold here must be made with enriched flour. It is just the opposite in Italy; nothing may be added to the flour. Some Italian pasta manufacturers, believing that Americans prefer more tender pasta, use a softer type of wheat flour for exported pasta. While the flavor difference may not be immediately noticeable, the point is that pasta made to be sold abroad is not the same as in Italy. By law they cannot even be made in the same factories.

Fortunately, there are enough reliable ingredients widely available to give Italian cooking in America a satisfyingly authentic accent. Without too much trouble, most of us can find canned Italian tomatoes; imported cheeses such as Parmigiano-Reggiano, pecorino romano, gorgonzola, and fontina; silky prosciutto from Parma; Italian medium-grain rice; extra virgin olive oil; imported olives, and Italian espresso coffee, to name just a few.

Rather than be disappointed at what I can't find on this side of the Atlantic, I prefer to think of America as a separate culinary region of Italy. Since Italian food has been and continues to be America's favorite and with so many Italians who emigrated here cooking their families' traditional dishes, this isn't so far-fetched. Even the name America is an Italian one!

Just as when I'm in Italy, I look for markets and shops in my area that make fresh, Italian-style ingredients such as sweet, creamy ricotta and fresh mozzarella. I also seek out good local bakeries where I can find Italian-style breads and breadsticks.

I develop recipes that adapt well to the best of both the native and imported products available here. If I can't find fresh porcini mushrooms, I substitute another meaty, flavorful variety like shiitake or portobello, or I combine dried porcini with bland white mushrooms to approximate the texture and flavor of the fresh. When the ripe tomato season has passed, I put away my fresh tomato recipes until summer comes again and use canned Italian tomatoes for sauces and soups. Just as a Sicilian cook would cook pasta with fennel and sardines instead of Piedmontese tagliatelle with white truffles, I avoid recipes that do not work well with ingredients I find here.

Many of the recipes in this book can be prepared in true Italian style with a minimum amount of time, ingredients, and equipment and still result in maximum flavor. There are recipes for every day—from quick meals to prepare after work to more elaborate dishes for special occasions or when time is not a problem.

My preference is for the uncomplicated food typical of good Italian home cooking. Since Italian cooks demand only the finest and freshest ingredients, not much needs to be done to coax out their best flavor. No more spices and seasonings are added than are necessary to enhance natural flavors. Typical cooking techniques are simple and straightforward. Sauces and dressings are used sparingly so as to balance other flavors and not overwhelm them.

I have tried to make the recipes as foolproof as possible by keeping the instructions clear and methodical. Each recipe has been tested several times. Despite this, it is impossible to factor in all of the variables, and a certain amount of personal judgment is called for. Do not hesitate to make adjustments for your equipment, ingredients, circumstances, and personal tastes.

Many Italian cookbooks published in this country give the impression that an Italian meal is a complicated, multicourse affair, but this is an outdated notion. Formal meals, especially in restaurants in Italy, are served in separate courses, but more often than not those are special occasions, not everyday events. Today many Italian women have full-time jobs and little help at home. Like most of us, they have less time for cooking than they used to. And even as much as Italians enjoy the pleasures of eating and drinking, health and dietary concerns have made overindulging very unpopular. After all, how can one present *la bella figura,* a good appearance, if one is out of shape?

At home and in casual restaurant situations, menus are flexible. Italians eat moderately but well. They might have just one dish, such as a pasta, soup, or even a plate of vegetables with bread, as their entire meal. Though I have arranged the recipes in this book in typical menu courses for the sake of convenience, there is no reason not to serve an antipasto as a main course, or a vegetable as an antipasto, or just a bowl of soup for dinner.

Though most of these recipes will be new to American cooks, there are some handy, staple recipes such as Quick Tomato Sauce, Fresh Egg Pasta, and Meat Broth that are an essential part of good Italian cooking and that no Italian cookbook would be complete without.

I have compiled the recipes for this book in several ways. Some are derived from my mother's cooking, recipes she learned from her mother and my father's mother, who both came to this country as adults in the early 1910s. When I travel, it always pleases me to note how similar these family favorites are to the way they are still prepared in Italy. Whenever possible, I just ask the good Italian cooks I meet how they have prepared their food. Since Italians like to talk about food as much as they like to eat it, I can often get a pretty good idea, even if it is a little sketchy, of how it was prepared. Sometimes, in a busy restaurant for example, there is no one to ask, so I simply work backward once I am in my home kitchen, relying on my taste memory and knowledge of Italian food to duplicate the flavors. Friends and family are my loyal and patient critics—and sometimes even recipe testers—as are my cooking school students who bring me their recipes and share family memories, favorite restaurants, and travel experiences.

My many years working as a test kitchen cook for various food magazines have proven invaluable in enabling me to piece together a recipe. And my collection of Italian cookbooks comes in handy for reference and fact checking, especially with regard to traditional dishes.

I have stacks of notebooks with handwritten comments and rough sketches of dishes eaten and wines tasted on all of my Italian trips. I also save menus from restaurants that are kind enough to give them to me. While others collect photographs of churches and monuments, I keep albums of snapshots of antipasto tables and dessert carts, fruits and vegetables growing in the fields, fish markets and fishermen, bakers and bread, cheesemakers, and winemakers to help me remember my favorite food adventures.

These are my impressions of food in Italy today, gathered over more than twenty-five years of traveling and eating around the country. Despite the pressures and influences of modern times, Italians maintain a passionate interest in eating well. Surprisingly, they have succeeded in maintaining many old traditions, even while adapting them to today's tastes. Italian food continues to be what it always has been: delicious, healthful, and appealing.

Fairs and Feasts

SAGRAS E FESTAS

Every season in Italy brings special holidays that are celebrated with fairs *(sagras)*, feasts *(festas)*, processions, music, and dancing. Some are small local events while others are celebrated throughout the entire country. They may commemorate the harvest, the changing of the seasons, a major holiday, or a minor holy day. Some make perfect sense while others may seem quite odd. One of the strangest festivals I have encountered is the *Sagra del Urlo,* held in Monforte d'Alba in Piedmont. It is basically a contest to see who can shout the loudest. No matter what their theme, these events offer an authentic taste of Italy today, something like a country fair. If you decide to visit any of these festivals, check with the local tourist authorities for the exact dates, since they are subject to change.

Winter

Feast of the Star A large star lights up a *presepio,* or crèche, that is placed on a cart and carried in procession through the streets of Sabbio Chiesa near Brescia in Lombardy. Everyone carries gifts of food for the Three Kings, mostly cheese, wine, and salami, which are consumed at a great dinner that follows.

Epiphany There are many feasts and special foods for the Epiphany. In the Veneto, everyone eats *la pinza de la Marantega,* a sweet bread made with cornmeal, white wheat flour, dried figs, anise seeds, and candied fruits.

The town of Andreis near Pordenone in Friuli-Venezia-Giulia celebrates with a sagra of bread and wine. Everyone drinks the local wine and eats a special fig and raisin bread baked in a wood-burning oven.

Sagra delle Luganighe At Cannobio near Novara in Piedmont, January brings the feast of the *luganiga,* a type of sausage, celebrated with heaps of boiled sausages, potatoes, and sauerkraut.

Festa di San Antonio At Volongo near Cremona in Lombardy, young people collect wood to build a pyre sixty feet high to burn an old witch made of straw who represents winter. Everyone eats *torta dura,* or hard cake, made with cornmeal and spices.

Spring

Feast of the Cherry Trees in Flower Held in Vignola near Modena in Emilia-Romagna in early April.

Sagra dei Garagoi At Marotta near Pesaro in The Marches, you will find this sagra dedicated to the *garagoi,* or sea snails. They are cooked in tomato sauce with lots of pepper. The locals say the best way to eat them is to take a sip of wine for every seven snails. Naturally, only the local wines such as Bianchello and Verdicchio from the *Colli Pesaresi* will do.

Sagra del Gnocco More than fourteen hundred pounds of potatoes are cooked for this feast at Teolo near Padua, and everyone eats potato gnocchi.

Sagra della Piè Fritta This fair honoring a small fried flatbread is held at Fontanelice near Bologna.

Sagra dello Stoccafisso The stockfish fair is held at Melazzo near Alessandria in Piedmont. Five chefs cook huge quantities of the dried fish with tomato sauce, olives, anchovies, tuna, and garlic. The day's events include a stockfish hurling contest.

Sagra del Biscotto This fair is held at Bomarzo near Viterbo in Latium. Ring-shaped cookies flavored with anise seed are dedicated to Saint Anselm, the patron saint of Bomarzo.

Sagra delle Uova Sode To celebrate Easter, a hard-cooked egg–eating contest is the highlight of this feast held at Tredozio near Forli in Emilia-Romagna.

Sagra del Carciofo Held at Ladispoli near Rome, this sagra features a mountain of *mammola* artichokes, the round, spineless variety for which the region is renowned. The piazza is surrounded by stands offering them cooked in different ways. At night there is a fireworks display.

Sagra del Pesce Held at Camogli near Genoa, in honor of the feast of San Fortunato, the patron saint of fishermen. The townspeople fry up fresh fish in an enormous pan and distribute it to all.

Summer

Festa del Lambrusco Held in July at Albinea in Emilia-Romagna. Fizzy, red wine is sampled with *gnocco fritto,* or fried puffs of pasta dough, accompanied by prosciutto and salami and *erbazzone,* a savory tart stuffed with greens, eggs, and Parmigiano-Reggiano.

Festa di Noiantri Held in Rome along the banks of the Tiber. *Noiantri* means "we others," which is the way the residents of the bohemian Trastevere neighborhood think of themselves, as a breed apart. Booths offer tastes of bruschetta and sell local crafts and foodstuffs.

Campionato Nazionale dei Mangiatori d'Anguria **National watermelon eating championship** Held at Sissa near Parma.

Sagra delle Melanzane Ripiene Held in Montanesi near Genoa for the feast of Saint Rocco. Wine and cheese accompany the stuffed eggplant.

Sagra del Pecorino At San Godenzo near Florence, fresh and aged sheep's milk cheese is tasted in the town square.

Sagra dell 'Anguilla Orbetello in Tuscany celebrates with eels either fried, marinated, or stuffed.

Autumn

The harvest season brings a wealth of gastronomic festivals throughout Italy. You could probably find one for every day of the month of September. The Festa of the Duck is held at Desenzano on Lake Garda, of the Wild Boar at Capalbio in Tuscany, of the Octopus at Portovenere in Tuscany, of the Mushrooms at Budoia in Friuli-Venezia-Giulia and Lucca in Tuscany. Among the many grape festivals, the most famous is probably that of Marino in the Castelli Romani in Latium where a huge fountain spouts white wine instead of water.

La Vendemmia del Nonno Held each year at Castagnole Monferrato near Asti in Piedmont, with the harvesting and stomping of the grapes in the old manner. Afterward there is a big dinner featuring polenta with anchovy sauce.

Sagra della Nocciola Held in Castellero in Piedmont. The highlight is a footrace through the hazelnuts. Homemade tortes, cakes, and sweets are handed out and prizes given for the best nuts.

Sagra delle Lepre Held at Selvatelle near Pisa. Cooks prepare potted hare, roasted hare, and pappardelle with hare sauce. For those who don't like hare, there are grilled steaks and roast pork.

Sagra degli Stacchioddi Held at Latiano in Puglia, this fair celebrates a type of homemade pasta that is shaped into little curved disks and served with a tomato sauce and sour ricotta cheese.

Regional Tastes
of Italy

A FEW YEARS AGO I *visited a restaurant and hotel training school in Salsomaggiore Terme near Parma. Our little group of food writers was assigned a student guide, a very poised young lady who took us through the classrooms and explained what was being taught. I was most impressed with our guide until we entered a kitchen classroom where several student chefs were flipping hamburgers on a grill. When we asked about it, she exclaimed, "At last! Fast food is coming to Italy!"*

My heart sank. Later, I told a friend, Dr. Mario Zannoni of the Consorzio di Parmigiano-Reggiano, how dismayed I was by the incident. But he was not concerned. He pointed out that it was only natural for a young person to be curious about something as beloved by teenagers everywhere as fast food. "Don't worry," he replied. "She will soon tire of the novelty. She is just experimenting and will return to our traditions when she is a little more mature."

I felt much better hearing that, and I think he was right. Though hamburger restaurants have managed to make their way into Italian cities and kids love them, though Italian women no longer have time to spend in the kitchen preparing multi-course meals, though young and old alike have become more health and weight conscious, Italian regional cooking is alive and well. You may have to search for it, but that, for me, is one of the joys of traveling in Italy.

On the pages that follow, you will find many recipes for some of the local specialties to be found in each region of Italy. These are just a sampling of the possibilities, however, so I have included lists organized by region of some of the other specialties that either do not translate well to our ingredients here or that I did not have the room to include in this book. Maybe the next one!

There are twenty regions in Italy (think of them if you will as states in this country), though I have paired some because they are so similar. These suggestions are based on my experiences and are by no means comprehensive. Foods and flavors can change drastically from one region to the next, and even one village to the next.

Abruzzi and Molise

Abruzzi and Molise, two regions in central Italy, share a common history and at several times in the past were considered as one region. Both regions are somewhat remote, and travel is difficult because of high mountains and poor roads. Few tourists go there except to visit the beautiful and rugged National Park of the Abruzzi.

Lamb and pasta are eaten everywhere, often seasoned with the fiery little red chili called *diavolillo,* or little devil. The town of Fara di San Martino is renowned for its manufactured pasta. Italians regard cooks from Abruzzi with the highest regard.

- *Maccheroni alla Chitarra* Square strands of homemade spaghetti cut on a wood-framed instrument strung with metal wires, called a guitar. The pasta is often sauced with a spicy lamb, tomato, and chili sauce, such as the one on page 110.

- *Torrone* Soft nougat candy studded with almonds or hazelnuts and sometimes flavored with chocolate.

- *Le Virtu* A thick soup made in spring with the first fresh vegetables of the season and the last of the stored winter staples. According to tradition, the soup is named for seven beautiful virgins who first prepared it. Each contributed ingredients, so seven kinds of legumes, seven pastas, seven types of greens, seven root vegetables, and, in the richer variations, seven kinds of meat are used. Naturally, the cooking time is seven hours.

- *'Ndocca 'Ndocca* A stew made with ribs, feet, ears, skin, and other less desirable parts of the pig flavored with rosemary and chilies.

- *Centerbe* A sweet liqueur flavored with many herbs.

- *Parozzo* A rustic almond and chocolate cake with a chocolate frosting.

- Wines White: Trebbiano d'Abruzzo. Red: Montepulciano d'Abruzzo.

Basilicata and Calabria

Basilicata was once considered so remote and inhospitable that during the Fascist regime of Mussolini, political undesirables were sent there in exile. Carlo Levi wrote an extraordinary book about this era called *Christ Stopped at Eboli.* Today things are considerably better, especially along the beautiful coastline, which attracts tourists from all over.

Calabria, the "toe" of the Italian boot, is just south of Basilicata and shares the same stretch of coast. Calabria has the added feature of the Silento, a large area of lovely rolling hills covered with trees, called the great wood. The beaches on the "sole" of the boot, along the Tyrrhenian Sea, are particularly fashionable.

The two regions have many similarities as far as food is concerned, relying primarily on vegetables, pasta, lamb, and pork.

- *Millecosedde* A local type of minestrone, made with several kinds of beans, cabbage, onion, celery, and other vegetables in season.

- *Sagne chine* The name is dialect for full lasagne, layers of fresh pasta with meatballs, hard-cooked eggs, and cheese. In springtime a sauce of artichokes and fresh peas is used.

- *Panzerotti* Little baked or fried dessert turnovers filled with a puree of chick peas, chocolate, and cinnamon.

- *Mostaccioli* Spiced cakes shaped like men, lambs, hearts, fish, and so on.

- Wines Red: Aglianico del Vulture.

Campania

South of Latium, Campania faces the Mediterranean Sea. The region's capital is Naples, a beautiful city dominated by Vesuvius, an active volcano. The rich volcanic soil and hot, sunny weather produce some of the finest vegetables, especially tomatoes, in all of Italy. Campania is the heartland of dried pasta. In Naples and all along the coast, seafood, pasta, and vegetables are eaten.

Though the Sorrento peninsula and the islands of Capri and Ischia are swamped with tourists, they are still devastatingly beautiful wherever they have not been overdeveloped. Pompeii and the quieter Herculaneum offer a fascinating peek at life in ancient Rome.

Inland, Campania is mountainous and the climate colder. Naturally, the cooking is hearty. The local prosciutto is particularly tasty.

- **Pizza** Naples is the birthplace of the modern pizza and it is truly an exquisite dish when eaten there. People eat pizza all day long, and with only a few exceptions, even the finest restaurants serve it. Forget designer pizza, the Neapolitans like their pizza toppings simple—often just crushed tomatoes, creamy mozzarella, and basil—on a crisp, chewy crust that is neither too thin nor too thick.

- **Mozzarella** I once watched a Neapolitan gentleman methodically eat an entire mozzarella the size of a large grapefruit, in between an antipasto, a bowl of pasta, a roasted fish, and a salad. But the mozzarella in this region is so good—so creamy, juicy, and tender—it is practically irresistible. Though most is made from cow's milk, the finest mozzarella of the region is made from the milk of rare water buffaloes.

- *Sfogliatelle* Crackling crisp layers of thin pastry stuffed with sweetened ricotta cheese flavored with spices and candied fruits. These clam-shell–shape pastries are best when they are eaten still warm.

- *La Pastiera* A traditional Easter cake made with ricotta, wheatberries, orange, citron, and cinnamon in a tender pastry crust.

- **Wines** Whites: Fiano di Avellino, Greco di Tufo, Lacryma Christi del Vesuvio (both white and red). Red: Taurasi.

Emilia-Romagna

Emilia-Romagna follows the Po River practically spanning north central Italy from west to east. Because the soil is so rich and fertile, the plains are densely cultivated, and there is plenty of land for raising dairy cows. The cooking of Emilia to the west is extremely rich with meat, butter, cream, and cheese, especially Parmigiano-Reggiano. Pasta making in this region is an art form, and there is a vast variety of egg-rich fresh pastas, both flat and stuffed with meat, cheese, and vegetables.

The fare is somewhat lighter in Romagna to the east, especially along the Adriatic Coast where rice, vegetables, and seafood take on greater importance.

- **Prosciutto di Parma** Tender, buttery, salt-cured hams. Exquisite flavor, especially when eaten as the locals do, with fresh bread and sweet butter.

- **Tagliatelle** In 1972 a law was passed to resolve centuries of disagreement over the correct width of these flat strips of fresh egg pasta first created, according to legend, in honor of Lucrezia Borgia's golden tresses. A legal tagliatella must be between 6.5 and 7 millimeters so that it can swell to 8 millimeters when it cooks. Tagliatelle are classically served with a rich, slow-cooked meat sauce; the dish is described as *alla bolognese.*

- **Tortellini, anolini, cappelletti** Plump pasta rings or disks filled with meat or cheese. Lovely served in broth, though rather heavy in a butter, meat, or cream sauce.

- *Squaquarone* A very soft, fresh cheese, something like sour cream. Delicious as the filling for an omelet.

- *Torta di taglierini* A pastry shell filled with orange-flavored custard and topped with crunchy golden strips of sugared fresh pasta and almonds.

- **Wines** White: Albana di Romagna. Reds: Lambrusco, Sangiovese di Romagna.

Friuli-Venezia-Giulia

The easternmost region of Italy, much of Friuli-Venezia-Giulia was, until after World War II, a part of Yugoslavia. The Slavic influence remains strong, and both the German and Slav languages are commonly spoken, as well as Italian.

I find the people here are especially warm and friendly, and there is much to see and do. The old Roman town of Aquilea has stunning fourth-century mosaics, a must for archeology buffs. Grado is a busy beach resort built on a little island. To the northwest, the mountainous Carnia region looks as if it has been untouched for centuries. The best strawberry ice cream I have ever eaten was in Udine. Sophisticated Trieste, to the southeast, is Italy's second largest port and home of Italy's best coffee producer, Illycaffè.

- **Prosciutto di San Daniele** Raw ham cured on the bone with the hoof still attached. San Daniele prosciutto is sweeter than other kinds and has a more delicate flavor.

- *Gubana* A large spiral-shaped yeast cake stuffed with fruits, nuts, cocoa, and spices.

- *La Jota* Cabbage and pork soup thickened with cornmeal.

- *Stinco di maiale* Tender roasted pork shanks.

- **Grappa** A type of brandy made all over northern Italy. The Nonino family distillery is famous for its highly sophisticated single vineyard grappas and fruit liqueurs.

- *Strucolo* Flaky dessert strudel stuffed with ricotta cheese, apples, or other fruits.

- *Montasio* A semi-firm cow's milk cheese used to make *frico,* the crispy wafers on page 52, but also wonderful for eating straight.

- **Wines** Whites: Sauvignon Blanc, Pinot Grigio, Tocai. Reds: Cabernet Sauvignon, Merlot. Dessert: Picolit.

Latium

I could happily live as a vegetarian, if I lived in Latium. During the spring I would eat lots of *puntarelle,* shoots of tender young chicory, which Romans devour by the bowlful as a spring tonic. Then there are the famous Roman artichokes, either deep-fried until crisp on the outside and creamy on the inside or more simply cooked with mint and olive oil. I would begin every meal with fava beans sautéed with *guanciale,* or cured pork cheek, or perhaps I would just have a light supper of raw baby fava beans with pecorino and good local bread. Somewhere in between I would eat the pale green, pointed Roman *broccolo,* a cross between broccoli and cauliflower; *rughetta,* crisp wild arugula; and stuffed squash flowers.

All of this bounty of flavorful vegetables plus fruits comes from *la campagna Romana,* the countryside just outside of Rome, which is dotted with little farms. Like much of Latium, the soil is very fertile, a legacy of the many long-dormant volcanoes that dot the area.

South of Rome are the Castelli Romani, sleepy little hill towns where city dwellers flock for a breath of country air during the summer months. There are lots of *osterie,* inexpensive restaurants where everybody eats *porchetta,* roast pork flavored with garlic and herbs on crisp rolls, and drinks cool, white Frascati wine by the pitcherful.

In Rome itself, the traditional dishes include milk-fed baby lamb prepared in several different ways and many dishes made with organ meats. The food of Rome's Jewish quarter, such as fried salt cod and pasta with chick peas, is particularly interesting.

- *Puntarelle* A springtime salad of young shoots of chicory that look like curled pale green ribbons, served with a zesty anchovy, vinegar, and garlic dressing.

- **Stuffed zucchini flowers** Melted mozzarella and anchovy oozes from zucchini or other squash blossoms fried in a delicate golden crust.

- *Maccheroni alla gricia* Thick strands of dried pasta with *guanciale,* or cured pork cheek, pecorino romano, and lots of black pepper.

- *Carciofi alla giudia* Jewish-style artichokes flattened and fried until crisp in olive oil.

- *Fave al guanciale* Fresh fava beans cooked with guanciale, onions, and white wine.

- *Scamorza alla griglia* Thick slabs of chewy scamorza, a drier form of mozzarella, are grilled until golden on both sides.

- **Wines** Whites: Frascati, Est! Est!! Est!!! Red: Colle Picchioni.

Liguria

Crescent-shaped Liguria is a thin sliver of a region bordered on the north by Piedmont and on the west by France curving along the Mediterranean Sea to the south. A ridge of high mountains protects Liguria from harsh weather, and temperatures are mild all winter long. Land is scarce so vineyards and farms are terraced into the rocky mountainsides that face the sea. Some farmers' plots are so remote that they can be reached only by small boats. Herbs, grapes, olives, and vegetables thrive on the sunny slopes.

Liguria is known for its fresh fish, vegetables, and unusual pastas. Without much grazing land, meat and cheese are rare. Since the region has at one time or another been a part of France, the cooking shares many similarities. *Socca,* the chick pea flour crepe of Nice, is called *farinata* in Genoa, Liguria's main city, while the Genoese *pissadella,* an onion, anchovy, and tomato pizza, is very similar to the Provençal *pissaladière.*

- *Corzetti* Handmade pasta disks, stamped with a star or other design on both sides to resemble coins. Corzetti may be made with chestnut, whole wheat, or white flour and can be dressed with a mushroom or a meat sauce.

- *Trofie* Little pasta twists, often served with pesto.

- **Pesto** True Ligurian pesto is delicate, creamy, and bright green, quite different from the clumsy, overwhelming sauces spread on everything from pizza to chicken salad in the United States. Always prepared fresh, Ligurian pesto is made with the local basil, said to be at its best when the herb is in flower, plus pine nuts, garlic, and a combination of pecorino and parmesan cheeses with

Ligurian olive oil. A dollop of pesto is added to the minestrone and the thin pasta strands called *trenette,* which are served with string beans and potatoes to lighten the intensity of the pasta and sauce.

- *Cima alla Genovese* A boneless breast of veal stuffed with ground meats, parmesan, eggs, and peas, served cold and thinly sliced.

- *Torta Pasqualina* A savory cake made from thirty-three layers of pastry, ricotta, eggs, swiss chard, artichokes, and other vegetables, traditionally served at Easter time. The thirty-three layers represent the years Christ lived.

- Wines White: Cinqueterre.

Lombardy

Sandwiched between Piedmont, Switzerland, the Veneto, and Emilia-Romagna, Lombardy is one of Italy's largest regions. It is also one of the wealthiest, with prosperity coming from major industries such as automobile manufacturing. To the north, the beautiful lake district attracts visitors from all over Italy and the rest of Europe. All or part of Lakes Como, Maggiore, Lugano, Iseo, and Garda are within Lombardy's borders. Milan vies with Rome in importance. It is Italy's fashion, design, and business center.

The cooking of Lombardy is rich with butter and cream. Some of Italy's finest cheeses are produced here as well. Risotto and polenta are more common than pasta, though around Mantua, on the Emilia-Romagna side of the region, the situation is reversed and pasta becomes more prominent.

- Gorgonzola A blue-veined cheese, gorgonzola can be *dolce*—soft, young, and creamy—or *piccante*—firmer, aged, and sharp. You can cook with gorgonzola, or eat it plain. Either way it is excellent.

- Mascarpone A soft, unaged dessert cheese halfway between sour cream and cream cheese. An essential ingredient for *tiramisù.*

- Taleggio A soft, ripe cheese with a full, buttery flavor.

- *Rosette* or *michette* Hard rolls that are all crunchy crust surrounding a pocket of air.

- *Pizzocheri* Buckwheat pasta tossed with cabbage, potatoes, garlic, and cheese.

- *Bresaola* Air-dried beef thinly sliced and served as an antipasto.

- *Tortelli di zucca* Mantua-style ravioli filled with winter squash and crushed amaretti.

- **Osso Buco** Thick slices of veal shank cooked with wine and vegetables. The name means bone with a hole.

- *Risotto milanese* Saffron-flavored risotto made with marrow. It is traditionally served with osso buco.

- **Panettone** It would not be Christmas in Milan, and many other parts of Italy, without this mushroom-shape, sweetened yeast bread studded with raisins and candied fruits.

- **Amaretti** Crisp cookies made with both sweet and bitter almonds for dunking in wine.

- **Wines** White: Franciacorta. Red: Valtellina.

The Marches

Le Marche, meaning the Marches, takes its name from the German word for boundary lines. During the tenth century, the region was divided into three zones, each called a *marca* and ruled by a marquis.

Located on the east coast of central Italy, The Marches is bounded by Umbria to the west, Tuscany to the north, the Abruzzi to the south, and the Adriatic Sea to the east. A large part of the region is mountainous but its long coastline is very popular with vacationers.

A friend from Ascoli Piceno, one of the region's chief cities, told me that Italians jokingly say "Better the tax collector at your door than a Marchigiano under your roof." The Marchigiani have a reputation for being voracious eaters and the kind of guests who never go home.

- *Olive all'ascolana* Jumbo green olives pitted and stuffed with ground meat and seasonings then deep-fried in a golden bread crumb crust.

- *Vincisgrassi* Lasagna noodles layered with meat, cheese, truffles, and béchamel sauce.

- *Fiadone* An Easter torte made with eggs, ricotta, cinnamon, and lemon zest baked in a pastry crust.

- *Brodetto* Fish stew flavored with saffron, garlic, and tomatoes.

- **Wines** White: Verdicchio.

Piedmont

Some of the finest and most sophisticated cooking in Italy can be found in the north-western Piedmont region. Bordered by France, Lombardy, Liguria, and the Valle D'Aosta, Piedmont is completely landlocked but does not lack for fine ingredients, or for that matter, fine cooks. Many of Italy's greatest wines come from Piedmont, and tourists travel from all over the world to visit the wineries and sample the local cooking in the area's many fine restaurants.

Fall and winter are white truffle season, and the whole area is fragrant with its incredible perfume. White truffles are never cooked, merely sliced thin and shaved over foods like pasta, risotto, and eggs, whose warmth accentuates their flavor.

- *Bagna Cauda* Literally a "hot bath" of anchovies, garlic, and oil in which to dip strips of raw vegetables like peppers, fennel, and celery. Eating bagna cauda is a cold weather ritual especially with young red barbera wine.

- *Tajarin* A dialect name for tagliatelle, these are rich in eggs and usually served with a meat sauce.

- *Insalata di carne cruda* Raw chopped veal dressed with lemon juice and olive oil and topped with shaved truffles.

- *Fonduta* Like a cheese fondue made with fontina cheese, served over risotto or toast.

- *Finanziera* A stew of sweetbreads, mushrooms, peas, chicken livers, and other ingredients in a rich sauce. It is named for the coat worn by bankers and financiers in Turin who apparently doted on this dish.

- *Brasato al barolo* Beef pot roast marinated in red wine and vegetables and cooked until tender. Served with polenta.

- *Panna cotta* Literally "cooked cream," this cloudlike confection of barely gelled cream is usually served with a caramel, chocolate, or fruit sauce.

- **Wines** Whites: Arneis, Gavi. Reds: Dolcetto, Barbera, Barbaresco, Barolo. Desserts: Moscato d'Asti, Asti Spumante.

Puglia

Puglia at the heel of the Italian boot has a long coast lined with sandy beaches on the Adriatic Sea and the Gulf of Taranto. Inland, the soil is fertile, and endless groves of olive trees and many kinds of fruits and vegetables thrive in the hot, sunny climate.

The landscape around the town of Alberobello is dotted with *trulli,* cylindrical stone houses with conical roofs. According to one legend, the trulli, which can easily be disassembled, were designed centuries ago to avoid the heavy taxes imposed on more permanently constructed houses by a feudal dictator.

- *Ceccamariti* Literally "blind husbands," leftover bread cubes and vegetables simmered together to form a thick, tasty soup. Supposedly, a housewife would make ceccamariti, which only *seems* complicated and time consuming, to fool her spouse into believing she had been working hard all day.

- *Fave e cicoria* A thick puree of dried fava beans topped with boiled chicory cooked in olive oil.

- *Carteddate* Fried pastry spirals filled with dried fruits and nuts and drenched in honey. A typical Christmas sweet.

- *Ricci di mare* Sea urchins, freshly plucked from the sea. The spiny shells are opened carefully and the tender coral roe inside is eaten raw with bread.

- *Lampascioni* Wild hyacinth bulbs with the flavor of bitter onions. Lampascioni are often boiled and coarsely mashed with extra virgin olive oil or cooked with eggs for a frittata.

- *Buratta* A tender mozzarella sack stuffed with a soft heart of mascarpone.

- Wines Red: Salice Salentino.

Sardinia

Sardinia is a large island south of Corsica in the middle of the Mediterranean Sea. To the northeast is the island's fabled Costa Smeralda, the Emerald Coast, lined with luxurious resort hotels frequented by wealthy European jetsetters. In sharp contrast, most of the rest of Sardinia is rocky and bare and people make their living farming and raising sheep.

Despite the fact that it is an island, the residents settled inland to avoid marauding pirates and the threat of malaria spread by mosquitos from the coastal marshes. As a result, meat is more important than fish in the local cooking, although Sardinian lobsters are excellent, as is the *bottarga,* dried pressed mullet, tuna, or other fish roe that tastes like a cross between anchovies and caviar—definitely fishy. Bottarga is good grated over spaghetti or thinly sliced on crostini.

- *Carta di musica* Cracker-thin crisp bread, the name means music paper for the crackling sound it makes when it is broken.

- *Maloreddus* Tiny gnocchi flavored with saffron usually served in a meat and tomato sauce.

- *Culigiones* Large filled pasta stuffed with ricotta and swiss chard.

- *Porceddu* Roast suckling pig cooked on a spit.

- *Sebada or seada* Sweet cheese fritters drenched in honey.

- Pecorino romano Sharp firm sheep's cheese for grating over tomato sauces, pasta, and soups

- Wines White: Vernaccia. Red: Cannonau.

Sicily

Centuries of conquests by Arabs, Normans, Romans, Greeks, Spanish, French, and other invaders have left a lasting influence on the Sicilian kitchen. It is Italy's largest island and one of the richest regions in the diversity of its cooking, but it can be difficult to find examples of good cooking in this region's restaurants, which are often lackluster. Getting to know a Sicilian family might not even be a help. When Charles and I visited his relatives in Naro, near Agrigento, we wrote ahead to tell them of our interest in Sicilian cooking. They prepared a lovely meal for us featuring *tortellini bolognese,* packaged stuffed pasta rings in a Bologna-style meat and tomato sauce, and veal milanese, fried breaded veal cutlets in the style of Milan. We later realized that they considered local dishes too humble for foreign guests. Some of my best Sicilian dining experiences were at the cooking school operated by Anna Tasca Lanza at the Regaleali winery in central Sicily.

- *Pasta con le sarde* Thick pasta tubes with a sauce of fresh sardines, onions, wild fennel, raisins, and pine nuts.

- *Sfinciuni* A thick, soft pizza topped with lots of cooked onions, anchovies, and tomatoes.

- *Pasta alla Norma* Named for the opera by Bellini, who was born in Catania, this dish is made with spaghetti topped with tomato sauce, fried eggplant slices, and ricotta salata cheese.

- *Stigghioli* Lamb's intestines seasoned with parsley, green onions, and grated cheese and grilled. Stigghioli stands are as ubiquitous in Palermo as hot dog vendors in New York.

- Orange salad A colorful salad of sliced oranges, olives, and mint dressed with olive oil. Especially good with fish.

- *Frutti di martorana* Almond paste confections molded into fantastic shapes resembling fruits, vegetables, lambs, and so on. Some are stuffed with pistachio or citron marmalade.

- Wines White: Nozze d'Oro. Reds: Rosso del Conte from Regaleali, Duca Enrico from Duca di Salaparuta. Dessert: Marsala.

Trentino-Alto Adige

High up in the Alps, this is Italy's northernmost region bordering on Switzerland and Austria. German is spoken as much if not more than Italian. Winters in the mountains are cold and snowy, though summers can be quite warm in the valleys. One summer, we were surprised to find that the temperatures in Trent were the same as in Palermo. Trentino-Alto Adige is paradise for skiers in winter and hikers in summer. The Dolomites, a younger mountain range than the Alps, have sharp craggy peaks and beautiful, pristine villages. The hearty local cooking is a mixture of Italian and German, too. Sausages, sauerkraut, and strudel share the menu with risotto, polenta, and gnocchi. Apple trees and grapevines thrive here.

- *Grostl* Small pieces of leftover beef or veal, potatoes, and onions browned together to form a crusty cake, sprinkled with fresh chives.

- *Canederli* Dumplings made from whole grain bread flavored with meat, cheese, or onions, served with melted butter.

- *Speck* Smoked, cured pork, sliced thin and served with horseradish.

- *Birolodi* Pork sausages flavored with raisins, spices, and nuts.

- *Torta di polenta nera* A buckwheat cake layered with red blueberry preserves and served with kirsch-flavored whipped cream.

- *Krapfen* Hot donuts filled with jam or preserves.

- Wines Whites: Pinot Grigio, Chardonnay, Riesling. Reds: Cabernet Sauvignon, Merlot.

Tuscany

Olive trees are the first thing that comes to my mind when I think of Tuscany. They grow happily all over the region as they do in many parts of Italy, but nowhere do they appear more beautiful than in Tuscany with their silvery, gray-green leaves waving in the slightest breeze and gnarled branches reaching toward the sun. Bordered by the Mediterranean Sea, Emilia-Romagna, Umbria, and Latium, Tuscany, especially the central region of Chianti, has the perfect climate for both olives and wine grapes.

Tuscan food is very simple but prepared with exceptional care. Soups are more important than pasta or risotto and meat is more prevalent than seafood. Beans are king here and meals are accompanied by loaves of hearty, unsalted bread. Extra virgin olive oil is an essential ingredient in Tuscan cooking. Marvelous red wines complete the meal.

- *Finocchiona* A large, coarse-grained salami flavored with fennel seeds.

- *Antipasto Toscana* A combination of crisp crostini spread with a spicy chicken liver pâté and assorted salami.

- *Acquacotta* Literally "cooked water," a mushroom and bread soup served with a poached egg in the center.

- *Cacciucco* A spicy fish stew made with seafood, garlic, tomatoes, and red wine.

- *Pappa al pomodoro* Tomato soup thickened with bread.

- *Pollo al mattone* Flattened chicken grilled under a brick until brown and crusty.

- *Bistecca alla fiorentina* Thick T-bone steak, preferably from Tuscan Chianina beef, grilled rare and drizzled with extra virgin olive oil.

- *Fagioli al fiasco* White beans slowly simmered until creamy in a large wine bottle with sage and olive oil.

- *Schiacciata con l'uva* Flatbread studded with grapes and sugar usually served at harvest time.

- *Biscotti di Prato* Hard, dry cookie slices filled with almonds, usually served with vin santo for dipping.

- *Ricciarelli* Soft almond cookies.

- **Wines** Whites: Galestro, Vernaccia di San Gimignano. Reds: Chianti, Vino Nobile di Montepulciano, Brunello, Carmignano. Dessert: Vin santo.

Umbria

Umbria is called "the green heart" of Italy because of its very central location and tree-covered hills. Though it is completely landlocked, surrounded by the regions of The Marches, Tuscany, and Latium, Umbria has plenty of water from the Tiber River and Lake Trasimeno.

There are no major cities in Umbria, although jewel-like medieval towns such as

Perugia, Orvieto, Spoleto, and Assisi dot the landscape. Black truffles are a feature of the local cuisine, usually grated on pasta and egg dishes. These truffles are much milder than the prized white truffles of Piedmont.

The town of Norcia is renowned for its excellent pork sausages and salami and Castelluccio for its tiny, delicious lentils. Umbrian olive oils are known for their rich olive flavor and are used as a condiment on soups and bread.

- *Torta sul testo* A pizzalike flatbread baked on a *testo,* a special stone griddle.

- *Schiacciata* Flatbread baked with coarse salt and sage.

- *Spaghetti alla norcina* Spaghetti dressed with truffles, garlic, and anchovies.

- *Porchetta* Suckling pig rotisserie-roasted with a stuffing of garlic, fennel, and other herbs.

- *Regina in porchetta* Carp flavored like porchetta with garlic, fennel, and rosemary.

- *Mazzafegati* Pork liver sausages flavored with raisins and pine nuts.

- *Serpentone delle monache* A pastry snake with an almond tongue and raisin eyes, filled with dried fruit and nuts.

- **Wines** Whites: Orvieto, Torre di Giano. Red: Rubesco.

Valle D'Aosta

One of my most delicious memories of the Valle D'Aosta is sitting in the wan spring sunlight outside a cheese dairy eating perfectly aged fontina cheese with fresh whole grain bread. The semi-firm cheese had a slight aroma of truffles and the bread was earthy and good.

The Valle D'Aosta, in the northwest corner of Italy, is bordered by France, Switzerland, and Piedmont. This is Italy's smallest region, yet it has the highest mountains in the country. A large part of the region is taken up by the Gran Paradiso, a national park that was formerly a royal hunting preserve. Game is abundant and cows summering in the grassy valleys produce the milk to make fontina.

- *Polenta concia* Yellow cornmeal cooked with milk, cheese, and butter.

- *Zuppa alla valpellinentze* Cabbage soup with ham, rye bread, and fontina.

- *Fontina Valle D'Aosta* A far cry from fontina produced in other places, this semi-firm cheese has a natural rind and a rich, buttery flavor and aroma. A fine eating and cooking cheese that melts beautifully.

- *Torcetti di Saint Vincent* Ultra-crisp cookie loops, reputedly a favorite of Queen Margherita of the House of Savoy.

- *Coppa dell'amicizia* The friendship cup is a round covered bowl with several spigots on top from which to drink its contents, hot coffee flavored with grappa, sugar, and orange zest. The bowl is passed from one diner to another until all of the liquid is consumed.

- Wines White: Blanc de Morgex.

The Veneto

Venice, known as *La Serenissima,* naturally dominates the Veneto region. There is nothing else quite like this romantic city built on 117 tiny islands, with its winding canals, gondolas, and artistic people. The best way to see the city is to walk (and walk) until you get lost in its endless maze.

Beyond Venice, the Veneto offers much more. Verona, the setting for Shakespeare's *Romeo and Juliet,* is an elegant city built on both sides of the Adige River. During the summer months, its beautiful Roman arena is the setting for operatic performances. Treviso, Padua, and Vicenza are lovely cities, too, and of course there is Lake Garda with its tropical climate and many quaint resort towns lining its shores. The town of Riva del Garda at the northern tip of the lake is especially appealing with its mountainous backdrop. Excellent olive oil is produced in the entire lake area.

- *Pastissada di cavalo* A specialty of Verona, horsemeat is stewed with spices, wine, and tomatoes and served over polenta.

- Risotto Venetians like their risotto "all'onda," meaning wavy or rippling because it is rather thin and soupy. There are many different flavor possibilities including peas, squid ink and squid, asparagus, seafood, and wild hops.

- *Bigoli con salsa* Thick whole wheat spaghetti in an anchovy, white wine, and onion sauce.

- *Pasta e fagioli* I once had an Italian teacher from the Veneto who was astonished to hear that other regions of Italy made pasta and bean soup. She obviously thought I was mistaken, and if I was not, those other versions were beneath considering. Veneto bean soup is very good. There are many variations usually made with reddish brown *borlotti* beans and homemade pasta.

- *Baccalà mantecato* Salt cod, boiled then pureed to a thick cream with potatoes and olive oil.

- Polenta White cornmeal often is used in this region because its flavor is more delicate with fish.

- Wines Whites: Soave, Bianco di Custoza, Prosecco. Reds: Valpolicella, Amarone.

Ingredients and Equipment

GOOD INGREDIENTS ARE THE *foundation of good Italian cooking. To shop Italian: have several ideas in mind when you go to the store. If the cheese looks dry or moldy or if the fish is less than pearly and moist, be flexible and buy something else.*

- Think seasonally, choosing vegetables and fruits at their peak of ripeness and avoiding those that are out of season.

- Learn to recognize the differences between foods that are at their best and those that are not.

- Remember that bigger is not always better, especially when it comes to produce. Sometimes larger fruits and vegetables are simply overgrown.

- Examine, smell, and, if possible, taste ingredients before adding them to your recipes to be sure they are right.
- Seek out sources in your area for the finest Italian or Italian-style ingredients.

What follows is a list of basic ingredients you'll need to keep on hand for the recipes in this book.

Anchovies ⋯ Acciughe

Flat fillets of anchovies are an essential ingredient in many Italian dishes. Although there are as many people who love anchovies as those who hate them, most in the latter group can't erase their first anchovy experience, when they made the mistake of eating a hot whole fillet with a bite of pizza. I have found time and time again that people who think they don't like anchovies are amazed at what a good taste they have when they are chopped up and added to sauces. Unless someone is allergic, I don't bother to mention that a dish contains anchovies unless asked to identify the flavor.

Anchovies packed in salt are common in Italy but they are hard to find in the United States. They must be rinsed to remove the salt and be filleted. It's easy since the two fillets zip right off the central rack of bones. Salted anchovies are meatier than oil-packed canned anchovies and have a firmer texture.

Oil-packed anchovies can be very good, too. Since they crumble as they get older, buy oil-packed flat fillets of anchovies in small jars as opposed to cans, if you can find them. This way, you can see what condition the fillets are in as opposed to canned anchovies, where you never know what's inside until you open the can.

Don't buy oil-packed anchovy fillets rolled around capers. These are meant to be used as a garnish, not for cooking.

Once opened, oil-packed anchovies quickly develop a tired, stale flavor so it is better to use them immediately than to try to keep the leftovers. If you must keep them, place them in a very small container and cover them completely with olive oil.

Anise ⋯ Anice

Anisette and Sambuca are two popular anise-flavored Italian liqueurs. From the same botanical family as dill, fennel, caraway, and cumin, anise has a mild licorice flavor. In Italy, anise seeds and extract are frequently used to flavor sweetened baked goods. To do so, lightly crush the seeds in a mortar and pestle or with the flat side of a heavy knife before adding to doughs or batters.

Basil ⋯ Basilico

Few foods have a more alluring aroma than fresh basil. I keep it on hand to flavor tomato sauces, to toss with salad greens, or to layer in a sandwich with roasted peppers or tomatoes.

I keep basil growing in pots in my garden or on the windowsill as long as possible, but since it is an annual, the plants do not winter over. Most of the year, I buy fresh basil in the supermarket.

Freshly picked basil is very delicate and does not last long. Unlike hardier herbs like parsley, basil cannot tolerate the cold of the refrigerator very well. If the leaves are chilled, they start to blacken and wither after just a day or two. Unless the weather is very hot, fresh basil keeps better in a jar of cool water on the kitchen counter than in the refrigerator. Try to use it up quickly. If the kitchen is very warm, loosely wrap the top of the bunch in dry paper towels for insulation and place the stem ends in about an inch of water. Invert a plastic bag over all and keep the basil in the refrigerator. It might last an extra day or two.

As a last resort, you can freeze basil. First rinse it in cool water and remove the leaves from the stems. Pat the leaves dry and place them in a small, heavy-duty plastic bag. The leaves will darken and the flavor fade somewhat, but frozen basil is better than no basil at all. Use the leaves directly from the freezer, preferably for sauces and other uses where the dark color and wilted texture will not be so noticeable.

I do not like basil preserved in olive oil. There is a slight but serious danger of botulism poisoning. Dried basil is unpleasant and tastes nothing like the fresh. If you have no fresh or frozen basil, substitute fresh parsley or mint.

An old Tuscan superstition maintains that cutting basil with a knife will attract snakes. The best way is not to cut the leaves, but to tear them into small pieces. In addition to ensuring that snakes won't show up, this technique has the added advantage of preventing the basil leaves from turning black.

Bouillon Cubes ⸭ Dadi

Bouillon cubes sold in the United States have very artificial colors and flavors. All they taste like is salt and stale dried herbs, so I was amazed to learn that many of my Italian friends use broth made from *dadi,* or bouillon cubes. Since their risotto and soup tasted great, I knew there had to be a difference.

I asked a representative of one of the large food companies that produces a popular brand of bouillon cubes in the States about this. She told me that though the same brand name is used, bouillon cubes have a different formulation in different countries. Many of the bouillon cubes sold in American stores are manufactured to suit the tastes of the large Hispanic market. They contain turmeric and other spices not used in Italy. So even if the brand name is the same as in Italy, the cubes most definitely are not. Now, whenever I travel, I buy boxes of Italian boullion cubes. They make a practical gift! Star is the best of the Italian brands that I have tasted.

Homemade broth is best, but if I am out of it or in a hurry, I use canned broth mixed with equal parts of water so that it will not be too concentrated. Taste several brands until you find one you like.

Bread Crumbs ⋯ Pan Grattato

One of my least favorite cooking chores as a child was making the bread crumbs. My mother would collect bread scraps in a roasting pan that she kept in the turned-off oven heated by a pilot light. When the scraps where good and dry, it was my job to grate them. Instead of a grater, we used the holes of the *scolapasta,* a big aluminum pasta colander that strained out the crumbs that were too coarse. It was hard work and my fingers would soon be numb and scraped. Then my sister would have to take over.

Bread crumbs are an essential ingredient in Italian cooking, particularly in the South where they sometimes take the place of cheese as a seasoning on pasta. Canned bread crumbs should not be used because they are made from spongy white bread, which contains sugar, milk, and additives. If you know a bakery that makes bread crumbs from leftover loaves of Italian or French bread, you can use those, or make them yourself as I do.

Place the ends and leftover slices of unsweetened French or Italian bread in a plastic bag in the freezer. When you have a batch of them, spread them in a shallow layer in a roasting pan and bake them in a low oven, about 275°F., until they are very dry. Let cool then grind the pieces in a food processor or blender. Store the crumbs in a jar in the refrigerator. They seem to keep indefinitely, though you should taste them from time to time to be sure that they have not gotten moldy.

Capers ⋯ Capperi

Capers are the green, unopened buds of the caper plant flowers. The plants grow wild in many areas around the Mediterranean, though they are also cultivated in parts of Sicily and Spain.

In springtime in Italy, fresh capers are a treat in salads and sauces but to preserve them, capers are either salted or pickled in vinegar. Capers preserved in salt retain more of the flavor of the fresh, but need to be soaked in several changes of cool water before they are added to dishes. Pickled capers are more widely available than salted but less of the caper flavor survives the harshness of the vinegar. Drain pickled capers before using. Some cooks like to rinse them briefly in cool water to eliminate some of the vinegar. Pickled capers keep indefinitely while the salted ones get mushy from the salt after a while and should be discarded. Both kinds should be stored in the refrigerator.

Small capers were at one time considered more desirable than large, but I suspect that had more to do with their perfect appearance than their flavor. Large capers are just as flavorful but chop them before adding to most dishes.

Cheese ⋯ Formaggio

You can't help but think of Parmigiano-Reggiano, or parmesan cheese, when you enter the city of Parma in Emilia-Romagna in northern Italy. The deep, warm ochre

When to Grate, When Not to Grate, and What Cheese to Grate

The Italians have very definite ideas about grating cheeses—when and which ones to use and when to use none at all. The idea is to employ grated cheese judiciously to enhance and balance the other flavors in a dish. Some foods, especially seafood teamed with pasta or rice, should never be topped with cheese. It would overwhelm the delicate seafood.

Once in a popular New York Italian restaurant that takes the authenticity of its cooking very seriously, an acquaintance ordered a seafood lasagne for his main course. When it arrived, he requested some Parmigiano to grate over the top. The waitress hesitated. She had been instructed not to serve cheese with this lasagne. She politely suggested that my friend try it the way the chef recommended it be eaten—without cheese. He was persistent, however, and she graciously argued no further. Just as she was about to grate cheese onto the lasagne, the maître d' suddenly appeared and grabbed her wrist to stop her. "What do you think you are doing?" he snarled. She answered calmly but emphatically, carefully enunciating each word: "The gentleman wants cheese." The maître d' skulked away as the savvy waitress grated a snowy mountain of Parmigiano over the lasagne.

Three cheeses are typically used as *grana,* or grating cheese, in Italy: Parmigiano-Reggiano, grana Padano, and pecorino romano. Other cheeses such as asiago, caciocavallo, or ricotta salata are sometimes grated, but they are regional and much less common. Parmigiano-Reggiano and its slightly milder cousin, grana Padano, can be used in similar ways, whereas pecorino romano with its sharp, pronounced flavor has more specific uses. I keep both Parmigiano and pecorino on hand at all times.

color of the buildings, a legacy of the Austrians who once ruled the city, is almost a perfect match to the color of a well-aged wheel of the famous cheese.

Italian law tightly regulates the making of Parmigiano-Reggiano, and the procedure remains basically the same today as it has been for more than seven hundred years. Parmigiano can be made only in a limited region around the cities of Parma and Reggio Emilia. The milk for the cheese must come from local cows, which are carefully bred for that purpose.

Parmigiano-Reggiano is an essential ingredient in many Italian dishes, especially those of northern Italian origin. It's also delicious for eating as a snack or with fresh

Buying, Grating, and Storing Hard Cheese

When shopping for cheese, avoid those called parmesan or romano that do not come from Italy. Even those that simply say imported may not be from Italy at all, and their flavor is usually a shadow of the real thing. Genuine Parmigiano-Reggiano should be a creamy straw color with no traces of dried edges. The name should be imprinted on the rind. Pecorino romano is white to slightly yellow and should also look fresh and moist. Buy the cheese in chunks that you can use up in a couple of weeks' time. Flavor and texture are lost when cheese is frozen.

Keep the cheeses tightly sealed in plastic wrap and store them separately in plastic bags in the refrigerator. Grate hard cheeses only as needed. All cheese is best when it is grated just before it is used. Even if your market sells cheese called "freshly grated," chances are that it will dry out and lose much of its delicate flavor before you have the opportunity to use it up. Besides, it is impossible to tell from grated cheese that you are really getting what you paid for. Grated cheese sold in jars and cans is of very poor quality and should not be used.

To grate hard cheese, I use the medium holes of an ordinary box-style cheese grater or a rotary grater of the kind made by Mouli or Zyliss. For large quantities, I sometimes use a food processor fitted with the steel blade. Don't try to grate hard cheese with one of the shredding disks; these cheeses are too firm and may damage the machine. The steel blade makes fast work of hard cheese, though it cuts it into small granules rather than grating it into fine shreds. To make flakes or shards to scatter over salads, use a swivel-blade vegetable peeler or paring knife.

or dried fruit for dessert. I buy it in big two- to five-pound pieces; that way, I always have some on hand when I want it. Parmigiano is too hard to cut into neat wedges and is best broken into small pieces. The Italians use a small knife with a wooden handle and an almond-shape blade that is made especially for this purpose. The cheese breaks along its natural grain, enhancing both the texture and flavor. As the cheese is eaten, you may notice some tiny white granules of calcium which are natural and an indication of the cheese's quality.

Grana Padano is similar to Parmigiano but it is made outside of the Parma-Reggio zone. Its flavor is slightly milder and milkier and the color is often lighter than Parmigiano. It can be used in any recipe where Parmigiano is called for and is also an excellent table cheese.

With little flat land for cows to graze, southern Italy is better suited to small animals such as sheep. The milk from these sheep goes into a number of different cheeses. The most famous sheep's milk cheese is pecorino romano, a firm white to pale yellow cheese with a pungent, salty flavor.

Its name is derived from *pecora,* the Italian word for ewe. Romano refers to the fact that much of the cheese was produced at one time in the area around Rome. Today, it is also produced nearby on the island of Sardinia. Locatelli, a brand of pecorino romano, has been so well marketed in the United States that it is often believed to be a distinct kind of cheese, but it is not. The flavor of pecorino romano is a natural complement to tomato sauces with olive oil, bread crumb stuffings and toppings, pasta, and soups. Thin chips or shavings are delicious in salads or as a topping for crostini.

Pecorino romano is the grating cheese I think of first for southern Italian cooking. As an Italian friend, restaurateur Nicola Marzovilla, explained it, "Where I come from [near Bari in Puglia], Parmigiano is practically an imported food."

Chilies ··· Peperoncini

Diavolicchi e vino fanno il sangue fino (little chilies and wine make good blood), according to an old saying from the Basilicata region, above the toe of the Italian boot. In many parts of central and southern Italy, chilies, either fresh or dried, add spice to sauces, vegetables, and soups. The most common are the tiny red *diavolicchi,* or little devils, about $1/2$ inch long and hot as blazes. Generally, they are used sparingly. Often they are heated in the cooking oil and then removed, leaving just a note of their spicy flavor behind. For a more pronounced flavor, the chili is crushed first, then added to the other ingredients. Small whole chilies can be purchased in many supermarkets or Asian markets or you can substitute crushed red pepper from the supermarket.

Chocolate ··· Cioccolato

Bittersweet or semisweet chocolate can be used for the recipes in this book. An imported brand such as Perugina, Callebaut, Lindt, or Tobler would be my first choice, though there are other good brands on the market. Milk chocolate is not suitable for these recipes. Don't use chocolate chips when the chocolate is to be melted. Chips are formulated with less cocoa butter so that they retain their shape in baking.

Cocoa ··· Cacao

Dutch process or alkalized cocoa is darker in color and less bitter than nonalkalized cocoa, but either can be used in these recipes. Most manufacturers make both kinds, so read the label carefully. Never use sweetened cocoa powder for recipes. Sift cocoa through a sieve before using it to eliminate any lumps and make mixing more even.

Measuring Wet and Dry Ingredients

Practically everyone had a grandmother, aunt, or neighbor who could whip up marvelous cakes and cookies by adding a pinch of this and a handful of that. With experience and practice, it is possible to bake that way. After making a cake a few times you will be able to judge when the batter looks and feels right or wrong. But even without experience, you can turn out excellent cakes, tarts, and cookies. The secret is measuring the ingredients correctly.

Flour and other dry ingredients for baking should always be measured with dry measuring cups, the stacking kind usually made of metal or plastic. Long-handled ones are best. Dip the appropriate measure into the flour or other dry ingredient and scoop up a heaping cupful. With a spatula or knife, sweep off the excess flour even with the rim of the cup. Do not press the flour down or tap it on the countertop; this will cause it to settle and give an inaccurate measurement.

Butter is easiest to measure by the number of tablespoons indicated on the paper wrapping of each stick. If you buy butter in bulk, measure it in a dry measuring cup. Let the butter soften at room temperature, then pack it into the cup with a spatula and level the top.

Liquids should be measured in a liquid measuring cup, usually made of glass or plastic with calibrations up the sides. Many give metric measures on one side and cup measures on the other. The cup has sufficient headroom so that even if it is filled to the maximum measured amount, it will not spill over as it would in a dry measuring cup. To measure any liquid accurately, pour it into a liquid measuring cup on an even surface. Bend over to check the measure at eye level.

Eggs ... Uova

For baking purposes it is essential to use the size eggs called for in a recipe. The small difference in size between a large egg and a jumbo egg can truly affect the outcome of delicate cakes and pastries. For this book, I have used large eggs exclusively, for baking and otherwise.

When cracking a quantity of eggs for baking or cooking, it is a good idea to break the eggs one at a time into a small bowl. As each one is cracked, you can easily scoop out any bits of shell, or a bad egg can be discarded without ruining a whole batch. Transfer the egg to a larger bowl before breaking and inspecting the remainder.

The same is true for separating eggs. Since egg whites will not beat up light and fluffy for cakes and desserts if there is any yolk mixed in, break an egg over one bowl, letting the white flow out of the shell. Place the yolk in a second bowl. Transfer the white to a third bowl before cracking the next egg.

Fennel Seed ··· Semi di Finocchio

Fennel is sometimes confused with anise and though the two plants are related, they are not the same. Fennel is somewhat stronger and is used more often in savory dishes while anise is used primarily for desserts. In Italy, fennel seeds often are added to pork dishes, especially sausages and roasts, or as a flavoring for olives, *taralli*, and certain other breads.

Flour ··· Farina

All of the recipes in this book were tested using unbleached all-purpose flour, except where indicated. When unbleached all-purpose flour is kneaded with water, gluten, the protein that gives structure to breads and cakes, develops. Bleached all-purpose flour has slightly less gluten than unbleached, but it can be substituted successfully for the recipes in this book. Bread flour, which has the most gluten, should be used only for bread recipes.

Garlic ··· Aglio

More is not always better when it comes to garlic. In most cases Italian cooks use it sparingly and many dishes do not call for it at all. Since fresh garlic is mild and sweet tasting and older garlic harsh and bitter, avoid garlic that is shriveled, yellowed, or sprouting green shoots. Look for firm, plump heads without any trace of bruises or mold. The outer skin should be pearly and attached to the cloves.

Garlic can be sliced, chopped, or cooked whole, depending on the degree of flavor desired in the dish. In some cases, where just a hint of garlic flavor is desired, the garlic may be cooked first in oil and discarded before the rest of the ingredients are added.

To separate the cloves from a head of garlic, place it on a countertop and press down firmly. The cloves will separate from the head. If they do not or if you prefer, simply break off as many cloves as required with your thumbs.

To peel a garlic clove, place it on a cutting board and lay the flat side of a heavy chef's knife against it. Smack the knife with the heel of your hand to partially smash the garlic. If the garlic is to be chopped and not sliced, smack it harder and the job will be half done. If there is a green shoot inside, remove it to make the garlic taste milder. I usually do this only if the garlic is going to be used raw. Cut off the stem end and remove all of the papery skin from the clove. The garlic can now be thinly sliced or finely chopped with a heavy chef's knife according to the recipe or your personal taste. I prefer to chop garlic rather than use a garlic press because it turns the garlic into a puree so fine that the flavor becomes heavy and very pungent. Besides, a press is a nuisance to clean. But a press is certainly quicker, and if you don't have the patience to chop garlic really fine—I hate biting into big pieces of garlic—by all means, use it.

Cooking Onions and Garlic the Italian Way

Many savory recipes begin with cooking onions or garlic in oil. To do this, Italian cooks, unlike the French, start with a cold pan to ensure that the vegetables soften and cook slowly without becoming brown and bitter.

For onions, place them in the skillet or saucepan with the oil. Turn on the heat to medium and cook until the onions are tender, pale golden, and translucent. Regulate the heat so that the onions don't brown. They should be done in five to seven minutes.

Garlic is handled the same way. The garlic and oil are placed in the cold pan and cooked until the garlic is pale gold and fragrant. Garlic cooks quickly—about one minute should be sufficient.

When a recipe begins with both onion and garlic, the onion should be cooked first since it takes longer. Add the garlic only after the onion is tender or it may become overdone.

Reserve a cutting board just for chopping garlic and onions to avoid transferring their strong flavors to delicate foods like cheese or fruits.

When cooking garlic in oil, place the two in a cold pan at the same time, then turn the heat on to no higher than medium. If you start with hot oil, the garlic can quickly overcook, blacken, and develop a sharp, acrid flavor. For most purposes, garlic cooked in oil (or butter) should be no darker than a pale to medium golden color. It is usually ready when you can smell its aroma, which takes less than a minute in an average pan once the oil is hot. If the garlic turns a dark brown, discard it and the oil too and start over. The sharp flavor of burnt garlic can ruin your dish.

Never substitute dried garlic powder or preserved garlic in any form. It has a sour, nasty flavor that will ruin your good cooking and make it difficult to digest. Do not use garlic-flavored oil. It is overpriced and the flavor is inappropriate. Nor should you make your own flavored oil by marinating garlic. Botulism bacteria can thrive when garlic is stored in oil, especially at room temperature.

Herbs ⋯ Erbe

In addition to parsley and basil, the most commonly used herbs in Italian cooking are rosemary, sage, mint, oregano, and marjoram. A few other herbs, like calamint *(Sat-*

Removing Food Aromas from Your Hands

Here is a neat trick for removing the garlic aroma from your hands after chopping. Hold your hands under cool running water while you rub them with a piece of stainless steel such as a kitchen spoon. The smell disappears like magic.

As an alternative, wash your hands first with cold water and lemon juice or coarse salt. Wash them again with soapy water. Repeat the procedure if any lingering traces remain.

---

ureja calamintha), called *nepitella* in Italian, chives, tarragon, and thyme are used in certain ways and in regional dishes, but they are much less common.

Fresh rosemary, sage, and mint are preferable to the dried, which can become bitter and musty. Fortunately, they are widely available in most markets, and they keep well if their stems are kept moist. If at all possible, grow herbs on a windowsill to pick fresh whenever you need them. Oregano and marjoram are the only herbs I use in the dried form, but they must be used sparingly or their flavors can be overwhelming.

Don't be tempted to muddle the flavors of Italian dishes by adding a lot of herbs. Though there are exceptions in this book, such as the Ragged Pasta with a Thousand Herbs (page 136), where the flavor is deliberately herbaceous, most dishes need only one or two herbs to give them a balanced flavor lift.

Juniper Berries ⋯ Bacche di ginepro

Juniper berries are the blue-black fruit of a small evergreen bush. They give the characteristic flavor to gin and are often used to season bird and game dishes, especially venison. Dried juniper berries are available in most gourmet shops. They keep well for about a year in a cool dark place. Before adding juniper berries to stews or other meat dishes, crush them lightly with the flat side of a heavy chef's knife or cleaver.

Lard ⋯ Sugna

Gigino Pizza a Metro is a pizzeria located in Vico Equense, a pretty little town outside of Naples. The huge restaurant, known as "the university of pizza," is packed night and day, inside and out, with big family groups who come for the fresh seafood, enormous antipasto assortment, and the pizza, which is sold by the meter. What makes Gigino's pizza so special? The answer is lard. Instead of drizzling the pizza with a stream of olive oil before baking it, Gigino's chefs anoint their pies with melted lard, which gives them an extra-rich, meaty flavor.

Although Italian cooking is often defined as Northern if it is butter based and Southern if it is oil based, in reality many places in Italy, especially the South, traditionally use lard as their primary cooking fat. Until fairly recently, butter and oil were too expensive and not widely available. In addition to adding flavor to sauces and stews, lard browns foods well and makes baked goods very tender and crisp, with a melt-in-the-mouth texture.

My grandmother always said olive oil was "too heavy" and butter was just for breakfast toast. My mother used to make her own fresh lard by melting down pure white pork fat until it became liquid. Then she would strain the fat and pour it, with a bay leaf for freshness, into jars, which she stored in the refrigerator. Sometimes she cooked the solid bits left in the strainer further until they were golden brown and crackling, then kneaded them into bread dough with lots of coarse black pepper. The dough was baked into big rings, which we ate sliced with strong provolone cheese, olives, and young red wine. I hated the smell of the rendering pork fat, but the aroma of the garlic and meat browning in the fresh lard for Sunday's pasta sauce is a very pleasant memory.

I once asked my Aunt Anna if she could remember how my grandmother made her Easter sweet bread, which she called *casatiella*. I had tried to duplicate it several times but could never get it quite right. "Of course," she said, "Grandma used plenty of eggs, orange flower water for flavoring, sugar, flour, yeast, and big scoops of fresh lard." No wonder the flavor was off—I had made it with butter.

Today many people prefer to use olive oil, a heart-healthy monounsaturated fat. My mother stopped using lard a number of years ago, and I use it only occasionally. Despite Grandma's pronouncement, olive oil is very good tasting. I suspect that the olive oils available in her day were not the fresh, high quality oils we find everywhere today.

I have substituted either straight olive oil or a combination of pancetta, for pork flavor, and olive oil in cooking many recipes that would have once been made with lard.

Lemons ... Limone

Fresh lemons are essential for salad dressings, garnishes, and desserts. I keep them in the refrigerator in the produce drawer, where they stay fresh for weeks. To get the most juice out of a lemon, let it warm to room temperature, then roll it on a flat surface pressing firmly with the palm of your hand to break down the cell walls and release the juices.

To grate lemon zest, I use a lemon zester. This device has a handle that is easy to grip. The business end is a flat piece of metal almost like a table fork, but instead of tines it has five tiny circles. By scraping the circles across the skin, you remove only the finest, narrowest strips of zest without digging into the bitter white pith below. Gather the strips of zest together on a cutting board and finely chop them. As an alternative, you grate the zest on the fine holes of a box grater. Turn the lemon frequently to avoid digging into the white pith below. Use a small pastry brush to remove the tiny bits of zest that collect in the ridges of the grater. Once a lemon has been zested, wrap it in plastic wrap and refrigerate it, so that the juice does not dry out before you can use it.

Mozzarella ... Mozzarella

Though Parmigiano-Reggiano and pecorino romano may reign elsewhere, mozzarella is the king of cheeses in Naples. A big ball of this creamy white semi-soft cheese often is served as an antipasto before meals and it is used in pasta, vegetable, and meat dishes and, of course, on pizza.

Freshly made mozzarella is tender, juicy, and delicate with a sweet milky flavor, not to be confused with the hard, yellowish, salty cheese found vacuum sealed in most grocery stores. Find a shop in your area where mozzarella is made fresh daily. Avoid refrigerating it, if using within hours, so that the cheese will retain its soft texture.

Nutmeg ... Noce moscato

Nutmeg is the seed of an evergreen tree. A pinch of it often is used in stuffing mixtures for pasta and vegetables as well as in desserts. Since the flavor fades quickly, nutmeg is best when it is ground just before using. Use the fine holes of a cheese grater or a specially designed nutmeg grater.

Nuts ... Noci

Nuts are used in Italian cooking in pasta sauces; stuffings for meat, fruit, and vegetables; and, of course, desserts. Since most nuts have a high fat content, they spoil easily. Always buy bulk almonds, hazelnuts, walnuts, and pine nuts from a store with good storage and a constant turnover so that you have a better chance of their being fresh. A health food store is often a good source, with prices more reasonable than at a food specialty shop. Some nuts come vacuum packed at the supermarket. At home, store shelled nuts in an airtight container, preferably in the freezer. Toasting brings out the flavor of nuts. To toast nuts, spread them in a single layer in a shallow pan. Bake in a 325°F. oven for five to ten minutes, or until lightly golden. Set a timer to remind you to check, since nuts go from toasty to burnt very quickly. Let the nuts cool before chopping or using in recipes.

Olive Oil ··· Olio d'oliva

A friend of mine came for dinner, then asked me for the recipe for the sautéed scallops that I had prepared. I wrote it down for her, but a few days later she called me to complain. She had tried it at home and it did not taste like mine, she said. She insisted that she had followed my directions exactly.

A few days later I stopped by to see her. As soon as I spotted the big bottle of olive oil on her counter, I knew what the problem was. She was using a brand that was not Italian. It was a very nice olive oil, but it had not been blended for Italian cooking. Its ripe olive flavor had a minty, herbaceous quality that may work with other foods but is not typical of Italian oils. It interfered with the delicate flavor of the scallops and changed the whole character of the dish.

Olive oils vary in flavor depending on where they are produced and the type and maturity of the olives used. Once the olives are pressed, the oils are classified on the basis of their acidity level. The highest quality oils are graded "extra virgin." In order to qualify for this designation, an oil must have an intense olive flavor and aroma and a very low level of oleic acid. Virgin oils have slightly higher acidity and good flavor.

Oils that have more acidity than extra virgin and virgin oils, or are otherwise less than perfect, are improved by refining and blending with some virgin olive oil for flavor. This grade of oil, available in big cans at the supermarket, was at one time called "pure," though most manufacturers today label it simply as "olive oil." Both extra virgin and olive oil are widely available here. A fourth grade, called "olive pomace oil" which is extracted with solvents from the olive mash left after processing for extra virgin or virgin oils, is rarely seen.

Some manufacturers also market olive oil that is labeled as "light." This is simply a refined or blended oil that has slightly less virgin oil added so it is lighter in flavor—not calories. All cooking oils, whether derived from olives, nuts, corn, or other vegetables, have 120 calories per tablespoon.

When I wrote my book *The Antipasto Table,* I specified extra virgin olive oil for practically all cooking purposes. As delicious as it can be, the flavor of extra virgin oil is fragile and is easily lost by cooking or heating. Also, extra virgin oil can be very expensive.

Since then, I have talked to a number of good Italian cooks I know. None of them uses extra virgin oil in that way. While it is essential always to use a good quality olive oil, they said, it is unnecessary to use extra virgin olive oil for all cooking purposes.

Now I buy at least two different kinds of Italian olive oil. I buy big cans of "olive oil" to use for cooking and sautéing or whenever the oil is to be exposed to high heat. This oil has a mild olive flavor that does not overwhelm the other ingredients in a recipe. It is relatively inexpensive and suited to many cooking purposes, even certain cakes and biscotti.

The other olive oil I keep on hand is a top quality extra virgin oil. This is a deep green oil with a pronounced fresh olive flavor. I use it when I want to add a distinc-

Pitting Olives

One of the best things about teaching is how much you can learn. A student in one of my cooking classes showed me his grandmother's way of quickly pitting olives. It works with all kinds.

Place an olive on a cutting board and lay the broad side of a chef's knife or cleaver on top. Smack the knife with the heel of your hand. The olive flesh should split open, and the pit can be easily removed.

tive olive flavor and smooth texture to salads, sauces, and vegetable dishes that will not be exposed to direct heat. Instead, I drizzle a spoonful into a bowl of soup or add it as a finishing touch to warm vegetables or pasta. The gentle warmth of the cooked food enhances the oil's flavor without damaging it.

The only way to judge an oil is by tasting it. Ask friends who are good cooks or the chef at your favorite Italian restaurant for recommendations. Then try a small bottle to see if it suits your taste. Each region's oil has its own flavor characteristics, so expect to try several brands before you find one or two you like.

Look for brands of extra virgin olive oil that are vintage dated, since the flavor fades as the oil ages. And don't buy more extra virgin olive oil than you can use in a month or two. Unopened, the oil maintains its flavor for about a year. Once the bottle is opened, the oil begins to deteriorate more rapidly. Keep it in a cool spot away from strong light to prevent rancidity. If you cannot use it all in a month or two, especially during hot weather, keep just a small container at room temperature and the remainder in the refrigerator. It may solidify, but it will become liquid again once it warms up slightly.

Olives ⋯ Olive

Olives can be crisp or soft in texture, chocolatey, spicy, or lemony in flavor, dry or juicy, but they are all delicious. The only olives that I find disappointing and inappropriate for Italian cooking are the tasteless ones that come in cans.

Olives are called black (though they can be brownish or purplish) if they are fully ripe or green if they are unripe. Green olives are generally crisper than black and more delicate in flavor. Black olives are richer tasting with a texture that ranges from soft to crisp. For most recipes, either type can be used; it just depends on the flavor and the texture that you want.

Slicing Onions Without Crying

A chemical found in onions called *propanethial S-oxide* is the guilty party that makes you cry when you chop or slice onions. When the onion is cut, the chemical fumes are released to combine with the tears in your eyes, forming sulfuric acid. This irritates your eyes and more tears are shed.

The best way to avoid crying is to store onions in the refrigerator. The cold helps somewhat to neutralize the effects of the chemical so your eyes will be less irritated.

Sweetening an Onion for Salad

The flavor of onions can be very strong. Cooking tames them and brings out their sweetness, but sometimes a bit of raw onion is nice in a salad. To sweeten onions, slice them thin, then soak the slices in ice water for ten to fifteen minutes. Drain the onion slices and pat them dry. Repeat if necessary.

For good tasting olives, find a food specialty shop in your area that stocks several kinds. My first choice for most cooking purposes is black Gaeta olives from near Rome. These are medium size with a semi-firm texture and a not too strong or salty flavor. Also good are Greek kalamata olives, which are stronger but still good, and they are widely available. Spanish manzanilla olives are a good choice for green olives as are the Greek Ionian. Try several varieties until you find the ones you like.

Taste the olives. If they taste salty, rinse off the brine. If they are still salty, soak them in several changes of cool water up to twenty-four hours. (For cooking purposes, don't buy seasoned olives unless their flavorings will complement your dish.)

Olives taste best when they are warm or at room temperature, but they should be stored in a covered container in the refrigerator. To heat them, place the olives in a shallow baking pan in a 350°F. oven and bake until they are warm, about fifteen minutes. Even quicker is the microwave oven. Place a cup of olives in a microwavesafe dish and heat on medium (50%) for thirty seconds. Stir the olives and heat for thirty seconds more if needed. Touch lightly to see that they are not too hot before biting into one.

Onions ··· Cipolle

A variety of onions are used in Italian cooking. Yellow onions are good for most cooking purposes. Sliced or chopped and cooked in olive oil or butter over medium heat, they become tender in about five minutes, golden and more flavorful in about seven minutes, though exact time depends on the pan and the kind of onion. To prevent onions from blackening and turning bitter during longer cooking, add a little water to the pan with the oil or butter.

Red, white, and green onions are milder than the yellow variety and best for salads or uncooked sauces, though they can be used for cooking when a less assertive onion flavor is preferred. Many people store onions at room temperature, but I prefer to keep yellow, red, and white onions unwrapped in the vegetable bin of my refrigerator. They last longer, at least a month, without sprouting and are less irritating to the eyes when cut. The flavor and aroma of most onions changes and becomes harsh once they are sliced or chopped, so I discard any leftovers.

Green onions or scallions have a much shorter shelf life than other varieties, less than a week. Since they have a strong aroma even when whole, I store them in the refrigerator in plastic bags, one over the bottoms and another over the tops, to prevent their aroma from reaching other foods.

Pancetta ··· Pancetta

Pancetta is made from the same cut of pork that is used for bacon. The meat is salted and flavored with black pepper and garlic, rolled up, and pressed into a log to be aged and cured. Pancetta is used for flavoring, especially in sauces and soups, or for barding, wrapped around lean meats or game birds to keep them moist while they roast or braise.

Many butcher shops and food specialty shops sell pancetta. Some slice the pancetta for you; others sell it precut in chunks shrink-wrapped in plastic. If you buy it sliced, ask for thin slices for wrapping around meats but thick slices for chopping.

Pancetta keeps for a long time in the refrigerator so I usually buy a large piece of it to have on hand. Assuming it is very fresh when you buy it, pancetta should last for three weeks. Pancetta can also be frozen. Divide it into small portions (one to two ounces is a practical size), and wrap them individually in plastic wrap. Store the packages in a heavy-duty freezer bag. The meat defrosts quickly, but it is easier to chop if it is still partially frozen. Slices can also be cut into small bits for cooking with kitchen shears.

Parsley ··· Prezzemolo

Italian parsley has a handsome dark green flat leaf. Its mild, fresh flavor is essential in many dishes so I keep a bunch on hand at all times. This is surprisingly easy to do since parsley keeps for a long time in the refrigerator, often as long as two weeks.

Buy the freshest bunch of parsley you can find. At home, snip off the base of the stems like a bunch of flowers. Discard any bruised or yellowed leaves. Fill a jar or vase with about one inch of cool water and place the parsley stems in the water. Invert a plastic bag over the top and refrigerate the jar until ready to use. Pull out a few branches of parsley to use as needed. Pinch off the leaves and discard the stems. Rinse the leaves and pat them dry before using. Change the water in the jar every day or two to keep the parsley fresh.

Curly parsley has very little flavor and is a pale substitute. Dried parsley should never be used. Since fresh flat-leaf parsley keeps so well and is readily available, I don't bother to freeze it.

Black Pepper ··· Pépe Nero

Once it is ground, black pepper becomes stale and loses its flavor quickly, adding only a bit of heat to food. Freshly ground black pepper is best for Italian cooking. White pepper is rarely used. Avoid ground black pepper sold in jars or tins.

Invest in a good peppermill or, better yet, two, so that you can have both fine pepper and coarse pepper whenever you want it without having to adjust the mechanism. A favorite kitchen gadget of mine is the Peppermate peppermill, which stores a generous amount of peppercorns, can be adjusted for coarse or fine grind, and has a handy cup to catch the ground pepper and keep it off the countertop.

Pine Nuts ··· Pinoli o Pignoli

Umbrella-shape stone pines are one of the most recognizable trees on the Italian landscape. From these graceful trees, called *Pinus pinea* in Latin, come large pine cones, whose seeds are known as pine nuts. They have a soft, creamy texture and mildly resinous flavor and are used for baking and in sauces, stuffings, salads, and many other dishes.

Italian pine nuts are long and resemble a grain of rice in appearance. Most pine nuts available in the United States today are the less expensive, shorter, somewhat triangular variety from China. The flavor of Chinese pine nuts is slightly stronger than those from Italy or other Mediterranean countries, but they can be used in Italian cooking. The most important thing is that the pine nuts be fresh. Since they contain a lot of oil, pine nuts tend to spoil quickly. Taste them before adding them to a dish to be sure they are not stale or rancid.

Store pine nuts in a tightly sealed container in the refrigerator or freezer. As with most nuts, the flavor of pine nuts is improved by toasting. Place them in a single layer in a shallow pan. Bake in a low 300°F. oven, shaking the pan occasionally, for five to ten minutes, or until lightly toasted. Pine nuts can also be toasted in a dry skillet on top of the stove. Place the nuts in the pan over medium heat. Cook, shaking the pan frequently, until the nuts are evenly browned.

Damon Lee Fowler, author of *Classical Southern Cooking* from Savannah, Georgia, with a strong background in Italian cooking tells me that for many years pine nuts were not widely available in his area. He discovered that pecans, which have a similar texture, make the best substitute for pine nuts in many Italian recipes.

Ricotta ··· Ricotta

Ricotta is made from whey, the cloudy liquid part of the milk that is left over after firm cheese is made. The liquid is cooked again (ricotta means recooked) until soft curds form. Ricotta may be salted and drained or left unsalted; it is best when it is eaten very fresh. If you can find a source for fresh ricotta, use it for the recipes in this book. It is less watery and its sweet milky flavor is exceptionally good. Otherwise, the packaged ricotta found in most markets can be used; taste several brands to find the best one. Avoid brands that have additives to thicken and preserve them and those that are too watery. Part skim milk ricotta can be used, but do not substitute lowfat ricotta.

Salt ··· Sale

Coarse or kosher salt is my first choice for cooking. If you look on the side of the box, you will see that its contents are simply salt. No additives or chemicals to make it free-flowing. It has the flavor of pure salt. Sea salt is also very good. Fine salt or table salt can have a metallic flavor—the difference is quite evident if you taste the two side by side.

As to which is the saltier salt, I find that it varies from brand to brand. When you are trying a new brand or type of salt, use what you consider to be a minimal amount and taste as you go along. Salt can always be added, though it cannot be removed.

Italians like their food quite salty, one of the reasons that food in Italy seems so tasty. Grilled meats often arrive with salt crystals melting on the surface. Since how much salt to use is a matter of personal taste, I do not give amounts of salt in most of the dishes in this book. Salt-free food is bland and boring while oversalted food soon becomes overwhelming. Learn to taste and salt foods judiciously as you prepare them, keeping in mind a balance of flavors and the changes the food will undergo as it is cooked. For example, if cheese is added to a soup or pasta at the end of cooking, the dish will seem saltier than without cheese. Long cooking will concentrate flavors and evaporate liquids, making foods seem saltier too.

Semolina ··· Semolino

Semolina is made from the ground endosperm or heart of durum wheat, a variety of hard wheat. Semolina is high in the protein gluten, which gives breads and pastas made with it a firm, chewy texture. Semolina also adds a pale straw color and nutty flavor. Finely ground semolina flour is used in many southern Italy recipes, but it should not be used to replace all-purpose flour unless indicated in the recipe.

Fine semolina mixed with water and rolled into tiny beads is called couscous. The Sicilians call it *cuscusu* and use it to make a wonderful fish stew. Semolina flour can be purchased in specialty food markets and many supermarkets. It should resemble very fine sand. If it is coarser than that, grind it in a food processor or blender for five minutes.

Sun-dried Tomatoes ⸪ Pomodori Secchi

Drying tomatoes in the sun was devised as a way to preserve them over the winter months. In Italy, their uses are limited: They are mostly marinated as an antipasto or chopped and tossed into a sauce for a rich tomato flavor. Most of the dried tomatoes sold in the United States are dried in ovens, not in the sun.

Oil-packed dried tomatoes in jars are often packed in inferior oil and have too many spices added. Buy the tomatoes dry and if they need to be reconstituted, soak them in warm water for five to ten minutes until softened. Pat them dry before using as directed in the recipe.

Tomatoes ⸪ Pomodori

Since fresh vine-ripened tomatoes have a very short season, canned tomatoes can be used for many sauces, soups, and stews. While they can never capture the unique flavor of fresh tomatoes at their peak of ripeness, canned tomatoes are far better than the pale, tasteless tomatoes available most of the year.

Canned tomatoes from Italy are the best for making sauces because they break down as they cook to form a thick, smooth sauce with just the right amount of sweetness. When shopping for tomatoes, look for the name San Marzano on the label, which refers to the variety used, and the words "product of Italy." They are packed when they are very ripe and have fewer seeds than other varieties. Buy only whole tomatoes so that you can see if they are fully ripe, not green at the stem, when you open the can. The tomatoes should look red from end to end and the liquid moderately thick, neither pasty nor watery. I buy 28- or 35-ounce cans; they are the most widely available and convenient size for sauces.

Truffle Oil ⸪ Condimento di Tartufo

Since fresh truffles here are often overpriced in relation to their quality, truffle oil can sometimes be used in a dish to give it an earthy truffle flavor at a fraction of the price. The oil is made by macerating shavings of white truffles in a bland vegetable or olive oil. Truffle oil should not be used for cooking; high heat would cause its flavor to be destroyed. Drizzle a drop or two on a hot baked potato, scrambled eggs, or toasted bread or sprinkle some on fresh fettuccine tossed with butter. The important thing about truffle oil is that it be used sparingly. Just a drop or two is enough in most cases.

Vinegar ··· Aceto

Though over the past few years balsamic vinegar has taken the United States by storm, it is little used and not very well known in Italy outside of its home region of Emilia Romagna. There it is used not so much for dressing salads but as a condiment to finish a sauce for veal or pork or to perk up berries for dessert. It is also used as a *digestivo,* a beverage that aids digestion when taken in tiny sips after a meal. While some aged balsamic vinegars can be exquisite, they are also very pricey. Most of the brands that are sold here are not very good. I think the reason balsamic vinegar has become so popular is that it is sweet, a taste that many people find appealing. Because of this sweetness, balsamic vinegar should not be used as a substitute for red wine vinegar. It has its uses, but it is not an all-purpose vinegar.

You will need both red and white wine vinegars for the recipes in this book. Try several brands to find one that you like. I've had good luck with the Paul Corcellet and Dessaux brands from France, though for red wine vinegar I prefer homemade (see page 46). Vinegars flavored with herbs, spices, and garlic are generally too aggressive and should not be used in Italian cooking.

Yeast ··· Lievito di Birra

Yeasts are tiny plants. When mixed with a liquid and flour, the yeast comes alive and begins to feed on the sugar and starch in the flour. As it feeds, it emits carbon dioxide which inflates the bread dough and makes it rise. A long slow rise ensures that the bread will have a good flavor.

All of the bread recipes in this book were tested with active dry yeast, the kind that comes in little envelopes. If you bake a lot of bread, you might want to buy a jar of active dry yeast, which turns out to be much less expensive than the envelopes. Fresh cake yeast can be substituted if you prefer. Follow the instructions on the package. Cake yeast does not have a long shelf life so be sure that it is very fresh before using it. Quick-rise yeast can be used, though it saves very little time, and some cooks feel it produces inferior results. Instant yeast, fairly new to the United States, is very good because it requires 25 percent less yeast per recipe and it does not need to be dissolved in water before using.

The most important thing to remember when baking with yeast is that it can be killed by overheating. Before adding it to water, check to see that the water temperature is between 105° and 110°F., using an instant-read thermometer. If the water is too hot, you may kill the yeast; if it is too cold, the rising process will be excessively slowed. If you will be kneading the dough in a food processor, use a cooler water temperature because the heat of the motor can overheat the dough.

Many bread recipes begin with proofing the yeast, or testing to see if the yeast is still alive. The only time I bother with this step is if I'm not sure that the yeast is still good, that is, if it is past the expiration date on the package or if it has not been stored

Making Red Wine Vinegar

Making your own red wine vinegar is easy; and if you use good wine to begin with, your vinegar will have a special flavor. The only problem may be in finding a starter, called a "mother." If you know someone who makes vinegar, ask him or her to share some mother with you. It may sound like a strange request to you, but people who make vinegar usually have plenty to spare—and are happy to get rid of it. The mother is a rubbery, jellylike substance that forms on top of vinegar as it develops. You may occasionally find some growing on top of a bottle of unpasteurized vinegar. If all else fails, a good mother can be purchased by mail order from companies that specialize in wine and vinegar-making supplies (see page 382).

Once you have your starter, you will need only two other things: a container and some red wine. While a wooden barrel adds complex flavors to vinegar, it is not essential. You can make your vinegar in a crock or glass jar. I use an old sun tea jar (with a frolicking Santa Claus painted all around). It holds about a gallon of liquid and has a wide mouth, which makes it easy to reach in and remove some of the mother when it gets too big. It also has a spigot near the bottom for drawing off the vinegar.

Pour whatever red wine you will be using into the jar or crock, filling it no more than halfway since the vinegar-making process needs plenty of oxygen. You can use leftover wine but never use a wine that

properly. To proof the yeast, put the required amount of warm water (105° to 110°F.) in a small bowl. Add half a teaspoon of sugar and stir until dissolved. Sprinkle the yeast on the surface and stir again. Let stand for five minutes. If the mixture becomes foamy, the yeast is active and ready to use. Pour the yeast mixture into the flour and proceed with the recipe.

Store yeast in a cool dry place, preferably in the refrigerator. Instant yeast comes in large packages. Store it tightly sealed in the freezer.

Pots and Pans

In practically every cooking class I teach, someone asks what type of pots and pans I recommend. Like most cooks, I have an assortment of different kinds and sizes made tasted spoiled as it will just make spoiled-tasting vinegar. Add the mother. Cover the jar with a piece of cheesecloth or a thin fabric, which will allow the air to circulate but keep dust particles out.

Put the container in a cool place with a fairly constant temperature. Choose a spot where you will not be bothered by the smell of the vinegar, which can get quite strong. In as little as two weeks in warm temperatures or as long as two months, you will notice a whitish film on the surface of the liquid. This is the mother, which will continue to thicken and grow. Do not move the jar unnecessarily or the mother will sink to the bottom. This is not a problem if it happens, but it makes it more difficult to remove. You can add more wine to the container if you like, but do not fill it more than two thirds full. Remove some of the mother from time to time or it will take over your container. Give it away to friends to start their own vinegar.

When the contents of the jar smell like vinegar, about two weeks after the mother has formed, you can extract some from the jar. Pour it into clean bottles, filling them as full as possible to exclude oxygen and stop the mother from reforming. Use a plastic or natural cork to seal the bottles. It is ready to use immediately or, better yet, it can be set aside to age and mellow for several months. Homemade vinegar is quite strong. It can be blended with water to tame its potency, if you like.

White wine vinegar is more difficult to make at home since white wine contains sulfites, which inhibit the growth of the mother. I mostly use homemade red wine vinegar, but I keep a small bottle of storebought white wine vinegar on hand for certain recipes where its lack of color is important.

from a variety of materials. I don't think any one type of equipment works for all cooking purposes.

My basic cookware is a good quality set of pots and saucepans made of stainless steel with a heavy aluminum-clad bottom. The six-quart Dutch oven, minus its original domed lid, which I never use, is my favorite for making risotto and tomato sauces. Its dimensions are ten by four inches. Two eight-quart pots are perfect for cooking pasta and soup or for boiling vegetables. I use nonstick skillets for sautéing chops or making frittatas. A heavy cast-aluminum or iron grill pan is useful for grilling a fish steak or two. I use enameled cast-iron pots when slow cooking stews or braising.

For the most part, I avoid restaurant cookware. It is designed to be used on a commercial range, which has a higher heating capacity output and larger burners than a household-type stove such as mine. Chances are a big restaurant skillet or other pot would be too large and the food around the edges of the pot would not cook evenly. While some small commercial pieces may work on an ordinary home range, high quality household cookware is more practical, unless you have a commercial stove. My only exception to this is a large stockpot I bought in a commercial cookware store. It is great for broth and bollito misto.

No matter what type pots you buy, avoid cheap, flimsy cookware. You can build up your pots and pans a piece or two at a time, but only buy high quality equipment. It cooks better and is easier to maintain. There are many good brands to choose from, including Farberware, Le Creuset, Calphalon, and Paderno.

saluti da procida

Antipasto ... Antipasti

ANTIPASTO DISHES ARE AMONG *the most intriguing foods in the Italian cooking repertory. They are so fascinating to me that I wrote a book, called* The Antipasto Table, *devoted to the subject. Though that book contains almost two hundred recipes, I had no difficulty finding new ones for this chapter, since the number of dishes that can be served as antipasto seems to be inexhaustible.*

Many restaurants in Italy prominently display all or part of the antipasto choices to catch the customer's eye, and the first thing I do upon entering a trattoria or ristorante is check out the day's offerings, which usually include seafood, grain, and vegetable salads, stuffed vegetables, cured meats, and egg dishes. There's always something that I haven't tried before.

In Italian homes, an antipasto course may or may not be served, but when it is, the dishes are usually very simple—a few slices of salami, some olives, or perhaps crostini. In restaurants, however, the antipasto course can be far more elaborate, with restaurants in the Piedmont region in northwestern Italy taking the prize for serving the greatest number at each meal. Menus are rarely presented. Antipasto is served in separate courses, each one a surprise for the diner. They usually include *carne cruda,* chopped raw veal seasoned with olive oil and lemon juice and crowned with thin shavings of fresh white truffles; miniature omelets; marinated cheeses; batter-fried trout; rabbit pâté; and roasted pepper wedges filled with garlic and anchovies—to name just a few. The most I have been offered is twelve, but I have heard of meals that began with even more.

Even though the word antipasto means before the meal, many of the recipes in this chapter are perfect as luncheon or side dishes. Those that can be made ahead are ideal for company. One of my favorite ways to entertain is to set out an assortment of antipasto dishes as a buffet and let my guests help themselves.

Some antipasto dishes should be served alone, such as the Parmesan Custards with Mushrooms, which is quite rich, while others can be combined to form an assortment. If serving several dishes at one time, mix and match them for a variety of textures, colors, and flavors. Grilled Mushrooms with Melted Fontina and Prosciutto, Thousand Herb Omelet, and Roasted Pepper and Wilted Onion Salad would be a good combination, for example.

Also, take a look at the antipasto shopping list. With these ingredients on hand, you can quickly improvise an easy antipasto assortment.

Antipasto Shopping List

Stock your shelves with these ingredients and you can make an antipasto in minutes.

In the cupboard

Canned Italian tuna in olive oil ••• *Canned anchovy fillets* ••• *Canned sardines* ••• *Imported green and black olives* ••• *Jarred pickled vegetables (giardiniera)* ••• *Dried dates and prunes* ••• *Capers* ••• *Breadsticks* ••• *Extra virgin olive oil* ••• *Dried tomatoes* ••• *Wine and balsamic vinegars* ••• *Breadsticks*

In the refrigerator

Celery, carrots, and lemons ••• *Parmigiano-Reggiano, provolone, or other hard cheeses*

In the freezer

Homemade roasted peppers ••• *Italian bread*

Instant Antipasti

A simple antipasto platter can be assembled from some jarred pickled vegetables, canned tuna, firm sharp cheese, olives, and breadsticks. Following are some additional quick-and-easy ideas:

- Pitted dates slit and stuffed with small pieces of Parmigiano-Reggiano.

- Thin slices of prosciutto, ham, or salami wrapped around thin breadsticks or cooked asparagus spears.

- Thin slices of prosciutto wrapped around wedges of pear or persimmon.

- Thin slices of smoked salmon wrapped around breadsticks.

- Roasted peppers dressed with capers, anchovies, garlic, and olive oil.

- Dried tomatoes, softened in warm water and drained, then pureed with garlic, olive oil, basil, and a bit of balsamic vinegar to spread on toast or crackers.

- Raw vegetables—fennel, belgian endive, carrots, celery—cut into spears to dip in extra virgin olive oil seasoned with coarse salt and freshly cracked pepper.

- Bite-size wedges of Parmigiano-Reggiano seasoned with a drop of fine balsamic vinegar.

- Fresh goat cheese drizzled with extra virgin olive oil, chopped garlic, crushed red pepper, and oregano, parsley, or basil.

- Balls or cubes of fresh mozzarella tossed with olive oil, chopped anchovies, parsley, and crushed red pepper.

- Thin slices of leftover focaccia or Italian bread brushed with olive oil and herbs and baked until crisp.

Have you ever made a grilled cheese sandwich and when the cheese drips out onto the hot surface of the pan it becomes lightly browned and a little crisp? That is what *frico* is like, although here grated cheese is intentionally placed in the pan to form toasted cheese wafers. Golden and crunchy, these lacy wafers are perfect with drinks or a glass of chilled white wine before dinner. They keep for a week if stored in an airtight container.

In Friuli, frico is made with a local semi-firm cow's milk cheese called montasio, similar to Swiss emmentaler in flavor and texture. If montasio is not available, substitute Parmigiano-Reggiano, asiago, or a mild provolone. And, a nonstick skillet is essential.

The technique for making frico is similar to that used in making crepes. The trick is to watch the cheese carefully. If it seems to be browning too much or too quickly, lift the skillet away from the heat until it cools down slightly. Once you become adept at making frico, you can use a larger skillet or a flat pancake griddle to make several wafers at one time.

I like to shape frico into small wafers but they are traditionally made larger and placed over the bottom of an inverted small cup. As they cool, the wafers become firm and take on the rounded shape of the cup. Sometimes the frico cups are served with a filling, such as sautéed mushrooms.

Cheese Wafers

FRICO

1 pound montasio
Vegetable oil

1 Grate the cheese on the largest holes of a cheese grater. Heat a large nonstick skillet over medium-low heat. Brush the skillet with oil. Spread about 2 tablespoons of the grated cheese in a circle about 3 inches in diameter. Be sure not to make the layer of cheese too thick, or the wafers will be chewy instead of crispy.

2 Cook the cheese, flattening it if necessary with a wooden spoon or plastic spatula, until melted and golden brown on 1 side, about 2 minutes. Flip the wafer over. Use a second spoon or spatula to push the wafer off if it sticks. Cook the wafer until golden and set, about 1 minute more. Take care not to let it darken to more than a light gold color or it may become bitter. Transfer the wafer to paper towels to drain. Brush out any crumbs from the pan and repeat with the remaining cheese.

3 When the wafers are completely cooled, they are ready to serve.

To make ahead: The wafers can be made up to 1 week before serving. Place them in layers separated by wax paper in an airtight container and store at room temperature.

Thousand Herb Omelet

FRITTATA CON MILLE ERBE

12 large eggs

2 tablespoons finely chopped Italian flat-leaf parsley

2 tablespoons finely chopped fresh basil

1 tablespoon chopped fresh chives

1 tablespoon chopped fresh tarragon

2 teaspoons finely chopped fresh marjoram

1 teaspoon finely chopped fresh thyme

1 teaspoon finely chopped fresh rosemary leaves

1 teaspoon salt

Freshly ground pepper, to taste

2 tablespoons olive oil

1 In a large bowl, whisk the eggs, herbs, salt, and pepper until well combined.

2 In a large flameproof skillet over medium-low heat, heat the oil. Add the egg mixture and reduce the heat to low. Cook, lifting the edges 2 or 3 times to allow the uncooked egg to slide under the cooked portion, until the omelet is set around the edges but still moist in the center, about 10 minutes.

3 If your skillet does not have a flameproof handle, wrap the handle in foil. Transfer the skillet to the broiler. Cook just until the center of the frittata is set, about 1 minute. Watch carefully so that the frittata browns only lightly, or the eggs will toughen.

4 Invert a large serving platter over the frittata. Protect your hands with oven mitts and invert the skillet with the platter. The omelet will slide out onto the platter. Cut into wedges to serve. The omelet is best hot or warm.

Livio Felluga may not be the youngest winemaker in Friuli, but he certainly is one of the most energetic. One day, the charming octogenarian took us on a tour in his Jeep through his vineyards that had me holding on for dear life as he calmly threaded his way up and down the steep rocky slopes. Afterward, I was exhausted, but Livio insisted we join him for dinner and a tasting of some of his excellent wines.

The restaurant he chose was Da Romea in the town of Manzano, where Leda della Rovere, the chef and owner, is known as one of the finest cooks in Friuli. She makes this antipasto omelet in the spring and summer when her garden is full of fresh herbs. Of course, it does not have a thousand herbs—the name is just a bit of Italian hyperbole—but it looks like it with bits of chopped parsley, basil, and other fresh herbs throughout. For twelve eggs, you will need a total of about three quarters of a cup of mixed fresh herbs. The combination suggested here is just a suggestion. You can use whatever fresh herbs you have on hand. Use dried herbs sparingly, if at all; their flavors can be overwhelming.

Before we left, I asked Signor Felluga how he managed to stay so young. Not surprisingly, he attributed his vitality and enthusiasm for life to the beneficial effects of the wines of Friuli.

Da Romea
Via Divisione Julia 15
Manzano (Friuli)

SERVES 4

My husband, Charles, nearly swooned with pleasure when he ate the white bean and shrimp salad at Romano restaurant in Viareggio on the Tuscan coast. Every ingredient was lovingly chosen and carefully cooked: fresh cannellini beans simmered to a creamy tenderness; the ripest, sweetest tomatoes; and barely cooked fresh shrimp dressed with a delicate olive oil.

My version of this popular salad is a little zestier than Romano's since it contains rosemary instead of basil and the shrimp are grilled instead of boiled. I find these substitutions more forgiving of the thawed frozen shrimp and dried beans available here in the United States. Though this salad is usually served as an antipasto, it makes a fine main course in larger quantities.

Romano
Via Mazzini, 120
Viareggio (Tuscany)

Warm Bean Salad with Grilled Shrimp

INSALATA DI FAGIOLI E GAMBERI

12 jumbo shrimp, peeled and deveined
2 large garlic cloves, finely chopped
2 tablespoons chopped fresh rosemary leaves
4 tablespoons olive oil
Salt and freshly ground pepper, to taste
1 cup dried cannellini or Great Northern beans, cooked and
*   drained (about 3 cups after cooking, or canned beans, rinsed*
*   and drained; see Step 1, page 96)*
1 large tomato, seeded and chopped
1 tablespoon fresh lemon juice
Sprigs of fresh rosemary, for garnish

1 In a bowl, combine the shrimp, half the garlic, 1 tablespoon of the chopped rosemary, and 2 tablespoons of the olive oil with salt and pepper. Stir well. Cover and chill for 1 hour.

2 Preheat a grill or broiler.

3 In a saucepan over medium heat, heat the remaining garlic, rosemary, and olive oil just until fragrant, about 1 minute. Stir in the beans. Cover and cook over low heat for 5 minutes, or until warm. Remove from the heat. Stir in the tomato, lemon juice, salt, and pepper.

4 Grill the shrimp until lightly browned and just opaque in the thickest part, about 5 minutes.

5 Spoon the bean mixture onto 4 plates and surround with the grilled shrimp. Garnish with rosemary sprigs and serve.

Fava Beans with Seven Salads

FAVE CON SETTE INSALATE

8 ounces dried peeled fava beans

2 to 4 tablespoons extra virgin olive oil

Salt, to taste

1 cup imported black olives, such as Gaeta or kalamata, pitted and chopped

1/2 cup thinly sliced red onion, separated into rings

1 cup arugula, tough stems removed

1/2 cup pickled peppers, drained and sliced

1 cup chopped fresh tomatoes

1 pound spinach, dandelion, or broccoli rabe, cooked and drained

1/2 cup thinly sliced radishes

1   Place the beans in a large bowl of cold water. Let stand in a cool place for at least 4 hours or overnight. If the weather is warm, place the bowl in the refrigerator.

2   Drain the beans and rinse them. Place the beans in a large pot. Add fresh cold water to cover the beans by 1 inch. Bring the water to a slow simmer and cook the beans over low heat until very soft and all of the liquid has been absorbed, about 1 hour. If necessary, add a little more water to prevent the beans from drying out. With a potato masher, mash the beans until smooth. Stir in the olive oil and season with salt.

3   Spoon the warm fava beans onto a warm shallow serving platter. Place piles of the seven salads around the edges. Serve immediately.

To make ahead: The fava bean puree can be made up to 3 days before serving. Add a little water and reheat over very low heat or use a double boiler.

In this dish from Puglia in southern Italy seven "salads" top a warm puree of dried fava beans, which is spread on a large shallow serving platter with the salads placed on top around the edges. The toppings are called salads, but they range from chopped tomatoes and sliced radishes to jarred pickled peppers and cooked spinach, and can be varied according to the season or the ingredients on hand. Seven is the typical number, but use fewer or more if you like. Exact proportions for the salads are not important and the amounts below are just a suggestion. This makes a great meatless antipasto or main course.

Dried peeled fava beans can be found in Italian, Greek, and Middle Eastern markets. Brown unpeeled favas can be used, but the skins, which are very tough, must be removed one by one from the beans after cooking, a chore that no one enjoys.

Dante Bernardis, owner of the Trattoria Blasut in Lavariano in the Friuli region, regaled us with stories and jokes as we nibbled these delicate fritters made with cantaloupe slices and basil leaves coated with a delicate batter.

Later, chef Andrea Bordignon, who had heard how much we enjoyed the fritters, stopped by our table to say hello, and when I inquired how he prepared them, he offered two useful tips. First, he uses sparkling mineral water to make the batter light and airy. Then, he dries the slices of melon between two pieces of white bread (paper towels also do the job) so that the batter will adhere and not slip off the fruit when it hits the hot oil. Serve these as soon as they are done with a glass of sparkling wine.

As we were leaving the restaurant, Dante, whose nickname Blasut means Shorty in the local dialect, invited us to return to Lavariano some future February to attend his annual *Festa di Maiale*, or pork festival, an all-day affair that begins at dawn with coffee and pastries. Throughout the day, people come from all over the region to feast on polenta, fresh pork ribs, and grilled pork tenderloin, washed down with the local red wine. Music and dancing accompany the festivities.

Trattoria Blasut
Via Garibaldi, 123
Lavariano (Friuli)

Cantaloupe and Basil Fritters

MELONE E BASILICO FRITTI

¹/₂ small ripe cantaloupe, at room temperature
1 small bunch of fresh basil or sage
1 cup all-purpose flour
1 teaspoon salt
2 large eggs
¹/₂ cup cold sparkling mineral water or club soda
Vegetable oil, for deep-frying

1 Peel and seed the cantaloupe. Cut it into pieces about 2 × 1 × ¹/₄ inch in size.

2 Remove 12 basil leaves from the stem. Rinse under cool running water.

3 In a small bowl, combine the flour and salt. Add the eggs, mineral water, and 1 tablespoon of the oil and whisk just until blended.

4 Fill a deep-fryer with oil according to the manufacturer's directions or pour 1 inch of oil into a deep heavy saucepan. Heat the oil to 375°F. on a deep-frying thermometer.

5 Pat the cantaloupe and basil leaves dry. Dip the pieces, one at a time, into the batter, then slide them carefully into the hot oil. Do not crowd the pan or the pieces will stick together. Turn the pieces to brown evenly. When golden brown and puffed, about 1 minute, remove the pieces with a slotted spoon and drain them well on paper towels.

6 Reheat the oil briefly. Fry the remaining melon and basil leaves. Serve immediately.

Deep-Frying

An electric deep-fryer is not essential for deep-frying, but it is very useful. It regulates the temperature automatically, so that the oil does not vary from the desired range of 350° to 375°F. Electric fryers are also deep and very stable so that there is little danger of the pot tipping or the oil boiling over. If you don't want to make the investment or if you don't fry food frequently, consider sharing one with a friend.

To fry on top of the stove use a deep-fryer with a basket or improvise with a deep heavy saucepan with a flat bottom, preferably without a long handle. If it does have a handle turn it toward the rear of the stove. To prevent overflows, never fill a deep-fryer more than halfway, since the oil will bubble up when food is added. Make sure the pan is perfectly dry before adding the oil to avoid spattering.

Attach a deep-frying thermometer to the side of the pan. Heat the oil over medium heat. When it reaches 375°F. the oil is ready. Learn to recognize when the oil is ready as insurance against a faulty thermometer. Drop a small piece of white bread or a bit of whatever you're frying into the oil. If it swims around rapidly and makes bubbles, the oil is ready. Try to keep the oil in the 350° to 375°F. range. The temperature will fall as food is added, then rise again as it cooks.

Add only as much food to the pan as can fit comfortably without crowding, or the pieces may stick together. Use a frying basket or long metal tongs to add the food or retrieve it from the oil. Dip the basket or tongs in the hot oil before adding the food, to prevent sticking. To drain the food, line a baking sheet with absorbent newspapers or brown paper bags beforehand and cover them with clean paper towels.

When you have finished frying, turn off the heat and leave the oil to cool completely before discarding it. Never reuse frying oil. The flavors and juices of the previously fried food will cause the oil to develop an off taste.

I never thought of stuffed cabbage as an Italian dish until I came across this version from Naples in a book called *A Napoli si mangia cosi* (Eating the Neapolitan Way) by Vittorio Gleijeses. The cabbage leaves are wrapped around pieces of fresh mozzarella and baked in a simple tomato sauce. Follow this antipasto with Pork Chops in Red Wine and Juniper (page 253) or a roast chicken (see pages 223–224), or any of the meat dishes that do not include tomatoes.

Mozzarella-stuffed Cabbage

INVOLTINI DI CAVALO

1 garlic clove, finely chopped
3 tablespoons olive oil
2 tablespoons chopped fresh parsley
2 large tomatoes, peeled, seeded, and chopped, or 2 cups chopped canned Italian tomatoes
1/2 teaspoon dried oregano
Salt and freshly ground pepper, to taste
8 large savoy cabbage leaves
8 ounces fresh mozzarella
1/4 cup grated Parmigiano-Reggiano

1 In a medium saucepan over medium heat, cook the garlic in the oil for about 30 seconds, or until pale golden. Stir in the parsley, then add the tomatoes, oregano, salt, and pepper. Bring the sauce to a simmer and cook for 15 to 20 minutes, or until thickened.

2 Bring a large pot of water to a boil. Add the cabbage leaves and salt to taste. Cook for 2 minutes, or until the leaves are tender. Remove the leaves with a slotted spoon or tongs and drain them on paper towels. Pat the leaves dry.

3 Preheat the oven to 375°F. Oil a 9-inch square nonreactive baking pan.

4 Spoon half of the sauce into the pan.

5 Cut the mozzarella into 8 pieces. Place 1 piece near the base of each cabbage leaf. Roll up the leaf, tucking in the sides to make a neat package. Place the cabbage rolls in the pan, seam side down. Spoon on the remaining sauce and sprinkle with the Parmigiano.

6 Bake the rolls for 30 minutes, or until the sauce is bubbling. Serve hot.

Spiced Eggplant

Melanzane con le Spezie

SERVES 8

This eggplant appetizer is similar to the sweet-and-sour caponata of Sicily. The combination of ingredients may seem odd, but the flavors come together harmoniously. In fact, chocolate in combination with eggplant appears in several southern Italian recipes, including an unusual crostata from the Naples area. Serve the eggplant plain or on slices of toasted bread.

2 medium eggplants (about 1 pound each)

Salt, to taste

$^1\!/_4$ cup raisins

1 ounce semisweet chocolate

2 tablespoons sugar

Pinch of ground cinnamon

$^1\!/_4$ cup olive oil

$^1\!/_4$ cup red wine vinegar

$^1\!/_2$ teaspoon grated lemon zest

$^1\!/_4$ cup pine nuts

$^1\!/_4$ cup coarsely chopped walnuts

1 Cut the eggplants into 1-inch cubes. Layer the pieces in a colander sprinkling each layer with salt. Place an inverted plate and a weight such as a heavy can on top. Place the colander in the sink or over a bowl to catch the drips and let stand for 1 hour. Rinse the eggplant pieces and drain well.

2 In a large pot, combine the eggplant with the raisins, chocolate, sugar, cinnamon, olive oil, vinegar, and $^1\!/_2$ cup water. Cover and cook over low heat, stirring occasionally, for 30 to 40 minutes, or until the eggplant is tender. Watch carefully so that it does not scorch. If the mixture becomes too dry, add a little water.

3 Stir in the lemon zest and nuts. Let cool. Serve at room temperature.

To make ahead: This keeps well, covered, for up to 1 week in the refrigerator. Bring to room temperature before serving.

One of the most passionate cooks in the Piedmont region in northeastern Italy is Claudia Verro. Together with her husband Tonino, she operates the Locanda Contea, a restaurant and inn renowned for its fine food and wine. The dining rooms at La Contea remind me of my grandmother's house. Massive, dark wood furnishings make the high-ceilinged rooms seem homey and old-fashioned. In winter, a cozy fire burns in the fireplace. The restaurant is always packed with visitors from all over the world who come for a taste of Claudia's inspired interpretations of classic Piedmontese cooking. During the white truffle season in November and December, a table must be booked weeks in advance.

One of Claudia's specialties is *tartrà*, a delicate parmesan and onion custard flavored with herbs, originally a farmer's rustic one-dish meal. Claudia has enriched it further by baking the mixture in puff pastry and garnishing it with white truffles and porcini mushrooms.

This simpler, yet equally delicious version, is adapted from one given to me by Roberto Donna, the personable chef/owner of several Washington, D.C., restaurants, including Galileo and I Matti, for an article I wrote for the *New York Times*. Like Claudia, Roberto hails from Piedmont, although these days he

Parmesan Custards with Mushrooms

TARTRÀ

1 cup heavy cream

1/4 cup milk

1 bay leaf

2 fresh sage leaves

1 tablespoon chopped fresh parsley

1 small sprig of fresh rosemary

2 tablespoons plus 2 teaspoons unsalted butter

1/4 cup finely chopped onion

2 large eggs

2 tablespoons freshly grated Parmigiano-Reggiano cheese

Pinch of freshly grated nutmeg

Salt and freshly ground pepper, to taste

8 ounces white mushrooms, quartered

Sprigs of fresh parsley, for garnish

1 Preheat the oven to 350°F. Butter four 6-ounce custard cups.

2 In a bowl, combine the cream, milk, bay leaf, sage, parsley, and rosemary. Let stand for at least 1 hour at cool room temperature or in the refrigerator.

3 In a small skillet over medium heat, melt 2 teaspoons butter. Add the onion and cook until tender, about 5 minutes. Let cool.

4 In a large bowl, beat the eggs until foamy. Strain the cream mixture into the eggs. Stir in the onion, cheese, nutmeg, 1/4 teaspoon salt, and pepper. Pour into the prepared custard cups.

5 Place a roasting pan in the oven. Pour about 1/2 inch hot water into the pan. Place the custard cups in the hot water bath. Bake for 50 to 60 minutes, or until the tops are lightly golden and the cus-

tards are just set. Remove the custards from the pan and let stand for 15 to 30 minutes.

6 In a medium skillet over medium heat, melt the remaining 2 tablespoons butter. Add the mushrooms and cook, stirring frequently, until lightly browned, about 10 minutes. Sprinkle with salt and pepper.

7 Run a small knife around the inside of the cups and invert the custards onto serving plates. Spoon the mushrooms to one side. Garnish with parsley sprigs. Serve warm.

To make ahead: The custards can be made ahead of time through Step 5, but the mushrooms should be cooked just before serving. Let the custards cool, then cover each cup with plastic wrap. Store in the refrigerator for several hours or overnight. To reheat, bring about 1/2 inch water to a simmer in a skillet or saucepan wide enough to hold the cups. Place the cups in the water and let stand for about 10 minutes, or until the centers are warm. Prepare the mushrooms, unmold the cups, and garnish with the mushrooms as described in Steps 6 and 7.

does his cooking on the other side of the Atlantic.

Tartrà is very rich. I like to serve it with a mushroom garnish as a first course followed by Quail with Rosemary and Garlic (page 242) or as a meatless main dish accompanied by asparagus or sweet peas.

La Contea
Piazza Cocito, 8
Neive (Piedmont)

Galileo
1110 21 Street NW
Washington, D.C.

I Matti
2436 18 Street NW
Washington, D.C.

Though their name sounds Italian, portobello mushrooms are a large variation of cremini, a brown version of white button mushrooms. I usually brush them with olive oil and garlic and grill them the way other large mushrooms, notably the illustrious porcini, are prepared in Italy. For this dish, the grilled portobellos are stuffed with prosciutto and cheese, a rich complement to their meatiness.

Grilled Mushrooms with Melted Fontina and Prosciutto

FUNGHI RIPIENI ALLA GRIGLIA

4 large portobello mushrooms

About 3 tablespoons olive oil

4 thin slices prosciutto

4 thin slices Italian fontina cheese, rind removed

2 teaspoons chopped fresh parsley

1 Preheat a grill or broiler. Set the rack 4 to 5 inches from the source of the heat.

2 Wipe the mushrooms clean with a damp paper towel. Remove the stems and set them aside for another use. Brush the mushroom caps on both sides with olive oil. Grill or broil the mushroom caps with the tops toward the source of the heat until tender and slightly browned, about 5 minutes. Turn the caps and grill the other side.

3 Place a slice of prosciutto and a slice of cheese inside each mushroom cap, folding the slices to fit. Grill or broil for 1 minute more, or until the cheese is slightly melted.

4 Sprinkle with parsley and serve immediately.

Roasted Olives with Fennel and Lemon

OLIVE AL FORNO

8 ounces imported black olives, such as Alfonso or Gaeta

4 garlic cloves, peeled

$^1/_2$ lemon, scrubbed and thinly sliced

$^1/_4$ cup olive oil

1 teaspoon fennel seed

Pinch of crushed red pepper

1 Preheat the oven to 350°F.

2 Spread the olives, garlic, and lemon slices in an 8-inch baking pan. Drizzle with the olive oil and sprinkle with fennel seeds and red pepper. Bake for 45 minutes, stirring the olives 2 or 3 times.

3 Transfer the olives to a serving bowl and serve warm.

To make ahead: These olives keep well, covered, in the refrigerator for up to 1 week.

Roasting black olives emphasizes their flavor and makes them taste almost chocolatey. Choose plump, meaty, not-too-salty olives like Alfonsos or Gaetas and serve them warm with crusty Italian or French bread. The leftover oil is sensational when used as a dip for good bread, or drizzle it over mixed salad greens.

For sweet, smoky roasted peppers, I usually place whole bell peppers under the broiler and turn them until the skin is charred and blistered. For this dish, however, the peppers are baked in the oven to loosen the skins and soften the peppers without charring, resulting in a flavor that is more delicate and peppers that are just as easy to peel. The pepper halves are then stuffed with tomatoes, olives, and mozzarella and baked briefly until the cheese is melted.

Roasted Pepper Rolls with Melted Mozzarella

INVOLTINI DI PEPERONI

4 large red or yellow bell peppers

2 large ripe tomatoes, peeled, seeded, and chopped

1/4 cup chopped pitted black olives, such as Gaeta

2 tablespoons grated pecorino romano

2 tablespoons chopped fresh parsley

2 tablespoons olive oil

Salt and freshly ground pepper, to taste

8 ounces fresh mozzarella, diced

1 Preheat the oven to 450°F.

2 Cut the peppers lengthwise in half and cut away the cores, seeds, and white membranes. Place the peppers, cut side down, on a roasting pan. Bake for 25 minutes, or until the skins are wrinkled and the peppers are tender when pierced with a knife. Place the peppers in a bowl and cover with plastic wrap. Let cool. Remove the skin.

3 In a bowl, combine the tomatoes, olives, pecorino, parsley, olive oil, salt, and pepper. Set aside 1/2 cup of the mixture. Stir the mozzarella into the remainder.

4 Oil a large baking pan. Place a spoonful of the mozzarella and tomato mixture in the center of each pepper half and fold over the ends to enclose the filling. Place the rolls in the pan. Spoon the remaining tomato mixture over the pepper rolls.

5 Bake for 15 minutes, or until the cheese is melted. Serve warm.

To make ahead: The peppers can be prepared ahead through Step 2. Cover and refrigerate for up to 24 hours.

Roasted Pepper and Wilted Onion Salad

INSALATA DI PEPERONI

*4 large red, yellow, or green bell peppers, or a combination of
colors*

1 large onion, very thinly sliced

3 tablespoons extra virgin olive oil

2 to 3 tablespoons fresh lemon juice

Salt and freshly ground pepper, to taste

2 tablespoons chopped fresh parsley

1 Broil or grill the peppers as described on page 66. Place them in a bowl and cover with foil or plastic wrap. Let stand until cool.

2 Bring a small saucepan of water to a boil. Add the onion. As soon as the water returns to a boil, remove the pot from the heat. Drain the onion and pat it dry. Place it in a serving bowl.

3 Peel and seed the peppers. Cut them into 1-inch strips and place them in the bowl with the onion. Strain the pepper juices over the vegetables.

4 Add the olive oil, lemon juice, salt, and pepper. Stir in the parsley. Serve immediately or let marinate for at least 2 hours.

To make ahead: This salad can be made up to 2 days before serving and stored in a covered container in the refrigerator. Bring back to room temperature before serving.

Red and yellow bell peppers are available year round (albeit at a stiff price in winter). Since they are nothing more than fully ripened green bell peppers, until recently they could be found only late in the summer growing season. When my mother used to shop for peppers, she looked for the ones turning from green to red that had the most red. Actually, we liked a combination of the two, both for the contrast in color and for the slight difference in texture and flavor. Green peppers are a bit crisper while red peppers are sweeter.

The first time I encountered yellow peppers was in Tuscany. I was not quite sure what they were when they arrived on my antipasto plate until I tasted them. They were slightly hot yet sweet, like a mild chili. The yellow peppers available in the United States lack that interesting touch of heat.

Although I most often dress roasted peppers with just garlic, olive oil, and a pinch of oregano or chopped fresh basil, this is another favorite combination, with onions, parsley, and lemon juice. A quick dip in boiling water wilts the onion slightly and renders it sweet and mellow.

Besides its role as an antipasto, this salad is good in a sandwich with drained canned tuna or anchovies or served with a frittata for a quick lunch or supper.

Four Ways to Peel Peppers— and One Way Not To

Peppers can be peeled several different ways. Here are the four methods I use, depending on how I will be using the peppers.

1. For very sweet-tasting peppers with no hint of smoke, bring a saucepan of water to a boil. Drop in the peppers, two or three at a time. Hold the peppers under the water with a spoon or small strainer for thirty seconds. Remove with a slotted spoon. Dry the peppers and let cool slightly. Peel off the skin.

2. My preferred method for peeling peppers for salads and crostini toppings is to roast them. Their flavor becomes intensely concentrated and slightly smoky, and the juices can be used in the salad dressing. Even though the peppers are called roasted, they are actually broiled or grilled.

   Place the peppers on a rack in a preheated broiler or place them on an outdoor grill. Broil or grill the peppers, turning them often so that the skin becomes blistered and lightly charred but the flesh of the peppers does not burn. When the peppers are evenly charred, transfer them to a bowl and cover with plastic wrap or foil to steam; this helps loosen their skins. Let cool.

   Many recipes recommend putting the peppers in a brown paper bag to steam and cool, but since such bags are made of recycled paper treated with chemicals not suited for human consumption, I prefer to put the peppers in a clean bowl, where the pepper juices collect—an added bonus. A brown bag has no magical properties that make removal of pepper skins any easier. When you peel the peppers hold them over a strainer set on top of a bowl to catch the juices and any seeds that drop. Peel off the skins and remove the stems, veins, and seeds.

3. The peppers can also be roasted in a hot oven. Preheat the oven to 450°F. Cut the peppers in half and remove the stems and seeds. Place the peppers on a rack in a roasting pan, cut side down. Roast for twenty-five minutes, or until the skins are blistered and slightly browned. Remove from the oven and place in a bowl covered with plastic wrap or foil. Let cool. Peel off the skins.

4. Peppers can also be peeled with a swivel-blade vegetable peeler. This is the best method to use if you want to have the pepper raw and crisp for salads.

One way *not* to peel peppers is to hold them over a stovetop burner. I find that the skin becomes very charred and flakes off in tiny bits and pieces rather than coming off in large strips. To remove the little flakes, some cooks wash the skins off under cold water, but this technique also washes away the juices and dilutes the peppers' flavor.

To Make Ahead: **When red and yellow peppers are in season and prices are reasonable, I buy them by the dozen to roast and freeze. I roast, peel, and seed them using the second method (grilling or broiling). Then I pack them in their own juices in 1- to 2-cup-size freezer containers. I place a piece of plastic wrap on the surface of the peppers so that there is no airspace between them and the inside of the lid. I do this to prevent freezer burn. Frozen this way, the peppers keep for months with little loss of texture or flavor. To thaw, place the container in the refrigerator overnight. Let the peppers come to room temperature before dressing and serving them.**

Rice Salad with Tuna and Roasted Peppers

INSALATA DI RISO AL TONNO

1 cup long-grain rice

Salt, to taste

1 large ripe tomato, chopped

1 or 2 roasted red bell peppers, cut into small dice (about 1 cup)

1/2 cup imported black olives, such as Gaeta, pitted and chopped

1 can (7 ounces) Italian tuna in olive oil, drained

2 tablespoons chopped fresh parsley

3 tablespoons extra virgin olive oil

2 tablespoons red wine vinegar

Freshly ground pepper, to taste

1/4 cup toasted pine nuts

1 Bring 2$\frac{1}{2}$ cups water to a boil in a medium saucepan. Add the rice and salt. When the rice returns to a boil, stir well. Cover the pan and cook over low heat until the water is absorbed and the rice is tender, about 18 minutes.

2 In a large serving bowl, combine the tomato, peppers, olives, tuna, parsley, olive oil, vinegar, salt, and pepper. Add the rice and stir well.

3 Just before serving, taste for seasoning. Sprinkle with the pine nuts and serve.

SERVES 6

Rice salads are very common in Italy, especially in the summer. While cold pasta tends to become flabby and lose its texture if made in advance, rice stays firm and is much more appealing as part of a cold buffet. For salads, I prefer American-style long-grain rice because the grains remain separate after they are cooked.

Prosciutto-wrapped Prunes and Almonds

Involtini di Prosciutto, Prugne, e Mandorle

California chef Charles Saunders prepared these little tidbits to serve with champagne at a dinner at the Gloria Ferrer winery in Sonoma. I love the way he reinvented a seventies appetizer—remember prunes stuffed with water chestnuts wrapped in bacon?—and updated it by adding prosciutto and toasted almonds. Though the concept is undeniably American, the combination of flavors has an Italian accent thanks to the prosciutto.

16 plump pitted prunes
16 almonds, toasted
4 ounces thinly sliced prosciutto

1 Preheat the oven to 350°F.

2 Stuff each prune with an almond. Cut the prosciutto into 4 × 1-inch strips. Wrap a piece of prosciutto around each prune. Secure the prosciutto with a toothpick. Place the prunes on a rack in a small roasting pan. Bake for 10 minutes.

3 Serve hot.

To make ahead: Stuff the prunes and wrap them in prosciutto up to 2 hours before baking. Cover tightly with plastic wrap. Bake just before serving.

ISOLA DI PROCIDA

Salads

At the Italian table, green or mixed salads are sometimes served as a side dish or following the main course. Green salads are made with many different mild to slightly bitter leafy vegetables. When I visit Italy, I look for two of my favorites, green radicchio and *rughetta,* a crisper, tastier version of the cultivated arugula grown in the United States. A mixed salad might also contain sliced radishes, celery, fennel, or grated carrots.

Forget what passes for "Italian dressing" in the States. Salad dressing in Italy is made with only three ingredients: oil (usually olive), an acid (usually wine vinegar or fresh lemon juice), and salt. A good rule of thumb is three parts oil to one part acid, but you can adjust the ratio according to your taste and the ingredients of the salad itself. The idea is to enhance the flavor of the vegetables, not drown or disguise it with a heavy dressing. There should be just enough dressing to coat the vegetables without leaving a puddle in the bottom of the bowl.

A salad that has such other ingredients as cheese, nuts, or fruit added to it or that has a heavier dressing made with mayonnaise or cream is usually served as an antipasto. I also serve such salads as a light luncheon dish.

Pear, Watercress, and Pecorino Salad

INSALATA DI PERE, CRESCIONE, E PECORINO

1 large ripe pear, cored and diced

2 to 3 teaspoons fresh lemon juice

2 tablespoons extra virgin olive oil

Coarse or kosher salt and freshly ground pepper, to taste

1 large bunch of watercress or arugula, washed, dried, and trimmed (about 4 cups)

1 piece of pecorino romano, at room temperature (about 1 ounce)

1 Combine the pear with the lemon juice, olive oil, salt, and pepper. Divide the watercress among 4 salad plates. Top with the pear.

2 With a swivel-blade vegetable peeler, shave thin flakes of pecorino romano over each salad. Serve immediately.

SERVES 4

Thin shavings of pecorino romano are a perfect contrast to the sweet pear and the peppery greens in this Roman salad. Use a swivel-blade vegetable peeler, the kind used for potatoes or carrots, to shave the thinnest possible slices of cheese. Shave the slices from a whole piece of cheese, preferably at room temperature. The delicate flakes that result have a melt-in-the-mouth quality that balances with the other ingredients. This technique works with many kinds of firm cheeses, including Parmigiano-Reggiano, which is used in the Spinach, Apple, and Pine Nut Salad (page 70).

Trent, in the Trentino-Alto Adige region in northern Italy, is the heart of Italian apple-growing country. At Ristorante Chiesa, many items listed on the menu are prepared with the local apples.

One evening when we arrived at the normally very busy restaurant, we were surprised to find it deserted. We ordered our meal, including this salad as an appetizer. It seemed strange that our waiter would disappear for long periods between courses and pouring our wine. Hearing a lot of noise and cheering coming from the kitchen, I peeked in and discovered the waiters, cooks, and busboys crowded around a small television set. It was the night of a major soccer playoff and everyone in Italy was watching it—except for a handful of tourists. By the time we left, the Italian team had won an important victory in the World Cup matches and the town spontaneously exploded with fireworks, marching bands, and cheering crowds. We just managed to drive away before all of the streets were completely blocked.

Chiesa
Via San Marco, 64
Trent (Trentino-Alto Adige)

Spinach, Apple, and Pine Nut Salad

INSALATA DI SPINACI, MELA, E PINOLI

8 ounces tender fresh spinach, trimmed, washed, and dried

1 Golden Delicious apple, peeled, cored, and thinly sliced

3 tablespoons extra virgin olive oil

2 tablespoons fresh lemon juice

Salt and freshly ground pepper, to taste

1/4 cup pine nuts, lightly toasted

1 piece of Parmigiano-Reggiano, at room temperature (about 2 ounces)

1 Tear the spinach leaves into 2 or 3 pieces. In a large bowl, combine the spinach and apple slices.

2 In a small bowl, whisk the oil, lemon juice, salt, and pepper. Pour the dressing over the salad and toss well. Arrange the salad on 4 plates. Sprinkle with pine nuts.

3 Using a swivel-blade vegetable peeler, shave the cheese into thin slivers. Scatter the slivers over the salad and serve immediately.

Baby Lettuce Salad with Goat Cheese and Black Olive Torta

INSALATA VERDE CON TORTA DI FORMAGGIO DI CAPRA

SERVES 6

Mesclun, or tender mixed baby greens, is perfect for this salad. You can buy it pre-washed and packaged in cellophane bags in many supermarkets. Wedges of a flavorful little cake of layered goat cheese and black olive puree accompany the greens. Serve it with slices of toasted Italian bread rubbed with garlic and drizzled with a robust extra virgin olive oil.

TORTA

1/2 cup imported black olives, such as Gaeta or Alfonso, pitted

2 anchovy fillets

1 small garlic clove

8 ounces fresh goat cheese, without rind

1 tablespoon extra virgin olive oil

SALAD

1/4 cup extra virgin olive oil

1 tablespoon red wine vinegar

Salt and freshly ground pepper, to taste

6 to 8 cups mesclun, washed and dried if necessary

1 To make the torta, line a 1 1/2-cup bowl with plastic wrap. In a food processor or blender, combine the olives, anchovies, and garlic. Puree until smooth. With a fork, mash the cheese and blend in the olive oil. Spoon about one third of the cheese into the bowl. Spoon half the olive mixture over the cheese. Make another layer with half of the remaining cheese, followed by the remaining olive mixture. Top with the last of the cheese. Smooth the surface. Cover with plastic wrap and top with a weight such as a heavy can. Place in the refrigerator for at least 4 hours or overnight.

2 To make the salad, just before serving, whisk the olive oil, vinegar, salt, and pepper until blended. Place the greens in a bowl and toss with just enough dressing to coat. Divide the greens among 6 salad plates.

3 Remove the plastic wrap and cut the olive torta into 6 wedges. Place a wedge on each salad and serve immediately.

Cook's note: Prepared olive paste can be substituted for the whole olives. Use ¹/₂ cup.

To make ahead: The torta can be prepared up to 3 days before serving.

SERVES 4

This salad is named for the grape pickers who have little time for a lunch break during the busy harvest season. I imagine a group of them sitting down under a shade tree, to share a refreshing salad. The combination of salty sardines and olives with grapes is Sicilian inspired. I prefer canned Norwegian sardines because they are lightly smoked before canning, which gives them good flavor. The salad is dressed with oregano-flavored oil, no vinegar. Instead you squeeze a lemon wedge over each portion. Serve the salad alone as an antipasto with a chilled pinot grigio or accompany it with sharp cheese and crusty bread for a light lunch.

Grape Pickers' Salad

INSALATA DI VENDEMMIATORE

2 medium-size ripe tomatoes, cored and cut into 1-inch pieces

1 small red onion, thinly sliced

1 can (3¹/₂ ounces) sardines, drained

1 cup green olives, pitted and halved

1 cup seedless red grapes, halved

4 cups torn romaine or Bibb lettuce leaves

¹/₄ cup olive oil

¹/₂ teaspoon dried oregano

Salt, to taste

Lemon wedges

1 In a large serving bowl, combine the tomatoes, onion, sardines, olives, and grapes. Tear the lettuce leaves into 1-inch pieces and add them to the salad.

2 Combine the olive oil, oregano, and salt. Pour the dressing over the salad and mix well.

3 Serve immediately with lemon wedges.

Endive with Tuna Dip

INDIVIA CON SALSA DI TONNO

1 can (7 ounces) Italian tuna packed in olive oil

4 anchovy fillets

1/2 cup mayonnaise, preferably homemade

2 tablespoons capers, drained

1 small garlic clove, peeled

1 1/2 to 2 tablespoons fresh lemon juice

3 heads of belgian endive

1   In a food processor or blender, combine the tuna with its oil, the anchovies, mayonnaise, capers, and garlic. Process until smooth, about 3 minutes, stopping to scrape down the mixture as necessary. Add lemon juice to taste. Scrape the tuna mixture into a small bowl.

2   To serve, place the bowl in the center of a large platter. Separate the endive into individual leaves. Surround the bowl with the endive and serve.

To make ahead: Prepare the tuna dip through Step 1. Cover with plastic wrap and store in the refrigerator for up to 24 hours.

SERVES 6

Vitello tonnato, a pairing of thin slices of cold poached veal with a tuna, anchovy, caper, and mayonnaise sauce, is a classic Italian summer favorite. The sauce is so good and so easy to prepare that I have devised a number of other ways to serve it: as a dip for belgian endive spears, red pepper strips, or other raw vegetables; over hard-cooked eggs; on toast; on poached chicken breasts; over steamed green beans or sliced tomatoes; or as a dollop in a hollowed-out new potato half. I keep the ingredients on hand, so it is the kind of thing I can put together in minutes.

Celeriac, also known as celery root or knob celery, is a homely looking vegetable from the same family as celery. The top of the plant resembles an undernourished stalk celery while the edible portion grows underground. It is covered with a rough brown skin that must be peeled away to get to the creamy white flesh inside. Celeriac has a mild celery flavor and is used a great deal in France where it is known as *céleri-rave*. This salad, combining celeriac, celery, and gruyère cheese in a creamy dressing, is a popular antipasto in Piedmont and reflects the influence of the region's neighbors, France and Switzerland, to its west and north.

Celeriac, Gruyère, and Celery Salad

INSALATA DI SEDANO, GROVIERA, E SEDANINO

1 medium bulb celeriac (about 10 ounces)

Salt, to taste

2 tablespoons fresh lemon juice

3 tablespoons olive oil

Freshly ground pepper, to taste

3 tablespoons heavy cream

2 to 3 tender celery ribs, sliced thin

4 ounces gruyère, cut into matchstick strips

4 large radicchio leaves

1 Peel the celeriac with a paring knife. Cut it in half, then into matchstick pieces. You should have about $2^1/2$ cups.

2 Bring a medium saucepan of water to a boil. Add the celeriac and salt. Cook for 1 minute after the water returns to a boil. Drain and cool under cold running water. Pat the pieces dry.

3 In a medium bowl, whisk the lemon juice, olive oil, salt, and pepper. Slowly whisk in the cream. Add the celeriac, celery, and cheese. Fold gently to coat with dressing. Cover and refrigerate for 1 hour.

4 Arrange the radicchio leaves on 4 salad plates. Spoon on the celeriac mixture. Serve immediately.

Smoked Salmon with Oranges and Fennel

INSALATA DI SALMONE AFFUMICATO

2 small fennel bulbs

3 navel oranges

1 to 2 teaspoons fresh lemon juice

2 tablespoons extra virgin olive oil

Salt and freshly ground pepper, to taste

4 to 8 large slices thinly sliced smoked salmon (about 6 ounces)

1 tablespoon chopped fennel leaves or fresh dill

1 tablespoon chopped fresh chives

1 Trim the fennel stalks even with the bulb, reserving some of the feathery green leaves, if any, for garnish. Trim away any bruised outer layers. Slice off the base of the fennel. Cut the bulbs lengthwise in half and remove the core. Slice the halves crosswise as thin as possible. You should have about 2 cups.

2 Squeeze the juice from one of the oranges. Peel the remaining oranges, removing all of the white pith, and cut into wedges.

3 Combine the orange juice, lemon juice, olive oil, salt, and pepper.

4 In a bowl, toss the fennel slices and orange wedges with half the dressing. Arrange the salad on 4 plates.

5 Lay the salmon slices over the salad. Drizzle with the remaining dressing. Sprinkle with the reserved fennel leaves or dill and chives. Serve immediately.

SERVES 4

Milan's Navigli district is similar to New York's Soho or Paris' Left Bank. *Navigli* means canals in Italian, and the two that give the area its name are all that are left of an extensive complex of waterways that once encircled Milan. A world apart from the elegant shops of Via Montenapoleone and the bustling commercial heart of Milan, the Navigli attracts artists, sculptors, and writers, who have moved into and renovated the old tenements that line the canals. There are little restaurants, some in floating houseboats, music clubs, and offbeat shops to explore, and the pace of life seems more relaxed than in the rest of the city.

I had this colorful salad of smoked salmon, fennel, and oranges at a little trattoria in the Navigli. Unfortunately that restaurant is gone now, but I love the way the creative chef combined a non-Italian ingredient like smoked salmon from northern Europe with fennel and oranges from southern Italy to create this harmoniously flavored salad. If only the European Economic Community could work together as well. Serve the salad as a first course, followed by Roasted Red Snapper with Green Olives (page 205) or in larger portions as a main course salad.

Crostini and Bruschetta

Although the styles of bread may differ from one region to another in Italy, all Italians have a deep respect for bread. Even though fresh bread is still purchased daily, nothing goes to waste. Day-old bread is soaked for salads or mixed with ground meat for meatballs and meatloaf. In southern Italy, toasted bread crumbs are sprinkled over pasta in place of cheese. Crumbs are also used as a coating or stuffing for meat, fish, and vegetables. Small pieces of bread are sautéed until crispy in butter or oil for soup or salad croutons.

Slices of bread, especially those cut from the rustic, country-style loaves, are grilled or baked to make toasts called *crostini,* or little crusts, or *bruschetta,* from the verb *abbrustolire,* to toast. The names are used interchangeably, though crostini are generally smaller and thinner slices, making them excellent for antipasto.

Toppings, from simple to imaginative, are piled on top of the toasted bread; these vary with the season, the region, and the cook. Chopped tomatoes mixed with herbs and olive oil are a classic both in Italy and in the United States. In Tuscany, crostini spread with chicken liver pâté accompanied by slices of salami is frequently served before an important meal. The most basic, yet possibly most irresistible, crostini is toasted or grilled bread rubbed with a fresh garlic clove and drizzled with extra virgin olive oil—the authentic version of garlic bread.

One Sunday, my husband and I stopped for lunch at a big, bustling family-style restaurant in Frascati outside Rome. The waiter took our order but soon returned to apologize that the kitchen was so busy, our order would be delayed. We didn't mind. We had no other plans, and it was a pleasure to sip our wine and watch the families and children eating, drinking, and having a wonderful time. But our waiter must have felt we needed sustenance. He brought out a big platter of warm garlic-rubbed bread generously doused with a rich extra virgin olive oil and accompanied by wedges of Parmigiano-Reggiano. Though we tried not to eat it all, we couldn't stop ourselves. Before we realized it, the platter was empty and we were mopping up the last traces of the olive oil with the bread crusts. When our dinner arrived, we could barely finish it.

Another type of crostini that is very popular is made with slices of firm polenta instead of toast. Polenta crostini can be browned in a skillet, on a grill, or in the oven. Sometimes they are served plain, usually as a side dish, or they can be topped with sautéed mushrooms, olive paste, or a soft or semi-soft cheese like gorgonzola or fontina.

Pheasant Hill Artichoke Crostini

CROSTINI DI CARCIOFI

4 medium artichokes

Salt, to taste

1 to 2 teaspoons fresh lemon juice

2 tablespoons extra virgin olive oil

Freshly ground pepper, to taste

8 slices of Italian or French bread, $^1/_2$ inch thick

2 large garlic cloves

1 With a large knife, trim off the top 1 inch of the artichokes. Rinse the artichokes under cold water, spreading the leaves open. Cut off the stem of each artichoke to make it even with the base so it will stand upright. Peel off the tough outer skin of the stems and reserve them. Bend back and snap off the small leaves around the base. With scissors, trim the pointed tops off the remaining leaves.

2 Place the artichokes and the stems in a pot just large enough for the artichokes to stand upright. Add enough water to reach a depth of 1 inch. Add salt. Cover and bring to a simmer over medium heat. Cook until the artichoke hearts are tender when pierced with a knife, about 45 minutes.

3 Let the artichokes cool slightly. Remove the leaves and reserve them for another use. Scrape the fuzzy chokes away from the hearts and discard. Mash the artichoke hearts and stems with a fork. Stir in the lemon juice, olive oil, salt, and pepper.

4 Grill or broil the bread until browned on both sides. Rub 1 side of the bread with a garlic clove. Spread the artichoke mixture on the toast. Serve immediately.

To make ahead: The puree can be made through Step 3. Cover and keep at room temperature for up to 3 hours.

In the Maremma, a remote part of Tuscany, a former New Yorker named Janet Hansen lives on a farm called *Collefagiano* (Pheasant Hill). She and her husband raise sheep and grow artichokes and other vegetables. An expert cook who has researched many historic Tuscan recipes, Janet also teaches Italian cooking classes several times a year. During the summer months, she serves family-style meals and rents rooms to guests seeking a quiet, get-away-from-it-all vacation.

Janet's artichoke heart puree inspired these crostini. Although the artichoke leaves are not used in this recipe, don't discard them. Serve them as a salad or appetizer with a dip of olive oil, lemon juice, salt, and pepper, or melted butter with lemon juice, or any vinaigrette dressing.

Azienda Agrituristica Collefagiano Montorgiali (Tuscany)

Antipasto

77

My favorite cheese for these crostini is a young, semi-firm pecorino. The Sini Fulvi Company of Rome produces a very good one; it comes either plain or spiced with flakes of crushed red pepper. Quality cheese shops in the United States carry it, but if it is not available, use another cheese, preferably something piquant like provolone, and add some crushed red pepper to the greens.

One of the more pungent members of the mustard family, broccoli rabe has a somewhat bitter flavor. Some people find the taste overpowering, especially the first time they try it. This is a good recipe for broccoli rabe first-timers because the cheese and bread cut its strong flavor.

Crostini with Broccoli Rabe and Melted Cheese

CROSTINI DI BROCCOLETTI DI RAPE E FORMAGGIO

1 pound broccoli rabe, rinsed

Coarse salt, to taste

3 tablespoons olive oil

2 large garlic cloves, thinly sliced

Crushed red pepper (optional)

8 slices of Italian or French bread, ¹/₂ inch thick, lightly toasted

8 slices fresh pecorino or mild provolone cheese

1 Trim about 1 inch off the bottom of the stems of the broccoli rabe. Cut it into 1-inch pieces. Bring a large saucepan of water to a boil. Add the broccoli rabe and salt. Cook for 5 minutes. Drain well and dry the pan.

2 In the same pan over medium heat, heat the olive oil, garlic, and red pepper, if using, until the garlic is fragrant, about 30 seconds. Add the broccoli rabe, red pepper, if using, and salt. Cover and cook for 5 minutes. If necessary, add 1 or 2 tablespoons warm water to prevent the vegetables from scorching.

3 Preheat the broiler.

4 Place the greens on the toasted bread. Top with the cheese.

5 Place the crostini under the broiler for 1 to 2 minutes, or until the cheese begins to melt. Serve immediately.

Cook's note: If you prefer, substitute a milder green like spinach or escarole, which requires no precooking, for the broccoli rabe. Begin the recipe at Step 2 and adjust the cooking time as needed. Spinach will need about 5 minutes; escarole may require 15.

Eggplant and Tomato Crostini

CROSTINI ALLA MELANZANA

1 small eggplant (about ³/₄ pound)

3 tablespoons extra virgin olive oil

Salt and freshly ground pepper, to taste

12 slices of Italian or French bread, ¹/₂ inch thick

1 large ripe tomato, cored and chopped

¹/₄ cup chopped fresh basil

¹/₂ cup chopped or crumbled ricotta salata or feta cheese (about
3 ounces)

1 Preheat the oven to 375°F. Place the eggplant on a piece of foil in a small baking pan. Bake for 1 hour, or until the eggplant is very soft. Let cool slightly. Remove the skin. Mash the eggplant pulp to a paste or puree it in a food processor. Add 1 tablespoon of the olive oil, salt, and pepper.

2 Heat a stovetop grill to very hot. Or turn on the broiler, placing the rack about 4 inches from the flame. Place the bread on the grill or broiler rack and grill or broil until lightly browned on both sides.

3 Combine the tomato with the basil, the remaining 2 tablespoons olive oil, salt, and pepper.

4 Spread the toast with the eggplant puree. Top with the chopped tomato mixture and the ricotta salata. Serve immediately.

SERVES 6

Here, toasted bread slices are topped with a spicy eggplant puree, chopped tomatoes, and crumbled ricotta salata cheese. Ricotta salata is made from fresh ricotta that is salted and pressed to extract the liquid. The cheese is semi-firm and tangier than fresh ricotta. It is good sliced as a table cheese, and it is also used frequently in southern Italy as a grating cheese for pasta and soups. Most Italian markets carry it but if you cannot find it, substitute a mild feta, which it resembles.

"A little old man whose name was Gepetto entered. He was often called Polendina by the bad boys of the neighborhood who liked to tease him because his yellow wig looked like a bag of yellow cornmeal. You must know, that is what polendina means in Italy, and it always made him angry to be called this."

Carlo Collodi, *Pinocchio*

Before lunch or dinner, Venetians like to stop for an *ombra,* a glass of wine at a neighborhood wine bar. Ombra means shade in Italian, and the tradition goes back to a time when wine was sold by itinerant salesmen. They would take up places in the shade of a palazzo to keep the wine cool, changing their position as the shade moved. Today's ombra is accompanied by small snacks called *cicchetti.* The snacks might be olives, slices of dried salami, a few sardines with onions and vinegar, or polenta crostini with different toppings. We tasted this one at Al Volto, one of our favorite wine bars, where you can sample many Italian wines by the glass.

Al Volto
San Marco 4081
Venice

Polenta Crostini with Watercress and Goat Cheese

CROSTINI DI POLENTA CON CRESCIONE E CAPRINO

1 bunch of watercress, rinsed and dried (about 6 ounces)
4 ounces mild goat cheese, at room temperature
1 tablespoon extra virgin olive oil
Freshly ground pepper, to taste
8 slices hot Polenta Crostini (page 192)

1 Remove the stems from the watercress.

2 In a bowl, mash the goat cheese with a fork, mixing in the olive oil and pepper.

3 Spread the hot crostini with the cheese. Top with watercress leaves and serve immediately.

Soup ... Minestre
e Zuppe

THE MANY DIFFERENT WAYS *to say soup in Italian are a*
clue to its importance. Minestra *is a soup containing rice or pasta with*
vegetables and/or beans cooked in broth or water. A minestrina *or* minestrella *is*
a light, clear version of a minestra while a minestrone *is a thick, hearty version.*
Minestraccia *is a bad soup. Then there is* zuppa, *distinguished from minestra by*
the fact that it contains sliced bread, usually toasted. It may also contain grains,
fish, meat, or vegetables. There is also a little soup, called variously zuppetta,
zuppettina, *or* zuppina, *and a big soup,* zuppone. *Ironically, the Italians often*
explain away confusing situations such as this one with an expression: Se non e

zuppa, e pan bagnato—if it's not soup, it's soaked bread—meaning one thing is much the same as another. Minestra, zuppa, and variations on the theme are often used interchangeably.

Whatever they are called, Italian soups are imaginative. Many are simple and quick, like Zucchini and Rice Soup, which takes only about thirty-five minutes cooking time; others like Tripe Soup have several steps and a number of ingredients that require longer cooking.

Some soups taste best made with a base of good broth, but many are made with plain water to keep the flavors pure and uncomplicated. Canned broths, while convenient, can be salty. Taste several brands to find one you like. Always dilute canned broth with an equal amount of water, or its flavor will be too concentrated, particularly in soups that need long slow cooking.

Italians eat soup in place of pasta or risotto as a first course, following the antipasto if one is served. A bowl of soup is also a typical evening meal, especially if lunch has been substantial. In contrast to American soups, which are generally served hot or cold, Italian soups are often served at room temperature. Extreme temperatures mask the flavors of soup, and more will come through if the soup is served lukewarm. This is especially true of some of the thick grain and bean soups.

Many thin, brothy soups are served with a sprinkling of grated cheese, usually Parmigiano-Reggiano or pecorino romano. Thick soups are more likely to be drizzled with a thin stream of flavorful extra virgin olive oil, especially in Tuscany.

Soup Shopping List

Making soup is especially easy if you keep the following ingredients on hand.

Meat or chicken broth ··· Pancetta ··· Garlic, onions, celery, and carrots ··· Lentils, dried or canned beans ··· Medium-grain rice, barley ··· Canned tomatoes, preferably San Marzano ··· Small pasta such as tubetti or ditalini ··· Parmigiano-Reggiano and pecorino romano ··· Extra virgin olive oil

Meat Broth

BRODO DI CARNE

2 pounds beef bones with meat

1 chicken

2 pounds bony chicken or turkey parts

2 celery ribs with leaves, cut into 3 or 4 pieces

2 carrots, trimmed and cut into 3 or 4 pieces

2 large onions, quartered

1 large tomato or 1 cup chopped canned Italian tomatoes

1 garlic clove, peeled

¼ cup fresh parsley leaves

1 Place the bones with meat, chicken, and chicken or turkey parts in a large stockpot. Add 6 quarts cold water and bring to a simmer. This will take about 1 hour.

2 With a large spoon, skim off the fat and foam that rise to the surface. It will take about 15 minutes for the foam to stop rising. Regulate the heat so that the water is barely simmering. If necessary, use a Flame Tamer.

3 Add the remaining ingredients. Cook for at least 2 hours; 3 hours is even better. Remove the meats and let the broth cool for 30 minutes.

4 Strain the broth and pour it into plastic storage containers. Let cool completely uncovered, then cover and refrigerate until chilled. Scrape off the fat on the surface.

5 Refrigerate for up to 3 days or freeze for up to 3 months.

Cook's note: Most of the flavor of the meat and chicken will go into the broth, but a thrifty Italian cook would still find a way to use the leftovers, either cut up and added to soup or tossed with other ingredients in a salad or chopped for a filling for ravioli or other stuffed pasta.

Giving a recipe for broth is like writing a recipe for a sandwich: A lot depends on your personal taste and what you have on hand. It is easier to say what not to add to your pot—namely strong-flavored ingredients such as lamb, pork, and vegetables with a high sulfur content like broccoli, cauliflower, or cabbage.

A combination of beef and chicken makes the most versatile broth for cooking soups, sauces, and risotto. Buy inexpensive meat cuts such as the neck or chuck. Use a whole chicken, plus necks, wing tips, and/or backs. If you can find it, a stewing hen, or older chicken, has better flavor than a young broiler. Veal or turkey parts can also be used, but use turkey with restraint since the flavor can be overwhelming. For chicken broth, omit the beef and beef bones in this recipe and reduce the amount of water to four quarts. Cook for two hours. This makes about two to three quarts.

Broth keeps for three days in the refrigerator, but I find it is most convenient to freeze it in half-pint containers for sauces and quart containers for soups and risotto. This recipe makes a lot, but you will be glad to have it on hand.

The mountainous Abruzzi region southeast of Rome is famous throughout Italy for its great chefs and good cooking like this unusual soup. Meat or chicken broth is ladled into bowls over rolled-up parsley and cheese crepes, called *scrippele* in the local dialect. Light and eggy, the crepes are an elegant touch. This is a perfect soup to serve for an important dinner.

Both the crepes and broth can be prepared a day or two ahead, making it easy to put this soup together at serving time.

Parsley and Cheese Crepes in Broth

SCRIPPELE 'MBUSSE

CREPES

5 large eggs

1/2 cup milk

2 tablespoons finely chopped Italian flat-leaf parsley

1/2 teaspoon salt

Pinch of freshly grated nutmeg

1 cup all-purpose flour

Vegetable oil

1/4 cup freshly grated pecorino romano

1/4 cup freshly grated Parmigiano-Reggiano

2 1/2 quarts Meat Broth (page 83) or chicken broth

1 To make the crepes, beat the eggs, milk, parsley, salt, and nutmeg until well blended. Place the flour in a flour sifter or sieve. Sift the flour over the egg mixture with one hand while beating with a fork held in the other hand. The mixture should have the texture of heavy cream.

2 Heat a 6-inch nonstick skillet over medium heat. Brush with oil.

3 Holding the skillet in one hand, pour in 2 tablespoons of the batter. Immediately rotate your wrist to turn the skillet and spread the batter into a thin layer. Place the skillet on the heat. After about 1 minute, the edges of the crepe will begin to lift away from the pan. With a pancake turner or your fingers, flip the crepe and cook it for 30 seconds on the other side, or until cooked but not browned.

4 Place the crepe on a plate. Repeat with the remaining batter. Stack the crepes as you finish them, placing a piece of wax paper between each crepe so that they do not stick together.

5 Combine the pecorino and Parmigiano. Sprinkle each crepe with a teaspoon of the cheese. Roll up the crepes to form 1-inch tubes.

6 When ready to serve, heat the broth until it is very hot. Season to taste. Divide the crepes among 6 heated soup bowls, placing them seam side down. Ladle the hot broth over them. Serve immediately.

To make ahead: The crepes may be made ahead through Step 4. Let them cool, then wrap the stack of crepes tightly in plastic wrap. Refrigerate for up to 3 days or freeze for up to 1 month. To thaw, place the crepes in the refrigerator overnight. Let stand at room temperature for about 1 hour, or until completely thawed.

Eggplant, Tomato, and Basil Soup

MINESTRA DI MELANZANA

1 medium eggplant (about 1 pound)

Salt, to taste

2 tablespoons olive oil

2 garlic cloves, finely chopped

2 large tomatoes, peeled, seeded, and chopped, or 2 cups chopped
*   canned Italian tomatoes*

1 small dried chili pepper, crushed, or a pinch of crushed red pepper

2 tablespoons chopped fresh basil

Freshly ground pepper, to taste

4 slices of Italian bread, toasted

2 tablespoons freshly grated pecorino romano

4 fresh basil leaves, for garnish

1 Trim the stem and base from the eggplant. Cut it lengthwise in half. Place the halves in a large pot with cold water to cover and a generous sprinkling of salt. Bring the water to a simmer. Cover and cook for 10 to 15 minutes, or until the eggplant is soft when pierced with a knife. Drain the eggplant and cut it into 1/2-inch pieces.

SERVES 4

The addition of a *peperoncino,* or small hot pepper, or some crushed red pepper gives a spicy edge to this soup from Calabria. Cooking the eggplant in salted water eliminates the bitter juices, just as salting would.

When buying eggplant, look for small- to medium-size ones; they have fewer seeds.

2 In a medium saucepan over medium heat, combine the olive oil and garlic. Cook just until the garlic is fragrant, about 30 seconds. Add the tomatoes, chili, and chopped basil. Bring to a simmer. Lower the heat and cook, stirring occasionally, until thickened, about 20 minutes. Add the eggplant, salt, and pepper to the tomato sauce. Add 2 cups water, bring to a simmer, and cook for 20 minutes more. If the soup is too thick, add more water.

3 Place a toasted bread slice in each of 4 soup bowls. Spoon on the hot soup. Sprinkle with cheese and garnish with a basil leaf. Serve immediately.

To make ahead: The soup can be made through Step 2 and refrigerated for up to 2 days before serving. Reheat gently.

Potato and Herb Soup

ZUPPA DI PATATE ALLE ERBE

3 tablespoons butter

2 tablespoons flour

2 tablespoons white wine vinegar

Salt, to taste

1¹/₂ pounds all-purpose potatoes, peeled and chopped

2 sprigs of fresh thyme, stems removed

6 fresh sage leaves

6 slices of Italian bread

1 In a large pot over low heat, melt 2 tablespoons of the butter. Add the flour and cook, stirring occasionally, for 1 minute. Add the vinegar, blending it into the flour mixture with a wire whisk. Gradually add 6 cups water and salt. Add the potatoes, thyme, and sage. Bring to a simmer and cook for 1 hour, or until the potatoes are soft.

2 Toast the bread and spread the slices with the remaining butter. Place the toast in 6 soup bowls. Add the soup and serve immediately.

SERVES 6

White vinegar, thyme, and sage add zest to this simple potato soup from the Alto Adige region in northeastern Italy. Serve it as a first course followed by Roast Loin of Pork (page 245) or any of the roast chickens (see pages 223–224).

Fennel and Leek Soup

ZUPPA DI FINOCCHIO E PORRI

2 large leeks

3 medium fennel bulbs (about 2^1/$_2$ pounds)

2 tablespoons butter

1 tablespoon olive oil

1^1/$_2$ pounds all-purpose potatoes, peeled and sliced

6 cups chicken broth

Salt and freshly ground pepper, to taste

Extra virgin olive oil, for drizzling

1 Trim the leeks of the roots and green tops. Cut them lengthwise in half and rinse well to eliminate all traces of sand between the layers. Coarsely chop the leeks.

2 Trim the fennel stalks even with the bulbs, reserving some of the feathery green leaves for a garnish. Shave a thin slice off the base. With a swivel-blade vegetable peeler, trim away any bruises or brown spots. Cut the fennel bulbs in half lengthwise, then cut crosswise into thin slices.

3 In a large pot, combine the leeks with the butter and olive oil. Cook over medium heat, stirring occasionally, until the leeks are tender, about 5 minutes. Add the fennel, potatoes, and broth. Season with salt and pepper. Bring to a simmer and cook for 1 hour or until all of the vegetables are soft.

4 Strain the vegetables and process them until smooth in a food processor or pass the vegetables and broth through a food mill set over a large bowl.

5 Return the vegetables and broth to the pot and reheat gently. Correct the seasoning. Transfer to a heated soup tureen.

6 Ladle the soup into soup bowls. Scatter a few of the reserved fennel leaves over each portion. Drizzle with olive oil and serve immediately.

To make ahead: The soup can be made ahead through Step 4 and refrigerated for up to 3 days before serving.

SERVES 6

Leeks and potatoes are a classic marriage in soups, most notably in French vichyssoise. Fennel further enhances the combination in this soup, which I first tasted at I Trulli, a Manhattan restaurant that specializes in Pugliese cooking.

Fresh fennel bulbs bear a resemblance to short, round celery though the leaves are feathery like dill. The season for fennel begins in the early fall and continues to spring. Many markets mistakenly label it as anise. Look for large round bulbs of fennel with no bruises or cracks. Store fennel in the refrigerator tightly sealed in plastic wrap.

I Trulli
122 East 27 Street
New York, New York

SERVES 6

When I was a child I thought it was very funny that a soup mixed with beaten eggs and cheese would be called *stracciatella,* or little rag-picker's soup. The eggs and cheese form yellow and white ribbons in the hot broth; they do resemble little scraps of cloth. This version of my childhood favorite contains escarole, but you can substitute spinach, if you prefer.

Escarole, Egg, and Cheese Soup

MINESTREA DI SCAROLA, UOVA, E CACIO

1 medium head escarole (about 1 pound)

2 tablespoons olive oil

2 medium onions, thinly sliced

2 medium carrots, chopped

1 celery rib, chopped

8 cups Meat Broth (page 83) or a combination of canned beef
    broth and water

Salt and freshly ground pepper, to taste

2 large eggs

1/3 cup freshly grated pecorino romano

1   Trim the base of the escarole and separate the leaves, discarding any bruised ones. Wash the leaves in several changes of cold water, paying special attention to the white part of each leaf where dirt tends to collect. Stack the leaves and cut crosswise into thin strips.

2   In a large pot over medium heat, heat the oil with the onions. Cook until tender and golden, about 7 minutes. Add the escarole, carrots, celery, and broth. Bring to a simmer. Cover and cook until the vegetables are tender, about 30 minutes. Add salt and pepper, keeping in mind that the cheese is salty. Remove the soup from the heat.

3   Beat the eggs with the cheese. Slowly stir the egg mixture into the hot soup. Taste for seasoning. Serve immediately.

Barley and Bean Soup

ZUPPA DI ORZO E FAGIOLI

1 cup dried cannellini or Great Northern beans

2 ounces sliced pancetta, finely chopped

1 tablespoon olive oil

2 celery ribs, chopped

2 carrots, chopped

1 medium onion, chopped

1 garlic clove, finely chopped

$1/2$ cup pearl barley, rinsed and drained

Salt and freshly ground pepper, to taste

$1/2$ cup chopped fresh parsley

1 Look over the beans and remove any shriveled beans or small stones. Rinse well. Place the beans in a large bowl with cold water to cover by 2 inches. Soak for at least 4 hours or overnight in the refrigerator.

2 In a large pot over medium heat, combine the pancetta and olive oil. Cook until the pancetta is lightly browned, about 10 minutes. Add the celery, carrots, and onion. Cook, stirring frequently, until the vegetables are golden brown, about 10 minutes. Stir in the garlic.

3 Drain the beans and add them to the pot with 2 quarts water. Bring to a simmer over low heat. Cook for 1 hour and 15 minutes, or until the beans are very tender. Coarsely mash them with a potato masher or the back of a large cooking spoon.

4 Add the barley, salt, and pepper. Cook for 30 minutes, or until the barley is tender. Stir frequently to prevent sticking. Add a little water if the soup becomes too thick.

5 Stir in the parsley. Serve hot or warm.

To make ahead: This soup can be completely made ahead and stored in the refrigerator for up to 3 days. Reheat before serving.

SERVES 6

Barley is believed to be one of the earliest foods cultivated by man. The grains were pounded and cooked into a forerunner of bread. Although the importance of barley declined in Europe as wheat and other grains became more available, barley still is eaten in many parts of northern Italy. It is excellent cooked like risotto (see page 170) with vegetables or seafood or in soups, especially those with beans or mushrooms. The term pearl barley simply means that the husk and bran have been removed. Pearl barley cooks faster and more evenly than whole barley.

In Italian, barley is called *orzo*. Do not confuse it with the small pasta shape that goes by the same name.

As we pulled into the courtyard at Regaleali, the Tasca family's wine estate in central Sicily, we were greeted by Anna Tasca Lanza coming toward us with a glass of white wine. We were surprised and delighted by her immediate appearance and warm welcome, but she laughingly explained that the wine was not to celebrate our arrival. She was carrying it to the kitchen for the wheat berry and vegetable soup she was preparing for our lunch. Soon we gathered in the courtyard in the warm sunshine, each with our own glass of wine, eating Anna's soup with homemade semolina bread and fresh sheep's cheese.

In springtime, Anna makes this soup with the wild fennel that grows in profusion all over Sicily. She feels that cultivated fennel is too sweet, so she recommends finishing the soup with a *battuto,* a blend of chopped herbs and grated pecorino romano cheese, as she does when fresh wild fennel is not available.

Regaleali Wheat Berry Soup

ZUPPA DI GRANO DURO

1 pound durum wheat berries or kamut (available at health food stores)

1 large onion, finely chopped

2 celery ribs, finely chopped

3 garlic cloves

1 1/2 cups peeled, seeded, and chopped fresh tomatoes or chopped canned Italian tomatoes with their juice

6 cups Meat Broth (page 83)

1 cup dry white wine

Salt, to taste

Pinch of crushed red pepper

4 cups cooked small white beans or 2 cans (16 ounces each), rinsed and drained

BATTUTO

1/4 cup chopped fresh parsley

1/4 cup chopped fresh basil

1 to 2 garlic cloves, minced

1/3 cup freshly grated pecorino romano

Extra virgin olive oil

1 Place the wheat berries in a large bowl. Cover with cool water by about 2 inches. Let stand overnight.

2 Drain the wheat and rinse it under cool water, rubbing the berries between the palms of your hands. In a large pot, combine the wheat, vegetables, broth, wine, salt, and red pepper. Bring to a simmer and cook over low heat for 30 minutes.

3 Add the beans and cook for 30 minutes more, or until the wheat berries are tender.

4 Combine the ingredients for the battuto. Spoon the soup into serving bowls. Drizzle each portion with a little oil. Sprinkle the battuto over the hot soup just before serving or pass it at the table.

5 Serve the soup hot or at room temperature.

Friulian Wild Mushroom Soup

MINESTRA DI FUNGHI

1 tablespoon olive oil

2 ounces sliced pancetta, finely chopped

1 medium onion, finely chopped

2 celery ribs, finely chopped

8 ounces white mushrooms, thinly sliced

8 ounces fresh wild mushrooms such as porcini or shiitake, thinly sliced

4 tablespoons chopped fresh parsley

2 garlic cloves, finely chopped

3 medium all-purpose potatoes, peeled and finely chopped

Salt and freshly ground pepper, to taste

8 cups Meat Broth (page 83) or 4 cups canned beef broth plus 4 cups water

¹/₂ cup pearl barley

SERVES 6 TO 8

On cold winter nights, families in Friuli gather around the *fogolar,* a square wood-burning fireplace that is the place to keep warm, socialize, and cook. At the cozy Trattoria Furlan in Tavagnacco near Udine, you can usually find the proprietor, Vicenzo Furlan, standing beside the fogolar in the dining room, grilling steaks, chops, and porcini mushrooms, the specialty of the house.

Plump, meaty, and full of flavor, porcini are the ultimate grilling mushroom. Their Italian name means little pigs, a reference to their succulence. Their botanical name is *Boletus edulis,* and they are known as *cèpes* in France. Porcini can also be found in forests in North America, but since they grow only in the wild, they are rare and quite expensive.

Though he won't reveal too many secrets, Signor Furlan says that he reserves the best porcini for grilling. All others can be used for sauces or soups, such as this

1 In a large saucepan over medium heat, cook the olive oil and pancetta until the pancetta is golden, about 10 minutes. Add the onion and celery and cook, stirring occasionally, for 5 minutes, or until tender. Add the mushrooms, 2 tablespoons of the parsley, and garlic. Cook, stirring, until the mushroom juices evaporate, about 10 minutes. Stir in the potatoes, salt, and pepper. Add the broth and bring to a simmer. Add the barley and cook, uncovered, over low heat for 1 hour, or until the barley is tender and the soup is thickened.

2 Sprinkle with the remaining parsley and serve.

markets.

When he has a minute to spare, Signor Furlan will proudly tell you about the time Ernest Hemingway came to dinner at his restaurant, and show you photos and newspaper clippings to prove it.

Trattoria Furlan
Via Nazionale, 130
Tavagnacco (Friuli-Venezia-Giulia)

Lentil and Escarole Soup

─────────

MINESTRA DI LENTICCHIE E SCAROLA

SERVES 4 TO 6

Lentils have a long history as a staple food in Italy. When excavations were made of the city of Pompeii, buried in an eruption of Vesuvius in 79 A.D., a large quantity of lentils was found in the market stalls.

According to Pliny, the Roman naturalist and writer who lived during the first century, a special ship had to be built to transport the Egyptian obelisk that now stands in front of Saint Peter's Basilica to Rome. To keep the obelisk from shifting, it was packed in lentils, almost three million Roman pounds of them!

Perhaps because they have always been cheap and widely avail-

2 tablespoons olive oil

1 medium onion, chopped

1 celery rib, chopped

1 medium carrot, chopped

1 garlic clove, finely chopped

1 medium tomato, peeled, seeded, and chopped, or ¹/₂ cup chopped canned Italian tomatoes

8 ounces brown or green lentils (about 1 cup)

A Fresh Taste of Italy

Salt and freshly ground pepper, to taste

1 large head of escarole (1 pound)

Freshly grated pecorino romano or Parmigiano-Reggiano
  (optional)

Extra virgin olive oil, for drizzling (optional)

1 In a large pot over medium heat, combine the olive oil, onion, celery, and carrot. Cook, stirring frequently, until the vegetables are soft, about 10 minutes. Stir in the garlic. Cook for 1 minute. Add the tomato and cook for 5 minutes more.

2 Rinse the lentils and pick them over to remove small stones. Add the lentils to the pot with the vegetables. Add 4 cups cold water and bring to a simmer. Cook for 30 to 45 minutes, or until the lentils are tender. Season with salt and pepper.

3 Trim the base of the escarole and separate the leaves, discarding any bruised ones. Wash the leaves in several changes of cold water, paying special attention to the white part of each leaf where dirt tends to collect. Stack the leaves and cut crosswise into 1/2-inch strips.

4 Stir the escarole into the lentils. Cover and cook for 10 minutes, or until the escarole is tender.

5 Serve hot or warm with grated cheese or a drizzle of olive oil.

able, lentils have historically been considered commonplace and often were despised. Platina wrote in 1475 that lentils were "the worst of all vegetables." It's not that lentils are bad-tasting, but without seasoning they are rather bland. The good thing about lentils is that they blend well with tastier foods like onions, garlic, and pork, accepting and extending their flavors. Also, lentils are high in iron, B vitamins, and fiber.

Brown or green lentils, available in most supermarkets, cook in forty-five minutes to an hour. Red lentils, available in health food stores, cook in about ten minutes, but they are not used much in Italian cooking. The caviar of lentils, tiny dark brown lentils from Castelluccio in the region of Umbria in central Italy, are more expensive than other kinds and hard to find in the United States. They cook in about thirty minutes, though their age, as with all lentils, is a factor in timing them.

Unlike most legumes, lentils do not need soaking. As they cook, lentils can go from firm to mushy in a matter of minutes. This is not a problem in soup but for a salad, the lentils should retain their shape, and so they must be carefully watched.

Spelt is an ancient grain, a precursor of modern wheat. Many people find it more digestible than wheat, and it seems to be enjoying a kind of renaissance in Italy. Many health food stores sell spelt, or you can substitute kamut, another ancient grain, or ordinary wheat berries.

Whether spelt or wheat is used, the grain will require precooking for this recipe. This can be accomplished while you chop and brown the other ingredients, or up to three days ahead of time. Keep the cooked grain in an airtight container in the refrigerator. One cup of spelt equals about three cups cooked.

This traditional Tuscan soup is a specialty at La Mora, an elegant restaurant just outside Lucca. Like many Italian soups, it is served warm, never hot, so that you can appreciate its complex flavor.

La Mora
Lucca (Tuscany)

Tuscan Bean and Spelt Soup

GRAN FARRO

1 cup spelt

Salt, to taste

2 tablespoons olive oil

4 ounces sliced pancetta, finely chopped

1 medium onion, chopped

2 medium carrots, chopped

1 celery rib, chopped

4 fresh sage leaves, chopped

1/2 teaspoon dried marjoram

4 cups cooked cannellini or Great Northern beans or 2 cans (16 ounces each), rinsed and drained

1 cup peeled, seeded, and chopped fresh tomatoes or canned Italian tomatoes

1 garlic clove, finely chopped

Freshly ground pepper, to taste

Extra virgin olive oil

1 Place the spelt in a colander and rinse it well under cold running water. In a large saucepan, combine the spelt and 4 cups water. Bring it to a simmer. Add salt. Cook over low heat until the spelt is tender and grains begin to pop open, about 1 hour.

2 Meanwhile, in a large pot over medium heat, heat the olive oil. Add the pancetta and cook for 5 minutes, or until lightly browned. Add the onion, carrots, celery, sage, and marjoram. Cook until tender, about 10 minutes. Stir in the beans, tomatoes, and garlic. Add 4 cups water and bring to a simmer. Cook for 30 minutes.

3 Strain the soup, reserving the liquid. Puree the beans and vegetables in a food processor, blender, or food mill.

4 Return the liquid and pureed solids to the pot. Add the cooked spelt, 2 cups water, salt, and pepper. Bring to a simmer and cook, stirring frequently, for 30 minutes, or until thick. Watch carefully that the soup doesn't scorch on the bottom of the pot. Add additional water if the soup becomes too thick. Season with salt and pepper.

5 Let the soup cool slightly before serving. Ladle into soup bowls and drizzle a little olive oil over each portion.

Zucchini and Rice Soup

MINESTRA DI RISO E ZUCCHINI

1 medium onion
¹/₄ cup olive oil
1¹/₂ pounds zucchini, scrubbed and chopped
4 cups chicken broth
¹/₂ cup Arborio or other medium-grain rice
Salt and freshly ground pepper, to taste
2 tablespoons chopped fresh parsley
¹/₄ cup freshly grated Parmigiano-Reggiano

1 In a large saucepan over medium heat, cook the onion in the olive oil until it is very tender and golden, 8 to 10 minutes. Add the zucchini and cook, stirring often, until soft, about 5 minutes. Add the broth and bring to a simmer. Add the rice, salt, and pepper. Cover and cook until the rice is tender, about 20 minutes.

2 Remove the soup from the heat and stir in the parsley and cheese. Serve immediately.

SERVES 4

This very simple soup is always satisfying. It exemplifies Italian home cooking at its best—and the whole thing takes less than thirty-five minutes from start to finish. This soup is made all over Italy with many variations, though the basic steps are always the same. First the onion is cooked gently in oil or butter until it is tender and golden. Then a vegetable—other than zucchini, this could be celery, cabbage, squash, tomatoes, escarole, spinach, asparagus, or some combination—is stirred in and cooked until soft. Broth is added, or you can use water. Rice or a small shape of pasta goes in next, and the soup is simmered until the rice is tender. A swirl of fresh parsley or basil, if you have it, and some grated cheese are the finishing touch.

Whenever I have a piece of Parmigiano-Reggiano I grate it right down to the rind to enjoy every last scrap of cheese. Even then, there is more to savor. Although the rind is hard, it is all cheese. Real Parmigiano-Reggiano has no plastic or wax coating so it is completely edible. I wrap the rind in plastic wrap and store it in the refrigerator. Then when I make minestrone or this soup, I scrub the outside of the rind with a brush under cool water and toss it into the soup. As it simmers, the rind softens and becomes chewy, releasing a rich cheese flavor that melts into the other ingredients. When the soup is done, the rind can be discarded as most of its flavor is gone, though you might want to consider cutting it into bite-size pieces and adding them to the soup.

The cheese rind is not essential to make this soup, just a nice addition.

Bean and Escarole Soup

MINESTRA DI FAGIOLI E SCAROLA

*8 ounces dried cannellini or Great Northern beans (about 1 cup)
    or about 3 cups cooked or canned beans*

1 small head of escarole (about $^3/_4$ pound)

1 medium onion, finely chopped

1 small celery rib

$^1/_4$ cup olive oil

2 large garlic cloves, finely chopped

*2 medium tomatoes, peeled, seeded, and chopped, or 1 cup
    chopped canned Italian tomatoes*

*1 piece (2 to 4 inches square) Parmigiano-Reggiano rind,
    scrubbed (optional)*

Salt and freshly ground pepper, to taste

*4 cups homemade Meat or Chicken Broth (see page 83) or use a
    combination of half water and half canned broth*

Freshly grated Parmigiano-Reggiano

1 If using cooked or canned beans, skip to Step 3. Otherwise, look over the beans and remove any shriveled beans or small stones. Soak the beans in cold water to cover by 2 inches for at least 4 hours or overnight.

2 Drain the beans and place in a pot with cold water to cover by 1 inch. Bring the water to a slow simmer. Cover and cook the beans over very low heat until tender, about 1 hour and 15 minutes. (Cooking time may vary according to the age of the beans.)

3 Trim the base of the escarole and separate the leaves, discarding any bruised ones. Wash the leaves in several changes of cold water, paying special attention to the white part of each leaf where dirt tends to collect. Stack the leaves and cut crosswise into $^1/_2$-inch strips.

4 In a large pot over medium heat, cook the onion and celery in the olive oil, stirring occasionally, until tender, about 5 minutes. Stir in the garlic. Add the escarole, tomatoes, and cheese rind, if using. Cover and cook for 30 minutes, or until the escarole is tender.

5 Add the beans, salt, and pepper. Add the broth and bring the soup to a simmer. Cover and cook for 20 minutes, or until thick.

6 Taste for seasoning. Serve hot with the Parmigiano.

To make ahead: This soup can be made up to 2 days before serving and refrigerated. Reheat gently.

The Soup of the Grain Threshing

MINESTRA DA BATE'L GRAN

1 small onion, finely chopped

2 tablespoons unsalted butter

8 chicken livers, trimmed

Salt and freshly ground pepper, to taste

2 teaspoons chopped fresh rosemary leaves

$1/2$ cup dry white wine

6 cups Meat or Chicken Broth (see page 83)

$1/2$ cup pastina or similar small pasta shape for soup

1 tablespoon chopped fresh parsley

2 tablespoons freshly grated Parmigiano-Reggiano

1 In a small skillet over medium-low heat, cook the onion in the butter until tender, about 5 minutes. Add the livers and cook until browned, about 2 minutes on each side. Sprinkle with salt and pepper. Add the rosemary and wine. Cook for 5 minutes more.

2 In a medium saucepan over medium heat, bring the broth to a simmer. Add the pastina and salt. Cook until just tender, about 8 minutes.

3 Add the contents of the skillet and the parsley. Cook for 1 minute more. Serve immediately with Parmigiano.

SERVES 4

Until recently, this Piedmontese country soup was served to the relatives and friends who came at harvest time to help with the grain threshing. It was considered light and refreshing, just what was needed after a day of toiling in the dust and hot sun. Today the work is done mostly by machine, but this tasty soup of chicken livers flavored with rosemary and white wine is still appealing.

I have read some older recipes that include tiny meatballs each "as large as a grape seed" as well as the chopped-up innards of chickens and rabbits plus homemade egg pasta cut into squares. This version is simpler and more contemporary in approach.

SERVES 4

A few years ago, friends of our spent five days in Rome. It was their first visit to Italy and they were traveling with their two young children. After a full day's sightseeing the children were tired and cranky at dinnertime—and so were their parents. Luckily, they were staying near Da Giggetto, a busy, friendly trattoria in Rome's Jewish quarter. They liked their first meal at the restaurant so much that they returned every night. Why take chances? By the time my friends left, the waiters knew the children by name, and our friends were welcomed to their special table like members of the family.

One of the dishes they raved about was the lentil soup. I served them this version one night, and though it was not the same as Da Giggetto's, which did not contain clams, they liked it very much.

Lentils are a delicious background flavor for the briny little clams. If tiny Manila clams or cockles are not available in your area, substitute another kind but chop them into small pieces if they are large.

Da Giggetto
Via Portico d'Ottavia, 21
Rome

Clam and Lentil Soup

ZUPPA DI VONGOLE E LENTICCHIE

2 pounds small clams, such as Manila clams or cockles, scrubbed

3 tablespoons olive oil

1 medium onion, finely chopped

2 tablespoons all-purpose flour

8 ounces lentils (about 1 cup)

1 large tomato, peeled, seeded, and chopped, or 1 cup chopped canned Italian tomatoes

2 bay leaves

1 celery rib, diced

1 carrot, diced

1 small zucchini, scrubbed and diced

Salt and freshly ground pepper, to taste

1 Put the clams in a large saucepan. Cover and place over medium heat. Cook until the clams open. As the clams open, remove them from the pot and continue to cook the remaining ones. Discard any that do not open.

2 Remove the clams from their shells, reserving the juice, and place them in a small bowl. Cover with plastic wrap and refrigerate. Strain the clam juice through a double thickness of dampened cheesecloth or a paper coffee filter. Combine the clam juice with enough water to equal 3 cups.

3 In a large pot over medium heat, combine the olive oil and onion. Cook for 5 minutes, or until tender. Add the flour and cook, stirring constantly, for 1 minute. Stir the clam juice into the pot. Bring to a simmer and add the lentils, tomato, and bay leaves. Cook for 45 minutes, or until the lentils are almost tender.

4 Add the celery, carrot, zucchini, salt, and pepper. Cook for 15 minutes more, or until the lentils are soft.

5 Add the clams. Serve hot.

Tripe Soup

MINESTRONE DI TRIPPA

SERVES 6 TO 8

1¹/₂ pounds fresh or thawed honeycomb tripe

1 tablespoon butter

2 tablespoons olive oil

1 large onion, chopped

1 carrot, finely chopped

1 celery rib, sliced

1 tablespoon chopped fresh rosemary leaves

1 garlic clove, finely chopped

Pinch of crushed red pepper

Salt and freshly ground pepper, to taste

8 cups Meat Broth (page 83)

¹/₂ cup chopped fresh tomato or chopped canned Italian tomatoes

4 medium all-purpose potatoes, peeled and chopped

4 cups cabbage strips (¹/₂ inch)

6 to 8 slices of toasted Italian bread

Freshly grated Parmigiano-Reggiano

1 The day before making the soup, rinse the tripe and cut it into 1 × ¹/₂-inch strips. Place the strips in a large bowl of cold water. Cover and refrigerate for 8 hours, changing the water several times.

2 Drain the tripe and place it in a large pot with cold water to cover. Bring the water to a simmer and cook for 5 minutes. Drain and rinse the tripe.

3 In a large soup pot over medium heat, melt the butter with the olive oil. Add the onion, carrot, celery, rosemary, garlic, and red pepper and cook for 5 minutes, or until the onion is tender. Stir in the tripe, salt, and black pepper. Cook for 15 minutes. Add the broth and tomato and bring to a simmer. Cover and cook for 2 hours, or until the tripe is tender but still slightly chewy.

Il trippaio, the tripe vendor, has been a welcome and familiar sight on the streets of Florence since at least the sixteenth century and even appears in an engraving from that era by the artist Annibale Carracci.

The vendor would go from door to door selling his product, suspended from a pole balanced over his shoulder. Eventually the pole was replaced by a wheeled cart where the different types of cleaned and precooked tripe could be displayed. Even today, tripe sellers can be found at special stalls in many open-air and indoor markets throughout Italy.

A few of the hand carts still exist in Florence, though now they are made of gleaming stainless steel with a glass-enclosed display case. At one tripe cart near the Porcellino market, workers and students line up to buy sandwiches made from crisp rolls stuffed with slices of tripe bathed in broth or topped with green sauce.

In the United States, tripe can be found in many supermarkets and butcher shops, though not often on restaurant menus. It seems to have fallen out of favor despite its importance in traditional American cooking. Tripe is the primary ingredient in Philadelphia pepper pot soup and Louisiana-style andouille sausage, and the Parker House restaurant in Boston was once famous for its fried tripe.

Honeycomb tripe, the most widely available, comes from the rumen, the largest section of a cow's four-part stomach. Rubbery-looking with an ivory white color, it is called honeycomb tripe because of its appearance. Tripe is sold thawed, washed, and partially cooked.

Tripe needs to soak for several hours before cooking, so plan accordingly. Some recipes call for cooking the tripe overnight or at least for several hours, but I find two to three hours is sufficient. It should remain slightly chewy.

Porcellino Market
Florence

4 Add the potatoes and cabbage and cook for 20 minutes, or until the potatoes are tender. Taste for seasoning.

5 Place a slice of toasted bread in each soup bowl. Add the soup. Sprinkle with Parmigiano-Reggiano and serve immediately.

To make ahead: The soup can be prepared ahead through Step 3 up to 2 days before serving. Cool and refrigerate. Reheat the soup and continue with the recipe.

Tripe in Sauce

Ancient recipe belonging to the Brotherhood of the Tripe of Moncalieri:
"For 4 persons cut 600 gms. of washed tripe into strips about 1 cm. large and 10 cm's long. Slice $1/2$ onion finely and golden it in 80 gms. of butter. As soon as the onion becomes a golden colour, add to it 70 gms. of lard and 2 chopped cloves of garlic. Fry it lightly then add 100 gms. of half a calf's leg, cleaned and boned, and the tripe.

"Season with salt, pepper and a hint of nutmeg. Leave it to simmer until the seasoning has nearly evaporated. At this stage add some meat stock and leave to cook for 7 to 8 hours, now and then adding some stock. Before serving dust with lots of grated parmesan cheese. Serve the tripe with slices of toasted bread."

Alberta Lantermo, *Piemonte in bocca*

A Fresh Taste of Italy

Sauces ... Salse

*N*OTHING IS MORE FIERCELY *debated in Italian cooking than the sauces used to dress pasta. With the possible exception of a few children under the age of five, every Italian has an opinion on the subject and, of course, insists that he or she knows the one, the best, and the most authentic recipe— usually his or her mother's.*

Before the tomato arrived in Italy from North America, most pasta was eaten with vegetables, cheese, butter, or lard. The typical Neapolitan seasoning was the pasta cooking water flavored with lard, cheese, and pepper. No wonder southern Italians adopted the tomato enthusiastically! It grows extremely well under the brutal sun of their region. When cooked quickly or slowly, with or without added meat, seafood, or vegetables, the sweet, spicy tomato is the perfect complement to naturally bland pasta.

Cooks in northern Italy use tomatoes for sauces, too, but relatively more meat goes into the pot and broth is used as an extender. Dried porcini mushrooms are sometimes added to give the sauce a rich, woodsy flavor.

Pasta sauces are the most personal expression of an Italian cook. Variations have evolved from convenience, necessity, and individual taste, using whatever ingredients were available, including vegetables, legumes, seafood, game, and meat, in whatever quantities people could afford.

The collection of sauces that follows is very versatile. Each can complement a wide variety of pasta shapes, so I have not linked them to any one type. Instead pasta suggestions are included with the recipes.

A sauce that contains a large proportion of meat and is cooked slowly over a long period of time is known in Italy as a ragù. All of the sauces in this collection can be made ahead of time, and the ragùs in particular improve in flavor overnight. Sauces with meat can be refrigerated up to three days, meatless sauces for up to 1 week. For longer storage, let the sauces cool completely, then freeze them in airtight containers for up to one month for sauces with meat, for up to three months for meatless sauces.

Peeled, Seeded, and Chopped Tomatoes

Many uncooked sauces, such as the one for the Ragged Pasta with a Thousand Herbs (page 136) or the Cold Pasta with Vegetable Confetti and Seafood (page 122), would lose their lightness and fresh appeal without fresh tomatoes. Others that are only slightly cooked, such as the Summer-style Fettuccine (page 137), would be dull and heavy with canned tomatoes. In these cases, consider making another recipe if good fresh tomatoes are not available. (I have indicated where substituting canned tomatoes in a recipe will do no harm.)

To peel, seed, and chop tomatoes, bring a saucepan of water to boiling. Gently lower 2 or 3 tomatoes into the pot. When the water returns to boiling, wait 30 seconds. Remove the tomatoes with a slotted spoon. When the water returns to boiling, repeat with the remaining tomatoes. Let cool briefly, then cut plum tomatoes lengthwise in half, round tomatoes in half crosswise and remove the stem end. Gently squeeze the tomatoes over a bowl to remove the juices and seeds. The skin should slip right off as you squeeze. Chop the tomatoes on a cutting board.

A Fresh Taste of Italy

Tomato Puree

SALSA DI POMODORO

2 pounds very ripe plum or Roma tomatoes

Cut the tomatoes lengthwise in half. In a large heavy stainless steel or enameled saucepan over medium-low heat, cook the tomatoes, covered, for 15 to 20 minutes, or until very soft. Stir occasionally and add 1 or 2 tablespoons water, if necessary, to prevent sticking. Pass the tomatoes through a food mill to eliminate the seeds and skins. The puree can be used immediately or stored.

To make ahead: The puree can be refrigerated or frozen. Let it cool completely and pour it into an airtight plastic container. Store in the refrigerator for up to 1 week or in the freezer for up to 3 months. This fresh tomato puree can be used in place of canned whole tomatoes in any of the recipes in this book, unless otherwise indicated.

MAKES ABOUT 3 CUPS, ENOUGH FOR 1 POUND PASTA

Our first apartment after we married was on the top floor of an old Brooklyn brownstone owned and occupied by three generations of an Italian-American family. One Saturday in September I awoke to the sound of excited voices in the backyard. I looked out the window and there was the entire family, from the eighty-six-year-old *padrone* to his five-year-old granddaughter canning tomatoes.

Bushel baskets of ripe red fruit were stacked in a corner of the yard. One person was busy washing wine bottles, another slicing the tomatoes in half, a third tending the huge pots of tomatoes boiling on a portable stove. Someone else fed the tomatoes through the *passapomodoro,* a food mill designed to separate the tomato pulp from the skins and seeds. The tomato puree was funneled into the well-scrubbed bottles and a leaf or two of basil was stuffed in (the five-year-old's job). Finally, the bottles were sealed with an old-fashioned metal cap like the ones on glass soda bottles.

I ran downstairs and offered to help, secretly hoping they would share some of the velvety red puree with me. We worked all day until we ran out of bottles. That night Signora Pina, the landlady, rewarded our hard work with a *spaghettata,* or spaghetti party. Of course, they gave me several bottles, which I hoarded all through the winter, using the exquisite puree only on special occasions.

This is my idea of fast food. I always keep canned tomatoes in the house and the sauce is prepared while the pasta cooks. In less than thirty minutes I have a pasta dinner on the table—much faster and thousand times better than a take-out pizza! When I have more time, I sometimes make a double batch and set aside half for another day. It freezes well, but I usually use it within a couple of days on pasta, over rice or vegetables, or on meatloaf, so I don't bother.

This quick sauce is based on canned tomatoes, which can be as good or better than fresh tomatoes, especially when true vine-ripened tomatoes are out of season.

Quick Tomato Sauce

SALSA PRESTO

2 large garlic cloves, very finely chopped
¹/₄ cup olive oil
1 can (28 or 35 ounces) Italian tomatoes with their juice or 2
* pounds ripe plum tomatoes, prepared as on page 102*
Salt and freshly ground pepper, to taste
Pinch of dried oregano (optional)
6 leaves fresh basil, torn into bits

In a large wide saucepan or skillet over medium heat, cook the garlic in the oil until just fragrant, about 30 seconds. Add the tomatoes with their juice and bring them to a simmer. Cook, crushing the tomatoes with the back of a wooden spoon. Adjust the heat so that the sauce is simmering rapidly but does not stick to the bottom of the pan. Add salt, pepper, and dried oregano, if using. Cook, stirring occasionally, until the sauce looks thick and rich and most of the liquid has evaporated, 20 to 25 minutes. Turn off the heat and stir in the fresh basil.

Cook's note: You can leave the tomatoes chunky or crush them fine, as you prefer. For a perfectly smooth sauce with no seeds, pass the tomatoes through a food mill *before* you add them to the pot.

Making Tomato Sauce

Fresh, vine-ripened tomatoes are incomparable for subtle, sweet, and delicate sauces. When they are in season, I prepare the tomatoes much as I did that day, though not in such enormous quantities. The puree can be used immediately or stored for later use. To preserve it, I freeze it instead of bottling it.

Plum or Roma tomatoes are best for sauces because they contain less water and fewer seeds than round tomatoes and thicken readily as they cook, but round tomatoes can be used. Two and a half pounds of fresh tomatoes make the equivalent of a twenty-eight- to thirty-five-ounce can of whole tomatoes.

Tomato sauce can be made in many ways. Sometimes I use a combination of butter and oil, or I cook an onion instead of, or along with, the garlic, or I add a chopped rib of celery and a carrot with the onion or use a pinch of dried oregano or chopped fresh parsley instead of basil. It all depends on what taste and texture I'm trying to achieve and how the sauce will balance with the other flavors of the meal. One thing is for certain, a simple tomato sauce is best when it is uncomplicated. Don't add too many herbs or vegetables, or any wine. That would mask the flavor of the most important ingredient—the tomatoes.

Good canned tomatoes are fully ripened before they are packed. You will not need to add sugar or other ingredients to enhance the sauce. Of course you have no way to tell until you open the can, so try several different brands until you find one you can trust. I have had the most success with San Marzano–type tomatoes imported from Italy. They are tender and fully ripened when they are packed, and as they cook, the juice condenses and the tomato pulp breaks down to a thick smooth sauce. Don't buy tomatoes packed in puree, which makes the sauce pasty, heavy, and too sweet. Also, always buy whole tomatoes, not chopped or pureed, so that you can see that they were fully ripe and red when packed.

An Italian market usually has a selection of imported canned tomatoes to choose from. Read the labels carefully, though. Some appear to be Italian, but the fine print on the back of the can indicates that the tomatoes were grown elsewhere. The words "product of Italy" should appear on the label. The San Marzano variety of tomatoes, which get their name from the region near Naples that reputedly produces the finest tomatoes in Italy, are best, and that name should also appear on the label.

To condense the tomatoes rapidly, use a wide saucepan or deep skillet. The pan should have a heavy bottom, so that the sauce does not scorch. Be sure to use one with a stainless steel, enameled, or nonstick surface that will not react with the acid in the tomatoes.

I watched Anna Tasca Lanza prepare this simple tomato sauce at Regaleali, her family's wine estate in Sicily. The gentle cooking brings out all the sweetness and flavor so that even canned tomatoes seem as delicate as fresh picked. Anna serves this sauce over spaghetti and tops it with either freshly grated pecorino romano or Parmigiano-Reggiano. Sometimes she substitutes fresh sheep's milk ricotta for these two cheeses, which makes the sauce pink and creamy. Sheep's milk ricotta is difficult to find here. A few cheese shops carry it, but since it is very perishable, it is not widely available. American-made sheep's milk ricotta does not taste like the kind made in Italy.

The best substitute would be ordinary cow's milk ricotta mixed with a tablespoon or two of pecorino romano. You will need about ⅔ cup of ricotta for a pound of spaghetti.

Anna's Tomato Sauce

SALSA DI POMODORO ALLA ANNA

1 can (35 ounces) Italian peeled tomatoes with their juice or
    2 pounds ripe plum or Roma tomatoes, halved lengthwise
1 medium onion, thinly sliced
1 garlic clove, chopped
2 tablespoons chopped fresh basil
Pinch of crushed red pepper
Salt and freshly ground pepper, to taste
2 tablespoons extra virgin olive oil
1 tablespoon unsalted butter

1 In a large pot, combine the tomatoes, onion, and garlic. Bring to a simmer. Cover and cook on low heat 20 minutes or until the onions are tender. Let cool slightly.

2 Pass the tomato mixture through a food mill. Return the puree to the pot. Add the basil, red pepper, and salt and pepper.

3 Bring to a simmer. Remove from the heat. Stir in the olive oil and butter.

To make ahead: Complete the sauce through Step 2. Let cool and then cover and refrigerate in tightly sealed containers for up to one week or freeze for up to 3 months.

Signora Agnesi's Ragù

IL RAGÙ DI SIGNORA AGNESI

1 ounce dried porcini mushrooms (about 3/4 cup)

2 tablespoons unsalted butter

2 tablespoons olive oil

1/2 pound veal for stew, cut into 1/2-inch dice

1/2 pound beef sirloin, cut into 1/2-inch dice

1 small onion, finely chopped

1 small celery rib, finely chopped

1 medium carrot, finely chopped

1 garlic clove, finely chopped

2 fresh sage leaves

1 bay leaf

1/4 cup chopped fresh parsley

1 teaspoon fresh marjoram or 1/2 teaspoon dried marjoram

2 tablespoons chopped pine nuts

1/2 cup dry white wine

Salt and freshly ground pepper, to taste

1 can (35 ounces) Italian tomatoes, passed through a food mill

1 Place the mushrooms in a bowl with 2 cups warm water. Let soak for at least 30 minutes. Drain the mushrooms, reserving the liquid. Strain the liquid through a paper coffee filter or strainer lined with dampened cheesecloth. Rinse the mushrooms well under running water examining each piece. Pay special attention to the stems which may have bits of soil clinging to the base. Drain well and chop.

2 In a large heavy saucepan over medium heat, melt the butter with the olive oil. Add the veal and beef and cook, stirring occasionally, until the meat is no longer pink. Add the mushrooms, onion, celery, carrot, garlic, sage, bay leaf, parsley, marjoram, and pine nuts. Cook until the vegetables are tender, about 10 minutes. Add the wine, salt, and pepper. Bring to a simmer, partly cover the pan, and cook for 30 minutes.

MAKES ABOUT 4 CUPS, ENOUGH FOR 1 1/2 POUNDS DRIED PASTA, SUCH AS ROTELLI, RIGATONI, OR PENNE, OR FRESH CAVATELLI (SEE PAGES 113 AND 145)

Vicenzo Agnesi revolutionized the fledgling dried pasta industry earlier this century by including the germ of the wheat in his pasta, giving it a better texture and flavor. Agnesi pasta is still famous in Italy for its high quality.

During Vicenzo's time, many members of the Agnesi family were involved in the business, so they worked and lived close to one another. At mealtimes, aunts, uncles, cousins, and in-laws, not to mention assorted friends, would gather to eat. Preparations were presided over by Maddalena Agnesi, Vicenzo's sister. Naturally, pasta was an important part of their meals, so when I came across this recipe for Signora Agnesi's Ragù in *A Tavola*, an Italian cooking magazine, I knew it had to be good.

3 With a slotted spoon, remove the meat and vegetables from the pan and chop them very fine. Discard the bay leaf. Return the chopped ingredients to the saucepan. Add the tomatoes and mushroom liquid. Season with salt and pepper. Cook, uncovered, over very low heat for 1 hour, or until the sauce has thickened. Stir the sauce occasionally so that it does not stick.

When fresh tomatoes are at their peak, I always buy too many. It does not matter if they are round beefsteaks, meaty Romas or plums, tiny cherries, or low acid yellow tomatoes, I can't resist them. Then I have to figure out what to do with them before they spoil. Most of the time I make this super-easy sauce using whatever tomatoes I have on hand. The oven heat concentrates their flavor, and the sauce tastes rich and sweet. Even less than perfect tomatoes are improved by this oven treatment. It can be made with just one variety of tomatoes or a combination.

Sometimes, instead of the basil, I toss the sauce and pasta with two cups of arugula torn into bite-size pieces. These tomatoes are good, too, as an antipasto spread on slices of chewy bread.

Roasted Tomato Sauce

SALSA DI POMODORI AL FORNO

2 pounds ripe tomatoes
3 large garlic cloves, finely chopped
Salt and freshly ground pepper
1/3 cup olive oil
1/2 cup chopped fresh basil or parsley

1 Preheat the oven to 400°F. Oil a 13 × 9 × 2-inch casserole dish or roasting pan.

2 For round or plum-shaped tomatoes, cut the tomatoes in half lengthwise and remove the stem ends. Cut the halves into 1/4-inch thick slices. For cherry tomatoes, cut the tomatoes in half.

3 Arrange half the tomato slices in the prepared dish. Sprinkle with the garlic, salt, and pepper. Top with the remaining tomatoes. Drizzle with the oil. Bake 30 to 45 minutes, or until the tomatoes are lightly browned and the tomato juices are reduced. Let cool slightly.

4 Just before serving, sprinkle the basil or parsley over the tomatoes.

To make ahead: Prepare the tomatoes through Step 3 as indicated. Let cool completely, then cover and refrigerate for up to 3 days. Reheat in a 350°F. oven for 15 minutes, or until hot.

The Butcher's Sauce

RAGÙ DEL MACELLAIO

¹/₄ pound boneless beef

¹/₄ pound boneless veal

¹/₄ pound boneless pork

¹/₄ pound boneless lamb

¹/₄ cup olive oil

1 medium onion, very finely chopped

¹/₂ cup dry red wine

1 pound ripe tomatoes, peeled, seeded, and chopped, or 2 cups
  chopped canned Italian tomatoes

3 cups Meat Broth (page 83)

Pinch of crushed red pepper

Salt, to taste

Trim all of the meats and cut them into ¹/₂-inch pieces. In a large saucepan over medium heat, heat the oil. Add the meats and the onion and cook, stirring occasionally, until the meat is browned, about 15 minutes. Add the wine. Simmer until most of the liquid has evaporated. Add the tomatoes, broth, red pepper, and salt. Bring to a simmer. Reduce the heat to low. Cook the sauce for 1 hour, stirring occasionally, until all of the meat is tender and the sauce has thickened.

MAKES ABOUT 3 CUPS,
ENOUGH FOR
1 POUND PASTA

Every so often my freezer fills up with small amounts of meat trimmings and leftovers—an extra pork chop, some scraps of lamb left after cutting up a leg, a small beefsteak—the kinds of trimmings that a butcher might have at the end of the week. Rather than see them go to waste, he would bring the odds and ends home to his wife to add to the pot for their Sunday ragù, which explains how this southern Italian sauce got its name.

I serve this hearty sauce over Ricotta Gnocchi (page 162), cavatelli (see page 145), or dried pasta such as rigatoni. Vary the meats according to what you have on hand. You will need one pound or a little more.

In many places in southern Italy, a branch of chili peppers was hung by the front door and people wore little golden charms shaped like long twisted chilies to keep away the *malocchio,* or evil eye. A small dried chili or a pinch of crushed red pepper is used in many sauces to add flavor, but don't get carried away—most sauces should be only mildly hot.

Chilies, bell peppers, onions, tomatoes, and ground lamb make a hearty sauce for pasta. Sometimes when I roast or grill a whole leg of lamb, I use the left-over roast lamb instead. You will need two to three cups of chopped leftover lamb. Prepare the cooked lamb exactly the same way as fresh lamb.

I would serve this with cavatelli (see page 145) or dried rigatoni, fusilli, or ziti (one pound for six people) and a sprinkle of pecorino romano cheese.

Spicy Lamb and Pepper Ragù

RAGÙ AL AGNELLO

2 tablespoons olive oil

1 medium onion, chopped

1 red bell pepper, seeded and chopped

1 small fresh chili, seeded and chopped, or crushed red pepper, to taste

2 garlic cloves, finely chopped

1 pound ground lamb

1 can (28 to 35 ounces) Italian tomatoes with their juice

Salt and freshly ground pepper, to taste

In a large saucepan over medium heat, cook the olive oil, onion, bell pepper, and chili until the vegetables are tender, about 7 minutes. Add the garlic and cook for 1 minute more. Add the lamb and cook, stirring often, until it is no longer pink. Stir in the tomatoes, crushing them with the back of the spoon. Add salt and pepper. Bring the sauce to a simmer and reduce the heat to low. Cook, stirring occasionally, until the sauce is thickened, about 1 hour.

To make ahead: The sauce can be refrigerated for up to 3 days or frozen for up to 1 month.

Pasta ... Pasta Asciutta

I NEVER TIRE OF EATING *pasta whether it's dried packaged pasta or fresh homemade pasta, dressed with a slowly cooked meat ragù, a quick tomato sauce, stir-fried vegetables, beans, or a fresh seafood sauce. In fact, I can think of very few things that pasta does not go with. I serve it all the time, when I'm preparing a family-style meal or a fancy dinner party, when I'm feeling extravagant or thrifty, when I'm in a hurry or have lots of time.*

Some form of pasta has been the Italian national dish for centuries. Its recorded history can be traced back to the Etruscans, a mysterious tribe who inhabited what is now Tuscany and central Italy in the sixth century B.C.

Historians are not quite sure where the Etruscans originated or how they got to Italy. Most of what is known about them comes from the well-preserved drawings on urns and amphorae excavated from their tombs. A number of these drawings clearly illustrate cooks using familiar-looking implements to make a type of pasta that resembles what is eaten today.

In northern Italy, fresh pasta is made with eggs and wheat flour. It is both delicate and rich, and it is meant to be eaten when freshly made and still pliable, though it can be dried for longer storage.

Fresh egg pasta, or *pasta all'uovo,* can be fashioned into many shapes, from flat ribbons of varying widths called fettuccine, tagliatelle, or pappardelle, to quill-shape tubes called *garganelle* to the bowtie-shape farfalle. Fresh pasta can be stuffed, as in ravioli or tortellini, or layered for lasagne. Every region has its favorites, which are known by different names in different places. At one time, fresh egg pasta was made at home on a daily basis, but today it is often storebought or made only on special occasions.

Though fresh egg pasta is not unknown in southern Italy, many traditional fresh pastas are made without eggs, with only flour and water. It may be rolled out flat or shaped, usually by hand, into individual pieces. Eggless pasta is chewier and more substantial than fresh egg pasta, but it does not lack flavor. It is the perfect complement to the hearty vegetable and meat sauces of the South.

Though stuffed pastas, especially ravioli and cannelloni, are made in southern Italy, they are less common than in the North, perhaps because meat, seafood, and cheese fillings are perishable and would not keep well in the hot southern climate. Besides, those ingredients are relatively expensive in the poorer South.

Italians consider *pasta secca* or *maccherone,* dried pasta like spaghetti or ziti, as an entirely different food from fresh egg pasta, neither better nor worse. Made from semolina flour and water, dried pasta developed in southern Italy where the sunny, hot, and dry climate afforded the perfect conditions for making it.

Northern Italians were slow to appreciate the appeal of dried pasta but Giuseppe Garibaldi, the visionary nineteenth-century hero of Italian unification, predicted its future. When he liberated Naples in 1860, Garibaldi declared, "It will be macaroni, I swear to you, that will unite Italy." He was correct. Today spaghetti exceeds even pizza in popularity. Inexpensive, quick, and healthy, dried pasta is eaten everywhere in Italy.

In the United States, marketers anxious to sell their much more costly, so-called fresh pasta product, have many consumers believing that dried boxed pasta is inferior to fresh, which is not at all true. Either one can vary from excellent to poor in quality, though I have tasted far more bad fresh pasta than bad dried pasta. How can something even be called fresh made with preservatives and powdered eggs, and with a six-month shelf life? Many of these commercial pliable pastas lack the springy texture and delicate flavor of well-made fresh pasta. When you try to cook them, the pieces jam together and are impossible to separate. Avoid these mass-produced "fresh" pastas and seek out shops that make their own on a daily basis.

If your recipe calls for fresh pasta but you do not have a source for it and no time to make your own, substitute dried without guilt. Some Italian cookbook authors, bound by custom and local traditions, cite vague rules concerning the pairing of fresh vs. dried pastas with certain sauces. While there is no denying that certain matches are better than others, I have rarely found it to be a disaster to make reasonable substitutions. The recipes that follow include suggestions for alternative pastas whenever possible.

When you consider the vast range of Italian pastas and sauces, the collection in this chapter is a limited one. Though I would like some day to write a book (really an encyclopedia would be needed) about pasta in all of its myriad forms, I have focused here on some of the more unusual recipes I have enjoyed at home and in my travels. I chose these recipes not only because they are unfamiliar to most Americans but also because they are so good and work so well with our native ingredients that they deserve to be better known.

In place of a broad selection of filled pastas, I have included a collection of some of my favorite hand-shaped pastas and a sampling of the many kinds of dumpling-like gnocchi made all over Italy. These unusual pastas are no more difficult to make than a batch of cookies.

Pasta Shopping List

For quick pasta meals, keep the following ingredients on hand.

Dried pasta in various shapes and sizes. The most useful: linguine, spaghetti, ditalini, penne, farfalle, and rigatoni ⋯ Canned Italian peeled tomatoes, preferably San Marzano ⋯ Garlic ⋯ Onions ⋯ Crushed red pepper ⋯ Fresh parsley and basil ⋯ Parmigiano-Reggiano and pecorino romano ⋯ Olive oil

Cooking Dried Pasta

Despite all that has been written in recent years about cooking dried pasta, many cooks still follow Fanny Farmer's advice in *The Boston Cooking School Cook Book* of 1923. Her instructions were that pasta should be cooked for twenty minutes, cooled in cold water to prevent sticking, then reheated in the sauce. This method guarantees you will end up with a plate of gummy, overcooked pasta.

Instructions on boxes of dried pasta are vague and don't take into account such variables as the size of the pot and the amount of water. Follow the instructions below, and I promise you'll cook perfect pasta every time.

- For one pound of dried pasta, choose a large wide pot, preferably stainless steel or enamel, six- to eight-quart capacity. Do not use a tall narrow stockpot; the shape of the pot will make it difficult to reach the pasta that sinks to the bottom when it first goes in.

- Fill the pot with cold water. Hot water has been resting in the hot water heater, where it loses oxygen and becomes flat tasting.

- Place the pot on the stove over high heat. Cover the pot and bring the water to a rolling boil. This takes about ten to fifteen minutes.

- Once the water is boiling, add at least two tablespoons coarse salt to the water. Coarse or kosher salt has a purer salt flavor and is preferable to table salt, which has a slight metallic edge from the additives used to make it free flowing. The amount of salt may seem too generous, but most of it will be poured down the drain with the cooking water. Only a small amount clings to the pasta, but it is necessary to bring out the flavor. Without it the pasta would be bland. (An easy way to measure the salt is the one my grandmother always used. She would take the box of salt and quickly pour it into the boiling water in a wide Z pattern as in Zorro. The quantity is exactly right.)

- Add the pasta to the boiling water all at once. Stir well with a wooden spoon.

- Stir the pasta two or three more times until the water returns to a boil to prevent the pasta from sticking together. Make sure the heat is on high. You can partially cover the pot to return the liquid to a boil faster, but do not cover it completely or the water will boil over.

- Never add oil to the cooking water. It is a waste of good oil. It does not prevent the pasta from sticking together, but it does prevent the sauce from coating the pasta properly.

- Pasta such as spaghetti or linguine will probably be too long to submerge completely in the boiling water. Unless you are using them for soup, they should not be broken. Wait a few seconds and the pasta will soften and become pliable enough to push down and stir into the water.

- Don't go away! Continue to stir the pasta every few minutes as it cooks.

- It is not possible to give an exact cooking time for pasta because it depends on the size and shape of the pasta, atmospheric conditions in your kitchen, the way it was manufactured, and a host of other factors. Every brand is slightly different. The times given on the package are not to be trusted. Pasta is done when it is cooked al dente, literally "to the tooth." The only way to judge is to look at it and taste it.

- Remove a piece or a strand of pasta from the water. Look to see if it has softened. It should be flexible yet retain its shape, the color slightly lightened, and the appearance slightly swollen and rounded compared to the dried state. Bite into the pasta. It should feel chewy but not hard. The center should not appear white and chalky.

- Very thin pasta like angel hair or capellini is virtually impossible not to over-cook. Even if you remove the strands from the water while still quite firm, they will continue to soften from residual heat. Though they are often used for pasta dishes in American restaurants, precisely because they are so quick cooking, they are better suited to soup, where a slightly soft pasta is more acceptable.

- Just before draining the pasta, scoop up about a half cup of the cooking water in a heatproof cup. Set it aside to add to the pasta and sauce if they need thinning. The slight starchiness of the cooking water also helps the sauce adhere to the pasta.

- Set a large colander over a large heatproof serving bowl in the sink. The hot water draining off the pasta will automatically heat the serving bowl.

- When the pasta is al dente, immediately pour it into the colander. Lift the colander carefully, letting the water drain off into the sink and serving bowl, if you have placed it there. If you forgot to save some of the water for the sauce, you can do it now.

- Shake the colander once to remove excess water but do not allow the pasta to become dry, or it will begin to stick together. It should remain moist.

- Unless the pasta is to be served at room temperature, do not rinse it. Rinsing removes the surface starch, which helps the pasta to bind with its sauce. The tap water will also cool the pasta, and this is not desirable for hot pasta dishes.

- Some recipe instructions recommend transferring the pasta to the pot containing the sauce and stirring the pasta and sauce together. This way, the pasta absorbs more of the flavors of the sauce. Other recipes suggest stirring the drained pasta and sauce together in a serving bowl. I tip the hot water out of the bowl, replace it with the drained pasta, and immediately toss it with the sauce.

- Never put the pasta into the serving bowl and pour the sauce on top without stirring them together. It may look pretty before it is stirred, but by the time the pasta is served, the pieces not covered with sauce will be dry enough to stick together.

- If the sauce seems thick, add a little of the reserved cooking water to liquefy it slightly. Toss again. Many Italian cooks also add a drizzle of extra virgin olive oil or a pat of butter at this point for added smoothness both of texture and flavor. Add cheese, if using. Toss the pasta well and serve it immediately.

- Serve the pasta in shallow rimmed soup bowls. The pasta will stay warm longer if you heat the bowls first in a low oven.

- After the pasta is drained, immediately fill the pasta pot with cold water for easy cleaning.

Massa Marittima is a typical Italian beachtown on the Adriatic coast. Row after row of brightly colored lounge chairs line the shore, and families frolic in the surf all day. At lunch time, there is a big rush to the striped blue or green and white tents, where women in uniforms prepare freshly made *piadina*, a flatbread baked on a griddle. The bread is folded and stuffed with prosciutto, sautéed greens, or cheese.

At night, the town's bustling outdoor restaurants are packed with hungry beachgoers downing pizza, seafood, and pasta. We chose one lively looking place, and I was about to order a pizza margherita when I saw a waiter flash by with steaming bowls of vivid red spaghetti. He saw my look of astonishment and laughingly called out, "It's spaghetti with rubies!" I ordered it, of course. The "rubies" were chopped beets and their brilliant juices stained the spaghetti vermilion red. It tasted great, too.

If the leafy beet tops are fresh, you can blanch and chop them and add them to the skillet with the beets. In this case, you can reduce the amount of beets to one bunch. The beets can be baked or microwaved (see page 284).

Spaghetti with Rubies

SPAGHETTI CON RUBINI

2 bunches of beets (8 medium beets, about 2 pounds)
1/3 cup olive oil
2 garlic cloves, finely chopped
Pinch of crushed red pepper, or to taste
Coarse salt, to taste
1 pound thin spaghetti or linguine

1 Preheat the oven to 400°F.

2 Trim the tops and stems off the beets. Wash the beets under cool running water and scrub them with a brush. Wrap the beets in aluminum foil and bake for 45 minutes, or until tender. Let cool, then peel and coarsely chop the beets.

3 In a skillet large enough to hold all of the pasta, combine the olive oil, garlic, and red pepper. Cook over medium heat for about 30 seconds, or until the garlic is fragrant and the oil is sizzling. Add the chopped beets and turn them in the oil mixture until just heated through.

4 Bring a large pot of cold water to a boil. Add salt and the spaghetti. Cook until the spaghetti is almost al dente, tender yet firm to the bite. Drain the spaghetti, reserving 1/2 cup of the cooking water.

5 Pour the spaghetti into the skillet with the beets. Add some of the cooking water. Simmer over medium heat, constantly turning the spaghetti with the beets, until the pasta is evenly colored, about 2 minutes.

6 Serve immediately.

Vermicelli with Walnuts and Garlic

VERMICELLI CON LE NOCI

2 garlic cloves, peeled

¼ cup olive oil

1 cup walnuts, finely chopped

Coarse salt, to taste

1 pound vermicelli or spaghetti

2 tablespoons chopped fresh parsley or basil (optional)

Freshly ground pepper, to taste

¼ cup freshly grated pecorino romano

1 In a large skillet over medium-low heat, cook the garlic in the olive oil until golden. Remove the garlic from the pan. Add the walnuts and cook, stirring, until lightly toasted, about 5 minutes.

2 Meanwhile, bring a large pot of cold water to a boil. Add salt and the pasta. Cook, stirring frequently, until the vermicelli is al dente, tender yet firm to the bite.

3 Drain the vermicelli, reserving ½ cup of the cooking water. In a large serving bowl, toss the vermicelli with the nuts and just enough of the cooking water to keep it moist. Add the parsley, if using, and sprinkle generously with pepper.

4 Add the cheese and toss again. Serve immediately.

SERVES 4

I'm always on the lookout for recipes that can be made quickly with ingredients I have on hand. This is one of my favorites since I usually have a can of walnuts in the refrigerator to use for baking plus pasta in the pantry. Leave out the parsley or basil if you don't have any fresh.

The town of Tropea in Calabria at the toe of the Italian boot is famous for its sweet onions. One way to eat them is in this simple, slightly creamy sauce, which combines tomatoes, ricotta salata, and a touch of hot pepper, with tubetti (little tubes) or ditalini (little fingers)—small pasta tubes that are more commonly used in soups.

Tubetti with Sweet Onion and Tomato Sauce

TUBETTI CON SALSA DI CIPOLLE

1 or 2 large white sweet onions, such as OSO Sweet, Bermuda, or Vidalia, chopped (about 1 pound)

$1/4$ cup olive oil

$1/4$ cup water

$3/4$ pound fresh tomatoes, peeled, seeded, and chopped, or $1^1/2$ cups chopped canned Italian tomatoes

Salt, to taste

Pinch of crushed red pepper, or to taste

1 pound tubetti or ditalini

$1/2$ cup shredded ricotta salata or $1/4$ cup fresh ricotta plus 2 tablespoons freshly grated pecorino romano

1 In a saucepan large enough to hold the tubetti, combine the onions, olive oil, and water. Cook, stirring occasionally, over low heat until the onions are very tender and translucent, about 15 minutes. Add a little more water if needed to prevent the onions from browning. Add the tomatoes, salt, and red pepper. Cook, stirring occasionally, until the sauce has thickened slightly, about 10 minutes.

2 Bring a large pot of cold water to a boil. Add the salt and tubetti. Stir well. Cook, stirring frequently, until the tubetti are almost al dente, tender yet firm to the bite.

3 Drain, reserving $1/2$ cup of the cooking water. Immediately add the tubetti to the simmering sauce. Stir in the cheese and reserved cooking water as needed to coat the tubetti with the sauce.

4 Remove from the heat and serve immediately.

The Flag

LA BANDIERA

SERVES 4 TO 6

1 garlic clove, finely chopped

1 small dried chili, crushed, or a pinch of crushed red pepper

¼ cup olive oil

1½ pounds plum tomatoes, peeled, seeded, and chopped, or 3 cups chopped canned Italian tomatoes

2 tablespoons chopped fresh basil

Salt and freshly ground pepper, to taste

3 medium potatoes, peeled and cut into ½-inch pieces (1 pound)

1 pound ditalini, tubetti, or other small pasta tubes

2 bunches of arugula, trimmed and torn into 2 or 3 pieces (about 4 cups)

⅓ cup freshly grated pecorino romano

Red, white, and green are the colors of the Italian flag—and the colors of this patriotic pasta from Puglia. The red is, of course, the tomatoes; the green, the arugula and herbs; and the white, the pasta and potatoes.

Be sure to cut the potatoes into pieces no bigger than half-inch dice, so that they are tender when the pasta is ready. When the cooked potatoes and pasta are drained and stirred into the sauce, their starch combines with it to create a velvety texture.

1 In a skillet large enough to hold all of the ingredients, cook the garlic and chili in the oil over medium heat until the garlic is fragrant and lightly golden, about 30 seconds. Add the tomatoes, basil, salt, and pepper. Bring to a simmer and cook, stirring occasionally, for 10 to 20 minutes, or until the sauce has thickened.

2 Bring a large pot of cold water to a boil. Add salt, the potatoes, and the ditalini. Cook, stirring frequently, until the potatoes and ditalini are al dente, tender yet firm to the bite.

3 Drain, reserving about ½ cup of the cooking water. Pour the potatoes, ditalini, and arugula into the pan with the simmering tomato sauce. Add some of the reserved cooking water as needed to moisten the pasta. Cook, stirring, for 1 to 2 minutes. Remove from the heat.

4 Stir in the cheese and serve immediately.

At one time, Catholics were not allowed to eat meat on Fridays. For a meatless dinner, my mother often made a frittata with vegetables or cheese and either pasta with beans or this pasta with peas, onions, and eggs.

Dishes similar to this one were served as a soup, with liquid added in the form of broth or the pasta cooking water. My family preferred the dish as a pasta, but its origin as a soup explains why broken spaghetti or linguine is used. Called *maltagliati* in Italian, meaning badly cut, broken pasta or scraps and end pieces of fresh pasta would ruin the harmony and appearance of a pasta dish. A frugal cook would never discard them but would hold them to use in soup, which is more forgiving of less-than-perfect pasta. Besides, the scraps and broken pieces fit comfortably in a soup spoon, though they might be hard to collect with a fork. My family liked the dish dry so that we could eat it with a fork, but my mother continued the tradition of broken pasta, as her mother did before her. Just snap a few strands at a time into two-inch lengths; these are large enough to eat with a fork.

The sugar in sweet peas quickly turns to starch, so unless I can get them freshly picked, I turn to frozen peas, which often taste better. Let them thaw just enough so that they are not in a solid block.

Broken Pasta with Peas and Onions

PASTA CON PISELLI

1/4 cup olive oil

1 large onion, halved and thinly sliced

2 1/2 cups fresh or frozen tiny peas, partially thawed

Salt and freshly ground pepper, to taste

1/2 pound linguine or spaghetti, broken into 2-inch lengths

2 large eggs

1/2 cup freshly grated Parmigiano-Reggiano

1 In a skillet large enough to hold all of the ingredients, cook the oil with the onion over medium heat, stirring occasionally, until the onion is tender and golden brown, about 10 minutes. Stir in the peas and cook for 2 minutes more. Season with salt and pepper.

2 Meanwhile, bring a large pot of cold water to a boil. Add salt and the linguine. Cook, stirring frequently, until al dente, tender yet firm to the bite.

3 Drain the linguine, reserving some of the cooking water. Add the linguine to the skillet. Stir well.

4 Beat the eggs with the cheese, salt, and pepper. Stir the mixture into the pasta. Cook over low heat, stirring, just until the eggs are lightly set. Add a little of the cooking water if the pasta seems dry.

5 Serve immediately.

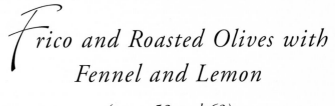

Frico and Roasted Olives with Fennel and Lemon

(pages 52 and 63)

Green Onion Pizza

(page 321)

Regaleali Wheat Berry Soup

(page 90)

Spaghetti with Rubies (page 116)

Ragged Pasta with
a Thousand Herbs

(page 136)

Whole Wheat Orecchiette
with Cauliflower and Bacon
(page 150)

Gardener's Risotto

(page 176)

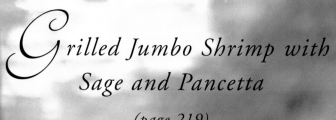

Grilled Jumbo Shrimp with Sage and Pancetta

(page 219)

Pasta and Potatoes

PASTA E PATATE

2 ounces pancetta, finely chopped

2 tablespoons olive oil

1 medium onion, finely chopped

1 small carrot, finely chopped

1 celery rib, finely chopped

1/4 cup chopped Italian flat-leaf parsley

1 pound all-purpose potatoes, peeled and cut into small dice
(about 3 medium)

1 garlic clove, finely chopped

2 cups chicken broth or water

Salt and freshly ground pepper, to taste

2 cups canned Italian tomatoes with their juice, cut up

1 pound tubetti or ditalini

1/2 cup freshly grated pecorino romano

1 In a saucepan large enough to hold the tubetti when cooked, cook the pancetta in the olive oil over medium heat until lightly browned. Add the onion, carrot, celery, and parsley and cook, stirring frequently, until lightly browned, about 8 minutes. Stir in the potatoes and garlic and cook for 2 minutes. Add the broth, salt, and pepper. Bring to a simmer and cook for 15 minutes. Add the tomatoes and their juice and cook until the potatoes are very tender, about 10 minutes more.

2 Meanwhile, bring a large pot of cold water to a boil. Add salt and the tubetti. Cook until the tubetti is almost done but still firm to the bite.

3 Drain, reserving 1 cup of the cooking water.

4 Stir the tubetti into the simmering sauce. Add cooking water as needed if the pasta seems too dry. Cook, stirring constantly, until the tubetti is al dente and coated with the sauce.

5 Transfer to a warm serving bowl. Stir in the cheese and serve immediately.

La cucina povera, literally "poor cooking," is a term used to describe dishes made from a few humble ingredients that turn out to be delicious and satisfying. *Pasta e Patate* from Naples is but one example of this type of home cooking.

The heart of the dish is the *battuto,* a combination of chopped aromatic vegetables including onion, carrot, celery, parsley, and garlic, cooked in oil until lightly browned. This preliminary cooking caramelizes the vegetables, tenderizes them, and brings out their flavors.

I serve Pasta and Potatoes thick enough to eat with a fork but many southern Italian cooks add more broth or even water and serve it as a soup. This is typical of la cucina povera—a dish can be stretched to feed as many mouths as needed, though for most people today serving it thick or thin is a matter of taste.

Cold pasta dishes or pasta salads are rarely found in Italy, so I was pleasantly surprised one hot summer afternoon to see this listed on the menu at Il Trigabolo, one of Italy's most highly acclaimed restaurants, in the sun-baked town of Argenta in Emilia Romagna. With its vibrant assortment of crunchy vegetables, herbs, and seafood, this has become my standard pasta dish when we have company on hot summer days. If I am serving a second course, I follow this pasta with Poached Salmon in Green Sauce (page 202).

Though the vegetables can be chopped ahead and the seafood precooked, wait until serving time to cook the pasta and vegetables and to assemble the dish. If prepared in advance and refrigerated, the pasta will become limp and the vegetables lose their flavor.

Chop the peppers and zucchini very, very fine so that they resemble confetti, or they will not cook sufficiently in the pasta water. You can use a food processor to chop the vegetables, but take care not to overprocess.

Il Trigabolo
Piazza Garibaldi
Argenta (Emilia-Romagna)

Cold Pasta with Vegetable Confetti and Seafood

PASTA FREDDA CON VERDURE E FRUTTI DI MARE

1/2 pound small to medium shrimp, shelled and deveined

Salt, to taste

1/2 pound bay or sea scallops, 1 cup chopped cooked lobster, or 1/4 pound crabmeat, picked over

2 medium-size ripe tomatoes, seeded and diced

1/4 cup snipped fresh chives

1/4 cup chopped fresh basil

1/4 cup extra virgin olive oil

Freshly ground pepper, to taste

1 pound linguine

3/4 cup very finely chopped red bell pepper (1/8- to 1/4-inch pieces)

3/4 cup very finely chopped yellow bell pepper (1/8- to 1/4-inch pieces)

3/4 cup very finely chopped zucchini (1/8- to 1/4-inch pieces)

2 small carrots, cut into matchsticks

1 In a medium saucepan, bring about 2 quarts of cold water to a boil. Add the shrimp and salt. Cook for 1 minute. Add the scallops, if using, and cook for 1 to 2 minutes more, or until all of the seafood is just cooked through. Drain the seafood and run it under cool water to stop the cooking. Pat the seafood dry. Chop it fine.

2 In a large serving bowl, combine the seafood, tomatoes, chives, basil, and olive oil. Season with salt and pepper.

3 Bring a large pot of cold water to a boil. Add salt and the linguine. Stir well. About 30 seconds before the linguine is ready, add the peppers, zucchini, and carrots. Stir well.

4 As soon as the linguine is al dente, tender yet firm to the bite, drain it and the vegetables in a large colander placed in the sink. The vegetables will be just slightly wilted. Cool the linguine and vegetables under cold running water until chilled. Drain well.

5 Add the linguine and vegetables to the tomato and seafood mixture. Toss well. Serve immediately.

Penne with Tomato, Sage, and Parmigiano

PENNE CON SALSA DI POMODORO E SALVIA

2 tablespoons olive oil

2 cups chopped canned Italian tomatoes, with their juice, or
    2 cups peeled, seeded, and chopped fresh tomatoes

4 fresh sage leaves or 1 teaspoon dried sage

Salt and freshly ground pepper, to taste

1 pound penne

2 tablespoons unsalted butter

1 to 2 teaspoons balsamic vinegar, to taste

3/4 cup freshly grated Parmigiano-Reggiano

1 In a medium saucepan, combine the oil, tomatoes, sage, salt, and pepper. Bring to a simmer over low heat. Cook, stirring occasionally, until the sauce is thick, about 20 minutes.

2 Meanwhile, bring a large pot of cold water to a boil. Add salt and the penne. Stir well. Cook over high heat, stirring occasionally, until the penne is al dente, tender yet firm to the bite.

3 Remove the tomato sauce from the heat and stir in the butter and balsamic vinegar.

4 Drain the penne and place it in a warm serving bowl. Add the sauce and stir well. Add the cheese and stir again. Serve immediately.

SERVES 4 TO 6

Two of Emilia-Romagna's star ingredients, Parmigiano-Reggiano and balsamic vinegar, combine with tomatoes and butter in this sauce. The sweet and sour flavors of the balsamic vinegar accent the corresponding flavor notes in the tomatoes, while the butter and a generous helping of cheese add a rich, smooth finish.

Fresh basil leaves look like spinach and taste like a whole new vegetable in this quick-cooking sauce. It cooks so fast, in fact, that it is a good idea to have the water boiling for the pasta before you begin to make the sauce. The scallops should be barely cooked so they don't have a chance to toughen. This sauce should be made only with a fresh tomato.

Spaghetti with Scallops, Tomato, and Basil

SPAGHETTI CON CANESTRELLI, POMODORO, E BASILICO

4 large garlic cloves, minced

¼ cup olive oil

1 pound sea or bay scallops, cut into ½-inch pieces

Pinch of crushed red pepper, or to taste

Salt, to taste

1 large ripe tomato, seeded and diced

2 cups fresh basil leaves, torn into 2 or 3 pieces

1 pound spaghetti or linguine

1 In a large skillet over medium heat, cook the garlic in the oil until the garlic is pale gold, about 30 seconds. Stir in the scallops, red pepper, and salt. Cook just until the scallops are opaque, about 1 minute. Stir in the tomato and basil. Cook for 1 minute, or until the basil is slightly wilted. Remove the skillet from the heat.

2 Bring a large pot of cold water to a boil. Add salt and the spaghetti. Cook, stirring frequently, until the spaghetti is al dente, tender yet still firm to the bite.

3 Drain the spaghetti and add it to the skillet. Toss well for 30 seconds. Serve immediately.

Linguine with Shrimp Sauce

LINGUINE AL GAMBERI

v.g.
6/10/97

1/2   1 pound medium shrimp, shelled and deveined, cut into $^1/_2$-inch
         pieces

      $^1/_3$ cup olive oil

1 1/2   3 large garlic cloves, finely chopped

      Salt and freshly ground pepper, to taste

2-3   4 to 5 ripe plum tomatoes, diced (about 2 cups)   *1 cup*

      $^1/_4$ cup capers, drained and chopped if large

1 1/2   1 pound linguine or spaghetti

1/4 $^1/_2$ cup chopped celery leaves, with some stems

1   Bring a large pot of cold water to a boil. Pat the shrimp pieces
dry.

2   In a skillet large enough to hold all of the ingredients, heat the
oil over medium heat. Add the shrimp, garlic, salt, and pepper.
Cook, stirring frequently, until the shrimp are lightly browned,
about 3 minutes. Add the tomatoes and capers. Cook, stirring, for 1
minute.

3   Add salt and the linguine to the water. Cook, stirring frequently,
until the linguine is al dente, tender yet firm to the bite. Drain, reserving some of the cooking water. Add the linguine and celery leaves
to the shrimp mixture.

4   Toss for 1 minute, adding some of the cooking water if needed.
Serve immediately.

Fresh celery leaves add a bright, fresh taste and a few chopped stems a bit of crunch to this quick pasta. Everything gets tossed together briefly in the skillet until the flavors of the sauce are absorbed by the linguine. The entire dish takes less than thirty minutes to prepare.

Prepare this dish only when tomatoes are in season. Canned tomatoes will make the flavor and consistency heavy.

When my husband's great-grandfather, Giuseppe Macaluso, was growing up in Palermo, Sicily, he made deliveries for the city's best baker. One of his stops was the Villa Igiea, a seaside estate on the outskirts of the city. The spectacular Moorish-Liberty style of the villa with its beautiful gardens and sweeping view across the bay must have seemed awesome to a poor delivery boy. Long after he had left Palermo for New York, he would reminisce about the villa. In fact, it was there that he met his bride-to-be, Maria, then just a schoolgirl. Family legend has it that Giuseppe was so taken by the sight of her that he dropped the coins he had just collected for his employer at the villa. She laughed at his dilemma, then stopped to help him. The rest is history.

Today the Villa Igiea is an expensive hotel. Though it is slightly rundown, you can still see the Belle Epoque detailing in its magnificent ballroom and some of the guest rooms.

While pesto is usually associated with Liguria, the Sicilians have their own versions. In Trapani pesto is made with crushed tomatoes and almonds. This recipe, which I adapted from a tuna pesto served at the Hotel Villa Igiea, is especially good in the summertime when you don't feel much like cooking. Cheese is not used in this version because of the tuna and anchovies.

Linguine with Tuna Pesto

LINGUINE ALLA VILLA IGIEA

1 cup tightly packed fresh basil leaves
³⁄4 cup tightly packed fresh parsley leaves
¹⁄3 cup pine nuts
2 medium garlic cloves, peeled
1 can (2 ounces) anchovy fillets, drained
¹⁄3 cup extra virgin olive oil
2 tablespoons fresh lemon juice
1 can (7 ounces) tuna in oil, preferably Italian tuna in olive oil
1 pound linguine

1 In a food processor fitted with the steel blade, chop the basil, parsley, pine nuts, and garlic. Add the anchovy fillets, olive oil, and lemon juice and process until smooth.

2 When ready to serve, bring a large pot of cold water to a boil. Mash the tuna with a fork.

3 Add salt and the linguine to the water. Cook, stirring frequently, until al dente, tender yet firm to the bite. Drain, reserving ¹⁄2 cup of the cooking water.

4 Immediately transfer to a serving bowl. Add the pesto, tuna, and some of the cooking water and toss well.

5 Add more water if the pasta seems dry. Serve immediately.

To make ahead: The pesto may be made ahead through Step 1. Scrape it into a bowl and let stand at room temperature for up to 1 hour.

Bowties with Leeks, Fontina, and Ham

FARFALLE CON PORRI E FONTINA

6 small leeks

2 tablespoons unsalted butter

Salt, to taste

1/2 cup heavy cream

6 ounces sliced cooked ham, cut into 1/2-inch squares

Freshly ground pepper, to taste

1 pound bowties (farfalle)

1 cup grated fontina, preferably Italian

1 Trim away the green tops and the root ends of the leeks. Cut them lengthwise in half and rinse well under cold running water. Drain the leeks and cut them crosswise into thin slices. You should have about 3 1/2 cups.

2 In a skillet large enough to hold the pasta when cooked, combine the leeks, butter, salt, and 1/2 cup water. Bring to a simmer and cook over low heat until the leeks are tender and slightly translucent and most of the liquid has evaporated, about 30 minutes. Add the cream and simmer for 5 minutes more, or until slightly thickened. Stir in the ham and pepper. Remove the sauce from the heat.

3 Bring a large pot of cold water to a boil. Add salt and the bowties. Cook, stirring frequently, until al dente, tender yet firm to the bite. Drain well, reserving some of the cooking water.

4 Add the pasta to the skillet with the leek sauce and toss well. Add the fontina and toss again. Stir in a little of the cooking water if the pasta seems too thick. Serve immediately.

To make ahead: The sauce may be made ahead through Step 2. Reheat gently if necessary when the pasta is ready.

SERVES 4 TO 6

My father, who was quite a good cook, and I used to sit together watching Julia Child's early television shows devoted to classic French cuisine. We were fascinated by her intricate recipes, so different from the simple Italian food we knew best. I couldn't wait to try them. I bought Julia's books, *Mastering the Art of French Cooking,* Volumes I and II, and proceeded to cook my way through them.

It was an excellent culinary education, but, unfortunately, I was not paying attention when Julia explained how to prepare leeks, which I had never eaten. They look a lot like big scallions, so I just rinsed, trimmed, and cooked them. It wasn't until I took a bite and got a mouthful of sand that I realized my mistake. Leeks grow in sandy soil, which gets trapped between the layers. They need a thorough rinsing inside and out. Large leeks tend to be tough, so use small to medium ones if possible. Cooked with butter and water, they become tender and soft without browning; their flavor stays mild and sweet.

In Italy, fava beans are one of the first vegetables to appear in the spring. In Rome, tender young beans are eaten raw at the end of a meal, together with fresh pecorino cheese. Sometimes favas, still in their long green pods, are tucked among the fruits in the fruit bowl.

If fresh fava beans are not available, use frozen favas. They can sometimes be found in Italian, Spanish, and Middle Eastern markets. The tough husk that surrounds each bean is left intact. Just drop the frozen beans into a pot of boiling salted water for one minute. Drain and cool them and the skins will peel off easily.

Fresh or frozen peas or lima beans can stand in for the favas, though the flavor will be different.

Bowties with Fresh Fava Beans

PASTA E FAVE

2 tablespoons olive oil

4 ounces pancetta, chopped

4 green onions, chopped

2 pounds fresh fava beans, shelled and peeled, or 2 cups frozen favas, blanched and peeled, or 2 cups partially thawed frozen lima beans

Salt and freshly ground pepper, to taste

8 ounces short wide pasta, such as bowties or orecchiette

1 In a skillet large enough to hold all of the pasta when cooked, heat the oil over medium heat. Add the pancetta and cook, stirring, until golden. Stir in the green onions and cook for 2 minutes, or until just tender. Add the fava beans and cook for 5 minutes. Season with salt and pepper.

2 Meanwhile, bring a large pot of cold water to a boil. Add salt and the bowties. Cook, stirring frequently, until the bowties are very firm. Drain, reserving 1/2 cup of the cooking water.

3 Add the bowties to the skillet. Cook, stirring, until the pasta and fava beans are tender, about 5 minutes more. Add some of the cooking water if the pasta seems dry.

4 Sprinkle generously with pepper. Serve immediately.

Dante and Beatrice's Pasta Cake

TORTA DI PASTA ALLA DANTE E BEATRICE

Salt, to taste

1 pound spaghetti

6 large eggs

¹/₂ cup freshly grated pecorino romano

Freshly ground pepper, to taste

2 tablespoons corn or other vegetable oil

2 ounces sliced Genoa salami, cut into thin strips

2 ounces sliced prosciutto, cut into thin strips

8 ounces mozzarella, preferably fresh, thinly sliced

1 Bring a large pot of cold water to a boil. Add salt and the spaghetti. Cook, stirring frequently, until al dente, tender yet firm to the bite.

2 Meanwhile, in a large bowl, beat the eggs with the pecorino and pepper. Drain the spaghetti and add it to the bowl. Toss well.

3 In a large skillet over medium heat, heat the oil. Toss the spaghetti again and add half to the skillet. Cover with half the salami and prosciutto strips. Make a layer of all the mozzarella slices. Cover with the remaining salami and prosciutto. Top with the rest of the spaghetti, pouring any remaining egg mixture over all.

4 Reduce the heat to low. Cook the spaghetti, flattening it with a spoon so that it sticks together and forms a cake. After about 5 minutes, slide a spatula around the rim of the skillet and lift the cake gently to be sure that it is not sticking. Cook for 15 to 20 minutes, or until the eggs are set and the pasta is golden.

5 Place a serving platter over the pasta. Carefully invert the skillet over the platter.

6 Serve hot or at room temperature cut into wedges.

SERVES 8

A large party was celebrating a happy occasion at Trattoria Dante e Beatrice in Naples. Several enormous golden cakes, which looked like dessert, were brought out. The waiter told us they were not dessert at all, but rather pasta tortes. He cut Charles and me two generous slices oozing melted mozzarella, prosciutto, and salami, then explained how it was made.

Cooked spaghetti is tossed with eggs, salami, prosciutto, and mozzarella then cooked in a skillet until the bottom is golden and the eggs are set, something like a frittata. It really is quite easy, though turning the skillet to flip the cake over can be somewhat clumsy, especially if you're using a heavy, cast-iron skillet. For this recipe, a lighter weight, nonstick skillet is a better choice. Have ready a large round serving platter somewhat larger than the skillet. Protect your hands with oven mitts, cover the skillet with the platter, then *Forza!*, as the Italians say, invert the skillet onto the platter without hesitation. The pasta cake will slip right out.

The cake can be made without meat, if you prefer. Just increase the mozzarella slightly or add some sautéed mushrooms. It is also very good served with a simple tomato sauce.

Trattoria Dante e Beatrice
Piazza Dante, 44/45
Naples (Campania)

MAKES ABOUT 1
POUND

Like riding a bicycle or rolling out a pie crust, making fresh egg pasta is not difficult to learn. It just takes practice. Explanations on paper can never take the place of actually handling the dough. Once you've got the feel of it, though, you'll have the satisfaction of turning out tender, satin-smooth fresh pasta in myriad shapes and sizes.

I've tried to make the instructions for making fresh egg pasta as clear as possible. If you've never made pasta before, or if you've not been successful, read the instructions carefully and choose a quiet time to try. Definitely don't invite a crowd over for a fresh pasta dinner until you feel completely comfortable about making it.

The dough can be made by hand or in a food processor or in a heavy-duty electric mixer. If you make the dough by hand, you can feel it change and develop from a mess of eggs and flour to a smooth, pliant dough. The machine method, however, is neater and faster.

Fresh Egg Pasta

PASTA ALL'UOVO

About 2¹/₂ cups unbleached all-purpose flour
4 large eggs

MAKING THE DOUGH

By Hand

1 Choose a countertop or a large wooden or plastic cutting board to work on. A plastic laminate countertop is better than a marble or granite surface. Stone countertops are too highly polished and slick. A cutting board should be reserved for pasta making, so that it does not pick up and transfer odors from strong smelling foods.

2 Pour the flour into a mound in the center of the board. With a fork, make a wide crater in the center of the mound. Crack the eggs, one at a time, into a small cup. Look them over to be sure there are no pieces of shells. Drop the eggs into the flour crater. Beat the eggs with a fork, gradually incorporating some of the flour from the inside of the crater. Use your other hand to support the wall of flour surrounding the eggs. Be careful not to take too much flour from any one spot or the eggs may spill out.

3 When the dough starts to form a ball and becomes too firm to stir, sweep any remaining flour to one side. Lightly flour your hands and begin kneading. Push the dough away from you with the heels of your hands and pull it back toward you with your fingertips. At first the dough will be very sticky but will become smoother as you knead it and the flour is absorbed. Gradually add in some of the reserved flour whenever the dough feels sticky. When enough flour has been added, the dough will feel moist but not sticky. Do not add more flour than is necessary to create a firm ball of dough or it may become too dry. (If you do go too far, moisten your hands with a little water and knead it in.)

4 Set the dough aside for a moment. Wash and dry your hands to remove scraps of dough. Use a dough scraper or metal spatula to clean the kneading surface and remove any hard bits of dough and excess flour that might later cause lumps in the pasta. Put the scrapings and flour into a sieve. Shake the sieve over the countertop and your hands to coat them lightly with flour.

5 Resume kneading until the dough is smooth and elastic, moist yet not sticky. This should take about 8 to 10 minutes. Do not skimp on the kneading time: The more the dough is kneaded, the lighter and better the pasta will be. Work as rapidly as possible so that the dough does not dry out.

6 Cover the dough with an inverted bowl and let it rest for 30 minutes or up to 2 hours at room temperature. This rest allows the flour to further absorb the moisture from the eggs and makes the dough pliable for rolling out.

In a Food Processor or Heavy-Duty Mixer

1 In a food processor with the steel blade or in a heavy-duty electric mixer with the flat beater attachment, beat the eggs. With the machine running, slowly add the flour by the tablespoonful. When most of the flour has been added and the dough forms a ball on the blade or beater, stop the machine. Pinch the dough. It should feel moist but not sticky and should be fairly smooth. If it is not, turn the machine on again and add more flour as needed.

2 Remove the dough from the machine and knead it on a lightly floured surface for 1 minute. This hand kneading is to ensure that the dough has the right consistency—firm, smooth, and moist, but not sticky.

3 Place the dough on a lightly floured plate and cover it with an inverted bowl. Let the dough rest for 30 minutes or up to 2 hours at room temperature. This rest allows the flour to further absorb the moisture from the eggs and makes the dough pliable for rolling out.

ROLLING OUT THE DOUGH

Have ready several jelly-roll pans, roasting pans, or rimmed trays covered with cloth kitchen towels for drying the pasta. (You use pans with raised sides so they can be stacked in a crisscross manner to take up less room.) Sprinkle the towels with flour. You can also drape the pasta over a wooden pole or dowel placed between 2 chair backs, or use a laundry drying rack, but I find that the pasta is more likely to break if dried this way and somebody is bound to bump into it. I favor drying it flat on pans.

By Hand

1 You will need a long, thin, wooden rolling pin at least 24 inches long and 1 1/2 to 2 inches wide. Choose a large flat surface such as a plastic or wooden cutting board or a plastic laminate countertop. Make sure the surface is perfectly flat and not warped, which would

---

An Ode to Macaroni

As I entered the door, I smelled
the aroma of ragù.
So . . . Take care . . . Goodbye . . .
I am leaving . . . If I sit
I might not go . . .

I am sure it is macaroni
I heard cracking
As I entered the door.
Could it be?

A tomato skin is resting
    on your arm
like a blood stain . . . Permit me?
I will remove it!
How fine your skin feels . . .
like silk, slipping under
    my fingers . . .

You look especially beautiful
    this morning
Your face reflects fire . . .
I am sure it's the macaroni . . .

I am going . . . Goodbye!
If I sit, I might not leave . . .
I might wait
'til you sit at the table,
to receive a ragù-flavore kiss!

Rocco Galdieri, from
"Sunday," Naples, 1932

make the pasta difficult to roll. A slightly rough or coarse surface will give the pasta sheet a better texture. Lightly dust the surface with flour.

2   Uncover the dough. It might feel moister and stickier than when you last handled it. Cut the dough into 4 pieces. While you work with 1 piece of dough, keep the remainder covered with an inverted bowl or plastic wrap.

3   Shape the dough into a round disk and place it on the board. Dust it very lightly with flour. Place the rolling pin in the center of the dough and push it away from you toward the edge. Rotate the dough a quarter turn, center the pin on the dough, and push it toward the edge once more. Repeat rotating the dough a quarter turn and rolling it out from the center 2 more times. Rotating the dough will help keep the shape round and the thickness even. Flip the disk over to be sure that it is not sticking. If necessary, dust with more flour.

4   Continue stretching the dough, rotating it and turning it over from time to time, until it is very thin and smooth. Work quickly so that the dough does not dry out. If it should tear, pinch it together to seal it or patch it with a small piece of dough from the edge. If necessary, lightly moisten the edges of the tear so that the dough will adhere. Sprinkle with flour and roll over the patch to smooth it.

5   Flip the dough over and rotate it frequently. When it is ready, the dough should be paper thin so that you can easily see your hand through it when the sheet is held up to a light.

With a Pasta Machine

1   Choose a location where you will have plenty of room to work. Following the manufacturer's directions, clamp the pasta machine firmly to your countertop or a sturdy table. Set the rollers of the pasta machine at the widest opening and dust them lightly with flour. Have extra flour handy for dusting the countertop, the pasta machine, and the pasta. (A large salt shaker or dredger filled with flour is ideal for this.)

2   Uncover the dough. It may feel moister and slightly stickier than when you last handled it. Cut the dough into 4 pieces. While you work with 1 piece of dough, keep the remainder of the dough covered with an inverted bowl or plastic wrap.

3   Flatten the dough into an oval disk. Turning the handle of the pasta machine with one hand, guide the piece of dough through the rollers of the machine. If the dough sticks or tears, dust it lightly with flour.

4   Remove the dough from the machine and fold it in thirds. Pass the dough through the machine again, flouring it if necessary. Repeat folding and passing the dough 5 or 6 times.

A Fresh Taste of Italy

5 Move the dial to the next notch. Pass the dough through the rollers. As the dough emerges from the rollers, lift it out straight so that it stays flat and smooth without wrinkling. Do not fold it.

6 Continue to pass the dough through the machine, moving the dial up 1 notch and narrowing the rollers each time, until the dough has reached the thinness you want. It should be thin enough to see your hand through it but not so thin that it will tear. You will have to judge the thinness for yourself since different manufacturer's machines have different settings. For stuffed pasta, such as ravioli, the dough should be as thin as possible, so you will probably need to go to the last setting. The second-to-the-last notch is usually thin enough for fettuccine or other flat pasta, where the dough can be slightly thicker.

7 Repeat with the remaining pieces of dough. As you roll out the strips, lay them side by side on the prepared towels without letting them touch one another. Let the strips dry for about 20 minutes, or until they are firm yet still pliable, turning them at least once before cutting.

CUTTING THE DOUGH

The dough should be cut while still flexible and not too dry or it will crack. The pasta can be cut with the cutting attachment for the pasta machine or with a large heavy chef's knife.

Fettuccine
Fettuccine should be about $^1/_4$ inch wide and 10 inches long.

If using the attachment, first cut the strip crosswise into 10-inch lengths. Feed one end of a piece of the pasta into the cutter. Crank the handle with one hand as you lift the fettuccine away from the machine with the other. (Enlist a helper if you can.) Separate the fettuccine and arrange the ribbons on the floured towels or on a drying rack to dry. Work quickly or they may stick together.

To cut the fettuccine by hand, loosely roll up the strip. Use a large heavy chef's knife to cut the rolled-up pasta crosswise into $^1/_4$-inch-wide strips. Separate the strips and dry them on towels or a drying rack.

Quadrucci, pappardelle, *tria*, and *stracci*, 4 other pasta shapes that are used in this book, need to be cut by hand since there is no pasta machine cutting attachment for them.

Other Shapes
For quadrucci, tiny pasta squares for soups and broth, first cut fettuccine. Stack a few strips at a time and cut them crosswise into $^1/_4$-inch slices to make little squares.

For pappardelle, wide pasta ribbons, follow the procedure for fettuccine, but cut rolled-up pasta into $^3/_4$-inch strips. Pappardelle is sometimes cut with a wavy-edge pastry wheel.

Tria, short ribbons slightly wider than fettuccine, are about $^1/_2$ inch wide by 4 inches long. First cut the pasta sheet into 4-inch lengths. Cut the lengths into $^1/_2$-inch-wide strips. Use a ruler or piece of cardboard as a guide, if necessary.

Stracci, literally rags, are cut with a fluted pastry wheel to give the edges a jagged shape. They should measure about 1 by 4 inches. To cut them, lay a strip of dough on the countertop or pastry board. With a fluted pastry wheel, press firmly to divide the strip crosswise into 4-inch lengths. Cut the pieces lengthwise into 1-inch strips. Use a ruler or other straight edge to guide you if necessary.

STORING FRESH EGG PASTA

Once it is cut, fresh egg pasta can be immediately cooked, refrigerated, or frozen, or it can be allowed to dry further for longer storage.

To keep the pasta fresh and pliable, let it dry for about 1 hour, or until it is leathery but still flexible. Put it in a plastic bag and tightly seal the bag. Refrigerate for up to 2 days or freeze for up to 1 month.

To dry the pasta, place the strands on pans lined with floured towels, stacking the pans one across the other so that air can circulate. Turn the strands once or twice to be sure that they are not sticking. Cover with a cloth towel, not plastic wrap or aluminum foil, which might cause the pasta to turn moldy. Place the pans in a cool dry spot, and let the pasta dry for several days. Rotate the pans daily. If the weather is damp or the pasta is thick, it may take up to a week to dry completely. When the pasta is completely dry, store it in plastic bags. It will be very fragile at this point so handle it carefully. It keeps indefinitely.

COOKING FRESH EGG PASTA

To cook 1 pound of fresh pasta, bring a 6- to 8-quart pot of cold water to a boil. Add 2 to 3 tablespoons salt. Add the pasta all at once. Immediately stir it with a wooden spoon. Stir frequently until the water returns to a boil. Cook until al dente, tender yet firm to the bite, 1 to 2 minutes, depending on how dry the pasta was before cooking. Test a few strands. The pasta should be somewhat chewy, never mushy. Drain the pasta and place it in a heated serving bowl. Immediately add the sauce and toss.

The Pasta Machine

A hand-cranked metal pasta machine with rollers, imported from Italy, is the best type of machine for rolling out pasta. It kneads, smooths, and stretches the dough to perfection. The only attachment I use is the fettuccine cutter, which makes even, professional-looking strands of pasta. Imported Italian pasta machines are available in cookware shops. If you have a choice, get a wider machine. It will make a broader rather than longer strip of dough; wider strips are easier to handle.

Machines that extrude the pasta by forcing it through a die make gummy, poor quality pasta that does not have the right texture for Italian-style pasta.

Keep your pasta machine in a dry place. To clean it, use a brush, a dry cloth, or damp towel. Never wash it or the parts may rust. Make sure it is perfectly dry and keep the machine covered with a cloth when not in use.

Pasta-Making Tips

- Flour varies according to the weather, its age, and how it is stored. These factors influence its ability to absorb the moisture from the eggs, so you may need to use more or less flour than is called for.
- Only unbleached all-purpose flour should be used, unless another type of flour is specified in the recipe. Unbleached all-purpose flour has the right amount of gluten, the protein in flour that gives pasta good elasticity and texture.
- Eggs vary in the amount of moisture they contain. The liquid in an egg evaporates as it ages, so you may need to use less flour with eggs that are not so fresh. The size of the eggs also makes a difference. I have used standard large eggs for all of the recipes in this book. If you use another size egg, adjust the flour accordingly.
- Some Italian cooks add a teaspoon of olive oil to the eggs before working them in the flour. This helps keep the dough pliable and is particularly helpful in a hot dry climate.
- Speed is essential when making fresh egg pasta. If you don't work fast enough, you're more likely to develop problems with drying, cracking, and tearing.

When life gets hectic, the Locanda dell'Amorosa outside of Sinalunga in Tuscany is the kind of place I dream about. I imagine driving up the narrow road lined with a double row of tall cypress trees that leads to the restaurant and inn, and I feel as if I am being transported to another time. Passing under a brick arch, I arrive in a peaceful medieval courtyard surrounded by several old stone buildings, some of which date back to the fourteenth century. Amorosa has several charmingly appointed comfortable rooms, and it is perfect as headquarters for touring the Tuscan countryside and visiting nearby Siena—if you can pry yourself away.

The chef, Walter Redaelli, who specializes in regional Tuscan recipes, uses olive oil, vegetables, and meats produced or grown on the surrounding farm, so that everything is perfectly fresh. This is his recipe for pasta "rags" made with handfuls of finely chopped herbs fresh from the inn's garden.

Locanda dell'Amorosa
Sinalunga (Tuscany)

Ragged Pasta with a Thousand Herbs

STRACCI DI PASTA CON MILLE ERBE

1/4 cup chopped Italian flat-leaf parsley

1/4 cup chopped fresh basil

1/4 cup chopped fresh tarragon

2 tablespoons chopped fresh mint

2 tablespoons chopped fresh marjoram

2 tablespoons chopped fresh thyme

2 tablespoons chopped fresh sage

2 teaspoons finely chopped fresh rosemary leaves

1/2 cup extra virgin olive oil

Coarse salt and freshly ground pepper, to taste

1 pound stracci (fresh egg pasta cut into 4 × 1-inch strips with a fluted pastry wheel) or fresh fettuccine (see page 130)

1/2 cup freshly grated pecorino romano

2 medium-size ripe tomatoes, peeled, seeded, and chopped

1   In a bowl large enough to contain all of the ingredients, combine the herbs, olive oil, salt, and pepper. Set aside.

2   Bring a large pot of cold water to a boil. Add salt and the stracci. Cook, stirring frequently, until the stracci is al dente, tender yet still firm to the bite, 1 to 2 minutes. Drain well.

3   Add the pasta to the bowl with the herb mixture and toss well. Add the cheese and toss again.

4   Scatter the tomatoes over the pasta and serve immediately.

Summer-style Fettuccine

FETTUCCINE DELL'ESTATE

1 medium onion, thinly sliced

3 tablespoons olive oil

3 medium-size ripe tomatoes, peeled, seeded, and chopped

2 small zucchini, scrubbed, trimmed, and chopped

2 red, green, or yellow bell peppers, roasted, peeled, seeded, and
thinly sliced (see page 66)

2 garlic cloves, finely chopped

1 tablespoon chopped fresh oregano or $^1/_2$ teaspoon dried oregano

Salt and freshly ground pepper, to taste

1 pound fresh fettuccine (see page 130)

$^1/_3$ cup freshly grated pecorino romano

6 large basil leaves

SERVES 4

Stop at your local farm stand for the ingredients for this light vegetable sauce to serve with fresh fettuccine. Look for small, tender zucchini, no more than six inches in length. Larger zucchini have tough seeds and contain more water, which makes them less flavorful.

1 In a large skillet over medium heat, cook the onion in the oil until golden, about 5 minutes. Add the tomatoes, zucchini, peppers, garlic, oregano, salt, and pepper. Cook, stirring occasionally, until the vegetables are tender, about 10 minutes.

2 Meanwhile, bring a large pot of cold water to a boil. Add salt and the fettuccine. Cook, stirring frequently, until the fettuccine is tender yet firm to the bite, 1 to 2 minutes. Drain, reserving 1 cup of the cooking water.

3 In a large heated bowl, toss the fettuccine with the sauce and cheese. Add some of the reserved cooking water if necessary to moisten.

4 Tear the basil into small pieces and sprinkle over the top. Serve immediately.

The first cookbook I bought when I got married was Anna Muffoletto's *Sicilian Cooking,* one of only a handful of cookbooks then available with authentic Italian recipes. Signora Muffoletto always referred to lentils as "pebbles" and that is just what they look like to me, too. Though lentils are more usual in salads or soups, they make a hearty yet simple sauce for pasta.

Pasta Ribbons with Pebbles

FETTUCCINE CON LE LENTICCHIE

¹/₄ cup olive oil

2 garlic cloves, peeled and lightly crushed

1 cup peeled, seeded, and chopped fresh tomatoes or chopped canned Italian tomatoes with their juice

Pinch of crushed red pepper

8 ounces lentils, rinsed and picked over to remove stones

Salt and freshly ground pepper, to taste

1 pound fresh fettuccine (see page 130) or dried small pasta, such as tubetti or ditalini

Extra virgin olive oil, for drizzling

1 In a large saucepan over medium heat, cook the olive oil and garlic. When the garlic is golden, stir in the tomatoes and red pepper. Bring to a simmer and cook for 10 minutes. Add the lentils and 4 cups water. Bring to a simmer. Cook for 30 minutes. Add salt and pepper. If the lentils become too dry, add a little more water. Cook until the lentils are completely tender and most of the liquid has evaporated, about 15 minutes more.

2 Meanwhile, bring a large pot of cold water to a boil. Add salt and the fettuccine. Cook, stirring frequently, until al dente, tender yet firm to the bite, 1 to 2 minutes. (Dried pasta will take longer.) Drain, reserving 1 cup of the liquid. Add the pasta to the lentils and toss well, adding a little of the reserved cooking water if needed.

3 Place the pasta in a large warm serving bowl. Drizzle with a small amount of extra virgin olive oil and serve.

To make ahead: The sauce can be made ahead through Step 1 up to 3 days in advance. When ready to use, add a little water and reheat gently.

Fettuccine with Porcini and Giblets

FETTUCCINE ALLA ROMANA

SERVES 4

1 ounce dried porcini mushrooms

3 tablespoons olive oil

2 slices pancetta, finely chopped

1 medium onion, finely chopped

8 ounces chicken giblets, trimmed and very finely chopped

1/2 cup dry white wine, such as Frascati

1 tablespoon dry Marsala

3 large fresh tomatoes, peeled, seeded, and chopped, or 3 cups
    chopped canned Italian tomatoes

1 cup Meat Broth (page 83)

Salt and freshly ground pepper, to taste

1 pound fresh fettuccine (see page 130)

1/3 cup freshly grated Parmigiano-Reggiano

1/4 cup freshly grated pecorino romano

Frascati, a little hill town not far from Rome, is best known for the white wine that bears its name. On Sundays and holidays, Romans flock to Frascati to enjoy the fresh air and dine in the many family-style trattorias. The wine is said to taste its best there, served foaming in flasks that are drawn directly from the barrel.

Ristorante Cacciani is one of the more elegant restaurants in Frascati. From its shady hillside terrace, you can see some of the fabulous nearby villas owned by royalty and other wealthy people. The restaurant was founded by Leopoldo Cacciani in 1922, and his descendants are still in charge. This recipe for fettuccine with porcini and chicken giblets is said to be an original recipe of the founder.

Ristorante Cacciani
Frascati (Latium)

1 Place the mushrooms in a bowl with 2 cups warm water. Let soak for at least 30 minutes. Drain the mushrooms, reserving the liquid. Strain the liquid through a paper coffee filter or strainer lined with dampened cheesecloth. Rinse the mushrooms well under running water, examining each piece. Pay special attention to the stem pieces which may have bits of soil clinging to the base. Drain well and chop.

2 In a large skillet over medium heat, heat the oil. Add the pancetta and onion and sauté until golden, about 5 minutes. Add the giblets and cook until lightly browned. Add the mushrooms, the mushroom liquid, white wine, and Marsala. Bring to a simmer and cook until most of the liquid has evaporated. Add the tomatoes and broth. Season with salt and pepper. Cook for 25 minutes more, or until the giblets are tender when pierced with a fork and the sauce is thick.

3 Meanwhile, bring a large pot of cold water to a boil. Add salt and the fettuccine. Cook, stirring frequently, until the fettuccine is al dente, tender yet firm to the bite, 1 to 2 minutes. Drain well.

4 Place the fettuccine in a warm bowl and toss with the sauce. Sprinkle with the cheeses, toss lightly, and serve immediately.

Fettuccine with Artichokes

FETTUCCINE CON CARCIOFI

3 medium artichokes

1 small onion, finely chopped

¹/₄ cup chopped Italian flat-leaf parsley

¹/₄ cup olive oil

1 garlic clove, finely chopped

¹/₂ cup dry white wine

Salt and freshly ground pepper, to taste

1 pound fresh fettuccine (see page 130)

1 tablespoon unsalted butter

More reliable than the first crocus as a sign the long winter is coming to an end is the arrival of the two Andys on the corner of Carroll Street in my Brooklyn neighborhood. Standing out in the watery spring sunlight, they sell fresh fruit and vegetables from the back of their beat-up red pick-up truck, piled high with wooden crates of fat green asparagus and tender little zucchini. Tall Andy always has good cooking advice to share with the local moms as he hands a juicy red strawberry to a cranky toddler. Meanwhile, short Andy slips an extra apple, maybe with a little bruise on it, into your shopping bag.

One day I was buying twenty-four artichokes for a class I was teaching at Macy's DeGustibus Cooking School. Tall Andy asked what I was going to do with so many artichokes, so I explained they were for a class. "Don't make it look too hard!" he exclaimed, his eyes widening. "Nobody wants to cook fresh artichokes any more because they think they're too much trouble."

1 Cut off the top ¹/₂ to ³/₄ inch of the artichokes. Rinse the artichokes under cold water, spreading the leaves open. Be careful to avoid the little thorns on the remaining tips of the leaves. Bend back and snap off all of the dark green leaves until you reach the pale yellowish cone of tender leaves at the center. With a vegetable peeler or paring knife, peel off the tough outer skin around the base and stems. Leave the stems attached to the base, but trim off the ends. Cut the artichokes lengthwise in half and scoop out the fuzzy chokes. Cut the artichokes lengthwise into thin slices.

2 In a large saucepan over medium heat, cook the onion and parsley in the olive oil until the onion is very tender, 5 to 7 minutes. Add the garlic and cook for 1 minute more. Add the artichoke slices, wine, salt, and pepper. Cover and cook for 10 minutes, or until the artichokes are tender when pierced with a fork.

3 Meanwhile, bring a large pot of cold water to a boil. Add salt and the fettuccine. Cook, stirring frequently, until the fettuccine is al dente, tender yet firm to the bite, 1 to 2 minutes. Drain, reserving 1 cup of the liquid. Add the fettuccine to the pan with the artichokes.

4 Add the butter and a little of the reserved cooking water if the pasta seems dry. Toss well until the butter is melted. Serve immediately.

Trimming artichokes is a bit of a nuisance, true, but it's not difficult, and the delicate flavor makes it worth the effort. If you want to prepare the artichokes an hour or two ahead of time, trim them but don't slice them, then place them in a large bowl with cold water to cover. Squeeze a lemon into the water to help prevent the artichokes from discoloring. They will darken somewhat, but the acid in the lemon slows down the process. Drain and slice the artichokes just before cooking.

Artichokes will stain your hands. Scrub them with a gentle nail brush and some mild soap and rub any stubborn stains with a cut lemon.

Battuto

Many Italian recipes start with a battuto, chopped aromatic vegetables lightly browned in oil or pancetta. The exact combination varies according to the other ingredients in the dish, and the ratio of ingredients may also change. Herbs are sometimes—but not always—added. The purpose of a battuto is to add a lively flavor to basically bland ingredients. In Pasta and Potatoes, the two starches act as carriers of the battuto. Beans or rice sometimes play the same role. Pancetta adds an extra note of richness, but a dish would still be very good (and a little lighter) without it.

Another kind of battuto is added as a final fillip at the end of cooking a soup or a stew, such as the Regaleali Wheat Berry Soup (page 90). This type of uncooked battuto is usually a mixture of chopped herbs and garlic. Gremolata, a Milanese-style battuto that is sprinkled on osso buco, features finely chopped lemon zest, garlic, and parsley.

When the New York Association of Cooking Teachers asked me to give a talk and cooking demonstration on Tuscan cooking, they specifically requested that I prepare pasta with rabbit sauce. To make this classic sauce, Tuscans use a hare, a large wild rabbit with a pronounced, gamey flavor. I wasn't able to find a wild hare, but not wanting to disappoint the club members, I did some research and discovered that pork sausages are sometimes added to the hare sauce for greater depth of flavor. I combined some sausages with a farm-raised rabbit and the results were delicious.

Pappardelle are ribbons of fresh pasta similar to fettuccine, only a bit wider. Substitute fettuccine, if you prefer.

Pappardelle with Rabbit and Sausage

PAPPARDELLE CON SALSA DI CONIGLIO E SALSICCIA

1 rabbit, fresh or thawed frozen, cut into 8 pieces (about 2¹/₂ pounds)

¹/₂ cup all-purpose flour

2 tablespoons unsalted butter

2 tablespoons olive oil

1 carrot, finely chopped

1 medium red onion, finely chopped

1 celery rib, finely chopped

¹/₄ cup chopped fresh parsley

8 ounces Italian-style pork sausage with fennel, casing removed, or 8 ounces ground pork plus 1 tablespoon crushed fennel seeds

Salt and freshly ground pepper, to taste

1 cup dry red wine

2 cups canned Italian tomatoes with their juice, chopped, or 2 cups peeled, seeded, and chopped fresh tomatoes

2 cups beef broth

Freshly grated nutmeg

1 rabbit liver, trimmed and finely chopped (optional)

1¹/₂ pounds fresh pappardelle or fettuccine (see page 130)

Freshly grated Parmigiano-Reggiano

1 Dust the rabbit pieces with flour and tap off the excess. In a large saucepan over medium heat, melt the butter with the oil. When the foam subsides, add the rabbit pieces and brown them on all sides. When browned, remove the rabbit pieces to a plate. Add the carrot, onion, celery, and parsley to the saucepan. Cook, stirring frequently, for 8 to 10 minutes, or until lightly browned. Add the sausage meat

or ground pork and fennel seeds to the vegetables. Cook, stirring to break up the chunks, until the meat is browned. Return the rabbit to the pan and sprinkle with salt and pepper. Add the wine and cook for 5 minutes, or until most of the wine has evaporated. Add the tomatoes, broth, nutmeg, salt, and pepper. Bring to a simmer and cook until the rabbit is tender, about 40 minutes. Remove the rabbit pieces. Stir in the liver, if using.

2 Remove the rabbit meat from the bones, being careful to discard the small bones. Chop the meat fine and return it to the saucepan. Cook for 5 minutes more.

3 Meanwhile, bring a large pot of cold water to a boil. Add salt and the pappardelle. Cook, stirring frequently, until al dente, tender yet firm to the bite. Drain and toss with the sauce.

4 Sprinkle with Parmigiano and serve immediately.

To make ahead: The sauce can be made ahead through Step 2 up to 24 hours before serving. Let the sauce cool. Cover and refrigerate until ready to use. Reheat gently.

Pasta As You Like It

The actress Anna Magnani, who became famous for her emotional portrayals in such Italian films as *Rome Open City* and *Mama Roma,* loved to cook simple, homey dishes—what the Italians call *cucina povera*—for her famous friends. One of her favorite menus was polenta with sausages, accompanied by Dom Perignon champagne, which she served to cinema stars such as directors Lucchino Visconti and Federico Fellini on her rooftop terrace with its sweeping view of Rome.

One day the filmmaker Roberto Rossellini, with whom Magnani had a stormy relationship, came to dinner immaculately attired in one of the white linen suits for which he was famous. No sooner had he arrived than he received a message from Ingrid Bergman, who was about to replace Magnani in his affections.

Noticing how distracted the director had become and suspicious of the letter's contents, Magnani asked sweetly as she mixed the pasta: "Is this the way you like it, Roberto?" "Yes, it's fine," he replied. "Would you like a little more *peperoncino?*" she asked. "It is perfect," he answered. "Then here it is!" shouted the fiery Magnani, as she dumped the pasta and tomato sauce all over the gorgeous linen suit.

Cavatelli, Orecchiette, Frusiudatti, and Strozzapreti

To most of us, homemade pasta means long sheer sheets of eggy dough either rolled out with a rolling pin or cranked out of a pasta machine. But in many parts of southern Italy, homestyle pasta is made without eggs, just flour, water, and salt, then hand molded into cavatelli (shells), orecchiette (fanciful little ears), or *frusiudatti* (fusilli in Pugliese dialect). The frusiudatti do not look like commercially made dried fusilli. Rather than partially uncoiled springs, these fusilli are tubes that are partially open along their length. In Calabria, a similar pasta is called *strozzapreti* (priest stranglers), or *strangolo.*

These pastas can be made with either semolina or whole wheat flour, depending on the flavor or texture you want to achieve. Semolina flour produces a creamy white, smooth pasta; whole wheat flour imparts a rough texture and medium brown color. Both kinds of pastas are chewy and substantial and go best with chunky vegetable, meat, and seafood sauces based on olive oil. Save your delicate cream and butter sauces for egg pasta.

Since the doughs are rather stiff, using a food processor or heavy-duty mixer is preferable to mixing by hand. Shaping the pasta on a wooden cutting board or a plastic board with a slightly grainy surface gives it a rougher surface texture, which allows the sauce to adhere to it more easily.

Once formed, the pasta can be used immediately, allowed to dry slightly, or frozen for up to one month. Complete drying of these pasta shapes may take several days, depending on the weather. The result is very hard pasta that takes a long time to cook, which is why I prefer not to dry them completely but to freeze them instead.

Unless you plan to use the pasta at once, have ready two jelly-roll pans, or trays with a shallow border—the borders will allow you to stack the pans crosswise so that air can circulate around the pasta without taking up too much counter space. Line the pans with linen or cotton tea towels or napkins, and dust the cloth lightly with flour. Do not let the pieces of pasta touch each other on the pans or they may stick together.

To freeze the pasta, place the filled pans directly in the freezer. Freeze until solid (about an hour or two), then transfer the pieces to plastic freezer bags, seal, and freeze them for up to one month. When you are ready to use them, do not thaw. Cook the same way as freshly made pasta, adding a minute or two to the cooking time.

Pasta Dough

PASTA FATTA IN CASA

SEMOLINA DOUGH

1 1/2 cups unbleached all-purpose flour

1 cup fine semolina flour

1 teaspoon salt

About 3/4 cup warm water

WHOLE WHEAT DOUGH

2 1/2 cups whole wheat flour

1 teaspoon salt

About 3/4 cup warm water

MAKES ABOUT 1
POUND

The semolina dough is used to make cavatelli, orecchiette, frusiudatti, and strozzapreti. The whole wheat dough is an alternative to semolina dough in making orecchiette.

MAKING THE DOUGH

Place the semolina and all-purpose flours or the whole wheat flour and the salt in a food processor or the bowl of a heavy-duty mixer. With the machine running, add just enough water to form a stiff dough. When the dough forms a ball, remove it from the processor. On a lightly floured surface, knead the dough until it is smooth and elastic, about 1 minute.

SHAPING PASTA DOUGH

Prepare the dough. Have at hand some flour for dusting. Line 2 large jelly-roll pans with clean dry dish cloths or napkins. Dust the cloths lightly with flour.

Shaping Cavatelli

1 Cut the semolina dough into 8 pieces. Take 1 piece and keep the remaining pieces covered with an inverted bowl as you work. On a lightly floured board or countertop, roll the piece into a long rope about 1/2 inch thick. Cut the rope into 1/2-inch lengths. Hold a dull-bladed knife with a rounded tip in 1 hand with your index finger pressed against the blade of the knife. Flatten each piece of dough, dragging it slightly so that the dough curls around the tip of the knife to form a shell shape.

2   Place the cavatelli to dry in a single layer on the prepared pans while you continue with the remaining dough.

3   Cook right away or dry or freeze as described on page 144.

Shaping Orecchiette

1   Cut the semolina or whole wheat dough into 8 pieces. Take 1 piece and keep the remaining pieces covered with an inverted bowl as you work. On a lightly floured board or countertop, roll the piece into a long rope about $\frac{1}{2}$ inch thick. Cut the rope into $\frac{1}{2}$-inch lengths. Hold a dull-bladed knife with a rounded tip in one hand with your index finger pressed against the blade of the knife. Flatten each piece of dough to form a shallow concave disk. Turn each disk inside out over the tip of your thumb. Another way to shape orecchiette is to cut the rope of dough into slices about $\frac{1}{16}$ inch thick. With the tip of your thumb, press each piece of dough in the center and drag it slightly to make a concave disk.

2   Place the orecchiette in a single layer on the prepared pans while you continue with the remaining dough.

3   Cook right away or dry or freeze as described on page 144.

Shaping Frusiudatti and Strozzapreti

1   Cut the semolina dough into 8 pieces. Take 1 piece and keep the remaining pieces covered with an inverted bowl as you work. On a lightly floured board or countertop, roll the piece into a long rope less than $\frac{1}{2}$ inch thick. Cut the rope into $\frac{1}{2}$-inch lengths. Press a bamboo skewer against 1 piece of the dough. Rock the skewer back and forth gently until the dough is elongated and almost wraps itself around the skewer. (As you become more adept, you can line up 2 or even 3 pieces of dough about 1 inch apart. Press the skewer against all of the pieces at once and proceed as above.)

2   Slide the pasta off the skewer onto the prepared pans in a single layer. Repeat with the remaining dough.

3   Cook right away or dry or freeze as described on page 144.

Cavatelli with Mussels, Beans, and Tomatoes

CAVATELLI CON LE COZZE

1/2 cup dried cannellini or Great Northern beans

1 medium carrot

1 celery rib

1 small onion

1 bay leaf

2 pounds small mussels or Manila clams

1/3 cup olive oil

2 large garlic cloves, minced

4 medium tomatoes, peeled, seeded, and chopped, or 2 cups
*   chopped canned Italian tomatoes with their juice*

1/4 cup finely chopped Italian flat-leaf parsley

1 pound cavatelli (see page 145)

Extra virgin olive oil (optional)

1 Rinse the beans and pick them over to remove any stones or shriveled beans. Soak the beans for 4 hours or overnight in the refrigerator in cold water to cover by 1 inch.

2 In a medium saucepan, combine the beans, carrot, celery, onion, and bay leaf. Add cold water to cover by 1 inch. Bring to a simmer and cook over low heat until tender, about 1 hour and 15 minutes. (Cooking time may vary considerably according to the age of the beans.)

3 Meanwhile, soak the mussels in cold water for 30 minutes. Drain and cut or pull off the beards.

4 In a large saucepan, combine the olive oil and garlic. Cook over medium heat for 30 seconds, or until the garlic is fragrant. Stir in the tomatoes and parsley. Add the mussels. Cover and cook until the mussels open, about 5 minutes. Turn off the heat. Remove the mussels and their juices from their shells and return them to the saucepan. Discard any mussels that have not opened.

Il Melograno is a luxurious inn and spa resort near Monopoli in Puglia. One night, a group of us were served a special dinner in a beautifully restored grotto that had once served as an olive oil mill. As we entered, fires were burning in several fireplaces carved into the stone walls of the cavernous room. The light played and flickered on the walls, making the room feel warm and cozy. Several unusual focaccias were served as starters and the roast kid seasoned with rosemary and olive oil was excellent, but this dish of homemade cavatelli, white beans, mussels, and a touch of tomato was the highlight of the meal.

In Puglia, the mussels are quite small, no more than three quarters of an inch long. They are nearly equal in size to the beans and cavatelli, which makes sense since larger mussels would overwhelm the other ingredients. Look for mussels no more than an inch in length; if they are not available, substitute small clams, such as cultivated Manila clams or New Zealand cockles.

Il Melograno
345 Contrada Torricella
Monopoli (Puglia)

5   Bring a large pot of cold water to a boil. Add salt and the cavatelli. Cook, stirring frequently, until the cavatelli are almost but not quite tender.

6   Drain the cavatelli and add them to the mussels sauce. Drain the beans, discarding the carrot, celery, onion, and bay leaf, and add them to the mussels sauce. Cook, stirring well, for 2 minutes, or until the cavatelli are tender.

7   Transfer to a warm serving bowl. Sprinkle with additional chopped parsley and olive oil, if necessary.

SERVES 4 TO 6

On our first visit to Sicily, it became a running joke with Charles and me to guess what would be on the dinner menu each night. We knew we would not be wrong if we said swordfish and eggplant, two of Sicily's favorite ingredients. They were the specials of the day wherever we went. Some years later, I tasted this fabulous dish in Milan. Since it contained swordfish and eggplant, I was not surprised to hear that the chef was Sicilian.

Cavatelli with Swordfish and Eggplant

CAVATELLI CON PESCE SPADA E MELANZANA

1 large or 2 small eggplants (about 1¹/₂ pounds)

Coarse salt, to taste

Corn or other vegetable oil, for frying

3 tablespoons olive oil

1 large garlic clove, very finely chopped

2 green onions, finely chopped

8 ounces swordfish, ¹/₂ inch thick, skin removed and cut into ¹/₂-inch pieces

Freshly ground pepper, to taste

2 teaspoons white wine vinegar

2 cups peeled, seeded, and chopped fresh tomatoes or chopped canned Italian tomatoes with their juice

1 teaspoon fresh oregano leaves or a pinch of dried oregano

1 pound cavatelli (see page 145)

¹/₃ cup freshly grated pecorino romano

Fresh oregano or fresh parsley, for garnish

1 Trim the ends off the eggplant and cut it into $1/2$-inch dice. Place the eggplant in a colander set over a plate or in the sink and sprinkle generously with salt. Let stand for 1 hour. Quickly rinse the eggplant pieces. Place the pieces in paper towels and squeeze until dry.

2 In a large deep skillet over medium heat, heat about $1/2$ inch corn oil. To test the oil, carefully place a small piece of eggplant in it. If it sizzles and cooks rapidly, the temperature is hot enough. Add enough eggplant to make a single layer. Cook, stirring occasionally, until crisp and browned. Remove the eggplant pieces with a slotted spoon. Drain well on paper towels. Repeat with the remaining eggplant. Set aside.

3 In a medium skillet over medium heat, cook the olive oil with the garlic and green onions for 30 seconds, or until fragrant. Add the swordfish cubes, salt, and pepper. Cook, stirring occasionally, until the swordfish is no longer pink, about 5 minutes. Add the vinegar and cook for 1 minute. Add the tomatoes and oregano. Bring to a simmer and cook for 15 minutes, or until slightly thickened.

4 Meanwhile, bring a large pot of cold water to a boil. Add salt and the cavatelli. Cook, stirring occasionally, until al dente, tender yet firm to the bite. Drain well.

5 In a large heated serving bowl, combine the cavatelli, sauce, and eggplant. Toss well. Stir in the cheese. Sprinkle with oregano or parsley and serve immediately.

The Cavatelli Machine

Cavatelli are easy to make by hand, so when Arlene Ward, director of Adventures in Cooking, a school and cookware shop in Wayne, New Jersey, suggested I try using a machine for a cooking demonstration, I scoffed. But since I had two large classes to make cavatelli for and Arlene was so enthusiastic, I decided to try it.

The machine is a hand-cranked metal gadget resembling an old-fashioned meat grinder that clips onto a countertop. You insert a rope of dough in one end, turn the handle, and out come perfectly shaped cavatelli. What they lack in hand-crafted charm, is more than compensated for by their uniform size, which makes the pasta cook more evenly, and the speed with which you can prepare a big batch. Needless to say, I bought the machine. And I use it often.

In this classic Pugliese dish, which I tasted at Il Melograno, the pasta and other ingredients are topped with either grated pecorino or seasoned bread crumbs just before serving. Bread crumbs are a common way to complete southern Italian pasta and vegetable dishes, since at one time even a small bit of cheese was too expensive for many households. Leftover bread crumbs added a pleasant crunch and a mild toasty flavor. In more prosperous times, the crumbs were enriched with olive oil and mashed anchovy fillets.

Pancetta is unsmoked rolled bacon seasoned with garlic, salt, and spices. Smoked pancetta is less common, but that is what is used in this hearty pasta dish. Thickly sliced bacon can be substituted.

The cauliflower should be cooked until it is fairly soft. The curved shape of the orecchiette catches and holds the nuggets of cauliflower, bits of bacon, and onion.

Whole Wheat Orecchiette with Cauliflower and Bacon

Orecchiette con Cavolfiore e Pancetta Affumicata

1 medium head cauliflower, trimmed and cut into 1-inch florets (about 1¹/₄ pounds)

Salt, to taste

2 tablespoons extra virgin olive oil

1 medium onion, finely chopped

8 ounces smoked pancetta or thickly sliced lean bacon, cut into ¹/₄-inch strips

Freshly ground pepper, to taste

1 pound whole wheat orecchiette (see page 146) or dried pasta, such as orecchiette or medium shells

¹/₂ cup freshly grated pecorino romano

1 Bring a large pot of water to a boil. Add the cauliflower and salt. Cook until soft, about 10 minutes. Remove the pieces with a slotted spoon or a small sieve. Reserve the water for cooking the pasta.

2 In a skillet large enough to hold all of the ingredients, heat the oil over medium heat. Add the onion and cook until tender, about 5 minutes. Add the pancetta or bacon and cook, stirring frequently, until crisp around the edges and lightly browned, about 10 minutes. Push the onions and bacon to the side and carefully tip the pan. Spoon off all but ¹/₃ cup of the fat. Stir in the cauliflower and season with salt and pepper.

3 Meanwhile, bring the cauliflower water back to a boil. Add salt and the orecchiette. Cook, stirring frequently, until al dente, tender yet still firm to the bite. Drain well, reserving about 1 cup of the cooking water.

4 Add the orecchiette to the skillet with the cauliflower. Cook, stirring constantly, for 1 minute, or until the ingredients are well combined. Add some of the cooking water if the pasta seems dry.

5 Sprinkle with cheese, stir well, and serve immediately.

Cook's note: To make a bread crumb topping, before cooking the orecchiette, heat 2 tablespoons olive oil in a small skillet. Add 4 anchovies or more to taste and cook, stirring constantly, until the anchovies have dissolved, about 2 minutes. Add ¹/₂ cup fine dry bread crumbs, preferably homemade from Italian or French bread. Cook, stirring, until the crumbs are lightly toasted, about 3 minutes. Sprinkle over the pasta.

The Pasta Reformer

Perhaps because it is so well loved, pasta has sometimes been a cause of controversy among the Italians. During the fifteenth century Fra Girolamo Savonarola, a fiery religious reformer, attempted to ban pasta, saying it was decadent and evil. He shouted this scathing indictment from his pulpit: "It is not enough for you to eat your pasta fried. No! You think you have to add garlic to it, and when you eat ravioli, it is not enough to boil it in a pot and eat it in its juice, you have to fry it in another pot and cover it with cheese!" The Florentines eventually became fed up with this kind of rhetoric and burned the priest at the stake.

The King's Pasta Problem

King Ferdinand II, who ruled Naples during the first half of the nineteenth century, had a problem. He liked to eat pasta but his chamberlain, Gennaro Spadaccini, felt that it was inappropriate and plebeian when entertaining important visitors and foreign dignitaries. Why? Rich and poor alike ate pasta with their fingers. Even without tomato sauce, eating pasta was undoubtedly a messy affair, no way for a king to impress his guests. The long, three-pronged forks in use at that time were better for holding down a cut of meat while carving than for eating pasta; they were in fact downright dangerous.

To please the king, who really missed his pasta and blamed the chamberlain for its absence at court meals, Spadaccini developed a shorter, four-tined fork, better suited to eating pasta and many other foods as well. This practical fork eventually came into common use in all of Italy as well as the rest of Europe.

Before dinner at Al Fornello da Ricci restaurant in Ceglie Messapico in Puglia, the cook demonstrated how to make the pasta called frusiudatti, a dialect word for fusilli or spirals. It is also known as *busiati,* or knitting needle pasta, because the dough is often shaped around a knitting needle. I use a thick wooden skewer.

At Al Fornello, the pasta was served with a tomato sauce and *rughetta,* or wild arugula. Rughetta is crisper and spicier than cultivated arugula, and it seems to pop out of every crevice and crack in Puglia's roads. As you walk along, you can't help but brush against it or crush it underfoot and release its tantalizing aroma. You'll have to use cultivated arugula in place of the wild.

Al Fornello da Ricci
Contrada Montevicoli
Ceglie Messapico (Puglia)

Homemade Fusilli with Arugula and Tomato Sauce

FRUSIUDATTI CON ARUGULA E POMODORI

3 tablespoons olive oil
2 garlic cloves, peeled and lightly crushed
2 pounds ripe plum tomatoes, peeled, seeded, and chopped, or
*   1 can (28 ounces) Italian tomatoes with their juice*
Salt and freshly ground pepper, to taste
1 bunch of arugula (about 6 ounces)
1 pound frusiudatti or strozzapreti (see page 146) or dried pasta,
*   such as penne or ziti*
2 ounces ricotta salata or feta cheese, shredded (about $^1/_2$ cup) or
* $^1/_4$ cup freshly grated pecorino romano and $^1/_4$ cup*
*   Parmigiano-Reggiano*

1 In a large saucepan, over medium heat, heat the oil with the garlic for 30 seconds, or until the garlic is fragrant and begins to color lightly. Add the tomatoes. If using canned tomatoes, crush them with the back of a spoon. Add salt and pepper. Bring the sauce to a simmer and cook for 20 to 25 minutes, or until thickened. Discard the garlic.

2 Wash the arugula well and trim off the tough stems. Dry the arugula in a salad spinner. Gather the arugula into a bunch and cut the leaves crosswise into thin strips. You should have about 2 cups.

3 Meanwhile, bring a large pot of cold water to a boil. Add salt and the frusiudatti. Cook, stirring frequently, until al dente, tender yet still firm to the bite, about 4 minutes for freshly made pasta. (Dried pasta will take longer.)

4 Drain the pasta and transfer it to a large heated serving bowl. Immediately add the sauce and half of the cheese and stir well.

5 Sprinkle with the arugula and remaining cheese and serve immediately.

Strozzapreti with Herb Sauce

STROZZAPRETI ALLE ERBE

SERVES 4 TO 6

Strozzapreti, or priest chokers, is a name given to many kinds of thick pasta throughout Italy. The story is that the pasta is so delicious a hungry priest greedily ate too much and choked. This Calabrian version is similar to the Pugliese frusiudatti (see page 146). An unusual touch is that the pasta water is flavored with fennel seed.

¹/₄ cup fresh basil leaves

¹/₄ cup fresh parsley leaves

2 tablespoons fresh mint leaves

1 tablespoon fresh thyme leaves

1 teaspoon fresh oregano leaves or ¹/₄ teaspoon dried oregano

¹/₂ cup olive oil

¹/₂ cup finely chopped red bell pepper

1 large garlic clove, finely chopped

2¹/₂ pounds fresh plum tomatoes, peeled, seeded, and chopped, or
    1 can (28 to 35 ounces) Italian tomatoes

Salt and freshly ground pepper, to taste

1 teaspoon fennel seeds

1 pound frusiudatti or strozzapreti (see page 146)

1 Finely chop the herbs. Place them in a small bowl with ¹/₄ cup of the olive oil. Set aside.

2 In a large heavy skillet over medium heat, heat the remaining ¹/₄ cup of olive oil. Add the red pepper. Cook, stirring frequently, for 5 minutes, or until the pepper is softened. Stir in the garlic and cook for 1 minute more. Add the tomatoes, salt, and pepper. Simmer for 20 to 30 minutes, or until thickened.

3 Meanwhile, bring a large pot of cold water to a boil. Add salt and the fennel seeds. Add the pasta pieces, a few at a time so that they do not stick together. Cook, stirring frequently, until almost tender. Drain the pasta and add it to the skillet with the sauce. Cook, stirring, for 2 minutes.

4 Add the herbs and stir well. Serve immediately.

Four Special Pastas

It never ceases to amaze me how many diverse forms pasta can take. Each of the four recipes in this section, for instance, is unique.

- The Spinach and Potato Strudel from Friuli starts with a dough similar to potato gnocchi that is wrapped around a spinach and cheese filling to make a salami shape. It is poached and served warm with a rich butter sauce.

- Old-style pasta from Parma is made from a semolina pudding that is baked and cut into squares to be simmered briefly and dressed with a fresh tomato sauce.

- Liguria's Triangular Ravioli are special in that they are made with white wine in the dough.

- Crispy Pasta with Chick Peas is from Puglia, where many unusual pasta dishes originate. Half of the pasta is fried and half is boiled, then they are combined in a tomato and chick pea sauce.

SERVES 6

Apple and other fruit strudels make fine desserts, but this savory strudel from Friuli in the northeastern corner of Italy is a revelation. Instead of flaky pastry, a soft potato dough of the kind used to make gnocchi is wrapped around the spinach and cheese filling. The strudel is formed into a salami shape, cooked, then sliced and drizzled with melted butter flavored with fresh sage. The green and white spiral slices are very attractive.

Starchy baking potatoes are essential for a light dough. Serve the strudel as a first course instead of pasta or soup. Follow it with Roasted Veal Shanks (page 263) or Pork Chops in Red Wine and Juniper (page 253).

Spinach and Potato Strudel

STRUCCOLO DI SPINACI

SPINACH FILLING

1 pound spinach, washed and trimmed

$1/4$ cup finely chopped onion

1 tablespoon unsalted butter

1 large egg, beaten

1 cup ricotta

$1/4$ cup freshly grated Parmigiano-Reggiano

Salt and freshly ground pepper, to taste

POTATO DOUGH

1 pound baking potatoes

1 large egg, beaten

Salt, to taste

$1^{1}/4$ cups all-purpose flour

A Fresh Taste of Italy

BUTTER SAUCE

8 tablespoons (1 stick) unsalted butter, melted

4 fresh sage leaves (optional)

¼ cup freshly grated Parmigiano-Reggiano

1   Put the spinach in a large pot over medium heat in just the water that clings to the leaves. Cover and cook for 2 to 3 minutes, or until wilted and tender. Drain and cool. Squeeze out as much water as possible. Finely chop the spinach.

2   In a small skillet over medium heat, cook the onion in the butter until tender, about 5 minutes. In a bowl, combine the spinach, egg, ricotta, and Parmigiano. Season with salt and pepper. Set aside.

3   Scrub the potatoes and place them in a large pot with cold water to cover. Cook until tender when pierced with a knife. Drain and let cool slightly. Peel the potatoes. Mash the potatoes with a potato masher or pass them through a ricer. Add the egg and salt. Stir in 1 cup of the flour. Stir well with a wooden spoon. Turn the dough out onto a board and knead until smooth. The dough will be slightly sticky.

4   Rinse and squeeze dry a double thickness of cheesecloth measuring about 12 × 16 inches. Spread the cloth on the countertop and sprinkle it with the remaining flour. Spread the potato mixture over the cloth into a rectangle 8 × 10 × ½ inch thick.

5   Spoon the spinach mixture over the potato layer leaving a ½-inch border of potatoes all around. Pick up a long end of the cloth and use it to lift and roll up the spinach and potato layers like a jelly roll. Pinch the dough together at the seam and at the ends to completely enclose the spinach filling. When the roll reaches the end of the cloth, wrap the cloth around it to enclose it completely. Tie the ends securely with string. Tie the roll twice more around the center to hold the cloth in place.

6   Choose a pot large enough to hold the strudel without bending it. Add cold water to a depth of 5 inches. Bring the water to a simmer and add salt. Carefully lower the roll into the pot. Cover and bring the water back to a simmer. Cook the strudel for 1 hour.

7   Meanwhile, in a small saucepan over low heat, melt the butter with the sage leaves, if using.

8   Remove the strudel from the pot. Drain and unwrap it. Pour about ¼ cup of the melted butter onto a warm platter. Cut the strudel into slices 1 inch wide and arrange them on the platter. Pour the remaining butter over the strudel and sprinkle with Parmigiano. Serve immediately.

"And my mother made pasta. People say Italians eat so well, they have this image of how much we adore pasta, how delicious, fabulous, even chic pasta is. The reason we ate so much pasta was simple: it hurts to have an empty stomach, and with pasta it is easy to fill it and not to hurt any more . . . it is a necessity. It is a taste cultivated in scarcity."

Renata Scotto,
More Than a Diva

La Greppia, located across from the Ducal Palace in Parma, is one of the city's best restaurants. The long white room is decorated austerely with antique farm tools. Through a large window at the rear, diners can watch the cooks as they effortlessly turn out a tempting assortment of the light eggy pastas Emilia-Romagna is known for, including tortellini and agnolotti. They also make this unique pasta with fine semolina, milk, and eggs. A semolina "pudding" is baked, then cut into small pieces and served with buttery tomato sauce. I don't know why Maurizio Rossi, the owner of the restaurant, who kindly gave me the recipe, calls it "old style," but that's how it is.

This sauce is also good on fresh fettuccine (see page 130), Potato Gnocchi (page 166), or Spinach and Ricotta Gnocchi (page 164).

La Greppia
Parma (Emilia-Romagna)

La Greppia's Old-style Pasta with Fresh Tomato Sauce

PASTA ANTICA

PASTA
2 tablespoons unsalted butter
1 cup milk
³/4 cup fine semolina
3 large eggs
¹/2 teaspoon salt
Freshly grated nutmeg
1 cup freshly grated Parmigiano-Reggiano

TOMATO SAUCE
3 tablespoons unsalted butter
2 tablespoons olive oil
1 small onion, finely chopped
2 pounds ripe plum tomatoes, peeled, seeded, and chopped
Salt and freshly ground pepper, to taste
¹/2 cup chopped fresh basil
¹/4 cup freshly grated Parmigiano-Reggiano
Basil leaves, for garnish

1 Preheat the oven to 350°F.

2 To make the pasta, in the top half of a double boiler set over simmering water, melt the butter. Whisk together the milk and semolina and stir the mixture into the butter. In a small bowl, whisk together the eggs, salt, and nutmeg and stir in. Cook, stirring frequently, until the mixture is very thick and holds a firm shape, about 10 minutes. Stir in the cheese.

3 Spread the semolina mixture in an 8-inch square pan. Pat the mixture until the surface is smooth. Cover with foil and bake for 15 minutes. Let cool, then chill, covered, until ready to use.

4 To make the tomato sauce, in a large skillet over medium heat, heat 2 tablespoons of the butter and the olive oil. Add the onion and cook, stirring occasionally, until golden, about 7 minutes. Add the tomatoes, salt, and pepper and simmer until thick, about 15 minutes. Stir in the chopped basil.

5 Bring 2 quarts of water to a simmer in a large saucepan. Cut the semolina mixture into $3/4 \times 1/4$-inch rectangles. Drop the pieces into the water and cook for 30 seconds, just until heated. Take care not to cook longer, or they may begin to break apart. Gently drain the pasta.

6 Add the pasta to the sauce. Add the remaining 1 tablespoon butter. Heat, stirring gently, until the butter is melted.

7 Spoon onto serving plates and sprinkle with cheese. Garnish with basil leaves and serve.

To make ahead: Cook the pasta and sauce through Step 4. Cover and refrigerate up to 2 days. Reheat the sauce gently before continuing with the recipe.

Macaroni à Foie Gras

An invitation to the Parisian home of Giocchino Rossini was much sought after by members of French society. Not only was there sure to be good music and witty conversation, but also fine food, often invented by Rossini himself and based on foie gras and truffles, two of his favorite ingredients.

One dish, which he called *macaroni à foie gras,* was made of thick strands of tubular spaghetti such as bucatini or perciatelli which were filled with goose liver pâté. To accomplish this, the composer used a specially made ivory and silver syringe to inject the pâté into the narrow opening. Rossini is said to have valued this tool as highly as his piano.

The recipe became so famous it was requested by Emperor Napoleon III who reportedly enjoyed it very much. No word on whether Rossini lent him his syringe.

In Liguria, these tri-cornered ravioli are filled with a mixture of borage and chard and a local fresh cheese called *prescinseua*. I do occasionally find borage available at my local farmers' market, but it is rare. Fortunately, spinach makes a good substitute. Ricotta stands in for the prescinseua. The pasta is made with white wine, which makes it very tender.

Triangular Ravioli with Walnut Sauce

PANSOTI CON SALSA DI NOCI

CHARD FILLING

1 pound chard, washed and trimmed

1/2 pound spinach, washed and trimmed

Salt, to taste

1 cup ricotta

1/2 cup freshly grated Parmigiano-Reggiano

1 small garlic clove, minced

1 large egg, beaten

Freshly ground pepper, to taste

PASTA

About 4 cups unbleached all-purpose flour

Pinch of salt

4 large eggs, beaten

1/3 cup dry white wine

WALNUT SAUCE

2 cups soft fresh bread crumbs, from the inside of a loaf of Italian or French bread

1/2 cup milk

2 cups walnuts

1 small garlic clove

Pinch of dried marjoram

1 cup ricotta

3 tablespoons extra virgin olive oil

3/4 cup freshly grated Parmigiano-Reggiano

Salt and freshly ground pepper, to taste

2 tablespoons unsalted butter

1   To make the filling, place the chard and spinach in a large pot with ¹/₂ cup water and salt. Cover and cook for 5 minutes, or until the vegetables are tender. Drain well and let cool. Squeeze the greens to extract the juice. Finely chop the greens. In a large bowl, combine the chopped greens, ricotta, Parmigiano, garlic, egg, salt, and pepper. Mix well. Cover and refrigerate until ready to use.

2   To make the pasta, in a large bowl combine 3¹/₂ cups of the flour, salt, eggs, and wine. Stir until a stiff dough forms. Transfer the dough to a lightly floured surface. Knead until smooth and elastic but not sticky, adding as much of the remaining flour as necessary. Let the dough rest under a bowl for at least 20 minutes.

3   Line 2 jelly-roll pans with cloth dish towels and lightly dust with flour.

4   Divide the dough into 4 pieces. Take 1 piece and roll it out into a strip using a pasta machine as described on page 132. Keep the remaining dough covered. Cut the pasta strip into 4-inch squares. Cut each square diagonally into 2 triangles.

5   Place a scant tablespoon of the filling slightly off the center of each triangle. Brush the edges lightly with cool water. Press the top over to form smaller triangles, molding the dough around the filling to eliminate air bubbles. Pinch the edges to seal. Place the filled triangles on the pans. Repeat with the remaining dough and filling. Let dry for at least 30 minutes, turning the pieces over twice to prevent sticking.

6   To make the sauce, soak the bread crumbs in the milk for 10 minutes. When the bread is soft, squeeze it, reserving the milk.

7   In a food processor, finely chop the walnuts, garlic, and marjoram. Add the bread crumbs, ricotta, olive oil, and ¹/₂ cup of the Parmigiano. Process until smooth and creamy, adding the reserved milk as needed until the sauce is the consistency of thick cream. Season with salt and pepper.

8   Bring a large pot of cold water to a boil. Add a generous amount of salt and the ravioli. Cook, stirring occasionally, until the ravioli are tender and rise to the surface, about 3 minutes.

9   Place the sauce in a large warm serving bowl. Drain the pasta, reserving 1 cup of the cooking water. Add the butter and cooking water as needed to the sauce to thin it. Stir well. Add the pasta and toss gently.

10   Sprinkle with the remaining Parmigiano and serve immediately.

Praise to Macaroni

Beautiful and white
As you emerge in groups
Out of the machine
If on a cloth
You are made to lie
You look to me like the
    milky way
Zounds!
Great Desire
Master of this earthly life,
I waste away,
I faint from the wish
To taste you
O maccheroni!

Filippo Sagruttendio, from
Le Laude de Li Maccarune,
Naples, 1646

Tria is a dialect name used in many places in southern Italy for a homemade pasta that resembles short strands of fettuccine. According to Luigi Sada, a food writer from Puglia and the author of many cookbooks, tria is derived from the Arabic word *itriya,* a kind of dried pasta eaten by nomadic people. He cites this as proof that pasta arrived in southern Italy from the Middle East via the Arab invasions of Sicily. This version of tria is made without eggs—just flour, water, olive oil, and salt. The dough is surprisingly easy to handle.

In this recipe from Puglia, the tria is cooked in a very unusual way. Half of the pasta is boiled while the rest is fried until crisp and lightly browned. Both pastas are added to a chick pea sauce. I have never tasted anything like it anywhere else in Italy.

Crispy Pasta with Chick Peas

CECI E TRIA

CHICK PEA SAUCE

2 tablespoons olive oil

1 small onion, chopped

1 small celery rib, chopped (about 1/2 cup)

1 can (16 ounces) chick peas, rinsed and drained

2 medium tomatoes, peeled, seeded, and chopped, or 1 cup chopped canned Italian tomatoes

2 tablespoons finely chopped fresh parsley

1 garlic clove, finely chopped

1 bay leaf

Salt and freshly ground pepper, to taste

TRIA

About 2 cups unbleached all-purpose flour

1 teaspoon salt

1/2 cup cool water

1 tablespoon olive oil

1   To make the sauce, in a large saucepan, combine the olive oil, onion, and celery. Cook over medium heat until tender, about 5 minutes. Add the chick peas, tomatoes, parsley, garlic, bay leaf, and 2 cups water. Season with salt and pepper. Bring to a simmer and cook for 45 minutes.

2   To make the tria, in a medium bowl, combine 2 cups of the flour and the salt. Add the water and the oil. Stir until a soft dough forms. Add more water a few drops at a time if the dough seems too dry. Turn the dough out onto a lightly floured surface and knead until a smooth dough forms. Let the dough rest, covered with an inverted bowl, for 30 minutes to 1 hour.

3 Line 2 jelly-roll pans with cloth kitchen towels and sprinkle lightly with flour.

4 Roll out the dough using a pasta machine as described on page 132. Cut into 3 × ½-inch strips. Lay the strips without touching on the pans until ready to use.

5 In a large skillet over medium heat, heat ½ cup oil. Add a fourth of the tria and cook, stirring, for about 4 minutes or until it blisters and begins to turn golden. Remove the pasta with a slotted spoon and drain on paper towels. Repeat with another fourth of the tria.

6 Bring a large pot of cold water to a boil. Add salt and the remaining uncooked tria. Cook for 1 to 2 minutes, or until barely tender. Drain well, reserving some of the cooking water.

7 If necessary, bring the sauce to a simmer. Remove and discard the bay leaf. Add the boiled tria. Stir in some of the cooking water if the pasta seems dry. The sauce should resemble a thick soup. Transfer to a warm serving bowl.

8 Add the fried pasta to the dish. Serve hot.

To make ahead: The sauce can be made ahead, covered, and refrigerated for up to 2 days. The pasta can be made ahead. The pasta has to be fried before it dries completely. Store the cooled fried pasta in a tightly sealed plastic bag up to 1 week.

CHIANCIANO
PROVINCIA DI SIENA

Anno 1895 - Il manifesto reclame di Chianciano Terme

You Are What You Eat

The beautiful actress Sophia Loren is often complimented on her good looks. To which *La Loren,* as the Italians call her, has been known to reply, "Everything you see I owe to spaghetti."

Gnocchi

In *The Decameron*, written in the fourteenth century, Boccaccio wrote of the mythical Paese di Bengodi, or Village of Good Cheer, located on the top of a mountain of grated parmesan cheese. The inhabitants did nothing all day but cook and eat macaroni, which they rolled down the mountain to coat with cheese. Boccaccio must have been writing about gnocchi since the rounded shape would roll easily down a parmesan mountain.

Made from almost any ingredients that can be formed into a dough, gnocchi are sauced and eaten much like pasta. Though they are usually boiled, they can also be baked with butter and cheese, deep-fried, or cooked in broth.

Gnocchi (pronounced NYOK-ee) are made in every region of Italy and take many different forms. In the Val D'Aosta near the Alps, they are made from buckwheat flour and covered with fontina cheese. Saffron colors the tiny gnocchi of the island of Sardinia, while pumpkin is used in Lombardy. Gnocchi in the Alto Adige near Austria are made with rye bread crumbs and dried mushrooms. Sweet gnocchi, made with a potato dough and plum or apricot filling, are eaten as a first course in Friuli.

SERVES 6

Ricotta and parmesan flavor these tender little gnocchi from Sicily. This dough is firm enough to use in a cavatelli machine, if you have one.

Ricotta Gnocchi

GNOCCHI DI RICOTTA

1 pound fresh ricotta or 1 container (15 ounces)

1¹/₄ cups freshly grated Parmigiano-Reggiano

2¹/₄ cups all-purpose flour

1 recipe Quick Tomato Sauce (page 104) or The Butcher's Sauce (page 109)

1 Line 2 large jelly-roll pans with cloth dish towels. Lightly dust the towels with flour.

2 In a large bowl, blend the ricotta and 1 cup of the Parmigiano. Gradually stir in as much of the flour as possible. When the dough becomes too stiff to stir, turn it out onto a lightly floured surface.

Knead in the remaining flour and continue to knead until the dough is smooth and forms a ball, about 5 minutes.

3   Divide the dough into 8 pieces. Take 1 piece and keep the rest covered with an inverted bowl. On a lightly floured surface, roll the piece of dough into a rope about $\frac{1}{4}$ inch in diameter. Cut the rope into $\frac{3}{4}$-inch lengths. Dip a table fork in flour. Holding the fork in one hand, roll each piece of dough over the back of the tines, using enough pressure to leave ridges on the outside of the gnocchi and a concave indentation on the inside. Drop the gnocchi onto the prepared pans without touching one another. Repeat with the remaining dough.

4   Bring a large pot of water to a boil and add salt. Simmer the gnocchi in 2 or 3 batches, dropping them in a few at a time to prevent sticking. After the gnocchi rise to the surface, cook for 1 minute more, or until tender. Remove with a slotted spoon or skimmer and drain well.

5   Meanwhile, bring the sauce to a simmer. Pour half into a heated serving bowl. Add the gnocchi and toss.

6   Top with the remaining sauce and Parmigiano and serve.

To make ahead: The gnocchi can be made through Step 3, covered with plastic wrap, and refrigerated for up to 1 day or frozen for future use. To freeze, place the pans with the gnocchi in the freezer for 1 to 2 hours until frozen solid. Transfer the gnocchi to a plastic bag and seal tightly. Store in the freezer for up to 1 month.

porto azzurro

ISOLA D'ELBA

These plump little green pillows make an elegant first course. I usually serve them with a sage and butter sauce, but a light tomato sauce, such as Anna's Tomato Sauce (page 106), can be substituted.

If you would like to follow these gnocchi with a meat course, I would suggest something simple, such as the Chicken with Fennel-Sausage Stuffing (page 228).

Spinach and Ricotta Gnocchi

GNOCCHI VERDI

2 pounds fresh spinach, rinsed and stemmed

2 tablespoons unsalted butter

1 small onion, finely chopped

$1/2$ cup finely chopped prosciutto

1 pound fresh ricotta or 1 container (15 ounces)

$1^1/2$ cups plus 2 tablespoons all-purpose flour

$1^1/2$ cups freshly grated Parmigiano-Reggiano

2 large eggs

$1/4$ teaspoon salt

$1/4$ teaspoon freshly grated nutmeg

$1/4$ teaspoon freshly ground pepper

SAGE BUTTER SAUCE

8 tablespoons (1 stick) unsalted butter

6 fresh sage leaves

Pinch of salt

1 Put the spinach in a large pot over medium heat with just the water that clings to the leaves. Cover and cook for 2 to 3 minutes, or until wilted and tender. Drain and cool. Squeeze out as much water as possible. Finely chop the spinach.

2 In a medium skillet over medium-low heat, melt the butter. Add the onion and cook until softened, about 5 minutes. Add the prosciutto and cook for 30 seconds. Stir in the chopped spinach. Transfer the mixture to a large bowl.

3 Line 2 large jelly-roll pans with wax paper.

4 With a wooden spoon, beat in the ricotta, $1^1/2$ cups of the flour, 1 cup of the Parmigiano, the eggs, salt, nutmeg, and pepper. The mixture will be soft.

5 Spread the remaining 2 tablespoons flour on a dinner plate. Lightly flour your hands and shape the gnocchi mixture into balls about ³/₄ inch in diameter, rolling them lightly in the flour. Put the gnocchi on the pans, cover, and refrigerate for up to several hours until ready to cook.

6 To make the sauce, in a small saucepan over low heat, melt the butter. Add the sage leaves and salt. Cook until the butter is lightly browned, 4 to 6 minutes. Keep warm over very low heat.

7 Bring a large pot of cold water to a simmer and add salt. Don't let the water boil or the gnocchi may break. Add the gnocchi in 2 batches, dropping them in a few at a time to prevent sticking. After the gnocchi rise to the surface, cook for 1 to 2 minutes more. Remove the gnocchi with a slotted spoon or skimmer and transfer to a warm platter. Drizzle with the sauce and sprinkle with the remaining Parmigiano.

To make ahead: These gnocchi can be made ahead completely up to 1 hour before serving. In Step 7, place the cooked gnocchi in a single layer in a well-buttered baking dish. Drizzle with the sauce, cover, and hold at room temperature. To reheat, sprinkle with the cheese and bake in a preheated 350°F. oven for 15 minutes, or until heated through.

The Pasta Cure

Scaramouche, a foxy old clown in the Italian Commedia dell'Arte, is notorious for his enormous appetite. One day he was not feeling well and sent for his doctor. The physician looked him over and announced that though he was indeed very ill, if he ate moderately, he might live eight days more.

"Are you sure?" asked Scaramouche. "Yes, sir," replied the doctor. "Well," said the clown, "eight days more or less is only a bagatelle for a man that has lived as much as I have and it is not worth the trouble to deprive myself of a good plate of vermicelli. Bring me a very large portion and go call my confessor."

by Maria Paleari Henssler, "Ora Pasta!", *Nuova Cucina*

Though no one seems to know why, Thursday is the day Romans eat potato gnocchi. Roman children even have a little chant: *"Ridi, ridi che la mamma ha fatto i gnocchi!"* (Laugh, laugh, Mamma has made gnocchi!).

Potato Gnocchi are more delicate than other kinds, so handle them with care. The drier the potatoes, the less flour will be needed to make a dough and the lighter the gnocchi will be. Cooking the potatoes with their skins on helps keep them from absorbing excess water. Don't pierce them any more than absolutely necessary as they cook.

As an alternative to the tomato sauce, serve them with melted butter and sage sauce (see page 164).

Potato Gnocchi

GNOCCHI DI PATATE

1 pound baking potatoes
About 1 cup all-purpose flour
Salt, to taste
1 recipe Quick Tomato Sauce (page 104)
$^1/_4$ cup freshly grated Parmigiano-Reggiano

1 Line 2 baking sheets with cloth dish towels. Dust the towels with flour.

2 Scrub the potatoes and place them in a large pot with cold water to cover. Cook until tender when pierced with a knife. Drain and let cool slightly. Peel the potatoes. Mash the potatoes with a potato masher or pass them through a ricer. Stir in $^3/_4$ cup of the flour and $1^1/_2$ teaspoons salt. Stir well with a wooden spoon. Turn the dough out onto a lightly floured board or countertop. Knead until smooth, adding in as much of the remaining flour as necessary to make a moist but nonsticky dough.

3 Divide the dough into 6 pieces. Take 1 piece and keep the rest covered with an inverted bowl. Roll the piece into a $^1/_2$-inch-thick rope about 15 inches long. Cut the rope into $^3/_4$-inch lengths. Dip a table fork in flour. Holding the fork in one hand, roll each length of dough over the back of the tines with the thumb of the other hand, using enough pressure to leave ridges on the outside of the gnocchi and a concave indentation on the inside. Drop the gnocchi in a single layer without touching one another onto the baking sheets. Repeat with the remaining dough.

4 Bring a large pot of cold water to a boil and add salt. Cook the gnocchi in 2 batches, dropping them in a few at a time to prevent sticking. Simmer until all of the gnocchi float to the surface, then cook for 30 seconds longer. Remove with a slotted spoon or skimmer and drain well in a colander.

5 Spoon half the sauce into a heated serving bowl. Add the gnocchi and spoon on the remaining sauce.

6 Sprinkle with cheese and serve immediately.

Rice, Barley, and Polenta ... Riso, Orzo, e Polenta

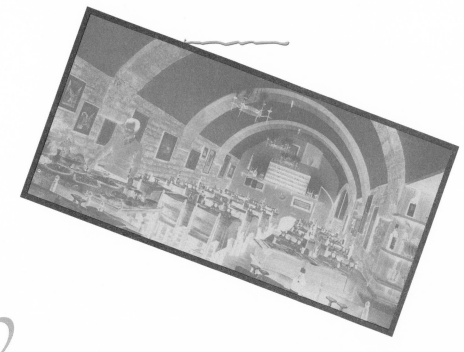

RICE, BARLEY, AND CORN *for polenta are just three of the many grains used in Italian cooking. The recipes in this chapter are served as first courses like pasta or occasionally as side dishes.*

Rice is a northern Italian staple grown mostly in Piedmont and Emilia-Romagna. It is believed to have been brought to Italy by the Arabs, who planted it first in Sicily. Eventually it made its way to the North where the growing conditions were more suitable. By 1787, Italy had become famous for the high quality of its rice. Thomas Jefferson, visiting on a diplomatic mission, was so impressed with it that he smuggled a few sacks of seed rice out of the country with him when he left, even though it was illegal. He brought the rice home to South Carolina where it was planted in hopes of revitalizing the American rice industry, which had been destroyed during the Revolutionary War.

Today rice appears mainly as risotto in Italy. I rarely order risotto in restaurants outside of northern Italy because few cooks beyond that area seem to cook it correctly. Risotto is a dish best made by a cook with some degree of devotion to the task. A number of special rice dishes exist in other parts of Italy, including the magnificent Sartù di Riso, a giant rice timbale filled with meat, mushrooms, and cheese, which originated in Naples. Rice is also eaten in stuffings for meats, vegetables, and poultry, and in desserts.

Barley is an ancient grain, often referred to in the Bible. During the Roman era, barley and other grains were made into a kind of porridge called *puls,* which fed the marching legions. Today barley is used mostly in isolated parts of northern Italy, where it is added to soups and breads or cooked into a kind of risotto.

Columbus brought back corn to Spain and Portugal on his return from the New World. From there it spread to Italy, probably arriving first in Venice, a major shipping port, around 1530. The new plant flourished, and by the seventeenth century it was grown in many areas of Italy. The peasants liked it because it was filling and cheap, much less expensive than wheat. Usually it was eaten in place of bread in the form of mush, or polenta, following the old Roman tradition of eating cooked cereals. The Italians called the new grain *granoturco,* or Turkish grain, since it was assumed that it had come from the East. The Turks, who knew they had nothing to do with it, called it *grano dei rum,* meaning Roman grain.

Polenta seems to be either loved or hated by Italians. There are those who are drawn to its golden color and soul-satisfying warmth, and those who were forced to eat it as children or during the lean years after World War II and swear they will never eat it again.

Polenta is at its best in a supporting role, as an accompaniment to stews and sauces, or in a casserole enhanced by the flavors of mushrooms and cheese. One very special dish in this chapter is the L'Infarinata, a cornmeal and vegetable porridge from Lucca, which is somewhere between a thick soup and a soft polenta dish flavorful with bits of vegetables and pancetta.

Risotto

Of all the different methods for cooking rice in various cuisines around the world, none is quite the same as risotto. Flavored with vegetables, meat, seafood, cheese, or even fruit, risotto is a savory rice dish, served as a first course in place of pasta or soup. The rice is cooked and stirred slowly with ladlefuls of hot broth added at intervals so that a creamy sauce forms around the grains. Because the method is unique, risotto is sometimes misunderstood.

A good risotto has grains of rice that are tender yet slightly firm to the bite. The consistency can be thick or thin, but the rice should be suffused with flavor. The very best risotto is made with homemade broth and fresh ingredients. Risotto cannot be made ahead and reheated, unless it's going to be used to make Risotto al Salto, crispy rice pancakes (see page 172).

Making good risotto is not difficult but it requires time, patience, and the cook's undivided attention. Since these elements are rarely available in restaurants, perfect risotto is seldom achieved commercially. But once you get the knack of it, it is quite easy to make at home.

Risotto can be simple or elaborate. No matter what ingredients are added, the basic technique for making risotto is always the same. First, chopped onion (or shallots or garlic) is cooked in butter, olive oil, or a combination of the two until soft and tender. Italian medium-grain rice (sometimes erroneously called short-grain rice) is added and stirred for two minutes, a very important step that coats the grains with the butter and helps them retain their shape through all of the cooking and stirring that follows. The Italians call this step the *tostatura,* or toasting, though no browning actually takes place. Next, a small amount of liquid, either broth, wine, water, or a combination, is added—about half a cup. As the rice cooks and the liquid is absorbed, more liquid is slowly added. Throughout the cooking, the rice needs constant stirring. The stirring helps the rice absorb the liquid and release its starch, which creates the creamy sauce that eventually surrounds the grains.

Meat, fish, or vegetables are added either at the beginning, middle, or end of the cooking time, depending on how much cooking they require. Specific information and cooking times are given in the individual recipes. Have all of these ingredients chopped and measured out before you begin cooking.

The final step in making risotto after removing the pot from the heat, is to add a pat of butter. The butter is vigorously stirred so that it binds with the creamy sauce around the rice and makes it even smoother. If you prefer and if it goes with the other flavors in the risotto, a fruity extra virgin olive oil can be used in the same way. Unless the risotto is made with seafood, freshly grated Parmigiano-Reggiano often adds a finishing touch.

Risotto Making Equipment

To cook risotto, choose a heavy pot that distributes the heat evenly. My favorite is a six-quart stainless steel Dutch oven with an aluminum clad bottom. The dimensions are ten by four inches, perfect for easy stirring without splashing the liquid over the sides. Use a wooden or plastic spoon or spatula to stir without scratching the pot.

Serving Risotto

In Italy, risotto is almost always eaten as a first course, instead of pasta or soup, and not as a side dish. This makes sense, since cooking risotto requires your full attention and it would be difficult to prepare something else simultaneously. The only time it is served as an accompaniment is with a few long-cooked dishes such as osso buco, and the braised spareribs on page 247. Since those dishes can be made ahead and actually taste better when reheated, they are easy to have ready at the same time as the risotto.

Risotto Cooking Tips

From my cooking classes, I have found that many cooks have similar problems when making risotto. Here are some important points to remember:

- Only about half a cup of liquid should be added to the rice at any one time. Choose a soup ladle with a half-cup capacity to make it easy. Cook and stir the rice with a wooden or plastic spoon until most of the liquid has been absorbed and only a small amount is left around each grain of rice. The spoon should leave a wide track when drawn across the bottom of the pan. If more liquid is added to the rice before the previous addition is absorbed, the rice cooks unevenly and develops a hard, chalky center. At the beginning the rice absorbs the liquid rapidly because it is very dry, but as it begins to become saturated, the absorption rate slows down. Don't try to speed things up by adding a lot of liquid at once—the rice will not cook any faster. If you find the stirring tiresome, enlist a friend to help you.
- Rice sometimes sticks to the bottom of the pan for a number of reasons. One is that the pan is too lightweight and thin. Another is that the rice became dry before the next ladleful of liquid was added. Having the cooking temperature too high may also cause sticking. To correct this, reduce the heat slightly, add more broth, and stir vigorously. Next time, use a heavier pot.

Risotto also makes a very good one-dish meal, especially if it contains meat or fish.

Risotto should be served in warmed shallow soup or pasta bowls. At home, I spoon the risotto directly from the pot into the individual bowls rather than into a serving dish. That way, it is less likely to cool off before it gets to the table. Risotto should be eaten with a fork.

A friend of mine who comes from Novara, in the heart of Italy's rice-growing region, showed me the Piedmontese way to eat risotto. You mound it in the center of the serving bowls, then each person flattens his portion slightly around the rim of the plate so that it cools enough to eat while the center stays hot.

Kinds of Rice for Risotto

Long-grain rice, the kind most commonly used in the United States, cannot be used to make risotto because it cooks up dry and fluffy. Medium-grain rice has the right amount of the right kind of starch to turn out creamy instead of dry and it withstands the slow cooking and stirring needed to make a good risotto. The best known variety of this kind of rice is Arborio, imported from Italy, which can be found even in supermarkets.

Though Arborio is the most widely distributed, two other Italian rice varieties can

- It is not possible to give an exact amount of the liquid needed to cook risotto because it depends on how high the heat is, how dry the rice is, what kind of rice is used, the moisture content of the other ingredients, and many other factors. For all these reasons, the amount will vary. Be prepared for this possibility by having a saucepan of hot water ready on the stove in the event that you run out of broth.
- Some cooks prefer their risotto dry and rather thick and others like theirs thinner and moister. I recommend a thinner risotto, at least until you have made risotto a couple of times. The finished rice continues to absorb liquid even as you are serving it, and chances are that by the time everyone is served, it will be thicker anyway. If you finish with a dry risotto, it may become too dry by the time it is served.
- The best way to judge when risotto is done is to taste a few grains. If they are hard and chalky and stick in your teeth, the risotto needs further cooking. When it's done, the rice should be firm, not mushy or soft. Like pasta, risotto should be served al dente. Once you have made risotto a few times, you will begin to recognize when the risotto is nearing completion. The rice grains will have swollen to three or four times their original size, the risotto will look creamy, and the grains will be milky white all the way through. Exact cooking time varies, but it is about twenty to twenty-five minutes from the first addition of broth.
- Risotto does not reheat well and should not be made in advance. It loses its creamy texture and becomes gummy and overcooked if it sits for too long. You can, however, assemble and prepare all the ingredients needed before starting. Cooking the onion, usually the first step, can be done in advance, but once the rice is added to the pot, you have to continue on, uninterrupted, to the end. Invite your guests to be seated at the table before the risotto is ready, then serve it as soon as it is done.

be found here: Carnaroli, a large wide-grain rice, and Vialone Nano, a smaller grain that cooks slightly faster than the other two. Italian markets and food specialty shops often stock these two varieties.

Some cookbooks refer to Arborio and other Italian varieties as short-grain rice. According to the United States Rice Council, however, rice is designated as long, medium, or short grain according to its starch characteristics and the length-to-width ratio of the individual grains. According to the Rice Council's standards, Arborio and the other Italian rices belong in the medium-grain category.

A medium-grain Arborio-type rice is being grown in California. It is sold in some health food stores and gourmet shops, but the supply is limited, and it may not be available everywhere. More of this type of rice is being planted, and distribution is expected to increase in the near future.

Buying and Storing Rice

Try to buy medium-grain rice at a store with a good turnover, and don't buy more than you can use in a relatively short time. Like most grains, rice can become stale if it is kept for too long, especially at warm temperatures. When you open the package, smell the rice to be sure that it's not rancid. Store the rice in a cool cupboard or, better yet, in the refrigerator or freezer in an airtight container. Let it come to room temperature before cooking.

Broth

The best broth for risotto is homemade. I make broth with a combination of meat, poultry, and vegetables for a rich flavor and wide variety of uses (see page 83). I prepare it in big batches and freeze it for long periods of time.

Canned broths can be used, but their flavor varies from good to awful, so taste several brands. Whichever brand you use, dilute it by half with water or the flavor will be too strong. Bouillon cubes are too salty and artificial tasting and should be avoided, though the Italian ones (see page 27) are good in a pinch, if you can find them.

Since rice absorbs hot broth better than cold broth, which would also prolong the cooking time, heat the broth for risotto to just below the simmer. Do not let it boil or too much will be lost to evaporation.

SERVES 4

The name of this dish refers to the way these crispy rice pancakes are quickly cooked in hot butter and flipped over in the pan. They can be made from leftover risotto, although they are so good you may want to make up a fresh batch to use this way. The cakes can be made ahead up to a couple of hours before serving, then spread on a baking sheet and reheated in a moderate oven. Miniature cakes are good for hors d'oeuvres, larger ones for lunch with a salad. They also make a fine bed for braised quail or rabbit. Some risottos hold together well enough that you don't really need to add the egg, but the cakes are easier to handle if you do.

Jumping Risotto

RISOTTO AL SALTO

1 large egg
2 cups cold leftover risotto (any kind)
1 tablespoon unsalted butter
Freshly grated Parmigiano-Reggiano (optional)

1 Beat the egg and blend it into the risotto.

2 In a medium nonstick skillet over medium heat, melt half of the butter. Use an ice cream scoop or ¼ cup dry measuring cup to scoop up the rice mixture. Flatten the scoops of rice into cakes about ½ inch thick.

3 Cook, turning once, until golden brown, about 6 minutes. Repeat with the remaining risotto. Serve hot, dusted with cheese, if you like.

A Fresh Taste of Italy

Gorgonzola Risotto

RISOTTO AL GORGONZOLA

2 tablespoons unsalted butter

1 tablespoon olive oil

$^1/_4$ cup finely chopped onion

$1^1/_2$ cups medium-grain rice, such as Arborio, Carnaroli, or
Vialone Nano

$^1/_2$ cup dry white wine

6 cups hot homemade chicken broth or a combination of half
canned broth and half water

Salt and freshly ground pepper, to taste

4 ounces imported Italian gorgonzola, rind removed, washed

1   In a large saucepan over medium heat, melt the butter with the olive oil. Add the onion and cook, stirring occasionally, until tender and golden, about 7 minutes. Raise the heat to medium-high. Add the rice and cook, stirring constantly, about 2 minutes more. Add the wine and cook, stirring constantly, until most of the liquid is absorbed.

2   Pour about $^1/_2$ cup of the hot broth over the rice. Cook and stir until most of the liquid is absorbed. The spoon should leave a wide track on the bottom of the pan yet there should be some liquid surrounding each grain of rice.

3   Continue adding broth about $^1/_2$ cup at a time, stirring after each addition. Adjust the heat, if necessary, so that the liquid simmers rapidly but the rice does not stick to the pan. Use only as much of the broth as necessary until the rice becomes tender yet firm to the bite. If you run out of broth, switch to hot water. Season with salt and pepper about halfway through the cooking time. Remove the risotto from the heat.

4   Add the cheese to the risotto, stirring until partially melted and creamy. Serve immediately.

Gorgonzola, a creamy cow's milk blue cheese from northwestern Italy, can be tangy or mild, depending on how long it has been aged. Young gorgonzola is called *dolce,* while the aged and more piquant cheese is called *stagionato.*

Use either one in this risotto, but make sure that the gorgonzola is fresh when you buy it. Ask for a sample. There should be no trace of ammonia in the smell or taste, and the color should be creamy white or yellow with blue or green streaks. Make a different dish if the cheese looks dried out or brownish.

Dionysius, a tyrant who ruled Siracusa in Sicily in the fourth century B.C., enlivened parties at his palace by having wild thyme, an herb believed to be an aphrodisiac, strewn about the floors. His guests would crush the thyme underfoot, releasing its intoxicating aroma.

Thyme is not used much in Italian cooking, but it does add a special flavor to this unique risotto. While many times risotto is finished with a bit of butter, a swirl of heavy cream makes this one extra smooth.

Creamy Lemon and Herb Risotto

RISOTTO ALL'ERBE

1 tablespoon unsalted butter

2 tablespoons olive oil

1/2 cup finely chopped onion

2 cups medium-grain rice, such as Arborio, Carnaroli, or Vialone Nano

6 cups hot homemade chicken broth or a combination of half canned broth and half water

1/2 cup chopped fresh basil

1 teaspoon chopped fresh thyme

1/2 teaspoon chopped fresh marjoram or 1/4 teaspoon dried marjoram

Salt and freshly ground pepper, to taste

1/4 cup heavy cream

1/2 teaspoon freshly grated lemon zest

1/2 cup freshly grated Parmigiano-Reggiano

1 In a large saucepan over medium-low heat, melt the butter with the olive oil. Add the onion and cook until tender and golden, about 7 minutes. Raise the heat to medium-high. Add the rice. Cook, stirring constantly, for 1 or 2 minutes, until the rice grains are shiny and evenly coated. Add about 1/2 cup of the broth. Cook, stirring constantly, until most of the liquid is absorbed. The spoon should leave a wide track on the bottom of the pan, yet there should be liquid surrounding each grain.

2 Continue adding broth about 1/2 cup at a time, stirring after each addition. Adjust the heat, if necessary, so that the liquid simmers rapidly but the rice does not stick to the pan. When half of the broth has been used, stir in the basil, thyme, marjoram, salt, and pepper.

3 Continue adding broth ½ cup at a time and stirring until the rice is tender yet still firm to the bite and a creamy sauce forms around the rice. If there is not enough broth, switch to hot water. Remove from the heat.

4 Add the cream and lemon zest and stir vigorously until the mixture looks creamy. Stir in the cheese and serve immediately.

Shrimp and Peas Risotto

RISOTTO CON GAMBERI E PISELLI

1 pound medium shrimp, shelled and deveined

4 tablespoons olive oil

2 tablespoons unsalted butter

Coarse salt and freshly ground pepper, to taste

1 medium onion, finely chopped

2 garlic cloves, finely chopped

3 tablespoons chopped Italian flat-leaf parsley

1 cup chopped peeled fresh tomatoes or drained chopped canned Italian tomatoes

½ cup dry white wine

2 cups medium-grain rice such as Arborio, Carnaroli, or Vialone Nano

6 cups homemade chicken broth or a combination of half canned broth and half water

1 cup fresh or thawed frozen tiny green peas

1 Cut each shrimp crosswise into 4 or 5 pieces.

2 In a large saucepan over medium heat, heat 2 tablespoons of the olive oil and 1 tablespoon of the butter. Add the shrimp. Cook, stirring, just until the shrimp turn pink, about 2 minutes. Sprinkle with

SERVES 6

Marcus Gavius Apicius, who lived in ancient Rome in the first century A.D., was a wealthy man who devoted himself to cooking, eating, and entertaining. He would spare no expense in providing the rarest delicacies, like nightingales' tongues, camels' heels, and ostrich, for his splendid banquets. When Apicius heard that enormous shrimp were being caught off the coast of North Africa, he quickly outfitted a ship and hired a crew to take him there to get some for himself. But even before reaching land, Apicius learned that the rumors were false and that the shrimp were quite ordinary. He lost all interest in the venture and ordered the ship to return home immediately.

Ordinary shrimp will do fine for this risotto, though. Other seafood, such as scallops, crab, or lobster, can be added. Since they need very little cooking, just stir them in about five minutes before the risotto is done.

salt and pepper. Remove the shrimp with a slotted spoon and set aside.

3   Add the remaining oil and the onion to the saucepan. Cook over medium-low heat until the onion is tender, about 5 minutes. Add the garlic and 2 tablespoons of the parsley and cook for 1 minute more. Add the tomatoes and cook, stirring constantly, for 2 minutes. Add the wine and bring to a simmer. Cook until most of the liquid has evaporated, about 2 minutes.

4   Add the rice and stir for 2 minutes. Add $1/2$ cup of the broth. Cook, stirring, over medium heat until most of the liquid is absorbed. The spoon should leave a wide track on the bottom of the pan, yet there should be liquid surrounding each grain of rice.

5   Continue adding broth about $1/2$ cup at a time, stirring after each addition. Adjust the heat, if necessary, so that the risotto simmers rapidly but does not stick to the pan. About halfway through the cooking time, add salt and pepper. If you run out of broth, switch to hot water.

6   When the rice is tender yet firm to the bite, stir in the shrimp and peas. Cook for 1 minute just until they are heated through. Remove from the heat.

7   Vigorously stir in the remaining 1 tablespoon butter and the remaining parsley. Serve immediately.

Gardener's Risotto

RISOTTO AL ORTOLANO

3 tablespoons unsalted butter

1 tablespoon olive oil

1 medium onion, finely chopped

$1/2$ cup diced carrot

$1/2$ cup diced celery

2 cups medium-grain rice, such as Arborio, Carnaroli, or Vialone Nano

Any scrap of arable land is turned into a vegetable garden in Italy. Peppers, eggplants, onions, and zucchini grow in profusion on vacant lots and highway medians. Even the gardens in front of many houses have basil and tomatoes planted among the hollyhocks and daisies.

No wonder such mixed vegetable dishes as Cianfotta (page 292) or Summer-style Fettuccine (page 137) abound in Italian

6 cups hot homemade chicken broth or a combination of half
*   canned broth and half water*

¹/₂ cup fresh or frozen baby lima beans or peeled fresh fava beans

1 cup finely diced zucchini

¹/₂ cup sliced mushrooms

4 plum tomatoes, seeded and diced

Salt and freshly ground pepper, to taste

¹/₄ cup finely chopped fresh basil

¹/₂ cup freshly grated Parmigiano-Reggiano

1 In a large heavy saucepan over medium heat, melt 2 tablespoons of the butter with the olive oil. Add the onion, carrot, and celery. Cook until the vegetables soften, about 5 minutes. Add the rice and cook, stirring, for 2 minutes. Turn the heat up to medium-high. Add $^1/_2$ cup of the broth and cook, stirring constantly with a wooden spoon, until most of the liquid is absorbed. The spoon should leave a wide track on the bottom of the pan, yet there should be a small amount of liquid surrounding each grain. Continue adding broth $^1/_2$ cup at a time and stirring constantly.

2 After 10 minutes, stir in the lima beans, zucchini, mushrooms, tomatoes, salt, and pepper. Continue adding broth $^1/_2$ cup at a time and stirring until the rice is tender yet firm to the bite and a creamy sauce forms around the rice. If there is not enough broth, switch to hot water. Remove from the heat.

3 Vigorously stir in the basil, cheese, and remaining 1 tablespoon butter. Serve immediately.

cooking. Use this recipe as a model, adding other vegetables, such as diced peppers, corn kernels, winter squash, or peas—whatever's in season—at the same time as the tomatoes.

The Rice Aria

Giocchino Rossini, who was born in Pesaro in Emilia-Romagna, was famous for his musical compositions, his great wit, and his devotion to good eating. He could write beautiful melodies seemingly without effort even while sitting with friends in a café or restaurant. His famous aria, *"Di tanti palpiti"* from the opera *Tancredi,* was written as the author waited for a plate of risotto with truffles. When word of the circumstances under which it was written got out, the romantic aria, which tells of the pangs of love, became known as the *aria dei risi,* or rice aria.

SERVES 4 TO 6

Foraging wild mushrooms is a activity many Italians indulge in during the spring and fall. Since mushrooms tend to pop up repeatedly in the same places, a wise mushroom hunter keeps his prime locations secret. Some limit their picking to the early morning hours when few people are up and about.

Many edible mushrooms grow in America's woods, too, but you have to know how to distinguish the edible ones from the poisonous ones. Fortunately, many wild varieties are now cultivated and sold in food specialty shops and some supermarkets. A combination of cultivated fresh and dried wild mushrooms are used in this recipe. Other kinds can be added or substituted.

Three Mushroom Risotto

RISOTTO AI TRE FUNGHI

1/2 ounce dried porcini or cèpes (1/2 cup)

3 tablespoons unsalted butter

1 tablespoon olive oil

1/2 cup chopped shallots or onion

2 cups medium-grain rice, such as Arborio, Carnaroli, or Vialone Nano

1/2 cup dry white wine

8 to 10 ounces fresh white mushrooms, wiped clean, trimmed, and coarsely chopped

1/4 pound fresh shiitake mushrooms, stems removed and caps coarsely chopped

4 to 5 cups hot Meat Broth (page 83) or a combination of half canned beef broth and half water

Salt and freshly ground pepper, to taste

1/2 cup freshly grated Parmigiano-Reggiano

1 Place the dried porcini mushrooms in a bowl with 2 cups warm water and let soak for at least 30 minutes. Drain the mushrooms, reserving the liquid. Strain the liquid through a paper coffee filter or strainer lined with dampened cheesecloth. Rinse the mushrooms well under running water examining each piece. Pay special attention to the stem pieces which may have bits of soil clinging to the base. Drain and chop.

2 In a large heavy saucepan over medium-low heat, melt 2 tablespoons of the butter with the olive oil. Add the shallots and cook until tender, about 5 minutes. Add the rice and cook, stirring, 2 minutes. Stir in the reconstituted dried mushrooms and the wine. Cook, stirring, until the wine has evaporated, about 2 minutes.

3 Turn the heat up to medium-high. Add half of the fresh mushrooms and 1/2 cup of the mushroom liquid and cook, stirring con-

stantly with a wooden spoon, until most of the liquid is absorbed. The spoon should leave a wide track on the bottom of the pan, yet there should be liquid surrounding each grain. Continue adding liquid 1/2 cup at a time and stirring constantly. When the mushroom liquid is finished, switch to the broth.

4 After 10 minutes, stir in the remaining mushrooms and salt and pepper. Continue adding broth as needed and stirring until the rice is tender yet firm to the bite and a creamy sauce forms around the rice. Remove from the heat.

5 Vigorously stir in the remaining 1 tablespoon butter and the cheese. Serve immediately.

Green Risotto

RISOTTO VERDE

1 pound fresh spinach

Salt, to taste

3 tablespoons unsalted butter

1 tablespoon olive oil

1 medium onion, finely chopped

2 cups medium-grain rice, such as Arborio, Carnaroli, or Vialone Nano

6 cups hot homemade chicken broth or a combination of half canned broth and half water

Freshly ground pepper, to taste

1/4 cup finely chopped fresh basil

1/4 cup finely chopped fresh parsley

1/3 cup freshly grated Parmigiano-Reggiano

1 Trim off the spinach stems and discard any bruised or yellowed leaves. Place the leaves in a sink or large basin and fill it with cold water. Swirl the spinach in the water then lift it out. Repeat, using fresh water, at least 2 more times until there is no trace of sand in the bottom of the sink.

SERVES 6

The wallpaper in my mother's kitchen in Brooklyn had pictures of a happy, smiling chef giving cooking advice. I don't remember all of his suggestions, but several have stuck with me, including "Wash vegetables in 3 waters." It was good advice then and it remains good advice now, especially when it comes to fresh spinach, which can be very sandy.

2 Place the leaves in a large pot with $1/4$ cup water and a pinch of salt. Cover and cook until the spinach is tender, about 4 minutes. Drain well, pressing the spinach to extract the excess moisture. Chop the spinach very fine. Set aside.

3 In a large heavy saucepan over medium heat, melt 2 tablespoons of the butter with the olive oil. Add the onion and cook until tender and golden, about 7 minutes. Raise the heat to medium-high. Add the rice and stir well for about 2 minutes, until the rice is coated and shiny. Add $1/2$ cup of the broth and cook, stirring constantly, until most of the liquid is absorbed. The spoon should leave a wide track on the bottom of the pan, yet there should be liquid surrounding each grain.

4 Continue adding the broth about $1/2$ cup at a time, stirring after each addition. Adjust the heat, if necessary, so that the liquid simmers rapidly but the rice does not stick to the pan. Add salt and pepper about halfway through the cooking time. The rice is done when it is tender yet firm to the bite and a creamy sauce forms around each grain. If you run out of broth, switch to warm water. Remove from the heat.

5 Stir in the spinach, basil, and parsley and mix well. Vigorously stir in the remaining butter and the cheese. Serve immediately.

SERVES 6

Fields of fava beans stretching as far as the eye can see are a harbinger of spring in many parts of Italy. This delicate, pale green risotto made with fresh favas and fennel is inspired by one I ate in Sicily. If serving it as a first course, I would follow it with something light, such as the Grilled Jumbo Shrimp with Sage and Pancetta (page 219) or Trout in Rosé Wine Sauce (page 210).

Fresh fava beans are available in many green grocers. Frozen favas can be found in many Middle Eastern, Italian, or Spanish

Risotto with Fava Beans and Fennel

RISOTTO CON FAVE E FINOCCHIO

$1^1/2$ pounds fresh fava beans, or $1^1/2$ cups frozen fava beans,
  blanched and peeled
1 large fennel bulb (1 pound)
2 tablespoons unsalted butter
2 tablespoons olive oil
$1/4$ cup finely chopped green onions

2 cups medium-grain rice such as Arborio, Carnaroli, or Vialone Nano

6 cups hot homemade chicken broth or a combination of half canned broth and half water

Salt and freshly ground pepper, to taste

³/₄ cup freshly grated Parmigiano-Reggiano

1   Shell the fava beans then peel off the thin skin that covers each bean. You should have about 1¹/₂ cups.

2   Trim off the dark green feathery leaves and stalks of the fennel down to the rounded bulb. Cut a slice off the stem end. With a vegetable peeler, trim away any brown spots or bruises. Cut the fennel lengthwise into quarters, then crosswise into thin slices.

3   In a large heavy saucepan, melt 1 tablespoon of the butter with the olive oil over medium-low heat. Add the green onions and cook until tender, about 3 minutes. Add the fennel and cook for 10 minutes, stirring occasionally.

4   Raise the heat to medium high. Add the rice and cook, stirring constantly, for 1 to 2 minutes, until coated and shiny. Add about ¹/₂ cup of the broth. Cook, stirring constantly, until most of the liquid is absorbed. The spoon should leave a wide track on the bottom of the pan yet there should be liquid surrounding each grain.

5   Continue adding the broth about ¹/₂ cup at a time, stirring after each addition. Adjust the heat, if necessary, so that the liquid simmers rapidly but the rice does not stick to the bottom of the pan.

6   After 15 minutes, stir in the fava beans. Add salt and pepper. Continue adding broth ¹/₂ cup at a time and stirring until the rice is tender yet firm to the bite and a creamy sauce forms around the rice and vegetables. Use only as much of the liquid as necessary. If you run out of broth, switch to hot water. Remove from the heat.

7   Vigorously stir in the remaining butter and the cheese. Serve immediately.

markets. If fresh or frozen favas are not available, substitute frozen baby lima beans, partially thawed. No peeling is needed.

"If you're depressed, risotto will lift you."

Giorgio Armani

At a restaurant in Mantua in the Lombardy region of Italy, the waiter brought me a platter heaped with this golden risotto. I could hardly wait to plunge my fork into it. After serving me a generous portion, he took away the partially filled platter. It was all I could do to keep from calling him back to ask for more.

In Italy, a large winter squash with brilliant orange flesh and gray-green skin is used for this risotto. Butternut squash is a near equivalent in flavor. The squash turns to a creamy smooth puree as it cooks and is absorbed by the rice.

Golden Risotto

RISOTTO D'ORO

4 tablespoons unsalted butter

1 tablespoon olive oil

1 medium onion

2 cups diced peeled butternut squash (about 1 pound)

6 cups hot homemade chicken broth or a combination of half
   canned broth and half water

2 cups medium-grain rice, such as Arborio, Carnaroli, or Vialone
   Nano

Salt and freshly ground pepper, to taste

1/2 cup freshly grated Parmigiano-Reggiano

1   In a large saucepan over medium heat, melt 3 tablespoons of the butter with the olive oil. Add the onion and cook, stirring occasionally, until tender and golden, about 7 minutes. Add the squash and 1/4 cup of the broth. Cover and cook over low heat for 10 minutes, or until the squash is very soft.

2   Raise the heat to medium-high. Add the rice. Cook the mixture, stirring occasionally, for 2 minutes. Add about 1/2 cup broth. Cook, stirring constantly, until most of the liquid is absorbed. The spoon should leave a wide track on the bottom of the pan, yet there should be liquid surrounding each grain.

3   Continue adding broth about 1/2 cup at a time, stirring after each addition. Adjust the heat, if necessary, so that the liquid simmers rapidly but the rice does not stick to the pan. Add salt and pepper about halfway through the cooking time.

4   Continue adding broth 1/2 cup at a time and stirring until the rice is tender yet firm to the bite and a creamy sauce forms around the rice. If there is not enough broth, switch to hot water. Remove from the heat.

5   Vigorously stir in the remaining butter and the cheese. Serve immediately.

Risotto with Apples

RISOTTO ALLE MELE VERDE

3 tablespoons unsalted butter

1 tablespoon olive oil

¼ cup finely chopped onion

2 medium Granny Smith or other tart green apples, peeled, cored,
    and chopped

Pinch of freshly grated nutmeg

2 cups medium-grain rice, such as Arborio, Carnaroli, or Vialone
    Nano

½ cup dry white wine

6 cups hot homemade chicken broth or a combination of half
    canned broth and half water

Salt and freshly ground pepper, to taste

½ cup freshly grated Parmigiano-Reggiano

1   In a large saucepan over medium heat, melt 2 tablespoons of the butter with the olive oil. Add the onion and cook until tender and golden, about 7 minutes. Add the apples and nutmeg. Cook for 8 to 10 minutes, or until the apples are very tender.

2   Raise the heat to medium-high and add the rice. Cook, stirring constantly, for 2 minutes. Add the wine. Cook, stirring constantly, until most of the liquid is evaporated. Add about ½ cup of the broth and cook, stirring constantly with a wooden spoon, until most of the liquid is absorbed. The spoon should leave a wide track on the bottom of the pan, yet there should be liquid surrounding each grain.

3   Continue adding broth about ½ cup at a time, stirring after each addition. Adjust the heat, if necessary, so that the liquid simmers rapidly but the rice does not stick to the pan. Add salt and pepper.

4   Continue adding broth ½ cup at a time and stirring until the rice is tender yet still firm to the bite and a creamy sauce forms around the rice. Use only as much of the liquid as necessary. If there is not enough broth, switch to hot water. Remove from the heat.

SERVES 6

Every spring I remember with nostalgia the year my husband, Charles, took a sabbatical from teaching and we spent the month of May in Rome. We often had dinner at a tiny trattoria called Pietro, where the specialty was strawberry risotto. It seemed strange when the waiter first suggested it, but after one bite the dish made perfect sense. The berries were the tiny, aromatic wild strawberries the Italians call *fragola del bosco*, and the risotto technique captured all of their delicate perfume. It was not sweet as I had expected but savory, with the flavors of the tart berries mingling with wine and Parmigiano-Reggiano.

Fruit risottos, while not exactly commonplace, are not unheard of in other regions either. In Trent, in the heart of the northern Italian apple-growing region, this green apple risotto was served during the harvest season as part of an all-apple menu. Cantaloupe found its way into a risotto flavored with prosciutto that we tasted in Friuli. Citrus risottos can also be very good.

Pietro
Via della Vetrina, 14
Rome

5 Add the remaining 1 tablespoon butter and stir vigorously until melted. Stir in the cheese and serve immediately.

SERVES 4

This risotto has no flavoring other than a bit of onion and, of course, the broth. It would be lovely with a shaving of white truffles, were you fortunate enough to have some. A few drops of white truffle oil has some of the aroma of the subterranean fungus but is a lot less expensive. You can find truffle oil in many upscale gourmet shops. Or serve the risotto plain with just some Parmigiano-Reggiano.

In Friuli, we had white risotto topped with braised spareribs (see page 247).

White Risotto

RISOTTO IN BIANCO

3 tablespoons unsalted butter

1 tablespoon olive oil

1 small onion, finely chopped, or ¹/₄ cup chopped shallots

2 cups medium-grain rice, such as Arborio, Carnaroli, or Vialone Nano

¹/₂ cup dry white wine

5 to 6 cups hot homemade chicken or Meat Broth (page 83) or a combination of half canned broth and half water

Salt and freshly ground pepper, to taste

¹/₂ cup freshly grated Parmigiano-Reggiano (optional)

1 In a large heavy saucepan over medium heat, melt 2 tablespoons of the butter with the olive oil. Add the onion and cook until tender, about 5 minutes. Raise the heat to medium-high. Add the rice and cook, stirring for 2 minutes. Stir in the wine. Cook, stirring constantly, until the wine has evaporated, about 2 minutes. Add about ¹/₂ cup of the broth and cook, stirring constantly with a wooden spoon, until most of the liquid is absorbed. The spoon should leave a wide track on the bottom of the pan, yet there should be a small amount of liquid surrounding each grain.

2 Continue adding broth ¹/₂ cup at a time and stirring constantly until the rice is tender yet firm to the bite and a creamy sauce forms around the rice. Add salt and pepper. Remove from the heat.

3 Stir in the cheese, if used, and the remaining 1 tablespoon butter. Serve immediately.

Barley Risotto

RISOTTO DI ORZO

3 tablespoons unsalted butter

1 tablespoon olive oil

1 small onion, finely chopped

1 cup pearl barley

$1/4$ cup finely chopped red bell pepper

$1/4$ cup finely chopped carrot

$1/4$ cup finely chopped celery

$1/2$ cup finely chopped zucchini

4 cups chicken broth

Salt and freshly ground pepper, to taste

2 tablespoons freshly grated Parmigiano-Reggiano

1 In a large saucepan over medium heat, melt 2 tablespoons butter with the olive oil. Add the onion and cook, stirring frequently, until tender, about 5 minutes. Raise the heat to medium-high and add the barley. Cook, stirring constantly, for 1 minute. Stir in half of the remaining vegetables and cook for 1 minute more. Add all of the broth and bring to a simmer. Cover and cook for 20 minutes.

2 Add salt, pepper, and the remaining vegetables. Cook, uncovered, for 10 minutes more, or until the liquid has evaporated and the barley is tender. Remove from the heat.

3 Beat in the remaining tablespoon of butter. Stir in the cheese and serve immediately.

Instead of rice, pearl barley, called *orzo* in Italian, is used to make a kind of risotto in Friuli. Do not confuse it with the rice-shape pasta called orzo in the United States.

The technique for barley risotto is simple, and the barley does not need constant stirring. Serve it like regular risotto as a first course or as a hearty side dish with Chicken with Fennel-Sausage Stuffing (page 228) or Roasted Veal Shanks (page 263).

A *sartù* is a large filled rice timbale that dates to the Bourbon reign in Naples. The name is derived from the French word *surtout* meaning "above all," since rice was expensive and scarce and not food for common people. Even today, sartù is eaten only on special occasions.

A sartù is a dramatic, impressive sight. The cooked rice is packed into a bowl or casserole dish, with meats, cheese, and sauce, baked, and then unmolded onto a platter. It looks like a golden brown cake but when cut, the savory mushroom sauce, tiny meatballs, and sausages that constitute the filling spill out.

Though it may seem complex, the version of sartù that follows is austere compared to some that I have read about. Those include chicken livers, hard-cooked eggs, cheese, salami, pancetta, prosciutto, and other ingredients. Several steps are involved, but none is difficult and the results are spectacular. The sartù can be made in stages, then assembled and baked before serving.

Serve the sartù on any festive occasion. It is particularly nice for a buffet dinner since it looks great and does not require a knife to eat it. I serve it as a one-dish meal followed by a green salad.

Rice Timbale from the Kingdom of the Two Sicilies

SARTÙ DI RISO

SAUCE

1 ounce dried porcini mushrooms (about ³/₄ cup)

1 medium onion, chopped

2 tablespoons olive oil

1 can (28 ounces) Italian tomatoes with their juice, passed through a food mill

Salt and freshly ground pepper, to taste

MEATBALLS AND SAUSAGES

8 ounces ground beef

¹/₃ cup fine dry bread crumbs

2 tablespoons freshly grated Parmigiano-Reggiano

1 small garlic clove, finely chopped

2 tablespoons chopped fresh parsley

1 large egg, beaten

Salt and freshly ground pepper, to taste

2 tablespoons olive oil

2 sweet Italian sausages

RICE

8 ounces mozzarella, preferably fresh, diced

1 cup partially thawed frozen peas

2 cups medium-grain rice such as Arborio, Carnaroli, or Vialone Nano

Salt, to taste

1 cup freshly grated Parmigiano-Reggiano

Freshly ground pepper, to taste

ASSEMBLY

2 tablespoons butter, softened

6 tablespoons fine dry bread crumbs

Chopped fresh parsley, for garnish

1   To make the sauce, place the mushrooms in a bowl with 2 cups warm water. Let soak for at least 30 minutes. Drain the mushrooms, reserving the liquid. Strain the liquid through a paper coffee filter or strainer lined with dampened cheesecloth. Rinse the mushrooms well under running water examining each piece. Pay special attention to the stem pieces which may have bits of soil clinging to the base. Drain well and chop.

2   In a large saucepan over medium heat, combine the onion and the olive oil. Cook, stirring occasionally, until tender, about 5 minutes. Stir in the chopped mushrooms. Add the tomatoes and the reserved mushroom liquid. Season with salt and pepper. Bring to a simmer. Cook over low heat, stirring occasionally, for 30 minutes, or until thickened.

3   To make the meatballs, combine the beef, bread crumbs, cheese, garlic, parsley, egg, salt, and pepper in a bowl. Mix well. Shape the mixture into 1-inch meatballs. In a skillet large enough to hold all the meatballs without crowding, heat the oil over medium heat. Add the meatballs and cook, turning occasionally, until browned on all sides, about 20 minutes. With a slotted spoon, remove the meatballs to a plate. Wipe out the skillet.

4   In the same skillet over medium-low heat, combine the sausages and 1 cup water. Cover and cook until the water evaporates and the sausages begin to brown. Cook the sausages, uncovered, turning them occasionally, until cooked through.

5   To assemble the sartù, cut the sausages into ¼-inch-thick slices. Combine the meatballs, sausage slices, mozzarella, and peas with half of the tomato and mushroom sauce and set aside.

6   In a large pot over medium heat, combine the remaining sauce with 4 cups water. Bring the mixture to a boil. Add the rice and 1 teaspoon salt. Bring the liquid back to a boil and stir once or twice. Cover and cook over low heat, stirring occasionally, until the rice is barely tender, about 17 minutes. Be careful that the rice does not stick to the bottom of the pot. Add a little more water if the rice seems dry. Remove from the heat. Let the rice cool slightly. Stir in the cheese. Season with salt and pepper.

7   Generously coat a deep 3-quart casserole or ovenproof bowl with

the butter. Sprinkle it with 4 tablespoons of the bread crumbs. Spoon about two thirds of the rice into the casserole, pressing it against the bottom and sides to make a shell about 1 inch thick. Spoon the meat mixture into the center, pressing it down with the back of the spoon. Cover with the remaining rice and smooth the surface. Sprinkle the top with the remaining bread crumbs.

8 About 2 hours before serving, preheat the oven to 350°F.

9 Bake the sartù for 1 hour, or until the surface is browned and the mixture is hot in the center. (Cooking time will be longer if the sartù components were made in advance and are cold.) To test for doneness, plunge an instant-read thermometer into the center of the sartù. The internal temperature should be about 130°F.

10 Let the sartù cool on a rack for 10 minutes. Run a knife or thin metal spatula around the inside of the casserole. Place a large platter over the casserole and invert the sartù onto it. Sprinkle with parsley. Cut into wedges to serve.

To make ahead: The mushroom and tomato sauce and the meatballs and sausages can be prepared ahead through Step 4. Cover and refrigerate separately for up to 24 hours. The sartù can be assembled and left to stand for up to 1 hour or refrigerate up to 4 hours. Do not refrigerate longer, as rice tends to harden if it is chilled.

Grandmother's Rice and Sausage Stuffing

RISO E SALSICCIA ALLA NONNA

1 large onion, chopped

2 tablespoons unsalted butter

2 tablespoons olive oil

1 medium red bell pepper, cored, seeded, and chopped

1 medium green bell pepper, cored, seeded, and chopped

2 large celery ribs, chopped

SERVES 8

My father's mother came from the tiny island of Procida off the coast of Naples. When she was a teenager, she was sent to work for a wealthy family in Marseilles. She learned to speak French and to cook and became quite sophisticated for a peasant girl. Eventually she returned to Procida and married my grandfather, who was a fisherman. They emigrated to America and settled in Brooklyn just after the turn of the century.

My mother lived with Grandma Scotto during World War II while

188

1 pound small white mushrooms, wiped, trimmed, and quartered

1 pound sweet Italian sausage

2 cups medium-grain white rice, such as Arborio, Carnaroli, or
Vialone Nano, or short-grain brown rice

Salt, to taste

1 cup turkey or chicken broth

1 In a large pot over medium heat, cook the onion in the butter and olive oil for 5 minutes, or until tender. Add the peppers, celery, and mushrooms and cook, stirring frequently, until the vegetables are very tender and begin to brown, about 20 minutes.

2 Meanwhile, remove the casings from the sausages and place the meat in a medium skillet. Cook over medium heat, stirring frequently to break up large lumps, until the sausage meat is lightly browned, about 10 minutes. Drain well with a slotted spoon.

3 In another pot, bring about 2 quarts of water to a boil. Add the rice and salt. Stir well. Cook, stirring occasionally, until the water returns to a boil. Continue cooking until the rice is tender, about 18 minutes for white rice and 35 minutes for brown rice. Drain well.

4 Add the sausage meat and rice to the vegetables and mix. Place the mixture in a large baking dish.

5 About 1 hour before serving time, preheat the oven to 350°F.

6 Add the broth to the casserole. Cover with foil and bake for 30 minutes, or until heated through.

To make ahead: The stuffing may be made ahead through the end of Step 4. Cover and refrigerate up to 4 hours. Bake as above.

my father was away in the army. Grandma taught her daughter-in-law to cook her way, and that included this recipe for an unusual turkey stuffing, which she had found in an Italian newspaper.

Over the years I have experimented with Grandma's recipe, but this is basically the same as hers. I like to use Arborio, Carnaroli, or Vialone Nano, imported Italian rices which were probably unavailable in this country during Grandma's day. Even better is short-grain *brown* rice, which has a nice chewy texture and nutty flavor. It can be found in health food stores. Sometimes I substitute fresh or reconstituted dried wild mushrooms such as shiitake or porcini for all or part of the white mushrooms.

My family always cooks the stuffing in a separate casserole dish instead of putting it inside the bird, but you can stuff the turkey, or a capon, if you wish. Let the rice mixture cool completely before placing it in the cavity.

"Rice was served sweet—like an English rice-pudding—only cooked in milk of almonds with a great deal of sugar or honey. Rice was also one of the chief ingredients of the bramagere, *which included in a recipe for twelve people, 4 fowls, 4 pounds of almonds, 2 pounds of lard, 1¹/₂ pounds of sugar, and an eighth of a pound of cloves. And when it is cooked and you serve it, sprinkle rose-water over the bowls, and sugar and white fried almonds and cloves. This dish must be white as snow, and thick, and potent in spices."*

Iris Origo, *The Merchant of Prato*

Polenta

Polenta is Italian cornmeal mush. The classic way of making it is to slowly dribble dry cornmeal into boiling water, then stir the mixture constantly for thirty to forty-five minutes, or until it is done. Made this way, it is difficult to avoid lumping, and all that stirring is a nuisance.

The method I prefer is from Craig Claiborne's *New York Times Cookbook,* which I have adapted to avoid using a double boiler as he recommends. The polenta turns out just as creamy as if it were made the traditional way, and there is no danger of lumping. Best of all, there is no need to stir constantly. Just be sure to keep the heat very low or use a Flame Tamer, if you have one. Stir the polenta every ten minutes or so to prevent scorching.

Coarsely ground cornmeal makes an excellent polenta. One brand that I find locally is Goya. It is inexpensive and always fresh, and it cooks up light and creamy. Italian polenta is usually made from yellow cornmeal except in the Veneto, where white cornmeal is preferred because it has a more delicate flavor that goes better with fish.

Unadorned polenta is very bland, making it the perfect partner for spicy stews or sauces. It goes with many kinds of meat, vegetable, seafood, and game dishes, such as Spareribs and Tomato Sauce (page 248), Spiced Venison or Beef Stew (page 272), or Broccoli, Pancetta, and Garlic (page 286). It can also be served like pasta, topped with a tomato sauce or ragù. To enhance the flavor of the polenta itself, you can cook it with half chicken broth or milk instead of water, or add butter, cream, or cheese at the end.

Italians like to serve polenta by pouring it out onto a cutting board. It is firm enough to form a smooth round disk, which can be cut into slices with a taut string. When I serve polenta with a saucy stew, I prefer to pour the polenta onto a large serving platter, then spoon the stew, or whatever I am serving with it, on top. It makes an impressive sight. Another alternative is to put the polenta in a separate bowl and serve it as a side dish, like mashed potatoes.

Polenta can be soft or firm. The former, made with more liquid, is better as a base for stew or topped with any of the ragùs. Firm polenta, made with less liquid, is better for crostini.

In Italy, an unlined copper pan called a *paiolo* is preferred for making polenta. There are even electric versions equipped with an automatic paddle for stirring. A saucepan with a heavy bottom to prevent scorching is a good alternative. The saucepan will be easy to clean if you fill it with cold water immediately after emptying it and let it stand until the crust is loosened.

Polenta

POLENTA

1 cup coarsely ground yellow cornmeal

About 2 teaspoons salt

2 tablespoons unsalted butter and $1/3$ cup freshly grated
   Parmigiano-Reggiano (optional)

1   In a medium saucepan over medium heat, bring 3 cups of water to a boil. In a small bowl, whisk together the cornmeal, salt, and 1 cup water. Pour the cornmeal mixture into the boiling water. Stir constantly with a whisk until it comes to a boil.

2   Reduce the heat to very low. Cook, stirring every 10 minutes or so, for 40 minutes, or until the polenta is thick and creamy. Use a Flame Tamer, if necessary, to keep the heat low enough to prevent the polenta from splattering. If the polenta becomes too thick, add more water. Remove the polenta from the heat.

3   Stir in the butter and cheese, if using.

To make ahead: Polenta can be kept warm for up to 1 hour. Do not add the butter and cheese. Cover the pot and place it in a larger pot filled with simmering water.

In the nineteenth century, a group of French and Italian writers, artists, and poets living in Paris formed an association known as The Order of the Polenta Eaters. The members included Luigi Denza, author of *Funiculì Funiculà,* the very famous Neapolitan song, and the novelist Emile Zola. The group gathered together over dinner to debate subjects ranging from art and gastronomy to politics and literature, but they all agreed on their love for polenta. One poet wrote of its beauty, describing the steaming polenta poured out onto a board as resembling the full moon rising in a mist. The club even had its own theme song that ended with the refrain "Hail, polenta, dish of kings. Your faithful lie prone at your feet. They sing in chorus of their admiration. Hail polenta, dish of kings!!!" Their motto was the six P's: *Per Patria prima, per Polenta poi* (For the homeland first, and then for polenta).

This is my favorite method of preparing polenta. If you wish, serve it plain or with butter and cheese.

SERVES 8

Once polenta cools, it becomes firm and can be cut into shapes and baked, fried, or grilled until crisp on the outside and soft in the center. Serve the crostini as a side dish or in place of toasted bread with a topping. The simplest topping for these is black olive paste, which some Italians call "poor man's caviar." It is available in jars in many gourmet shops.

Polenta Crostini

CROSTINI DI POLENTA

1 recipe Polenta (recipe precedes)
Olive oil

1 As soon as the polenta is cooked, spread it out about ¹/₂ inch thick on a baking sheet. Let cool.

2 When ready to cook, cut the polenta into 2-inch squares. (Firm polenta can also be cut with a cookie or biscuit cutter into circles or other shapes.)

IN THE OVEN

Preheat the oven to 400°F. Lightly oil a baking sheet. Arrange the polenta slices on the sheet. Brush the tops with oil. Bake for 30 minutes, turning once, until crisp and golden.

ON THE GRILL

Heat a grill or griddle until very hot. Brush the slices with oil on both sides. Grill, turning once, about 2 minutes on each side until crisp and golden.

IN A SKILLET

Heat 1 teaspoon of oil in a nonstick skillet over medium-high heat. Add the slices in a single layer without crowding. Cook, turning once, about 5 minutes on each side, or until crisp and golden.

To make ahead: The polenta can be made up to 3 days ahead. Cover and refrigerate. The crostini can be made ahead of time and kept warm in a low oven for up to 1 hour.

Polenta and Vegetable Porridge

L'Infarinata

2 tablespoons olive oil

2 ounces chopped pancetta (about 4 thick slices)

1 small onion, coarsely chopped

1 celery rib, coarsely chopped

2 large carrots, coarsely chopped

2 tablespoons chopped fresh parsley

2 tablespoons chopped fresh basil

1 tablespoon chopped fresh rosemary leaves

3 garlic cloves, finely chopped

2 cups chopped savoy cabbage

2 large potatoes, peeled and chopped

2 cups coarsely ground yellow cornmeal

2 cups cooked red kidney beans, or 1 can (16 ounces) red kidney beans, rinsed and drained

Salt, to taste

Extra virgin olive oil

Freshly ground pepper, to taste

In Lucca, this cornmeal porridge with vegetables and beans is served lukewarm in a soup plate with a drizzle of extra virgin olive oil on top and sometimes a sprinkling of grated pecorino. It is the kind of earthy dish that warms and satisfies, the ultimate expression of stick-to-your-ribs food.

The recipe makes a lot, so you will probably have some left over—which is the idea. As it cools, the mixture becomes firm enough to slice. These slices can be browned in a skillet for crusty appetizers to go with drinks the next day or to be served as a side dish with stews or braised meats.

1 In a large pot, combine the olive oil, pancetta, onion, celery, carrots, parsley, basil, and rosemary. Cook over medium heat, stirring occasionally, until softened, about 10 minutes. Add the garlic and cook for 1 minute more. Add the cabbage and potatoes and cook for 10 to 15 minutes, stirring frequently, until the cabbage is wilted. Add 4 cups cold water and bring to a simmer.

2 In a bowl, whisk the cornmeal with 2 cups cold water. Pour the mixture into the pot along with the beans. Cook, stirring, until the mixture comes to a simmer. Add salt. Cover and cook over very low heat, stirring occasionally, for 30 minutes, or until the mixture is thickened. Watch carefully so that the polenta does not scorch on the bottom. If it seems too thick, add more water. Taste for salt.

3 Serve in shallow soup bowls drizzled with extra virgin olive oil and lots of pepper.

Cook's note: To make crostini, spread leftover porridge $^3/4$ inch thick in an oiled pan. Let cool. Cover and chill. (Can be kept up to 3 days.) Just before serving, cut into squares. Heat a small amount of oil in a skillet. Pat the pieces dry and cook until crisp and lightly browned on both sides, about 5 minutes per side. Drain on paper towels and serve as an appetizer or side dish.

Polenta Baked with Mushrooms and Cream

PASTICCIO DI POLENTA

1 ounce dried porcini mushrooms (about $^3/4$ cup)

2 tablespoons unsalted butter

1 tablespoon olive oil

10 ounces fresh white mushrooms, wiped, trimmed, and sliced $^1/4$ inch thick

1 large garlic clove, finely chopped

2 teaspoons chopped fresh rosemary leaves

$^1/2$ teaspoon dried marjoram

Salt and freshly ground pepper, to taste

2 cups coarsely ground yellow cornmeal

4 tablespoons freshly grated Parmigiano-Reggiano

4 ounces fontina cheese, preferably Italian, thinly sliced

$^1/2$ cup heavy cream

SERVES 6 TO 8

One Sunday we were invited to lunch at a farmhouse in Piedmont owned by a banker from Milan. The banker spent most of his time in the city while his wife ran the farm and winery. On weekends, she liked to invite city people to enjoy the country air and share an old-fashioned meal. On this beautiful autumn day, there were forty guests in all, mostly members of the Milan Lions Club. Dinner was an amazing series of satisfying yet simple dishes. Our hostess and her helpers dashed back and forth to the kitchen while the banker and his guests took turns toasting each other's health. Later, the banker confided in me his secret formula for orange grappa while his wife shared this recipe. It makes a fine meatless main course or it can be served as a first course followed by Grilled Quail with Sausages (page 241).

1 Soak the porcini in 1¹/₂ cups lukewarm water for 30 minutes. Lift the mushrooms out of the soaking liquid. Strain the liquid through a sieve lined with dampened cheesecloth or a paper coffee filter, reserving the liquid. Wash the porcini thoroughly under cold running water to eliminate all traces of soil, paying special attention to the stem ends. Chop coarsely and set aside.

2 In a large skillet over medium heat, melt the butter with the olive oil. Add the fresh mushrooms, garlic, rosemary, and marjoram. Cook, stirring frequently, for 10 minutes, or until the mushrooms begin to brown. Stir in the porcini and their liquid. Cook until most of the liquid has evaporated, about 3 minutes. Season with salt and pepper and set aside.

3 In a large pot, bring 6 cups water to a boil. In a medium bowl, combine the cornmeal with 2 cups cold water and 1¹/₂ teaspoons salt. Stir the cornmeal mixture into the boiling water. Cook over medium heat, stirring constantly, until the liquid comes to a boil. Reduce the heat to low and cook, stirring occasionally, for 40 minutes. (A Flame Tamer will prevent the polenta from scorching on the bottom. If it gets too thick, add a little more water and stir well.)

4 Preheat the oven to 350°F. Butter a shallow 2-quart casserole or baking dish.

5 Pour half the polenta into the baking dish. Sprinkle with half of the Parmigiano. Spoon on the mushrooms in an even layer. Arrange the fontina over the mushrooms. Spread the remaining polenta on top, smoothing the surface.

6 Pour on the heavy cream and sprinkle with the remaining Parmigiano. Bake for 40 to 45 minutes, or until the top is browned and bubbling.

7 Let stand for 10 minutes before serving.

To make ahead: Prepare the recipe through Step 5 without preheating the oven. Cover the dish with plastic wrap. Hold at room temperature for 1 hour or refrigerate overnight. About 1 hour before serving, preheat the oven. Pour the cream over the polenta and sprinkle it with the remaining 2 tablespoons of cheese. Bake for 60 to 75 minutes, or until the top is browned and the polenta is heated through.

Seafood ... Pesce e Frutti di Mare

SINCE ITALY HAS MANY *lakes and rivers and is a peninsula surrounded by the Mediterranean and Adriatic seas, fish and seafood are abundant. Many more kinds are available in Italian markets than are found in the United States, and many of these are unique to local waters.*

Often in better restaurants and trattorias, whole fish and seafood are displayed in a refrigerated case for your inspection. Some may be brought to the table for a closer look. Fish is left whole with the head and tail intact, so that you can see it is fresh by looking at its bright eyes and moist, pearly skin. Once it is cooked, the waiter will bone the fish for you, usually at a small nearby service table so that you can watch and be sure you are getting the fish you chose.

In homes as in restaurants, cooking methods are very simple. More often than not, fish and seafood are grilled or roasted whole and seasoned with just lemon juice and a few drops of olive oil. Italians go out of their way to get the freshest seafood. Whatever sauce, seasoning, or cooking method they use, it is meant to enhance the natural flavor of the fish, not overpower it.

SERVES 2 TO 4

In Praiano along the Amalfi Coast, we ate fresh anchovies on the balcony of a restaurant facing the little island that was once the home of the dancer Mikhail Barishnikov. The tiny fish had been marinated in lemon juice, garlic, vinegar, and mint. Fresh anchovies are hard to find in the United States, but this marinade goes well with many kinds of dark-fleshed fish, especially bluefish, which is plentiful in the Northeast during the summer months. Mackerel or sardines would also be good. Fish cooked this way is also good cold.

Bluefish with Lemon, Garlic, and Mint

PESCE AZURRO AL LIMONE, AGLIO, E MENTA

2 large garlic cloves, finely chopped

2 tablespoons olive oil

2 tablespoons red wine vinegar

$1/2$ teaspoon freshly grated lemon zest

2 tablespoons fresh lemon juice

Salt and freshly ground pepper, to taste

$1/4$ cup chopped fresh mint

1 pound bluefish or mackerel fillets, cut into 4 pieces

1 In a shallow bowl, whisk together the garlic, olive oil, vinegar, lemon zest, lemon juice, salt, and pepper. Stir in the mint. Add the fish, turning it to coat on all sides. Cover and marinate for 1 hour.

2 Preheat the broiler or grill.

3 Place the fish on the broiler rack, skin side down, and cook, basting it once with the marinade, until it is lightly browned and just barely cooked through, 5 to 7 minutes, depending on the thickness of the fish. There is no need to turn the fish.

4 Serve hot or at room temperature.

Roasted Cod with Potatoes and Mushrooms

MERLUZZO AL FORNO CON PATATE E FUNGHI

4 tablespoons olive oil

3 teaspoons chopped fresh marjoram or 1 teaspoon dried marjoram

2 tablespoons fresh lemon juice

1 small garlic clove, finely chopped

Salt and freshly ground pepper, to taste

1 pound thick cod, halibut, or turbot fillets or steaks

1/4 pound shiitake mushrooms

4 small baking potatoes, scrubbed and thinly sliced (about 1 1/2 pounds)

1   Preheat the oven to 450°F. Oil a 15 × 10 × 1-inch jelly-roll pan.

2   Combine 1 tablespoon of the olive oil, half of the marjoram, lemon juice, garlic, salt, and pepper. Pour the mixture over the fish and let marinate while you prepare the vegetables.

3   Wipe the mushroom caps with a damp paper towel. Remove and discard the stems. Thinly slice the caps. Combine the mushrooms, potatoes, remaining olive oil, remaining marjoram, salt, and pepper. Spread the mixture evenly in the pan. Bake for 20 minutes, or until the potatoes begin to brown. With a metal spatula, turn the vegetables over. Bake for 10 to 20 minutes more, or until the potatoes are browned all over.

4   Place the fish on top of the potatoes. Bake for 10 to 12 minutes, depending on the thickness, until the fish is just barely opaque in the thickest part.

5   Serve immediately.

SERVES 4

When I tasted this dish at a restaurant in Milan, it was made with sturgeon and fresh porcini. But since those ingredients are not readily available, I suggest substituting cod and shiitakes. The flavors are not the same, but they are equally good, with the mushrooms perfuming the potatoes and complementing the meaty texture of the fish. Marjoram is an herb similar to oregano, though milder and slightly lemony. Oregano would be too powerful here, but thyme could be substituted for the marjoram.

The potatoes will become brown and crisp if you use a large, shallow roasting pan. A heavyweight pan made of enameled cast iron ensures even browning.

For many Italians, the year-end holidays begin with *Il Cenone*, the big seafood dinner held on Christmas Eve. Some families have seven kinds of fish (a reminder of the seven sacraments) while others have twelve, representing the Apostles. Baccalà, or salt cod, is essential for most.

I remember coming home from school to find a basin full of dried slabs of salted cod soaking in the laundry sink, and the tap left slowly running so a steady stream of cold water drizzled over the fish to wash away the excess salt. Then my mother would fry the fish in batter or cook it in a spicy tomato sauce, and even though my sister and I would howl about its strong aroma, it always tasted much better than it smelled.

Salt cod comes in several forms, either on the bone or boneless, with or without skin. The flesh is partially dry and stiff and must be kept refrigerated. Do not confuse baccalà with *stoccofisso*, or stockfish. *Stoccofisso* is not salted, merely dried.

Fresh fish can be substituted for the baccalà in this recipe. Use a firm-fleshed fish such as monkfish or bass. If using an unsalted fresh fish, begin the recipe at Step 2.

For baccalà, the exact soaking time will vary according to the salting method used in preparing the fish and its thickness. Figure on a minimum of twenty-four hours; longer soaking may be required. Taste the fish after twenty-four hours to see if it needs longer soaking.

Baccalà Salad

INSALATA DI BACCALÀ

1 pound baccalà

1 celery rib

1 pound waxy boiling potatoes, scrubbed

Salt, to taste

¼ cup olive oil

3 tablespoons fresh lemon juice

3 tablespoons chopped fresh parsley

1 large garlic clove, finely chopped

Freshly ground pepper, to taste

2 red or yellow bell peppers, roasted, seeded, and peeled
    (see page 66)

1 Wash the baccalà under cool running water. Cut the fish into 3 or 4 pieces. Place the pieces in a bowl and cover with cool water. Refrigerate for 24 hours, changing the water at least 5 or 6 times.

2 In a large pot, bring about 2 inches of fresh water to a boil. Reduce the heat to low. Add the baccalà and celery. Bring to a simmer and cook for 5 minutes, or until the fish is tender. Drain the fish and let cool slightly. Using your fingers, remove the bones. Cut or break the fish into bite-size pieces.

3 Place the potatoes in a medium saucepan with cold water to cover and salt. Bring to a simmer and cook until tender when pierced with a knife, about 20 minutes. Drain and thickly slice.

4 Whisk together the olive oil, lemon juice, 2 tablespoons parsley, garlic, salt, and pepper.

5 In a large bowl, combine the fish, potatoes, and peppers. Pour half the dressing over the salad and toss gently. Chill for up to 2 hours.

6 Toss with the remaining dressing and sprinkle with the remaining parsley just before serving.

Salmon Carpaccio

CARPACCIO DI SALMONE

SALAD

4 cups arugula or watercress

2 tablespoons olive oil

1 tablespoon fresh lemon juice

Salt and freshly ground pepper, to taste

1 tablespoon olive oil

1 pound salmon fillet, cut into thin slices

Salt and freshly ground pepper, to taste

1 Rinse the arugula in several changes of cool water. Pinch off the tough stems and dry the leaves thoroughly. Cut into 1-inch pieces and place them in a bowl. Just before cooking the fish, whisk together the olive oil, lemon juice, salt, and pepper. Set aside.

2 Heat the olive oil in a large nonstick skillet over high heat. Add enough fish to make a single layer. Cook until lightly browned on the bottom yet still undercooked on top, about 1 minute. With a large spatula, remove the salmon from the skillet and turn it, browned side up, onto a large serving platter. Sprinkle with salt and pepper. Cook the remaining salmon in the same way and add it to the platter.

3 Toss the arugula with the dressing. Pile the salad on top of the salmon. Serve immediately.

Carpaccio is said to have been invented at Harry's Bar in Venice. Owner Giuseppe Cipriani came up with the recipe to please an important and fussy client who was on a special diet. He had his chef thinly slice the finest raw beef and dress the slices with a caper and mayonnaise sauce. He named it carpaccio after the famous artist because the colors resembled those he had seen in his paintings.

Today there are many variations made with meat, fish, or vegetables. The only thing they seem to have in common is that the ingredients are thinly sliced and sometimes raw or only partly cooked. In this version, thin slices of browned salmon fillet are topped with a lemony arugula salad.

Pike, a freshwater fish, is usually served this way in Modena in the Lombardy region of northern Italy, but any firm-fleshed fish will do. I like salmon fillets: They are always available, and they look pretty with the green sauce.

The fish should be served at room temperature. It can be accompanied by slabs of hot grilled polenta (see page 192), though boiled new potatoes are also good. Pour a fresh white wine such as an Italian sauvignon blanc. Puiatti is an excellent producer from the region of Friuli-Venezia-Giulia.

Poached Salmon in Green Sauce

SALMONE IN SALSA VERDE

1 cup dry white wine

2 carrots, sliced

1 celery rib, sliced

1 small onion, sliced

5 whole peppercorns

2 whole cloves

1 piece cinnamon stick (about 2^1/$_2$ inches)

Coarse salt, to taste

1^1/$_2$ pounds pike, salmon, red snapper, or grouper fillets

GREEN SAUCE

^{1}/$_4$ cup extra virgin olive oil

4 anchovy fillets

2 garlic cloves, minced

3 tablespoons chopped fresh parsley

^{1}/$_4$ cup minced onion

^{1}/$_4$ cup finely chopped pickled pepper

2 tablespoons chopped drained and rinsed capers

2 tablespoons white wine vinegar

1 teaspoon grated lemon zest

1 In a deep skillet, combine the wine, carrots, celery, onion, peppercorns, cloves, cinnamon, and salt to taste. Add cold water to a depth of 1 inch. Bring the liquid to a simmer and cook for 25 minutes.

2 Cut the fish into 2 or 3 pieces that will fit in the pan without overlapping. Place them in the pan. If the liquid does not completely cover the fish, add more water. Cover the pan and cook until the fish is just opaque when cut at the thickest point, 8 to 10 minutes, de-

pending on the thickness of the fish. With a slotted spoon, remove the fish from the pan. Discard the poaching liquid and vegetables.

3 In a small saucepan over low heat, heat the oil with the anchovies and garlic. Cook, stirring, until the anchovies are dissolved. Add 2 tablespoons of the parsley and the remaining sauce ingredients except the lemon zest and cook for 2 minutes more.

4 Remove the skin and any bones from the fish. Cut or break the fish into 1-inch pieces and place them on a serving platter. Sprinkle the fish with the lemon zest and pour the sauce evenly over it.

5 Scatter the remaining parsley over all and serve at room temperature.

Salmon with Cabbage and Pancetta

SALMONE AL CAVOLO STUFATO

1/2 small head of cabbage, preferably savoy

2 tablespoons olive oil

1 tablespoon unsalted butter

1 medium onion, chopped

2 ounces thickly sliced pancetta, cut into narrow strips

1 garlic clove, finely chopped

2 tablespoons white wine vinegar

Salt and freshly ground pepper, to taste

4 thick slices salmon fillet, with skin

1 Rinse the cabbage and trim away the core. Cut the cabbage into thin strips. You should have about 8 cups, loosely packed.

2 In a large skillet over medium heat, combine the oil, butter, and onion. Cook until the onion is tender, about 5 minutes. Add the pancetta and cook for 2 minutes, or until it is golden. Add the garlic and cook for 1 minute more. Stir in the cabbage, 1/2 cup water, vinegar, salt, and pepper. Turn the heat to low. Cover and cook, stirring occasionally, for 20 minutes, or until the cabbage is tender.

SERVES 4

Italian cooks are as interested in foreign cuisines as Americans are. Their food and wine magazines feature Tex-Mex and Asian recipes as well as Italian. I suspect that this recipe has crossed the Atlantic both ways several times since I have seen similar French and American recipes. But I like this Italian interpretation, which I tasted in Milan made with pancetta and savoy cabbage, the kind with crinkly leaves. It has a milder flavor and is more tender than ordinary cabbage. Napa cabbage can also be used. Cooking the salmon with the skin side toward the heat keeps the flesh moist while the skin gets crisp.

3 Preheat the broiler or grill. Oil the grill rack.

4 Run your fingertips over the salmon and remove any bones. Sprinkle with salt and pepper. Place the salmon on the grill rack with the skin side facing the source of the heat. Cook the salmon for 5 to 8 minutes, depending on the thickness of the fillets, or until it is almost cooked through. The flesh should remain slightly translucent in the center. There is no need to turn the fish.

5 Arrange the cabbage and pancetta on 4 plates. Top with the salmon, skin side down, and serve immediately.

Crazy water is a Neapolitan term for a poaching liquid used to cook several different foods, though fish is the most common. It is a light broth made by simmering the classic Neapolitan ingredients—garlic, parsley, tomatoes, and wine—in water. Some cooks say that sea water is essential. The first cookbook to mention *acqua pazza* was written by Ippolito Cavalcanti, Duke of Buonvicino, more than 150 years ago. The preparation is still very much in use today.

In this recipe, the whole fish is cooked in the broth. It makes a dramatic presentation, but if you do not feel comfortable filleting the cooked fish, use fillets. Just be sure to choose firm fillets that will not break apart, such as snapper, mahi-mahi, or halibut.

Sea Bass in Crazy Water

SPIGOLA ALL'ACQUA PAZZA

¹/₄ cup olive oil

2 garlic cloves, finely chopped

2 tablespoons chopped fresh parsley

1 large tomato, peeled, seeded, and chopped, or 1 cup coarsely chopped Roma or plum tomatoes

1 cup dry white wine

Pinch of crushed red pepper

Coarse salt, to taste

1 sea bass or red snapper, dressed with head and tail intact (about 2 pounds)

Fresh parsley leaves, for garnish

1 In a skillet or saucepan just large enough to hold the fish, combine the oil, garlic, chopped parsley, tomato, wine, crushed red pepper, and salt. Add water to reach a depth of 1 inch. Bring the mixture to a boil over medium heat. Reduce the heat to low and simmer for 15 minutes.

2 Place the fish in the pan. Baste it with the broth. Cover the pan and cook for 8 to 10 minutes, or until the fish is opaque when cut near the bone.

3 With a large metal spatula, transfer the fish to a deep serving platter. Spoon on some of the cooking juices and garnish with parsley leaves. Fillet the fish and serve it in shallow soup plates with fish broth spooned over each portion.

Roasted Red Snapper with Green Olives

PESCE AL FORNO CON OLIVE VERDE

2 red snappers, pompano or sea bass, dressed (about 2 pounds each)

2 garlic cloves, finely chopped

1/2 cup fresh parsley leaves

1/4 cup olive oil

1/4 cup white wine vinegar

Salt and freshly ground pepper, to taste

1 cup green olives, pitted and chopped

2 tablespoons chopped fresh parsley

1 Preheat the oven to 400°F. Oil a roasting pan just large enough to hold the fish.

2 Rinse the fish well and pat dry with paper towels. Place the fish side by side in the pan. Stuff the fish with the garlic and parsley leaves. Drizzle with olive oil and vinegar and sprinkle with salt and pepper. Scatter the olives over the fish.

3 Roast the fish, basting once or twice, for 25 minutes, or until the flesh near the bone is just barely opaque.

4 Transfer the fish to a serving platter. Pour the pan juices over the fish and sprinkle with the chopped parsley.

5 Serve immediately.

SERVES 4 TO 6

Though all olives are green to start with, they gradually darken and turn black as they ripen. Some olive varieties taste best when they are picked green, others when black or fully ripe. Green olives contain less oil than black olives, and their flesh is firmer. Since they are also milder, they complement the delicate flavors of the fresh fish in this recipe.

Ask the fish seller to "dress" the fish for you, meaning the fish will be scaled and gutted, the gills and fins removed, and the tail trimmed. Removing the head is optional. In Italy it is left on.

Carlo Mastroberardino smiled knowingly when I told him that I had fallen in love with Naples. Carlo comes from nearby Atripalda, where his family makes some of the finest wines in all of Italy. He said he finds that many visitors react the same way.

Carlo and his wife Kelle enjoy cooking and matching Mastroberardino wines to food. Kelle, who is an American, is just as frustrated about getting American ingredients in Italy as we are about getting just the right Italian ingredients here—maybe even more so. She substitutes smoked pancetta for American-style bacon, but finding the right variety of potatoes for baking still eludes her.

Kelle is very enthusiastic about the Mastroberardino family's traditional recipes, and she gave me several from her collection including this one. Carlo suggests serving this dish with a dry white wine such as his Fiano di Avellino.

Swordfish in a Spicy Sauce

PESCE SPADA IN SALSA PICCANTE

3 tablespoons olive oil

4 swordfish, tuna, or shark steaks, about $3/4$ inch thick

2 garlic cloves, chopped

$1/2$ cup dry white wine

2 cups peeled, seeded, and chopped fresh tomatoes or chopped canned Italian tomatoes with their juice

$1/2$ cup imported black olives, such as Gaeta or kalamata, pitted and coarsely chopped

2 tablespoons drained capers, chopped

4 anchovy fillets, chopped

2 tablespoons chopped fresh parsley

Pinch of crushed red pepper

Salt and freshly ground black pepper, to taste

1 In a large skillet over high heat, heat the oil. Pat the swordfish steaks dry with paper towels. Slip them into the hot oil and brown on both sides. Remove the steaks to a plate.

2 Reduce the heat to medium. Add the garlic to the skillet and cook for 30 seconds. Add the wine and bring it to a simmer. Cook until most of the liquid evaporates. Add the tomatoes and cook, stirring occasionally, until the tomatoes are slightly thickened, about 10 minutes. Stir in the olives, capers, anchovies, 1 tablespoon of the parsley, the red pepper, salt, and black pepper. Cook over low heat for 5 minutes.

3 Return the fish steaks to the skillet and baste them with the sauce. Cook for 1 to 2 minutes more, or just until slightly pink in the center.

4 Transfer the fish to a large serving platter. Spoon on the sauce and sprinkle with the remaining parsley. Serve immediately.

Swordfish with Orange Sauce

PESCE SPADA ALL'ARANCIA

2 large navel oranges

Flour

4 swordfish or shark steaks, about $^1/_2$ inch thick

2 tablespoons olive oil

Salt and freshly ground pepper, to taste

$^1/_2$ cup chicken broth

2 bay leaves

$^1/_8$ teaspoon ground cloves

1 Grate the zest of one of the oranges and squeeze the juice from both. There should be 1 teaspoon of grated zest and $^1/_2$ cup juice. Set aside.

2 Spread the flour on a piece of wax paper. Lightly dip the swordfish in the flour, shaking off the excess.

3 In a large skillet over medium heat, heat the oil. Add the swordfish and cook for 2 minutes on each side, or until golden. Sprinkle with salt and pepper. Remove the swordfish from the pan and keep warm. Pour off the oil and wipe out the pan.

4 Add the broth, bay leaves, and cloves. Cook for 5 minutes, or until the broth is reduced to 3 tablespoons. Stir in the orange juice and zest and bring to a simmer. Add the swordfish and baste once or twice with the orange sauce.

5 Serve immediately.

SERVES 4

Meaty swordfish steaks in a light orange sauce are quick to prepare when you have little time for cooking. Serve this with Escarole with Raisins and Garlic (page 293). If you have a bit more time, Risotto with Fava Beans and Fennel (page 180) would be an excellent first course.

"We were a Wonder Bread and Cheez-Whiz-eating family. The biggest place that I always notice I'm different from my sisters is food—that I know about arugula, that I know about buffalo mozzarella. I never try to pretend that I grew up with all of that. But I could, and no one would know . . . Arugula is how I define my cities. I go to the grocery store, and either you can get arugula or you can't. And I really don't want to be anywhere you can't."

Cindy Crawford, *Bazaar* magazine, quoted in *The San Francisco Chronicle*

In southern Italy, thin slices of swordfish are cut and pounded into thin cutlets, much as veal for scaloppine. The cutlets are rolled around a filling of tomatoes, seasoned bread crumbs, or seafood. The rolls are skewered, then grilled or broiled.

If your fish seller is not willing to prepare the cutlets, you will probably have to do it yourself. Have the steaks sliced as thin as possible, less than half an inch thick. Trim off the skin. Place a piece of fish between two sheets of plastic wrap and pound gently to flatten it to an even quarter of an inch thickness. Handle the fish carefully so it does not break apart. An inexpensive plumber's rubber mallet, sold in most hardware stores, is perfect for flattening out the fish.

Using two skewers side by side helps to secure the rolls without their breaking or unrolling, a clever trick I learned from Mario Lo Menzo, the Tasca family chef at the Regaleali wine estate. For best results use flat metal skewers. You will need at least four skewers, depending on their length, for this recipe.

These crusty fish rolls call for some kind of salad. If ripe tomatoes are available, combine them with sweet onions, olive oil, and basil or serve a mixed green salad. For a mixed seafood grill, serve the swordfish rolls along with skewered shrimp (see page 219).

Swordfish Rolls

SPIEDINI DI PESCE SPADA

1 pound swordfish, pounded as described above to 1/4 inch thickness

1/2 cup bread crumbs, toasted

1/4 cup grated Parmigiano-Reggiano

2 tablespoons chopped drained capers

2 tablespoons chopped fresh parsley

1 large garlic clove, very finely chopped

Salt and freshly ground pepper, to taste

3 tablespoons olive oil

1 tablespoon fresh lemon juice

Lemon wedges, for garnish

1 Preheat the broiler or grill.

2 Cut each piece of swordfish into 2 × 3-inch rectangles. You should have 8 swordfish cutlets.

3 Combine the bread crumbs, cheese, capers, parsley, garlic, salt, and pepper. Add 2 tablespoons of the olive oil and mix well. Taste the mixture for seasoning.

4 Place 1 tablespoon of the crumb mixture at 1 end of a piece of fish. Roll up the slice to enclose the filling completely. Continue until all are done.

5 Combine the remaining oil and lemon juice. Brush over the rolls. Sprinkle the rolls with the remaining bread crumb mixture.

6 With one hand, hold 2 skewers parallel to each other about 1 inch apart. Thread the rolls on the skewers, pressing the rolls together until they are lightly touching.

7 Grill the fish 3 to 4 minutes on each side, or until the crumbs are browned and the fish feels just firm to the touch. Do not overcook.

8 Slide the rolls off the skewers. Serve hot with lemon wedges.

To make ahead: The rolls can be prepared through Step 6 up to 2 hours before serving. Cover and refrigerate until ready to cook.

Tuna Steaks with Mixed Mushrooms

BISTECCHE DI TONNO AI FUNGHI

8 ounces white mushrooms

4 ounces shiitake, stems removed, or other mushrooms

4 tuna steaks, about 3/4 inch thick

1 tablespoon chopped fresh rosemary leaves or 1 teaspoon dried rosemary, crumbled

Salt and freshly ground pepper, to taste

2 tablespoons olive oil

2 tablespoons unsalted butter

1 garlic clove, finely chopped

Pinch of dried marjoram

1/2 cup dry white wine

2 tablespoons chopped fresh parsley

1 Wipe the mushrooms clean with a damp paper towel. Cut the white mushrooms and shiitake caps into thin slices.

2 Sprinkle the tuna with rosemary, salt, and pepper.

3 In a skillet large enough to hold all of the tuna comfortably in 1 layer, heat 1 tablespoon of the olive oil over medium heat. Add the tuna and cook for 1 to 2 minutes on each side, or until browned. Remove the tuna steaks to a platter.

4 Add the remaining tablespoon of oil and the butter. When the butter is melted, add the mushrooms, garlic, marjoram, salt, and pepper. Cook, stirring frequently, until the juices have evaporated

SERVES 4

Nothing quite comes up to a thick, juicy beefsteak topped with buttery sautéed mushrooms. Much the same effect is created in this recipe with thick tuna slices standing in for the beefsteak. The advantage here is that tuna is much lighter than beef. Mix several mushroom varieties to make the dish more interesting.

and the mushrooms are browned, about 10 minutes. Add the wine and parsley. Bring to a simmer and cook for 1 minute.

5   Push the mushrooms to 1 side and return the tuna to the skillet. Spoon the mushrooms over the tuna. Cook for 1 to 2 minutes for medium rare, or until the tuna is done to taste. Do not overcook.

6   Transfer the tuna steaks to a serving platter and top with the mushrooms. Serve immediately.

Trout in Rosé Wine Sauce

TROTA IN SALSA PICEDO

¹/₄ cup all-purpose flour
Salt and freshly ground pepper, to taste
4 small salmon trout or brook trout fillets, skinned (about
    1¹/₂ pounds)
4 tablespoons extra virgin olive oil
¹/₂ cup chiaretto di Picedo or other dry rosé wine
2 medium-size ripe tomatoes, peeled, seeded, and chopped
2 tablespoons small capers, drained and rinsed
15 fresh basil leaves, torn into pieces

1   On a piece of wax paper, combine the flour with salt and pepper. Lightly dredge the trout in the flour mixture, shaking off the excess.

2   In a large skillet over medium heat, heat 2 tablespoons of the olive oil. Add the trout, skin side up, in a single layer. Cook until lightly browned, about 2 minutes. Carefully turn the fillets with a slotted spatula. Cook for 2 to 3 minutes more, or until barely cooked through. Transfer to a plate and keep warm.

3   Add the wine to the skillet and simmer, scraping the pan with a wooden spoon, until most of the liquid has evaporated. Add the tomatoes, capers, basil, salt, and pepper. Simmer for 1 minute. Remove from the heat and stir in the remaining oil.

4   Pour the sauce over the fish and serve immediately.

SERVES 4

Chiaretto di Picedo is a light rosé wine produced in the area around Lake Garda. Alberto Rossi of the Hotel/Restaurant Laurin said that the chef devised this recipe as a way to highlight the local wine and fresh trout from the lake. Any rosé will do. Serve the rest of the wine lightly chilled with the fish.

Hotel/Restaurant Laurin
Viale Landi, 9
Salò (Lombardy)

A Fresh Taste of Italy

Tuna Stew with Beans

TONNO IN UMIDO CON FAGIOLI

2 tuna steaks, at least 1 inch thick (about 1¹/₄ pounds)

2 tablespoons olive oil

Salt and freshly ground pepper, to taste

1 large red bell pepper, seeded and cut into 1-inch pieces

1 medium-size ripe tomato, cored and diced

1 large garlic clove, finely chopped

1 teaspoon chopped fresh rosemary leaves

2 cups cooked cannellini beans, drained, or 1 can (16 ounces) cannellini beans, rinsed and drained

1   Trim dark brown portions from the tuna steaks. Cut them into 1¹/₂ inch chunks. Pat the pieces dry with paper towels.

2   Heat the oil in a large skillet over medium heat. When it is hot, add the tuna pieces. Cook, turning the pieces occasionally, until lightly browned on all sides. Transfer the pieces to a plate. Sprinkle with salt and pepper.

3   Add the bell pepper to the skillet and cook, stirring occasionally, until it begins to brown, about 10 minutes. Add the tomato, garlic, rosemary, salt, and pepper. Bring to a simmer. Add the beans, cover, and reduce the heat to low. Cook for 10 minutes.

4   Stir in the tuna and cook for 2 minutes more, or until the tuna is slightly pink in the center.

5   Serve immediately.

SERVES 4

If you can make a stew with beef or lamb, why not one with tuna? In this recipe, the tuna is treated much like meat. Since tuna, unlike meat, does not have muscles that need tenderizing, it requires far less cooking. This hearty stew can be ready to serve in less than half an hour.

Until I started to work on this book, I didn't realize how well the flavors and textures of seafood and legumes complement each other and how frequently they are paired in Italian cooking. Try Clam and Lentil Soup (page 98), Warm Bean Salad with Grilled Shrimp (page 54), and Cavatelli with Mussels, Beans, and Tomatoes (page 147).

Have you ever wished you had a private chef to cook just for you? The closest I have ever come to fulfilling that dream was at a small restaurant not far from the northern tip of Lake Garda. On the side of a hill in the tiny town of Nago stands a small stone lookout tower that was built centuries ago. Today it is the home of Da Sergio, an elegant restaurant. One Sunday, my husband and I and two friends made reservations for lunch. We did not realize that the restaurant served only fish, which one of our guests could not eat in any form. Sergio was dismayed, but he offered to prepare one vegetarian and three fish meals. He would choose the menu. We agreed.

Sergio told us that he makes all the first and second courses while his wife prepares all the desserts and bakes all the bread. That day, he was like a one-man band, not just cooking our improvised meal, but serving it along with a series of appropriate wines, and clearing and resetting the table after each course. Fortunately, we were the only customers. This simple dish of fish fillets braised with fennel, leeks, and sun-dried tomatoes was the centerpiece.

Da Sergio
Nago (Trentino-Alto Adige)

Turbot with Fennel and Dried Tomatoes

FILETTI DI PESCE BIANCO CON FINOCCHIO E PUMATE

1 medium fennel bulb

2 small leeks

6 dried tomatoes, cut into thin strips

1/2 cup dry white wine

Salt and freshly ground pepper, to taste

1 pound turbot, monkfish, or other firm-fleshed white fish fillets

2 tablespoons fresh lemon juice

2 tablespoons extra virgin olive oil

2 tablespoons chopped fresh parsley

1 Trim the fennel stalks to the point where the bulb becomes rounded. Pare off any bruised or brown spots. Cut the bulb lengthwise into quarters and remove the core. Thinly slice the fennel.

2 Trim the leeks of the root ends and all but 1 or 2 inches of green. Cut the leeks lengthwise in half and wash very thoroughly between each layer. Cut the leeks crosswise into thin slices.

3 Put the leeks, fennel, dried tomatoes, and wine in a large skillet. Season to taste with salt and pepper. Cover and bring to a simmer. Cook until the fennel is crisp-tender, about 10 minutes.

4 Cut the fish into 4 pieces. Sprinkle with the lemon juice, salt, and pepper. Place the fish over the vegetables, basting with some of the juices and vegetables. Drizzle with the oil. Sprinkle with the parsley.

5 Cover the skillet. Cook until the fish is barely opaque in the center, about 5 minutes, depending on the thickness of the fish.

6 Serve immediately.

Brodetto, Grado Style

BRODETTO GRADESE

4 garlic cloves, peeled

3 tablespoons olive oil

1¹/₂ pounds assorted firm-fleshed fish, such as halibut steaks,
*   monkfish, tilefish, skinned, boned, and cut into 2-inch chunks,*
*   or large sea scallops*

Salt and freshly ground pepper, to taste

¹/₃ cup white wine vinegar

1 Lightly crush the garlic cloves with the side of a heavy chef's knife.

2 In a large skillet over medium heat, cook the garlic in the oil until the garlic is a rich brown color. Remove with a slotted spoon. Pat the seafood chunks dry with paper towels and add them to the skillet. Sprinkle with salt and pepper. When the fish is brown and crusty on 1 side, about 3 minutes, turn the pieces over and add the vinegar and ¹/₃ cup water. Bring the liquid to a boil and cook until it is slightly reduced and the fish is just opaque in the center.

3 Serve immediately.

SERVES 4

One evening we were sitting in the small covered courtyard of a popular restaurant in the beach resort town of Grado, east of Venice, when suddenly the sharp aroma of browning garlic and vinegar wafted through the air. Andrea Felluga, the son of Livio Felluga, one of the Friuli region's outstanding winemakers and our host, sniffed the air, smiled, and asked: "Do you smell that? It means someone is making *brodetto.*" Brodetto is Grado's classic white fish stew. Unlike other stews of the same name from elsewhere in Italy, this brodetto does not contain tomatoes or spices. The only ingredients are oil, garlic, vinegar, water, and seafood. As a result, the flavors are uncomplicated. This is not a saucy stew at all—very little liquid is left when the fish is cooked.

For best results, use several types of firm fish or seafood. Large sea scallops are especially good. Brodetto is usually served with soft polenta made without butter or cheese.

At Al Cavallino Bianco Restaurant in Pollesine Parmense outside of Parma, I tasted this unusual fish salad containing shavings of Parmigiano-Reggiano. Since Italians usually shy away from combining fish and cheese, especially in northern Italy, I found the combination surprising. But Luciano Spigaroli who owns the restaurant with his brother Massimo, who is the chef, told me that the recipe is an authentic one that dates back to the heyday of the royal Farnese family in the sixteenth century. Perhaps it was a show of wealth for the family to be able to serve both fish and cheese together, and the concept of keeping the two separate developed sometime later.

Al Cavallino Bianco
Via Sbrisi, 2
Polesine Parmense (Emilia-Romagna)

Fish Salad in the Manner of the Farnese Dukes

INSALATA DI PESCE IN SALSA FARNESE

1 medium onion, coarsely chopped

1 medium carrot, coarsely chopped

2 celery ribs with leaves, coarsely chopped

1 bay leaf

5 peppercorns

Salt, to taste

1 pound pike fillets or other firm-fleshed white fish fillets, such as scrod or orange roughy

2 tablespoons extra virgin olive oil

2 tablespoons fresh lemon juice

2 tablespoons chopped Italian flat-leaf parsley

Freshly ground pepper, to taste

About 3 ounces Parmigiano-Reggiano in 1 piece

1 In a saucepan large enough to hold the fish in a single layer, combine 2 quarts water, the onion, carrot, celery, bay leaf, and peppercorns. Bring to a simmer and cook until reduced by half. Strain and discard the vegetables. Return the liquid to the pan.

2 Bring the liquid to a simmer and add salt. Add the fish fillets and cook on low heat until the fish is just opaque, about 4 minutes, depending on the thickness of the fish. Remove the fish from the liquid with a slotted spatula. Place the fish on a serving plate and drain off any liquid that accumulates. Cut or break the fish into $1/2$-inch pieces.

3 In a small bowl, whisk together the olive oil, lemon juice, parsley, salt, and pepper. Pour the dressing over the fish.

4 With a swivel-blade vegetable peeler or paring knife, shave the Parmigiano-Reggiano into thin scales. Scatter the pieces over the fish. Serve at room temperature.

Seafood Couscous

CUSCUSU DI PESCE

1¹/₂ cups chicken or fish broth (optional)

1¹/₂ cups couscous

Salt

1 large onion, chopped

¹/₄ cup olive oil

2 garlic cloves, very finely chopped

1 bay leaf

*2 large tomatoes, peeled, seeded, and chopped, or 2 cups chopped
   canned Italian tomatoes with their juice*

4 tablespoons chopped Italian flat-leaf parsley

Pinch of ground cinnamon

Pinch of ground cloves

Pinch of freshly grated nutmeg

Pinch of saffron threads, crumbled

Pinch of cayenne

Salt and freshly ground pepper, to taste

*1¹/₂ pounds assorted firm-fleshed fish, such as swordfish, halibut,
   monkfish, or sea bass, and shellfish*

1 Bring 3 cups water or 1¹/₂ cups water and 1¹/₂ cups broth to a
boil. Place the couscous in a heatproof bowl, stir in the boiling liquid, and salt to taste. Cover and let stand for 10 minutes, or until all
of the liquid is absorbed. Fluff the couscous with a fork.

2 In a pot large enough to hold the fish in a single layer, cook the
onion in the oil over medium heat until tender, about 5 minutes.
Add the garlic and bay leaf and cook for 1 minute more. Add the
tomatoes, 2 tablespoons of the parsley, the cinnamon, cloves, nutmeg, saffron, and cayenne. Cook for 5 minutes. Add 2 cups water
and salt and pepper. Bring to a simmer.

3 Remove any skin or bones from the fish. Cut the fish into 2-inch

The Arabs, who ruled Sicily
from 827 to 1061 A.D., left
behind a legacy of art, culture,
and food. One such food is couscous, a tiny, bead-like pasta, most
frequently associated with the
lamb and vegetable dish of North
Africa. The Sicilian interpretation, made in the area around
Trapani on the western coast of
the island, contains different
kinds of fish simmered in a tasty
broth flavored with spices, which
give the dish an exotic taste and
tantalizing aroma. At one time,
cooks would make the beads of
couscous from scratch, rubbing a
combination of coarse and fine
semolina flour mixed with water
and saffron between their fingers.
The pasta beads were dried, then
cooked in a kind of colander
called a *pignatta di cuscusu* placed
over steaming broth. Today cooks
everywhere use precooked couscous to save time.

Use a variety of fish in this
recipe or just one, as you prefer.
Practically any fish will do, with
the exception of such very tender
fish as sole or flounder, which
will not hold their shape when
cooked. Shrimp or sea scallops
also are good but add them only
during the last five minutes of
cooking.

chunks. Add the fish to the pot. Cover and cook for 5 to 10 minutes, or until the fish is just cooked. With a slotted spoon, remove the fish to a warm plate. Cover and keep warm.

4 Add the couscous to the pot. Cover and cook for 5 minutes, or until hot. Taste for seasoning.

5 Transfer the couscous to a serving platter. Top with the fish. Sprinkle with the remaining parsley and serve immediately.

Stewed Baby Octopus

POLPETTI AFFOGATI

2 pounds cleaned baby octopus
2 cups peeled, seeded, and chopped fresh tomatoes, or chopped
    canned Italian tomatoes
1/4 cup olive oil
4 tablespoons chopped Italian flat-leaf parsley
2 large garlic cloves, finely chopped
1/2 teaspoon crushed red pepper, or to taste
Salt and freshly ground black pepper, to taste
16 slices Italian or French bread, toasted

1 Rinse the octopus and drain well. Remove the hard beak, if any, at the base of the tentacles.

2 In a large heavy saucepan, combine the octopus, tomatoes, olive oil, 3 tablespoons of the parsley, the garlic, red pepper, salt, and black pepper. Bring to a simmer. Cover the pot and cook on a very low flame, stirring occasionally, for 45 minutes. Uncover and cook for 15 minutes more, or until the sauce is thickened and the octopus is tender when pierced with a fork.

3 Place 2 slices of toast on each of 4 plates. Top with the stewed octopus and sauce. Sprinkle with the remaining parsley and serve.

SERVES 8

On my first visit to Sicily, I ordered *fritto misto,* a mix of small fish and seafood dipped in a thin flour coating and then fried until crisp. A platter arrived heaped with greaseless small fish and seafood including sardines, whitebait, shrimps, calamari, and tiny octopus, *polpetti.* Both large and small octopus are frequently used in Italian seafood stews and salads, but I was shocked to discover that this one still contained the ink sac. When I stuck my fork in, the black ink spurted out across the plate!

The ink from octopus and squid is completely edible. Sicilian cooks have access to freshly caught octopus and squid, and they like to leave the ink with its surprisingly fresh, briny flavor inside as an added flavoring.

In the United States, Italian, Spanish, Greek, and Asian fish markets sell baby octopus—without the ink sacs. Octopus marinated with olive oil, lemon juice, and garlic and grilled has become quite trendy in many restaurants here. In this recipe, little octopus are stewed with tomatoes and garlic and served over crisp slices of Italian bread,

To make ahead: The stew can be made up to 24 hours before serving. Cook the stew through Step 2. Let it cool, then cover and refrigerate until ready to serve. Reheat gently and serve with the toast as described in Step 3.

Grilled Stuffed Calamari

CALAMARI RIPIENI

1 pound cleaned medium-size squid, each about 5 inches

1/2 cup fine dry bread crumbs

5 tablespoons olive oil

2 tablespoons freshly grated pecorino romano

2 tablespoons finely chopped fresh parsley

2 garlic cloves, finely chopped

Salt and freshly ground pepper, to taste

Lemon wedges

1 Rinse the squid inside and out under cold running water. Make sure that the sacs are empty of sand and the jelly-like viscera. If they seem sandy, nick a small cut in the pointed end and flush them out with cool water. Rinse the tentacles and check to see that the beak, a hard round object at the base, has been removed.

2 Preheat the broiler or grill.

3 Combine the bread crumbs, 3 tablespoons of the olive oil, cheese, parsley, garlic, salt, and pepper. Use a small spoon to stuff the mixture loosely into the sacs of the squid. Do not pack the crumbs in tight. Tuck the base of the tentacles into the tubes and secure them with a wooden pick. Roll the calamari in the remaining oil.

4 Grill about 3 inches from the flame until browned, about 5 minutes on each side. Do not overcook or the squid will be tough.

5 Serve immediately with lemon wedges.

though polenta can be substituted.

If baby octopus are not available, calamari can also be prepared this way. Clean them and cut them into rings as described on page 220.

SERVES 3 TO 4

Calamari, the Italian name for squid, become crisp and brown when cooked on a very hot barbecue grill or broiler. The tentacles, which I think are the best part, open like flowers. You will need no more than two or three teaspoons of filling for each squid since the sacs shrink as they cook. Don't overstuff them or the filling will ooze out.

Most fish markets sell squid already cleaned, but few do a thorough job of it. Look them over carefully to be sure they are ready for cooking.

A tiella is a shallow pottery casserole dish from Puglia in southern Italy. It lends its name to foods cooked in it, such as this combination of mussels, rice, tomatoes, and potatoes. It is similar to a Spanish paella—which is also made with rice, vegetables, and seafood and cooked in a wide, shallow pan. The similarities may be more than a coincidence, since the Spanish ruled southern Italy during the seventeenth century and influenced the food and language.

Cut the potatoes as thin as possible so that they will be cooked when the rice is finished.

Tiella of Rice and Mussels

TIELLA DI RISO E COZZE

3 pounds mussels

3 medium potatoes, peeled and very thinly sliced

2 medium onions, thinly sliced

1¼ cups Arborio or other medium-grain rice

2 cups chopped canned Italian tomatoes with their juice

1 garlic clove, finely chopped

½ cup chopped fresh parsley

½ cup freshly grated pecorino romano

Salt and freshly ground pepper, to taste

4 tablespoons olive oil

1 About 1 hour before you plan to cook the mussels, scrub them and soak them in a bowl of cold water. Scape off any barnacles. Discard any mussels that do not close tightly or that have cracked shells.

2 Place the mussels in a large pot over medium heat. Cover and cook until the mussels open, about 5 minutes. Remove the mussels from the pot. Shell the mussels reserving their liquid. To remove any traces of sand or shells, strain the liquid through a sieve lined with dampened cheesecloth or a paper coffee filter. Pour the liquid into a measuring cup and add enough water to equal 3 cups. Set aside.

3 Preheat the oven to 400°F. Oil a shallow 3-quart flameproof casserole, such as a paella pan.

4 Make a layer of half of the potatoes and half of the onions. Pour the rice evenly on top. Top with half of the tomatoes, garlic, parsley, and cheese. Sprinkle with salt and pepper. Arrange the mussels on top and drizzle with 2 tablespoons of the olive oil.

5 Make a second layer with the remaining potatoes, onions, tomatoes, garlic, parsley, and cheese. Drizzle with remaining 2 tablespoons of the olive oil and sprinkle with salt and pepper.

6 Pour the mussel liquid around the side being careful not to disturb the layers.

7 Place the casserole on top of the stove and bring the liquid to a simmer. Cover tightly with foil and bake for 20 minutes. Remove from the oven and let stand for 10 minutes before serving. Test the potatoes with a sharp knife to be sure they are tender. If not, leave the casserole covered for 5 minutes more.

8 Serve hot or warm.

Grilled Jumbo Shrimp with Sage and Pancetta

GAMBERONI ALLA GRIGLIA

12 thin slices pancetta
12 jumbo shrimps, peeled and deveined
12 fresh sage leaves

1 Preheat the broiler or grill.

2 Unroll the pancetta slices and wind each slice around a shrimp. Tuck a sage leaf between the shrimp and pancetta. Thread 2 or 3 shrimps on each skewer.

3 Place the skewers on the grill rack or broiler pan about 4 inches from the source of the heat. Cook for 2 to 3 minutes on each side, or until the shrimps are cooked through and the pancetta is crisp.

4 Serve immediately.

SERVES 6

The Antica Osteria del Bai is located in a little stone building that was once a lookout post for the nearby port of Genoa. From the beach below, Garibaldi and his thousand, as his troops were called, embarked on their heroic journey south that eventually led to the unification of Italy. The age-old look of the building has been carefully preserved even to the maritime pines sprouting among its crumbling roof tiles. Inside, though, the restaurant is quite modern. We feasted on fat, juicy shrimps wrapped in a jacket of pancetta and cooked on the grill. Serve these at a barbecue with Green Bean, Cucumber, and Tomato Salad (page 295) and the Spring Potato and Watercress Salad with Horseradish (page 300). Terre Alte, a dry complex white wine from Livio Felluga, is perfect with the shrimp.

Antica Osteria del Bai
Via Quarto, 12
Quarto dei Mille (Genoa)

Cherry tomatoes are used in this salad in Naples, but if the plum tomatoes or beefsteaks at your market look better, cut them into bite-size pieces and use them instead.

If you've ever eaten calamari, or squid, with the texture of rubber bands, it surely was overcooked. The secret to cooking squid without toughening it is to cook it either very quickly, one minute is sufficient, or very slowly, for at least twenty minutes. For salads, one minute of cooking is enough; for soups, stews, and pasta sauces, the squid needs twenty minutes or more.

Calamari and Tomato Salad

INSALATA DI CALAMARI E POMODORINI

1 pound cleaned squid

Salt

3 tablespoons extra virgin olive oil

2 to 3 tablespoons fresh lemon juice

1 small garlic clove, minced

Pinch of dried oregano

Freshly ground pepper, to taste

1 pint cherry tomatoes, halved

1 bunch of arugula, trimmed and cut into bite-size pieces
   (about 2 cups)

1 Rinse the squid and look them over carefully to be sure they have been well cleaned. Check to see that the beak, a hard round object, has been removed from the base of the tentacles and the jelly-like viscera removed from the body sacs. If they seem sandy, nick a small cut in the pointed end and flush them with running water. Cut the sacs crosswise into $1/2$-inch rings. If they are large, cut the tentacles in half through the base.

2 Bring a medium saucepan of water to a boil. Add the squid and salt. Cook for 1 minute, or until the squid are opaque. Immediately drain the squid and rinse them under cold water to stop the cooking. Drain well and pat dry.

3 In a large bowl, combine the squid with the olive oil, 2 tablespoons lemon juice, garlic, oregano, salt, and pepper. Toss well. Cover and chill for up to 2 hours.

4 Add the tomato halves and arugula. Toss well and taste for seasoning. Add a few more drops of lemon juice, if necessary.

5 Serve immediately.

Chicken and Other Birds ... Pollame

*A*DA BONI IS ITALY'S *Fanny Farmer. Her classic Italian cookbook,* Il Talismano della Felicità, *is full of advice and recipes from around the world, though it is perhaps a bit outdated. In the chapter on poultry, Boni advises the cook to start always by purchasing a very fresh chicken: "Open the beak of the animal and there must not be any bad odor. The eye must be still lively and not have a glassy expression." Good advice, no doubt, but it is not often that most of us meet a chicken face to face.*

Whenever I can, I buy chickens at my local farmers' market. The birds come from a farm on Long Island where they are allowed to wander around and eat what they please so that the meat becomes firm and tasty. These chickens are on the small side, and they are fairly lean, with just a small amount of fat to keep the meat moist as it cooks.

The northeastern Veneto region produces most of Italy's poultry. In addition to chicken, Italians use lots of other poultry, but I have limited the recipes in this chapter to chicken, capon, turkey, duck, and quail, because those we find here closely resemble their Italian counterparts.

Until I tasted quail in Italy, I never liked these little birds much because many American restaurants, influenced by *nouvelle cuisine,* served them rare. To me, they were undercooked, stringy, tough, and unpleasant. Italian-style quails are stewed with a little wine, tomato sauce, or broth, and the birds are cooked until they are well done and the meat is tender, flavorful, and almost falling from the bone. Another good way to prepare quail is to grill or barbecue it. The skin becomes brown and slightly crisp while the meat remains juicy. Since quails weigh only about four or five ounces each, you should count on two per serving. They are available fresh or frozen. I find the frozen ones are very reasonably priced and the quality is excellent. Sometimes you can find partly boned quails, which are especially good for grilling.

A Sad Day

Rossini claimed to have cried only twice in his adult life, "once when my mother died [and] once when I was on a boating party having lunch and a roasted chicken filled with truffles fell overboard."

A Fresh Taste of Italy

Basil and Garlic Roast Chicken

POLLO AL BASILICO E AGLIO

1 bunch of basil, rinsed and stemmed (about 1 cup leaves)

4 garlic cloves, minced

Salt and freshly ground pepper, to taste

2 tablespoons olive oil

1 chicken (about 3¹/₂ pounds)

¹/₂ cup dry white wine

¹/₂ cup chicken broth

1 Preheat the oven to 450°F.

2 Finely chop the basil with the garlic. Add salt and pepper and 1 tablespoon of the olive oil.

3 Rinse the chicken and pat it dry inside and out. Remove the excess fat from the cavity. Fold the wing tips behind the back. Loosen the skin around the breasts and legs. Stuff half the basil mixture under the skin of the chicken. Put the remainder inside the cavity. Tie the legs together. Brush the skin of the chicken with the remaining oil. Place the chicken breast side down in a roasting pan.

4 Roast for 20 minutes. Reduce the heat to 375°F. Turn the chicken breast side up. Roast for 45 to 60 minutes, or until the juices are clear when the thigh is pierced with a fork. Tip the chicken so the juices run into the pan. Transfer the chicken to a serving platter and keep it warm.

5 Spoon off the excess fat from the pan. Place the pan on top of the stove over medium heat. Add the wine and broth. Simmer for 2 minutes, or until the juices are slightly reduced.

6 Carve the chicken and serve with the sauce.

According to legend, Helena, mother of Emperor Constantine, was told in a dream that she would find the remains of the true cross in a place where the air was scented with perfume. Sure enough, she located the cross buried in a patch of basil.

I once read a decadent-sounding recipe where sliced black truffles are inserted under the skin of a chicken to perfume the flesh of the bird with the truffles' earthy aroma. The same method works well here, using a bunch of fresh basil and a generous amount of chopped garlic in place of the costly truffle.

We once rented a cottage for a month in the village of Bottai just outside of Florence. Before we arrived there, I fantasized about spending the mornings sightseeing and shopping in the local markets, and then cooking us a fine evening meal accompanied by wines acquired at the many nearby wineries.

We soon learned why Florence is called the "oven on the Arno" by local residents who flee to the seashore and the mountains during the summer, abandoning the city to tourists from all over the world. To make matters worse, there was a drought that year, and our adorable cottage frequently had no water. Several times during our stay we had to trudge over to the owner's nearby *casa* (or *hasa* as it is pronounced in Florentine dialect), to get a pail of water.

I did not do much cooking, but we did explore many off-the-beaten-track trattorias. The owner of the local Conad store, a kind of Tuscan 7-Eleven, directed us to a run-down looking farmhouse. Despite the unimpressive appearance of the place, the food was simple and homey. The highlight of our meal was this plump chicken flavored with garlic, herbs, and lemon.

Country-style Roast Chicken with Lemon, Sage, and Rosemary

POLLO ALLA PAESANA

1 chicken (about 3¹/₂ pounds)

3 large garlic cloves, finely chopped

3 tablespoons chopped fresh sage

2 tablespoons chopped fresh rosemary leaves

Salt and freshly ground pepper, to taste

¹/₂ large lemon, thinly sliced

2 tablespoons olive oil

¹/₂ cup dry white wine

2 tablespoons fresh lemon juice

¹/₄ cup chicken broth or water

1 Preheat the oven to 450°F.

2 Rinse the chicken and pat it dry. Remove the excess fat from the cavity. Combine the garlic, sage, rosemary, salt, and pepper. Place about three quarters of the herb mixture and all of the lemon slices inside the chicken. Truss the legs and tuck the wing tips behind the back. Combine the remaining herb mixture with the olive oil and rub the mixture over the skin. Place the chicken breast side down in a roasting pan.

3 Roast for 20 minutes. Reduce the heat to 375°F. Turn the chicken breast side up and roast until golden, 45 to 60 minutes more, basting occasionally with the pan juices. Combine the wine and lemon juice and pour it over the chicken. Cook for 10 minutes more or until the juices run clear when the thigh is pierced with a fork. Remove the chicken from the pan. Cover and keep warm.

4 Spoon off most of the fat from the pan. Place the pan on top of the stove and add the chicken broth. Bring to a simmer and cook, scraping the pan occasionally, until the liquid is reduced by half.

5 Carve the chicken and serve with the sauce.

Chicken Breasts with Gorgonzola

PETTI DI POLLO CON SALSA DI GORGONZOLA

2 whole boneless and skinless chicken breasts, split

1/3 cup all-purpose flour

Salt and freshly ground pepper, to taste

2 tablespoons unsalted butter

1 tablespoon olive oil

1/4 cup finely chopped shallots

1/4 cup chicken broth

1/4 cup dry white wine

4 ounces gorgonzola, preferably dolce, rind removed

1 Place the chicken breasts between 2 pieces of plastic wrap and pound gently with a rubber mallet or meat pounder to an even 1/4-inch thickness.

2 Combine the flour, salt, and pepper. Dip the chicken breasts in the mixture. Shake to remove excess.

3 In a large skillet over medium heat, heat the butter and olive oil. When the butter has melted, add the chicken and cook, turning once, until golden brown, about 4 minutes on each side. Remove the chicken to a plate and keep warm.

SERVES 4

Many years ago we stayed at a beautiful hotel on the shores of Lake Garda. Dinner was included in the price of the room, and we entered the formal dining room with its starched white tablecloths and silver place settings anticipating a fine meal. Unfortunately, the kitchen was not on a par with the rest of the hotel. As he removed our barely touched plates, the waiter asked if we would like some cheese. We said yes, and he brought us a slab of perfectly ripe gorgonzola and a bowl of pears. Charles brightened at the sight and ordered a bottle of Bertani Amarone, a big, hearty wine with a hint of dried fruit flavor, from a particularly fine vintage that he had spotted on the wine list. The wine and cheese were so good and perfectly matched that we ordered the same thing for dinner every night of our four-night stay.

Gorgonzola, an excellent dessert cheese, especially when paired with pears, fresh or dried figs, or walnuts, is also good for cooking, most commonly as a pasta sauce or in risotto (see page 173). Here it makes an elegant topping for boneless chicken breasts. Serve this with Glazed Mushrooms and Onions (page 297) and a steamed green vegetable such as peas or spinach.

4 Add the shallots to the skillet and cook for 1 minute. Stir in the broth and wine, scraping up the browned bits from the bottom of the pan. Cook for 1 minute, or until the liquid is slightly thickened. Reduce the heat to low. Return the chicken to the skillet and turn it in the sauce.

5 Cut the gorgonzola into 4 pieces and place it on top of the chicken. Cover the skillet and cook just until the cheese is slightly melted, 1 to 2 minutes. Serve immediately.

SERVES 4

Tuscans are known to serve beans with steak or grilled sausages, but this roast chicken on a bed of beans is inspired by a recipe from the Veneto, where beans are revered almost as much as they are in Tuscany. These flavorful, creamy beans are so good in fact, I often make them alone or as a side dish with other meats, such as pork chops or ribs. I serve this chicken with a red wine from the Veneto, such as Campo Fiorin from Masi.

Roast Chicken with Bean Sauce

POLLO ARROSTO CON SALSA DI FAGIOLI

1 chicken (about 3¹/₂ pounds)

2 tablespoons olive oil

Salt and freshly ground pepper, to taste

2 slices pancetta

2 garlic cloves, peeled

1 sprig of fresh rosemary

¹/₂ cup dry white wine

BEANS

2 tablespoons olive oil

1 medium onion, finely chopped

1 garlic clove, finely chopped

2 ounces sliced pancetta or sopressa salami, chopped

4 anchovy fillets, chopped

1 tablespoon chopped fresh parsley

2 tablespoons chopped fresh basil

1 sprig of fresh rosemary

4 cups cooked cannellini or Great Northern beans with their
liquid or 2 cans (16 ounces each), rinsed and drained

Salt and freshly ground pepper, to taste

1   Preheat the oven to 450°F.

2   Rinse the chicken and pat it dry. Remove the excess fat from the cavity. Rub the chicken all over with the olive oil. Sprinkle inside and out with salt and pepper. Place the pancetta, garlic, and rosemary inside the bird. Truss the legs and fold the wing tips behind the back. Place the chicken breast side down on a rack in a small roasting pan.

3   Roast for 20 minutes. Reduce the heat to 375°F. Turn the chicken breast side up. Add the wine. Roast for 45 to 60 minutes more, basting occasionally. The chicken is done when the juices run clear when the thigh is pierced with a fork.

4   While the chicken cooks, prepare the beans: In a medium saucepan, combine the oil, onion, garlic, pancetta, anchovies, parsley, basil, and rosemary. Cook over low heat, stirring occasionally, for 10 minutes, or until lightly browned. Add the beans, about 1 cup of their liquid (or 1 cup water if using canned beans), salt, and pepper. Simmer for 5 minutes.

5   Place the chicken on a platter and keep warm. Spoon off the fat from the pan juices. Place the pan over medium heat on top of the stove. Cook, scraping up the browned bits, until the juices are reduced and slightly syrupy. If the pan is dry, add ¼ cup of water.

6   Carve the chicken. Place the beans on a warm platter. Top with the chicken. Pour the pan juices into a sauce boat and pass separately.

To make ahead: The beans can be made completely ahead of time and reheated when ready to serve.

To someone who enjoys cooking, chicken, basically an ordinary kind of bird, can be turned into a small masterpiece since it willingly accepts different spices and seasonings, stuffings and coatings that give it character and flavor. This roast chicken stuffed with fennel-flavored pork sausage is a case in point. The stuffing makes the bird seem special. It is perfect for a small dinner party or family Sunday dinner. Serve it with Fried Potatoes with Garlic and Hot Pepper (page 304) and Green Beans for the Feast of Saint Anna (page 296).

Chicken with Fennel-Sausage Stuffing

POLLO CON RIPIENO DI SALSICCIA

1 chicken (about 3¹/₂ pounds)

6 ounces Italian-style pork sausage with fennel (2 sausages), or ground pork plus 1 teaspoon crushed fennel seeds and ¹/₄ teaspoon coarsely ground black pepper

4 ounces chicken livers, trimmed and diced

2 ounces sliced pancetta, chopped

1 tablespoon chopped fresh rosemary leaves

2 garlic cloves, finely chopped

2 tablespoons olive oil

Salt and freshly ground pepper, to taste

1 Preheat the oven to 450°F.

2 Rinse the chicken and dry it thoroughly inside and out. Remove any excess fat from the cavity.

3 Remove the sausage meat from the casing. In a bowl, combine the meat with the chicken livers, pancetta, rosemary, and garlic. Mix well.

4 Stuff the cavity of the chicken with the sausage mixture. Brush the skin with olive oil and sprinkle all over with salt and pepper. Place the chicken breast side up on a rack in a roasting pan.

5 Roast for 20 minutes. Reduce the heat to 375°F. Roast, basting occasionally, for 60 to 75 minutes more, or until the internal temperature of the stuffing registers 140°F. on an instant-read thermometer. Remove the chicken from the oven. Cover loosely with foil and let it rest for 10 minutes before carving.

6 Spoon off the fat from the pan juices. Place the pan over medium heat on top of the stove and add 1 cup water. Bring the juices to a simmer and cook, scraping the pan, until the juices are reduced and slightly thickened.

7 Carve the chicken and serve with the pan juices.

Chicken in the Pot with Red Wine

POLLO AL TEGAME

1 chicken, cut into 8 pieces (about 3¹/₂ pounds)

2 tablespoons olive oil

4 garlic cloves, peeled

6 fresh sage leaves

Crushed red pepper, to taste

Salt, to taste

¹/₂ cup dry red wine

1 cup chicken broth

3 tablespoons raisins

2 tablespoons pine nuts

1 tablespoon chopped fresh parsley

1 Rinse the chicken pieces and pat them dry. Trim off the wing tips.

2 In a large skillet over medium heat, heat the olive oil. Add the chicken pieces, garlic, sage, and red pepper. Cook until the chicken is browned on all sides, about 15 minutes. Tip the pan and spoon off the excess fat. Sprinkle the chicken with salt. Add the wine and cook for 1 minute, scraping the bottom of the pan. Add the broth, raisins, and pine nuts.

3 Cover and cook, turning the chicken occasionally for about 20 minutes, or until the chicken is very tender and the juices reduced and slightly thickened. Add a little more broth or water if necessary to keep the chicken moist. If there is too much liquid, remove the chicken and reduce it over high heat.

4 Transfer to a serving platter and sprinkle with parsley. Serve immediately.

SERVES 4

While exploring Treviso, an old city with a medieval center, frescoed houses, and canals instead of streets, we stayed nearby at the Villa Condulmer. Once a private home, the sprawling villa has been converted into a comfortable hotel with a swimming pool, tennis courts, and two golf courses. When the concierge learned that we were Americans, he proudly showed us his autographed photo of President and Mrs. Reagan, who stayed at the hotel. For lunch the chef prepared this chicken cooked in red wine with raisins and pine nuts. I serve it with Fennel Mashed Potatoes (page 305).

Villa Condulmer
Zerman (Veneto)

Through friends of friends, we once rented an apartment in Rome. The living room had two tiny terraces from which you could see a bit of the Coliseum, quite a thrilling sight. On the other side of the apartment, our neighbor's kitchen window faced ours across a narrow air shaft, and each evening I would catch a glimpse of her preparing dinner for her family. Sometimes, we could hear her daughter singing "Blue Moon."

One day I met *la signora* as she was returning home from the market. I asked what she was cooking that night. "Nothing special," she replied. "This is the way we make chicken in Rome." Here is her recipe for Roman-style chicken cooked in a lively tomato sauce and served over crunchy slices of toasted bread. Serve it as the Romans would with a bottle of chilled white Frascati.

Chicken with Tomatoes and Crostini

POLLO ALLA ROMANA

2 ounces pancetta, finely chopped

2 tablespoons olive oil

2 tablespoons chopped Italian flat-leaf parsley

1 chicken, cut into 8 pieces (about 3^1/$_2$ pounds)

Salt and freshly ground pepper, to taste

^{1}/$_2$ cup dry white wine

1 garlic clove, finely chopped

1 teaspoon dried marjoram

*2 large ripe tomatoes, peeled, seeded, and chopped, or 2 cups
    chopped canned Italian tomatoes, with their juice*

8 slices Italian bread, toasted (^{1}/$_2$-inch thick)

1 In a large skillet over medium heat, combine the pancetta, olive oil, and parsley. Cook, stirring frequently, until the pancetta is golden brown, about 5 minutes.

2 Rinse the chicken pieces and pat dry with paper towels. Add the chicken to the skillet and cook, turning occasionally, until the pieces are browned on all sides, about 15 minutes. Tip the pan and spoon off the excess fat. Sprinkle the chicken with salt and pepper. Add the wine, garlic, and marjoram to the skillet and cook for 1 minute. Add the tomatoes and their juice. Bring to a simmer and cook, stirring occasionally, for 20 to 30 minutes or until the chicken is tender and cooked through. Taste the sauce for seasoning.

3 Arrange the slices of bread around the edges of a serving platter. Spoon the chicken and sauce into the center. Serve immediately.

Chicken with a Brown Crust

POLLO ROSOLATO

1 chicken, cut into 8 pieces (about 3 1/2 pounds)

Salt and freshly ground pepper, to taste

1/3 cup fine dry bread crumbs

2 tablespoons chopped Italian flat-leaf parsley

2 tablespoons freshly grated pecorino romano

1 large garlic clove, minced

About 2 tablespoons olive oil

1 Preheat the broiler.

2 Rinse the chicken pieces and pat them dry. Sprinkle with salt and pepper. Place the pieces, skin side down, on the broiler rack set in the broiler pan. Broil the chicken for 10 minutes. Turn the chicken and broil for 10 minutes more on the skin side.

3 Combine the bread crumbs, parsley, cheese, garlic, salt, and pepper. Add just enough oil to make a thick paste.

4 Set the oven heat to 350°F.

5 Sprinkle the skin side with the crumb mixture, patting it so that it adheres. Place the pan in the oven and bake for 10 to 15 minutes, or until the juices run clear when the chicken is cut near the bone.

6 Serve hot or cold.

SERVES 4

Cheese, bread crumbs, and garlic form a crusty brown coating on this easy chicken. It's quick enough to do after work or whenever you're in a hurry. Serve it with Minted Beet Salad (page 285) or Cabbage and Caper Salad (page 288).

This bread crumb topping has many uses in Italian cooking. Scatter it on fish fillets, clams on the half shell, or shrimp before baking in a hot oven or use it as a stuffing for baked mushroom caps or braised artichokes.

"I especially like chicken before I sing."

Luciano Pavarotti with William Wright, *My World* (New York: Crown, 1995)

This Neapolitan-style chicken was a childhood favorite passed down from my grandmother. My sister and I would argue over the "picky pieces," as we called the bonier parts that best absorb the spicy flavors.

Have the butcher cut up the chicken for you, or do it yourself using a chef's knife or a cleaver. After cutting, rinse the pieces under cool water and trim off any small splinters of bone. Pat the pieces good and dry before cooking, or they will not brown. Store the back and wing tips in a plastic bag in the freezer to add them to the pot the next time you make broth. A good red wine vinegar is essential. As tasty as balsamic vinegar is, it is too sweet for this dish.

Chicken with Vinegar and Hot Pepper

POLLO AL'ACETO

2 tablespoons olive oil

1 chicken, cut into 2-inch pieces (about 3^1/$_2$ pounds)

Salt and freshly ground pepper, to taste

3 large garlic cloves, finely chopped

^{1}/$_2$ teaspoon crushed red pepper

^{2}/$_3$ cup red wine vinegar

1 In a skillet large enough to hold all of the chicken in a single layer, heat the olive oil over medium heat. Dry the chicken pieces well. Place them in the skillet in a single layer and brown on all sides. Do not crowd the pan. If there is too much chicken to fit comfortably, cook it in 2 batches. Tip the pan and spoon out all but 1 tablespoon fat. Sprinkle the chicken with salt and pepper.

2 Scatter the garlic and red pepper around the chicken pieces. Add the vinegar and stir the chicken, scraping up the brown bits on the bottom of the pan with a wooden spoon. Cover and cook, stirring occasionally, until the chicken is tender and most of the vinegar has evaporated, about 15 minutes. If there is too much liquid left at the end of the cooking, remove the cover and simmer it until reduced. Add 1 or 2 tablespoons of warm water if the sauce becomes too dry.

3 Spoon the chicken pieces into a serving dish and pour the pan juices over all. Serve hot or at room temperature.

Florentine Fried Chicken

POLLO FRITTO ALLA FIORENTINA

1 small chicken (about 2¹/₂ pounds)

2 large eggs

Salt and freshly ground pepper, to taste

1 cup all-purpose flour

Vegetable or olive oil, for frying

Lemon wedges

1 Cut the chicken into 2-inch pieces. (Set aside the wing tips and back to make broth.) Rinse well and remove any bone splinters. Pat the pieces dry.

2 In a large bowl, beat the eggs with salt and pepper. Place the flour on a sheet of wax paper.

3 Add the chicken to the eggs and stir until the pieces are well coated. Remove the pieces one at a time and roll them in the flour. Tap off the excess.

4 Heat about ¹/₂ inch of oil in a large deep skillet. Test to see that the oil is hot enough by dropping in a bit of the egg mixture. When it sizzles and cooks quickly, add enough chicken pieces to fit comfortably in the pan without crowding. Fry the pieces, turning occasionally with tongs, until cooked through, 15 to 20 minutes. The chicken should be crisp and brown on all sides. As the pieces are done, remove them to drain on paper towels. Keep warm in a low oven. Continue cooking the remaining chicken.

5 Serve hot or at room temperature with lemon wedges.

Fried chicken may not come to mind when you think of Tuscan food, but in fact, it is a typical Florentine dish, sometimes served with artichoke hearts fried in the same batter. Rabbit is often prepared this way, too. One of the best places to taste this classic dish is at Trattoria Biba, in Scandicci, outside of Florence. The trattoria is a little hard to find since it's down a winding country road, but the cars parked along the road outside should provide a clue. Sit in the shady garden so you can hear the ripple of the stream that passes nearby while you eat.

Olive oil is used for frying in Tuscany, but I prefer the lighter flavor of vegetable oil.

Trattoria Biba
Scandicci (Florence)

SERVES 4

After a long walk in the rain through the streets of Pisa, we arrived at our destination, Al Restoro dei Vecchi Macelli. As we entered the trattoria, we were dismayed to find a big-screen TV in the center of the dining room, blaring the midday news. We feared we had made a terrible choice, but soon we were escorted into a private dining room off to one side. The television, it seems, was for the benefit of the local office workers, who ate lunch together at a big communal table.

We enjoyed a delicate monkfish salad with warm fresh cannellini beans, steamed scampi in a light basil sauce, and a chicken salad served at room temperature. The chef used citron in the salad, a large citrus fruit grown in the Mediterranean area and in Florida that resembles a big, bumpy lemon. It is rarely available in the United States, so I have substituted lemon zest, which works well with the flavors of the chicken, oranges, and fennel. After lunch we strolled back to the center of town for a second cup of espresso and some pastries at Salza, Pisa's best *pasticceria* and caffè.

Al Ristoro dei Vecchi Macelli
Via Volturno, 49
Pisa (Tuscany)

Pasticceria Salza
Via Borgo Stretto, 44
Pisa (Tuscany)

Lemon Chicken Salad

INSALATA DI POLLO AL LIMONE

1 chicken (3^1/$_2$ pounds)
2 celery ribs
1 medium onion, peeled
1 carrot, peeled
1 garlic clove, peeled
Salt, to taste

SALAD DRESSING
^{1}/$_4$ cup extra virgin olive oil
2 to 3 tablespoons lemon juice
1 to 2 teaspoons freshly grated lemon zest
Salt and freshly ground pepper, to taste

1 cup thinly sliced fennel
2 oranges, peeled and cut into segments
^{1}/$_4$ cup golden raisins
6 cups mixed baby lettuce leaves
^{1}/$_4$ cup toasted pine nuts

1   In a pot deep enough to hold the chicken, combine the chicken with cold water to cover. Bring to a simmer and cook over low heat until the foam rises to the surface, about 10 minutes. Skim off and discard the foam. Regulate the heat so that the water is barely simmering. Add the celery, onion, carrot, garlic, and salt. Cook for 30 to 45 minutes, or until the chicken is just tender when pierced with a fork. Remove the chicken from the broth and let cool slightly. Discard the skin and bones. Cut the meat into bite-size pieces.

2   To make the salad dressing: In a bowl, combine the olive oil, lemon juice, lemon zest, salt, and pepper. Whisk until blended.

3 In a large bowl, combine the chicken, fennel, oranges, and raisins. Add half of the dressing and toss gently. Toss the greens with the remaining dressing.

4 Place the dressed greens on a platter. Top with the chicken mixture. Sprinkle with the pine nuts and serve immediately.

Turkey Cutlets with Mixed Salad

SCALOPPINE DI TACCHINO CON INSALATA

TURKEY CUTLETS

4 turkey breast cutlets (about 1 pound)

2 large eggs

1/2 cup grated Parmigiano-Reggiano

1 tablespoon chopped fresh parsley

1 tablespoon chopped fresh basil

1 small garlic clove, minced

Salt and freshly ground pepper, to taste

1 to 2 tablespoons all-purpose flour

1/4 cup corn or vegetable oil

SALAD

2 tablespoons extra virgin olive oil

2 teaspoons red wine vinegar

2 teaspoons balsamic vinegar

Salt and freshly ground pepper, to taste

1 medium-size ripe tomato, diced

4 cups mesclun or other mixed tender greens, rinsed, dried, and torn into bite-size pieces

1/4 cup thinly sliced red onion

SERVES 4

Though formal meals often are served with a salad following the main course, family-style meals in Italy frequently include the salad on the same plate. More than just a matter of convenience, the crispness of the salad and the dressing on the greens make a pleasing complement to the richness of the meat. Somewhere along the line, this became a trend both in the United States and in Italy. In Milan, the classic veal Milanese, a flattened chop that is breaded and fried, is now often served with a salad on top. At Da Gianni, an incredibly busy trattoria in Bologna, I liked this version made with turkey breast slices in an herbed egg and cheese coating.

Da Gianni is one of dozens of terrific small restaurants in Bologna, but it is not easy to find. To get there, go to Salsamenteria Tamburini, the renowned food store and *rosticceria* near the Bologna market. Just a glance in the window will work up an appetite for tortellini. Buy some Parmigiano for nibbling and a bottle or two of balsamic vinegar to take home. Then make a left as you leave the store and another left at the corner, a short distance. Walk along the side of the building and turn left when you reach the corner. One more left takes you down an alleyway, and there is Da Gianni. Don't be surprised if you have to wait.

Da Gianni
Via Clavature, 18
Bologna (Emilia-Romagna)

Salsamenteria Tamburini
Via Caprarie, 1
Bologna (Emilia-Romagna)

SERVES 8

Pomegranates are the caviar of fruits. Their ruby red seeds explode in your mouth with red juice and sweet-tart flavor. The fruit juice complements the rich flavor of capon and basting turns the skin a deep mahogany color. Serve capon for Christmas dinner as they do in Italy, or at any fall or winter dinner party.

Extracting the juice from the pomegranates isn't difficult, but it can be messy since the pomegranate seeds and juice seem to fly all over no matter how careful you are. The best method I have

1 The turkey cutlets should be about $1/4$ inch thick. If they are thicker, place them between 2 pieces of plastic wrap and flatten them gently with the flat side of a meat pounder or rubber mallet.

2 Beat the eggs with the cheese, parsley, basil, garlic, salt, and pepper. Beat in enough flour to make a smooth paste just thick enough to coat the turkey.

3 In a large skillet over medium heat, heat the oil until a drop of the egg mixture sizzles when it is added.

4 Dip the cutlets in the egg mixture until well coated on both sides.

5 Place the cutlets in the pan in a single layer. If there is not enough room, cook the cutlets in 2 batches. Cook the cutlets until browned, about 2 minutes on each side. Drain the cutlets on paper towels. Keep warm while you cook the remainder. Arrange the cutlets on a serving dish.

6 In a large bowl, whisk the oil, vinegars, salt, and pepper. Add the salad ingredients and toss well.

7 Arrange the salad over the cutlets and serve immediately.

Christmas Roast Capon with Pomegranate Glaze

CAPONE AL MELOGRANO

1 capon (about $7^1/2$ pounds)
Salt and freshly ground pepper, to taste
2 garlic cloves, peeled
8 fresh sage leaves, plus more for garnishing
Olive oil
3 large pomegranates

A Fresh Taste of Italy

1 Preheat the oven to 325°F.

2 Rinse the capon thoroughly inside and out and dry well. Remove the excess fat from the cavity. Sprinkle the inside with salt and pepper. Place the garlic and 8 sage leaves in the cavity. Tuck the wing tips behind the back and tie the legs together. Rub the skin all over with olive oil and place the capon breast side up on a rack in a large roasting pan. Place in the oven and roast for 1 hour.

3 Meanwhile, roll the pomegranates on a counter, pressing down with the palm of your hand to loosen the seeds. Cut the fruit crosswise in half. Set aside 1 half. Break up the other 5 halves and scoop out the seeds with your fingers or a spoon. Drop the seeds into a food mill set over a bowl. Pick out any pieces of white membrane. Crush the seeds to extract the juices. You should have about 1 cup of juice. Remove the seeds from the remaining pomegranate half and set aside.

4 After 1 hour, juices from the capon should collect in the bottom of the pan. Set aside ¼ cup of the pomegranate juice for the sauce. Baste the capon with the pan juices and remaining pomegranate juice. Continue basting every 20 minutes or until the capon is done, about 1 hour and 20 minutes more. The skin will be a rich brown and the juices will run clear when the thigh is pierced with a fork.

5 Remove the capon from the pan and place it on a cutting board. Cover loosely with foil and let rest for 10 minutes.

6 Spoon off the fat from the pan juices. Place the roasting pan over medium heat on top of the stove and add the reserved ¼ cup of pomegranate juice. Bring to a simmer, scraping up the browned bits on the bottom of the pan with a wooden spoon. Add a little water or chicken broth if necessary. Strain the juices into a small saucepan and reheat gently.

7 When ready to serve, carve the capon and place it on a warm serving platter. Pour some of the juices over the meat. Place the remainder in a gravy boat to pass separately. Sprinkle the reserved pomegranate seeds over the carved meat and garnish the platter with the remaining sage leaves. Serve immediately.

To make ahead: Seed the pomegranates and squeeze the juice up to several hours before roasting the bird. Cover and refrigerate the juice and seeds until you are ready to proceed.

found is to crush the seeds in a food mill. Wear old clothes when you do this.

Capon is larger and tastier than chicken, yet much more elegant than turkey. Roasting time is about twenty minutes to the pound. If you prefer, substitute a large roasting chicken or a small turkey and adjust the cooking time accordingly.

Oh, oh I'm dying!
Make me a coffin of ricotta,
With ropes of sausage round
*   the sides.*
And with a pillow made of two
*   cooked capons,*
And two young girls as
*   candlesticks,*
And a flask of wine instead of
*   holy water.*

Traditional Sicilian carter's song

Though farm-raised ducks are fine for this recipe, a wild duck, such as the kind used in Italy, will make this rich sauce even more flavorful. You probably need to make the acquaintance of a duck hunter to get one.

In the area around the town of Arezzo in Tuscany, this sauce is served in one of two ways. Sometimes the duck meat is cut into small pieces and stirred into the sauce. Then the meaty sauce is tossed with the pasta. Or the duck is removed from the sauce and kept warm while the meat-flavored sauce is served with pasta as a first course. Then the duck is cut into serving-size pieces and eaten as a second course with vegetables of the season. I favor the first method, serving the sauce with fresh fettuccine (page 130) or a dried pasta like penne or rigatoni.

If you do not have a pot large enough to brown the duck whole, it can be cut into quarters before cooking.

Duck Ragù

RAGÙ DI ANATRA

1 duckling (about 5^{1}/2 pounds)
2 tablespoons olive oil
Salt and freshly ground pepper, to taste
2 ounces pancetta, chopped
2 medium onions, chopped
2 medium carrots, chopped
2 celery ribs, chopped
6 fresh sage leaves
Pinch of freshly grated nutmeg
^{1}/2 cup dry white wine
1 can (28 to 35 ounces) Italian tomatoes with their juice
^{1}/2 cup freshly grated Parmigiano-Reggiano

1 Rinse the duck inside and out and remove any loose fat from the cavity. Drain the duck and pat it dry. Dice the liver and set aside.

2 In a saucepan large enough to hold the duck, heat the oil over medium heat. Add the duck and cook, turning occasionally, until browned on all sides. Sprinkle with salt and pepper. Remove the duck to a platter. Spoon off the excess fat from the pot.

3 Add the pancetta, onions, carrots, celery, sage, and nutmeg. Cook for 5 to 10 minutes, or until the vegetables are wilted. Add the wine and simmer for 1 minute.

4 Pass the tomatoes through a food mill. Add the tomatoes to the pot with the duck and 1 cup of water. Bring to a simmer. Partly cover the pan and cook, stirring occasionally, for 2 hours, or until the duck is very tender when pierced with a fork. Remove the pan from the heat.

5 To serve the duck meat in the sauce, remove the duck from the pan. Discard the skin and remove the meat from the bones. Cut the meat into ^{1}/2-inch pieces. To serve the duck as a second course, leave it in the sauce.

6 Let the sauce cool briefly. Skim the fat from the surface. Add the diced duck liver.

7 If you will be serving the meat in the sauce, add it back now. Bring the sauce to a simmer and cook for 5 minutes. Taste for seasoning and serve with hot, cooked pasta as suggested above and cheese. If serving the duck as a second course, remove it from the sauce and keep warm. Serve the sauce with pasta. Cut the duck into serving pieces and serve after the pasta.

Quail with Tomatoes and Peas

QUAGLIE IN TEGAME

8 quails, fresh or thawed if frozen

2 tablespoons olive oil

2 ounces pancetta, chopped

1 tablespoon chopped fresh rosemary leaves

Salt and freshly ground pepper, to taste

¹/₂ cup dry white wine

1¹/₂ cups peeled, seeded, and chopped ripe tomatoes or canned Italian tomatoes

1 cup fresh or partly thawed frozen peas

1 Rinse the quails under cool water and drain well. Pat them dry inside and out. Tuck the wing tips behind the backs of the quails and tie the legs together with kitchen twine.

2 In a skillet large enough to hold all the quails in a single layer, combine the olive oil and pancetta. Cook over medium heat until the pancetta begins to turn brown. Add the quails and brown on all sides. Sprinkle the quails with rosemary, salt, and pepper. Add the wine and simmer for 1 minute. Add the tomatoes. Cover the pan and reduce the heat to low. Cook, turning the quails occasionally, until very tender, 45 minutes to 1 hour. If the liquid is too thin, remove the cover during the last 10 to 15 minutes of cooking.

3 Add the peas and taste for seasoning. Cook for 5 minutes more.

4 Serve immediately.

SERVES 4

Little birds like quail served on a mound of polenta are so appreciated in Verona that the local pastry chefs even invented a dessert that imitates this dish. I did a double take when I first saw the after-dinner version of *polenta e osei*, polenta and little birds in the local dialect, in a pastry shop near the Castelvecchio. Bright yellow frosting under a sparkling sugar coating covered a dome-shape cake that was topped with little birds made of chocolate. Though it was charming to look at, it was too sugary for me. I would rather eat the savory version.

These quails are cooked in a rich red tomato sauce spangled with peas. Serve the quail on a bright golden cloud of soft polenta (see page 191).

Onions, quail, and liver pâté on crisp toast is always a winning combination. Serve one quail per person as a first course or two as a main course. Serve your finest Chianti with this dish, such as Frescobaldi Montesodi or Ruffino.

"Italians fancy themselves as hunters. In Carrara there were 15,000 men with gun permits and about six small birds. You couldn't walk through the vineyards in autumn without meeting a gun pointed in your direction, and lead pellets rattled against the shutters. So where do all these quails come from? Once they were caught in nets as they flew in from Africa, were fattened on maize, and brought to the market. Now they are raised."

Patience Gray, *Honey from a Weed*

Braised Quails with Onions and Liver Crostini

QUAGLIE CON CROSTINI DI FEGATO

8 quails, fresh or thawed frozen

4 garlic cloves, halved lengthwise

8 bay leaves

8 thin slices pancetta

3 tablespoons olive oil

3 medium onions, thinly sliced

Salt and freshly ground pepper, to taste

1 cup dry white wine

1 cup chicken broth

4 ounces chicken livers, trimmed

2 tablespoons capers, rinsed and drained

CROSTINI:

2 tablespoons olive oil

8 thin slices toasted Italian bread

1 Rinse the quails and pat them dry. Tuck the wing tips behind the backs. Trim off the necks, if necessary. Place half of a garlic clove and a bay leaf inside each quail. Wrap a slice of pancetta around each. Truss the birds, securing the pancetta with kitchen twine.

2 In a skillet large enough to hold the quails in a single layer, heat the oil over medium heat. Add the quails. Cook, turning frequently, until browned on all sides. Scatter the onions around the quails. Cook until the onions are golden, 5 to 10 minutes more. Sprinkle the quails and onions with salt and pepper. Add the wine, turning the birds once or twice. Add the broth. Cover and cook, turning the quails occasionally, until the birds are very tender, 45 to 60 minutes. At the end of the cooking time, the onions should remain quite saucy. Add a little more broth or water if they seem dry.

3 To make the crostini: Just before serving, heat the oil in a small skillet over medium heat. Add the livers, capers, salt, and pepper. Cook, stirring often, until the livers are browned on the outside but still pink inside, about 5 minutes. Coarsely mash the livers with a fork. Spread on the toasted bread.

4 Place the crostini on a warm serving platter. Top each slice with a quail and bathe with the onions and pan juices. Serve immediately.

Grilled Quail with Sausages

QUAGLIE E SALSICCIA ALLA GRIGLIA

6 quails, fresh or thawed if frozen

¼ cup olive oil

¼ cup dry white wine

2 large garlic cloves, finely chopped

2 tablespoons chopped fresh rosemary leaves

Salt and freshly ground pepper, to taste

4 mild pork sausages, cut into 1-inch chunks (12 pieces)

12 whole fresh sage or dried bay leaves

1 With kitchen shears or a heavy chef's knife, divide the quails into halves by cutting them along the backbone and the breastbone. Rinse the quails and pat them dry.

2 In a shallow bowl, combine the olive oil, wine, garlic, rosemary, salt, and pepper. Add the quail halves, stirring to coat them well with the marinade. Cover and let stand for at least 1 hour at room temperature or for several hours in the refrigerator.

3 Preheat the broiler or grill.

4 Remove the quails from the marinade and pat them dry. Thread the quails and sausage pieces on flat skewers alternating the pieces with sage leaves.

5 Grill over glowing coals or broil about 4 inches from the heat source, basting occasionally with the marinade, until browned on all

SERVES 6

When I was researching my antipasto cook-book, a friend recommended I try Restaurant Zocchi in Pratolino outside of Florence. The antipasto selection was vast, but what I really enjoyed were the little birds, sausages, and other meats cooked on skewers in the enormous rotisserie.

Thrushes, called *tordi*, are available in Italy, but quails can be substituted. Use a mild pork sausage, such as luganega, available at many Italian pork butchers. Avoid sausages that are overly seasoned. Chicken and turkey sausages often fall into this category because manufacturers feel they have to compensate for the meat's lack of flavor. If you must cut back on fat, eliminate the sausages from this recipe altogether and make more quails instead.

Ristorante Zocchi
Pratolino (Tuscany)

sides and the sausages are cooked through, 15 to 20 minutes.

6 Slide the quails and sausages off the skewers onto a heated serving platter and serve immediately.

Quail with Rosemary and Garlic

QUAGLIE AL ROSMARINO

8 quails, fresh or thawed if frozen

8 sprigs (1 inch each) of fresh rosemary

4 garlic cloves, thinly sliced

Salt and freshly ground pepper, to taste

8 thin slices pancetta

Butter

1 cup dry white wine

1 Preheat the oven to 375°F.

2 Rinse the quails inside and out and pat dry. Stuff each quail with a sprig of rosemary and some of the garlic slices. Sprinkle with salt and pepper. Tuck the wing tips behind the back of each bird and wrap each quail in a piece of pancetta. With a piece of kitchen twine, tie the legs together and secure the pancetta against the body of the quail.

3 Butter a large ovenproof casserole with a tight-fitting lid just large enough to hold the quails. Add the quails and wine. Cover and bake for 1 hour. Uncover and baste the quails with the pan juices. At this point the quails will be pale looking. Cook, uncovered, for 30 to 40 minutes more, basting every 10 minutes, or until the birds are browned and the meat is very tender.

4 Place the casserole over medium heat on top of the stove and bring the cooking juices to a simmer. Cook until reduced and slightly thickened. Turn the quails and baste with the juices. If there is not enough liquid, add a little water or chicken broth.

5 Pour the juices over the quails and serve immediately.

SERVES 4

Quails, stuffed with rosemary and garlic and wrapped in pancetta, then slowly braised in wine, become so tender the meat all but falls off the bones. The technique here is unusual in that the quails are not browned first. All the ingredients are put into the pan cold and the quails brown toward the end of the long cooking time.

242

Meat and Game ...
Carne e Cacciagione

I ONCE HEARD AN *explanation of how spaghetti and meatballs, which is not an Italian dish, got started in the United States. It seems that when the droves of immigrants from Italy arrived in America in the early 1900s, most of the social workers they met were of English or German descent. These well-meaning women were appalled by the lack of meat and potatoes, then considered essential for good health, in the Italian immigrants' diet. As in most Mediterranean and Asian countries, Italian cooking never was centered on meat. Because of a lack of space and food to spare for large animals, beef cattle were—and still are— comparatively rare and cows were raised primarily for milk and cheese.*

The social workers advised the immigrants to change their diets. The Italians readily accepted the idea of eating more meat, since they considered even inexpensive ground meats, which they could fashion into meatballs, a luxury. In most places, meat, and tough cuts at that, was a once-a-week occasion, if at all. But the Italians refused to do without pasta. So the social workers suggested they substitute pasta for the potatoes on their plate. Anxious to become Americanized and accepted in their new country, the immigrants followed their suggestion and Italian-American cooking was born. Spaghetti with meatballs became symbolic of Italian cooking even though you won't find it in Italy.

Though Italians can now afford to eat more meat than they once did, portion sizes are still relatively small and most meals have a larger proportion of grains and vegetables than meat. To take the edge off their appetite, Italians begin a meal with a small dish of pasta, soup, or risotto, sometimes preceded by a light antipasto. Pork, lamb, veal, rabbit, and goat are more typical than beef for the meat course.

Braised Pork Loin with Grapes and Tiny Onions

BRASATO DI MAIALE CON L'UVA

SERVES 6

Little pearl onions and green grapes give tang to this braised pork loin. Since it is cooked with moist heat in a covered pot, there is no need to worry about overcooking. In fact, the entire dish can be cooked ahead of time and reheated. This method of braising a large cut of meat in a small amount of liquid is typically Italian. The meat cooks in its own juices and in the end tastes more like itself and less like the liquid in which it was cooked. The flavors are simple and uncomplicated.

Serve the pork with Browned Cabbage with Hot Pepper (page 289) and Crusty Potatoes with Tomatoes and Onions (page 301). Start with the Spinach, Apple, and Pine Nut Salad (page 70).

1 pound pearl onions

2 tablespoons olive oil

1 small boneless pork loin, rolled and tied (2¹/₂ pounds)

¹/₄ cup all-purpose flour

Salt and freshly ground pepper, to taste

¹/₄ cup white wine vinegar

1 pound seedless green grapes, stemmed (about 3 cups)

1 Bring a large pot of water to a boil. Add the onions and cook for 30 seconds. Drain and cool under cold running water. With a paring knife, shave off the tip of the root ends. Do not slice off the ends too deeply or the onions will fall apart during cooking. Remove the skins. Set aside.

2 In a heavy pot not much larger than the meat, heat the olive oil over medium-high heat. Roll the pork loin in the flour. Place it in the pot and brown well on all sides. Tip the pot and spoon off the

fat. Sprinkle the pork with salt and pepper. Add the vinegar and bring it to a simmer, scraping the bottom of the pot. Add the onions and 1 cup water. Cover the pot. Reduce the heat to low and simmer for 1 hour and 15 minutes.

3 Add the grapes. Cook for 1¼ hours more, or until the meat is very tender when pierced with a fork. Remove the meat to a cutting board and cover with foil to keep warm.

4 If there is a lot of liquid remaining in the pot, remove the grapes and onions to a bowl with a slotted spoon. Bring the liquid to a boil over high heat. Cook until the liquid is reduced and slightly syrupy. Reduce the heat and return the onions and grapes to the pot to reheat.

5 Slice the pork and arrange it on a warm platter. Spoon on the grape and onion sauce and serve immediately.

To make ahead: The entire roast can be made ahead up to 1 hour before serving and reheated just before.

Roast Loin of Pork

ARISTA DI MAIALE ALLA MIA MANIERA

2 tablespoons chopped fresh rosemary leaves

2 large garlic cloves, finely chopped

2 tablespoons olive oil

Salt and freshly ground pepper, to taste

1 pork loin, boned and tied with the bones (4½ pounds)

1 cup dry white wine

1 Preheat the oven to 425°F.

2 Make a paste with the rosemary, garlic, olive oil, salt, and pepper. Place the meat bone side down in a large roasting pan. Rub the meat all over with the paste, pushing some between the meat and the bones. Roast for 20 minutes. Reduce the heat to 350°F. Roast for 40 minutes more. Add the wine. Cook for 30 to 45 minutes more, or until an instant-read thermometer inserted at the center of the roast

SERVES 8

In Umbria, roast pork loin is called *arista*. The name is attributed to a Greek ambassador who attended a banquet in Florence during the fifteenth century. When he tasted the juicy browned roast perfumed with garlic and rosemary, he proclaimed it *arista*, meaning "the best," and so it has been called ever since.

Not too long ago, experts recommended roasting pork until it was well done, to an internal temperature of 170°F. Today pork is bred under more sanitary conditions. The animals are much leaner and a pork roast will dry out if it is cooked to such a high temperature. All bacteria are killed in the 137° to 145°F. range. A roast is perfectly safe to eat when it is cooked to medium,

155°F. on an instant-read thermometer, and it tastes better. The cooking time is about twenty minutes to the pound for a boneless roast.

To tell when a roast is done, remove the meat from the oven and insert an instant-read thermometer in the thickest portion of the meat without letting it touch the bone. Wait thirty seconds. The temperature should read 155°F. If the meat is done, cover it loosely with foil. Allow it to rest for about ten minutes before slicing so that the juices, which travel to the surface as the meat cooks, can retreat back to the center.

If the meat is not done, remove the thermometer and return the roast to the oven.

For this recipe, I like to use a pork loin roast that has been boned, the bones trimmed, and the roast tied against the rack that results. Prepared this way, the roasted meat is easy to carve, tasty, and moist. The roasted bones with bits of meat are a delicious bonus, either served alongside the meat or reheated under the broiler the next day until browned and crisp. Ask the butcher to prepare the roast by boning it and saving the rack of bones. Have him remove the chine (backbone), leaving the ribs in a rack that can be tied against the meat. My butcher calls this "pork in the cradle" which is just what it looks like.

reads 155°F. Remove the meat from the pan. Cover with foil and keep warm for at least 10 minutes before slicing.

3   Spoon off the fat from the pan juices. Place the pan over medium heat on the top of the stove and bring the juices to a simmer. Cook, scraping the pan, until the juices are reduced and slightly thickened. Strain the juices and skim off the fat.

4   Slice the meat and arrange it on a warm serving platter. Drizzle with the juices and serve.

To make ahead: This roast can also be served at room temperature. In that case, chill the pan juices slightly to make it easier to remove all traces of fat, then reheat.

Braised Spareribs

SPUNTATURE DI MAIALE

1/2 cup all-purpose flour

Salt and freshly ground pepper, to taste

2 pounds pork spareribs, cut into individual ribs

2 tablespoons olive oil

1 medium onion, chopped

1 large carrot, chopped

1/2 cup dry white wine

1 1/2 cups Meat Broth (page 83)

1 On a sheet of wax paper, combine the flour, salt, and pepper. Roll the ribs in the mixture, then tap them to remove the excess.

2 In a Dutch oven or deep heavy skillet with a cover, heat the olive oil over medium heat. Add as many ribs as will fit in a single layer and brown them well on all sides. Remove the ribs to a plate. Spoon off all but 2 tablespoons fat.

3 Add the onion and carrot to the pot. Cook, stirring occasionally, until lightly browned. Add the wine and cook, scraping the bottom of the pan, for 1 minute. Return the ribs to the pan and add the broth. Bring the liquid to a simmer. Reduce the heat to very low, cover, and cook, stirring occasionally, until the meat is very tender when pierced with a fork, about 1 1/2 hours. Add more broth or water if the meat becomes too dry.

4 Serve hot.

To make ahead: The spareribs can be completely cooked up to 2 days before serving and reheated.

Italians usually serve rice as a separate course, usually the first course, in place of pasta or soup. Until I tasted this dish, the only exception I had ever seen was osso buco, braised veal shanks, which frequently are served with saffron-scented risotto Milanese.

At the home of winemaker Franco Furlan of Castelcosa in Friuli, I was introduced to another exception. Signora Furlan and her daughter-in-law, Adriana, prepared tender pork spareribs in a rich brown sauce and served them with Risotto in Bianco, a simple risotto flavored with onion and white wine (see page 184).

SERVES 4

One of my favorite Roman restaurants is Vecchia Roma in Piazza Campitelli. It has a series of small, softly lit rooms beautifully decorated with frescos on the walls and ceilings. The food is classically Roman, yet not what you find in most restaurants. They serve the famous Roman lamb, *abbacchio*, for example, with scrambled eggs, a surprising yet amazingly good combination.

In addition to the regular list, special menus appear according to the season. For spring, there is an artichoke menu with artichoke soups, pasta, crostini, and stews. For winter, the special menu is a *fantasia di polenta*, with both crisp-fried and soft polenta and a variety of toppings. Tender, meaty spareribs cooked in a rich tomato sauce and served over soft polenta is one of my favorites from the polenta menu.

Vecchia Roma
Via della Tribuna di Campitelli, 18
Rome

Spareribs and Tomato Sauce with Polenta

POLENTA CON SPUNTATURE

2 tablespoons olive oil
2 pounds pork spareribs, cut into individual ribs
Salt and freshly ground pepper, to taste
1 medium onion, finely chopped
1 medium carrot, finely chopped
1 small celery rib, finely chopped
2 garlic cloves, finely chopped
1/2 cup dry white wine
2 cups tomato puree or canned Italian tomatoes passed through a food mill
2 tablespoons chopped fresh parsley
4 cups hot Polenta (page 191)
1 to 2 tablespoons freshly grated pecorino romano

1 In a large flameproof casserole over medium heat, heat the oil and brown the ribs well on all sides. Remove the ribs to a plate. Sprinkle with salt and pepper.

2 Spoon all but 2 tablespoons of the fat from the casserole. Add the onion, carrot, and celery, and cook for 5 minutes. Stir in the garlic. Add the wine and bring to a simmer, scraping the bottom of the pan. Add the ribs, tomato puree, parsley, salt, and pepper. Cook for 1 to 1 1/2 hours, or until the ribs are very tender and the meat is coming away from the bones. Remove any loose bones.

3 Pour the polenta onto a platter. Top with the ribs and sauce. Sprinkle with pecorino and serve.

To make ahead: The ribs can be cooked completely up to 1 or 2 days before serving and reheated in the sauce.

Salmon Carpaccio (page 201)

Grilled Quail with Sausages

(page 241)

Bollito Misto
(page 257)

Braised Lamb Shanks with Carrots, Celery, and Prosciutto

(page 268)

Roman Artichoke Stew

(page 279)

Beans with Onion Spoons

(page 283)

*Strawberries in Red
Wine, Mascarpone,
and Bread*

(page 331)

Apple Lattice Tart

Grilled Pork Tenderloin with Horseradish Sauce

FILETTO DI MAIALE CON SALSA DI CREN

2 pork tenderloins (about 1 1/2 pounds)

2 tablespoons chopped fresh sage

2 tablespoons chopped fresh basil

2 tablespoons chopped fresh chives

1 tablespoon chopped fresh rosemary leaves

1 bay leaf

1 garlic clove, finely chopped

Freshly ground pepper, to taste

4 tablespoons extra virgin olive oil

1 small piece fresh horseradish

Salt, to taste

1 In a shallow bowl, combine the pork with the herbs, garlic, pepper, and 2 tablespoons of the olive oil. Cover and marinate for several hours at room temperature or overnight in the refrigerator, turning the meat occasionally.

2 Peel and grate enough horseradish to make 1/2 cup. Stir in the remaining 2 tablespoons oil. Set aside.

3 Preheat the grill or broiler.

4 Grill the pork, turning to brown on all sides, 10 to 20 minutes, or until the meat is just slightly pink in the center. Sprinkle with salt. Let the meat rest on a cutting board for 10 minutes.

5 Slice the pork and serve it with the horseradish sauce.

SERVES 6

In Friuli, grated fresh horseradish is served with the local San Daniele prosciutto, though the ham is so good it really needs no adornment. San Daniele is less salty than other prosciuttos and it is easy to recognize even without tasting it since the hoof is left attached. Many experts consider it the best prosciutto. (San Daniele prosciutto exported to the United States has had the hoof removed.)

Horseradish is a member of the mustard family, and like mustard, it has a sinus-clearing, pungent flavor that goes well with pork, including this simple grilled dish. To use the fresh root, peel off the skin and any greenish-colored flesh. Grate the horseradish on a metal grater just before using or it will discolor and turn brown. If you cannot find fresh horseradish, serve the meat with radishes sliced and tossed with olive oil, salt, and pepper. You could also use prepared horseradish, though it lacks the flavor of fresh.

The splendid city of Orvieto in Umbria sits atop a plateau, like a crown on the head of a king. As you approach it, it seems to rise up magically before your eyes, a most dramatic sight. Its strategic location was especially important during the Middle Ages when it was used by Pope Clement VII as a hideaway after Charles V sacked Rome.

We stayed just outside Orvieto at the Hotel La Badia, a former Benedictine abbey that has been restored and converted into a hotel with antique furnishings and comfortable rooms. In the dining room, we ate spaghetti with the local black truffles and this dish of skewered marinated pork and chicken livers cooked on a spit in the huge open hearth. Our waiter was a fresh-faced young man who shyly presented me with a majolica water pitcher I had admired.

La Badia
Orvieto (Umbria)

Skewered Pork and Chicken Livers

SPIEDINI DI MAIALE E FEGATINI

1 teaspoon juniper berries

2 large garlic cloves, finely chopped

3 tablespoons chopped fresh sage

1 1/2 teaspoons fresh rosemary leaves

1 teaspoon salt

Freshly ground pepper, to taste

2 tablespoons olive oil

1 pound trimmed boneless pork loin, cut into 2 × 2 × 2-inch pieces

8 ounces chicken livers, halved

4 ounces thinly sliced pancetta, cut into 3 × 1-inch strips

1 medium red bell pepper, cored, seeded, and cut into 1-inch squares

1 medium yellow bell pepper, cored, seeded, and cut into 1-inch squares

1 Crush the juniper berries with the flat side of the blade of a heavy chef's knife. In a large bowl, combine the juniper with the garlic, sage, rosemary, salt, pepper, and olive oil. Add the pork and stir well. Cover and refrigerate for 24 hours, stirring occasionally.

2 Preheat the broiler or grill.

3 Wrap each liver half in a strip of pancetta and thread the pieces alternately with pieces of pork and pepper on 6 metal skewers. Broil or grill about 5 inches from the heat source, turning occasionally, until the pork is cooked through, about 15 minutes. Serve immediately.

Pork Chops with Pickled Peppers

BRACIOLE DI MAIALE CON PEPERONI

1 tablespoon olive oil

4 pork loin chops, about 1 inch thick

Salt and freshly ground pepper, to taste

4 large garlic cloves, thinly sliced

1 cup dry white wine

1/2 cup white wine vinegar

1 cup seeded and sliced hot or sweet pickled peppers, drained

1 In a large skillet over medium heat, heat the olive oil. Pat the chops dry and brown them on 1 side, about 2 minutes. Turn the chops and sprinkle with salt and pepper. Scatter the garlic slices around the chops and brown the other side. Sprinkle with salt and pepper. Add the wine and vinegar, turning the chops once or twice. Reduce the heat to low.

2 Cover and cook for 1¼ to 1½ hours, or until the chops are tender when pierced with a fork and most of the liquid has evaporated. If the chops become too dry, add a little water. Stir the peppers into the pan juices and cook for 5 minutes more.

3 Place the chops on a serving platter and spoon the peppers and pan juices over them. Serve immediately.

SERVES 4

Pork is bred so lean nowadays that chops often dry out by the time they are done. I find the best way to cook pork chops is to braise them a long time, until the meat is tender and falling from the bone. These tangy chops are simmered with wine, vinegar, garlic, and pickled peppers. If you like, add a few hot pickled peppers to the sweet, but not so many that their flavor is overwhelming. Barley and Bean Soup (page 89) would be a good first course, and the chops can be served with Broccoli Rabe with Garlic and Hot Pepper (page 286).

Pot-roasted beef simmered in a savory onion sauce and served over pasta is a classic Neapolitan dish, despite the fact that it's called Genoa-style beef by the Neapolitans. The explanation is that during the 1600s many of the trattorias in Naples were operated by cooks from Genoa, and a simpler version of this beef dish was their specialty. The salami and prosciutto were not added until sometime later, probably during the 1800s.

This recipe comes from my father's mother, Antoinetta Scotto. She taught it to her children, who in turn passed it along to their children. My cousin Joanne told me that when my aunt Donna gave her the recipe, included in the list of ingredients was "one small can of tomato paste with the label removed." The can was to be used not for its contents but as a tool to push the softened onions through a sieve. I remember my grandmother and mother making the sauce that way, though these days I use a food processor.

The onion sauce for this recipe is abundant because it is meant to be served over dried pasta as a first course. My mother preferred mafalde, a shape I rarely see anymore, which looks like a narrow, wavy-edged lasagna. Long fusilli or rotelle would also be good.

Grandmother's Pot Roast with Pasta and Onion Sauce

LA GENOVESE

2 tablespoons olive oil

3 pounds pot roast, such as bottom round or rump

Salt and freshly ground pepper, to taste

3 pounds yellow onions, very thinly sliced

4 large carrots, thinly sliced

2 ounces Genoa salami, cut into thin strips

2 ounces prosciutto, cut into thin strips

1 pound mafalde or fusilli

Freshly grated Parmigiano-Reggiano (optional)

1 Preheat the oven to 325°F.

2 In a large ovenproof casserole or Dutch oven over medium heat, heat the oil. Add the meat and brown it well on all sides. Sprinkle it with salt and pepper. Remove the meat from the pot and drain off the fat. Pour in 1 cup water and scrape the bottom of the pot with a wooden spoon to loosen any browned bits. Add the onions, carrots, salami, and prosciutto to the pot. Place the roast on top. Cover the pot and bring the liquid to a simmer. Place the pot in the oven.

3 Cook, turning the meat occasionally, until the meat is very tender when pierced with a fork, 2¹/₂ to 3 hours. Remove the meat to a platter and keep warm.

4 Spoon the sauce into a food processor or blender and puree until smooth. Season to taste. Return the sauce and the meat to the pot and reheat gently over low heat. Watch carefully so that the sauce does not scorch.

5 In a large pot of boiling salted water, cook the pasta until tender yet firm to the bite. Drain well.

6 In a large serving bowl, combine the pasta with just enough of the sauce to coat it lightly, reserving the rest of the sauce for the meat.

Serve the pasta with the cheese, if desired, as a first course.

7 Gently reheat the meat and sauce. Slice the meat and serve it with the sauce.

To make ahead: The pot roast can be completely cooked through Step 4 up to 2 days before serving and reheated.

Pork Chops in Red Wine and Juniper

BRACIOLE DI MAIALE AL VINO ROSSO E GINEPRO

2 tablespoons olive oil

4 pork loin chops, about 1 inch thick

8 garlic cloves, peeled

Salt and freshly ground pepper, to taste

6 juniper berries

1 cup dry red wine

1 bay leaf

1 In a large skillet over medium heat, heat the olive oil. Add the pork chops and the garlic. Cook, turning the chops once, until browned on both sides. Sprinkle with salt and pepper. Spoon off the excess fat.

2 Crush the juniper berries with the flat side of the blade of a heavy chef's knife.

3 Add the juniper berries, wine, and bay leaf to the skillet. Bring to a simmer. Reduce the heat to low and cover the pan. Cook, turning the chops occasionally, for 1 hour, or until the meat is tender when pierced with a fork. There should be just a few tablespoons of concentrated liquid left in the pan. Add a little water if the juices become too dry.

4 Remove the bay leaf and serve.

SERVES 4

Red wine stains these chops a deep mahogany red while the garlic cloves become sweet and mellow. Serve the chops with Fennel Mashed Potatoes (page 305).

When meat was scarce, southern Italians devised ways to make the most out of very little. In this dish, for example, a flattened slice of beef was rolled around a stuffing to give it the look of a small roast. The stuffing varied according to what the cook could afford. This one, from the Mastroberardino winemaking family, is rich with eggs, prosciutto, pine nuts, and raisins. Sometimes a simple stuffing of bread crumbs, parsley, and garlic would be used. The stuffed and rolled meat is braised in a tomato sauce, both to tenderize it and to impart its flavors to the sauce. The sauce is served with pasta as a first course, and the meat is sliced like a roast and served as a second course. The fact that such recipes survive in times of plenty is a tribute to how good and satisfying they are.

Serve the sliced meat with Smothered Cauliflower (page 287) or Broccoli Rabe with Garlic and Hot Pepper (page 286). A Mastroberardino Lacryma Christi del Vesuvio Rosso would round out the meal very nicely.

Stuffed Beef Roll, Neapolitan Style

BRACIOLA ALLA NAPOLETANA

1 pound boneless beef top round, about 1 inch thick

Salt and freshly ground pepper, to taste

Pinch of freshly grated nutmeg

2 ounces sliced prosciutto

2 hard-cooked eggs, thinly sliced

2 tablespoons pine nuts, toasted

2 tablespoons raisins

1 tablespoon chopped fresh parsley

1 garlic clove, finely chopped

1/4 teaspoon dried oregano

1/4 cup olive oil

1 medium onion, finely chopped

1 cup dry red wine

4 cups tomato puree or canned Italian tomatoes passed through a food mill

2 tablespoons chopped fresh basil

8 ounces penne or ziti

1 Place the beef between 2 pieces of plastic wrap and pound gently with a meat pounder or rubber mallet to a 1/4- to 1/8-inch thickness. Sprinkle the meat with salt, pepper, and nutmeg. Cover it with the sliced prosciutto. Lay the egg slices on top. Sprinkle with the pine nuts, raisins, parsley, garlic, and oregano. Carefully roll up the meat to enclose the filling. With kitchen twine, tie the roll at 1-inch intervals.

2 In a large saucepan over medium heat, heat the oil. Add the beef roll and brown it on 1 side. Turn the meat and add the onion. Cook, turning the beef occasionally, until it is browned and the onions are translucent, about 5 minutes. Add the wine and bring it to a simmer. Cook for 2 minutes. Add the tomato puree and basil.

3 Cover and cook on low heat, turning the meat occasionally until it is tender when pierced with a fork, about 2 hours. Add a little water if the sauce becomes too thick.

4 Just before serving, bring a large pot of water to boiling. Add salt to taste and the pasta. Cook, stirring occasionally, until the pasta is al dente, tender yet firm to the bite. Drain well and toss with some of the sauce. Serve the pasta as a first course.

5 Cut the beef roll into thick slices and remove the twine. Spoon some of the remaining sauce on a heated platter and arrange overlapping slices of beef on top. Serve at once.

To make ahead: Cook the meat entirely through Step 3. Let cool, then cover and refrigerate for up to 2 days. Reheat gently and proceed with the recipe.

Roman-style Oxtail Stew

CODA ALLA VACCINARA

¹/₄ cup olive oil

3¹/₂ pounds oxtail, trimmed and cut into 1¹/₂-inch pieces

1 large onion, chopped

2 garlic cloves, minced

4 whole cloves

Salt and freshly ground pepper, to taste

1 cup dry white wine

1 can (35 ounces) Italian peeled tomatoes, chopped

6 celery ribs, coarsely chopped (about 3 cups)

3 tablespoons pine nuts

3 tablespoons raisins

1 tablespoon grated bittersweet chocolate

1 In a large Dutch oven over medium heat, heat the olive oil. Pat the meat dry. Add the oxtail a few pieces at time and brown on all

> *"Going on strike in Rome is much more a matter of style than it is of economics. Rome is a very loony city in every respect. One needs but spend an hour or two there to realize that Fellini makes documentaries."*
>
> Fran Lebowitz

Once Charles and I were stranded at a railroad station in Rome because of an unexpected—but typically Italian—*sciopero*, or strike. The ticketmaster assured us that the train to Genoa would arrive late in the afternoon, so we had several hours to kill. Since it was a Sunday, the baggage room was closed. Hungry, tired, and burdened with luggage, we headed for the bustling Trattoria Checchino dal 1887 unannounced at the height of the lunch service. Located on Monte Testaccio in front of the city's former slaughterhouses, Trattoria Checchino built its reputation by serving classic Roman cuisine, which abounds in tasty ways to use innards and other less-than-prime animal parts, such as oxtails.

We explained our plight to Francesco Mariani, one of the

restaurant's owners, who immediately took pity on a pair of exhausted travelers. Our baggage was whisked out of sight, and a splendid lunch featuring oxtail appeared. We even had time to visit the restaurant's awe-inspiring wine cellar, built into a veritable mountain of discarded Roman amphorae, which act as a natural method of insulation. Later, Francesco insisted on driving us, restored and refreshed, back to the station to make sure we would catch our train.

Oxtail is one of the boniest, yet tastiest meats you will ever eat. Serve this stew plain or with polenta or lots of good bread to soak up the sauce. Any leftover sauce can be served with pasta. A hearty shape like rigatoni goes best.

Trattoria Checchino dal 1887
Via Monte Testaccio, 30
Rome

sides. Remove the pieces to a plate as they are browned. Spoon off all but 2 tablespoons of the fat. Add the onion, garlic, cloves, salt, and pepper. Sauté until golden. Add the wine and simmer until most of the liquid has evaporated. Add the oxtail, tomatoes, and 2 cups water. Bring to a simmer. Reduce the heat, cover, and cook, stirring occasionally, until the meat is very tender and falls away from the bone, about 3½ hours.

2 Meanwhile, bring a large pot of water to a boil. Add the celery and return the water to a boil. Cook for 1 minute. Drain well.

3 When the oxtail is tender, spoon about 2 cups of the sauce into a small saucepan. Add the blanched celery, pine nuts, raisins, and chocolate. Bring to a simmer over medium-low heat and cook for 5 minutes.

4 Transfer the oxtails to a serving platter. Spoon the celery and sauce over the meat and serve hot.

To make ahead: The oxtail can be cooked completely up to 2 days ahead of time. Any leftover sauce can be served over pasta.

RISTORANTE
NUOVO
MARCONI

37121 VERONA - Via Fogge, 4 - Tel. 045/591910-595295
CHIUSO DOMENICA

Mixed Simmered Meats with Green Sauce

BOLLITO MISTO

2 celery ribs with leaves, cut into 2-inch lengths

2 large carrots, quartered

1 large onion, peeled

1 large ripe tomato or 2 canned plum tomatoes

2 pounds beef brisket or rump

Coarse salt, to taste

1 whole veal shank, trimmed and tied (about 2^1/$_2$ pounds)

1 veal tongue or beef tongue (about 2 pounds)

1 zampone (about 2 pounds) or cotechino sausage (about 1 pound)

1 whole chicken (about 3^1/$_2$ pounds)

1 pound fresh quadrucci or fettuccine cut into 1-inch lengths

Parmesan (optional)

Green Sauce (optional; recipe follows)

Mostarda di Cremona (optional)

1 In a 16- to 20-quart stockpot or two 8-quart pots, combine the vegetables and 8 quarts of cold water. Bring to a simmer over medium heat.

2 Add the beef and a little salt. (If using beef tongue instead of veal tongue, add it now.) Bring the liquid back to a simmer and cook for 1 hour. Skim off the foam that forms on the surface throughout the cooking time. Add the veal shank and veal tongue, if using, to the pot and return the liquid to a simmer. Simmer for 45 minutes.

3 Meanwhile, place the sausage in a large saucepan with water to cover by 2 inches. Cover the pot and bring it to a simmer. Simmer for 1^1/$_2$ hours. (Do not be tempted to add the sausage to the stockpot; it will make the broth greasy.)

In Emilia-Romagna and other regions of northern Italy, *bollito misto,* an assortment of meats simmered in a rich broth, is a sumptuous feast. First the broth is served, usually with homemade pasta and a generous sprinkling of Parmigiano-Reggiano. Next the meat and poultry, including chicken or capon, *zampone* or *cotechino* sausage, and various cuts of beef and veal, are sliced and served with sauces that differ from region to region. In Piedmont it might be a creamy garlic sauce; in other places tomato sauce is served. In Emilia-Romagna, the sauces usually include green sauce made with capers, garlic, and parsley, and *mostarda di Cremona,* gem-like whole fruits preserved in a sweet and hot mustard syrup. (The word *mostarda* is used in different areas of Italy to apply to other foods, including a sweet grape syrup or preserve derived from *mosto,* or grape must. When asking for the fruits in mustard syrup for bollito, be sure to specify mostarda di Cremona.)

Restaurants specializing in bollito misto, such as Diana in Bologna and Arnaldo in Rubiera, have specially constructed stainless steel carts with deep wells to hold both broth and meat. When a customer orders the bollito, the waiter wheels the cart over and removes the meats one by one for inspection and selection.

Obviously, a full-fledged bollito misto feeds a crowd. It is a great excuse for a party, and once a year when the weather is cold in January or February, I have a bollito misto dinner at my house. The aroma of the simmering meats is incredible. Though the cooking is long, bollito misto needs very little attention, so there is plenty of time to set the table and relax before guests arrive.

Two of the ingredients for a classic bollito misto may require some shopping around, so plan ahead. *Zampone* is a boned pig's foot stuffed with delicately spiced minced pork and pork skin. The skin makes the sausage tender and gelatinous and each savory bite seems to melt in your mouth, leaving lingering hints of clove, cinnamon, and nutmeg behind. *Cotechino* is a sausage very similar to zampone, except that the spiced ground meat is enclosed in pork skin instead of the foot. If you live near an Italian pork butcher, ask if he makes it, especially around Christmas time. (Eating zampone with lentils on New Year's Day is said to bring good luck.) Otherwise, both zampone and cotechino can be ordered by mail from a number of sources. While hunting for the sausages, also look for the mostarda di Cremona, which is put up in jars.

You'll need a very large pot to make bollito misto. Mine is a 20-quart heavy aluminum stockpot that was surprisingly inexpensive at a restaurant-supply store. If you don't have a large enough pot, try to borrow one, or divide the recipe

4 Add the chicken to the stockpot with the beef. If necessary, add additional water so that the meats are covered. Bring back to a simmer. Simmer for 1 hour, or until all the meats are tender when pierced with a fork.

5 Remove the tongue and split the skin with a small knife. Peel off and discard the skin, gristle, and any bones. Return the meat to the pot to reheat.

6 Skim the fat from the broth. Taste for salt. The meats can stay warm in the broth for at least 1 hour.

7 To serve the broth as a first course with pasta, bring a large pot of water to a boil. Cook the pasta until tender yet firm to the bite. Spoon some of the broth into a tureen and add the pasta. Serve with grated parmesan. Slice part of the meats and sausage as needed, keeping the rest submerged in the broth. Serve the slices on a warm plat-

Ode to a Sausage

Giocchino Rossini, the great Italian composer, lived in Paris for many years and longed for the food and wines of his native Italy. He signed his letters during that time with the phrase *Senza maccheroni!!!!!,*—without pasta, but with five exclamation points.

He especially loved *zampone*, a sausage made from ground spiced pork stuffed into a pig's foot, and once said that a zampone from Modena in his stomach was worth more to him than any medal on his chest. Friends and admirers, knowing his penchant for good food and drink, were constantly sending him cheeses, olives, truffles, cakes, wine, and sausages. He penned the following immodest poem as a thank-you note for a gift of his favorite sausage and wine:

"I received the zampone and ate it,
I received the lambrusco and drank it
The food was exquisite, worthy of Rossini,
The wine was worthy of the gods of Homer."

ter moistened with broth. Pass bowls of Green Sauce and mostarda di Cremona, if using.

Cook's note: Leftover bollito misto makes a wonderful soup. Cut the meats and sausage into bite-size pieces and store them in the broth. After a day or two, reheat the broth and add some fresh noodles or pasta. If you like, add some diced cooked vegetables, too. Serve hot with Parmigiano.

Mostarda di Cremona

Mostarda di Cremona is made from whole small fruits like apricots, cherries, figs, and tangerines, and cut-up larger fruits such as pineapples and peaches. The fruits are poached in a series of mustard-flavored syrups with different sugar densities until most of their moisture is extracted. The fruits remain whole and their colors bright, enhanced by the syrup glaze.

Mostarda di Cremona is widely distributed in the United States. Dondi and Sperlari are the brands I most often see, and others are available in Italian groceries and specialty food shops. Look for a fresh batch, not one that has been sitting on the shelf for years. The liquid should be clear to light golden and the colors of the fruits vivid and jewel-like. All brands are sweet, but some are insipid. Others have a pungent mustard flavor, which I prefer. In Milan, Peck's, a not-to-be-missed food emporium located near the Duomo, sells an excellent version made for them exclusively. Unfortunately, it is not exported, so I always bring home a jar or two. I also have been known to bribe friends who are traveling to Milan to bring back a couple of jars for me. The pay-off: a bollito misto dinner for two. Mostarda di Cremona keeps well in the refrigerator. It is also good as a condiment for roast pork or chicken or grilled spareribs.

into two smaller pots, switching the meats from one to the other halfway through the cooking. The total cooking time is about four hours. The beef, which takes the longest, needs at least three hours and it takes almost an hour to bring that much water to the simmer. Allow a little extra time to be sure the meat is very tender.

To keep the meats hot and succulent when done, leave them submerged in the warm broth as much as possible. Keep the sausage warm in its separate pot. Slice only as much of the meats and sausage as needed at one time and serve them on a warm platter moistened with broth.

Once the meats are cooked, they will keep hot for up to an hour in partially covered pots, or they can be gently reheated. This recipe will feed a small crowd, but don't attempt to serve it buffet style; it's too messy. For a smaller number of guests, the recipe can be scaled down. Eliminate the sausage and tongue, for example; it will still be quite a feast.

Along with the meats, serve a bowl of colorful steamed whole vegetables such as white onions, carrots, and zucchini. Mostarda di Cremona is optional, but I would not leave out the Green Sauce (recipe follows).

Diana
Via Indipendenza, 24
Bologna (Emilia-Romagna)

Arnaldo-Clinica Gastronomica
Piazza 24 Maggio 3
Rubiera (Emilia-Romagna)

Next to tomato sauce, green sauce is one of the most versatile sauces in the Italian repertoire, though most Americans are unfamiliar with it. Some versions take vinegar instead of lemon juice, others call for garlic or onion instead of shallots, some add prepared mustard for flavoring or soaked bread for thickening. Green sauce tastes wonderful on all kinds of meat, poultry, and fish (see the recipe for salmon in a slightly different green sauce on page 202). It is even good on cooked vegetables like green beans or potatoes, on sliced tomatoes, and on hard-cooked eggs. The color stays bright green and the flavor remains tangy up to one week stored in the refrigerator. Green Sauce should be served at cool room temperature.

Green Sauce

SALSA VERDE

$1/4$ cup chopped Italian flat-leaf parsley
$1/4$ cup chopped drained capers
2 tablespoons finely chopped shallots
1 can (2 ounces) anchovy fillets, drained and chopped
1 garlic clove, finely chopped
2 tablespoons fresh lemon juice
$1/2$ cup extra virgin olive oil

In a bowl, whisk together the parsley, capers, shallots, anchovies, garlic, lemon juice, and olive oil. Cover and let stand at room temperature for 1 hour, or refrigerate for up to 1 week. Stir and taste for seasoning before serving.

This simple dish is a Neapolitan version of a boiled dinner, much less lavish than the grand bollito misto since only one kind of meat is used. When the meat is tender, it is cut up and either added back into the broth with dried pasta or tossed with celery and onion to make a warm second-course salad.

Neapolitan Boiled Dinner

MANZO BOLLITO ALLA NAPOLETANA

SOUP
$2^{1}/2$ pounds beef chuck roast
2 celery ribs, sliced
2 medium carrots, sliced
2 medium-size ripe tomatoes, peeled, seeded, and chopped
1 large yellow onion, chopped

3 medium potatoes, peeled

Salt and freshly ground pepper, to taste

8 ounces small pasta such as ditalini or small elbows

Freshly grated Parmigiano-Reggiano

SALAD (OPTIONAL)

2 celery ribs with leaves, thinly sliced

1 medium red onion, thinly sliced

2 tablespoons olive oil

4 tablespoons red wine vinegar, or to taste

Salt and freshly ground pepper, to taste

1 Place the beef in a large pot. Add 3 quarts cold water. Bring the water to a simmer. Simmer the beef for 2$\frac{1}{2}$ hours, skimming off the foam that rises to the surface. Add the vegetables, salt, and pepper. Simmer for 20 to 30 minutes more, or until the meat and potatoes are tender when pierced with a knife. (If the potatoes are done before the beef is tender, remove them so that they do not overcook.) Remove the meat and potatoes from the pot and set aside.

2 Add the pasta to the soup and cook, stirring occasionally, until tender, about 10 minutes.

3 Cut the meat and potatoes into bite-size pieces. If you are not making the meat salad, add the meat and potatoes to the soup and reheat gently. Taste for seasoning. Serve hot with cheese.

4 To make the salad, place the meat and potatoes in a large serving bowl. Add the celery and onion. Whisk together the oil, vinegar, salt, and pepper. Pour the dressing over the salad and toss well. Serve at room temperature or lightly chilled.

To make ahead: The soup can be made through Step 1 up to 2 days before serving. Reheat and proceed with the recipe just before serving.

"When I stopped by the only café in the central market of Florence, I found that its specialty was a meat sandwich—veal the day I was there. The sandwich maker carved slices from a large piece of veal that was sitting on a platter in an inch or two of juice. Then he chopped the slices into finer pieces. Then he took a bun, sliced it in two, placed both halves in the veal platter inner side down, and, with an index finger on each half, submerged them in the juice. Then he packed up the dripping bun with the veal, added what appeared to be about a quarter cup of salt, and handed it over. Breakfast."

Calvin Trillin, "Full Market Basket,"
Travels with Alice

Cheese-stuffed Roast Breast of Veal

Winter is the perfect time of year to be in Parma in Emilia-Romagna. The frosty weather gives you an appetite for the rich butter and cheese-based cooking of the region. At Croce di Malta restaurant, this cheese-stuffed breast of veal was served with potatoes, carrots, and onions roasted to a rich caramel brown to bring out their sweetness. Actually, the veal needs little more than a steamed green vegetable, such as broccoli or spinach to accompany it.

Veal breast can be extremely fatty. Trim it well or have the butcher do it for you but be sure to leave a pocket between the meat and the ribs for the stuffing. To sew the pocket closed, I use a big stainless steel upholstery needle threaded with unwaxed dental floss. The floss is strong and convenient.

Croce di Malta
Borgo Palmia, 8
Parma (Emilia-Romagna)

PETTO DI VITELLO ALLA PARMIGIANA

3/4 cup fresh bread crumbs from the inside of a loaf of Italian or French bread

1/4 cup milk

1 cup freshly grated Parmigiano-Reggiano

2 large eggs, beaten

Salt and freshly ground pepper, to taste

5 pounds veal breast, trimmed with a pocket left for stuffing (6 ribs)

2 tablespoons unsalted butter

2 tablespoons vegetable oil

1/2 cup finely chopped onion

1 tablespoon chopped fresh rosemary leaves

1/2 cup dry white wine

1 Soak the bread crumbs in the milk for 10 minutes. Lightly squeeze the crumbs to eliminate excess liquid. In a large bowl, combine the bread crumbs, cheese, eggs, salt, and pepper. Stuff the mixture into the veal pocket. Sew up the opening with dental floss or heavy cotton thread.

2 In a casserole large enough to hold the veal, heat the butter with the oil, onion, and rosemary. Add the veal and cook over medium heat, turning once, until browned on both sides. Sprinkle with salt and pepper. Add the wine and bring to a simmer. After 1 minute, partially cover the pan and turn the heat to low. Cook, turning the meat occasionally, until it is very tender and browned, 2 to 2$1/2$ hours. If necessary, add a little water to prevent the meat from sticking. Transfer the meat to a cutting board and keep warm.

3 Tip the pan and skim off the fat. Add 1/4 cup water to the pan juices and bring to a simmer over medium heat. Cook, scraping the bottom of the pan, until the juices are slightly reduced.

4 Carve the veal and serve with the pan juices.

Roasted Veal Shanks

STINCO DI VITELLO AL FORNO

2 tablespoons unsalted butter

2 tablespoons olive oil

2 veal shanks, trimmed (about 2$\frac{1}{2}$ pounds each)

Salt and freshly ground pepper, to taste

1 cup dry white wine

2 garlic cloves, thinly sliced

2 small sprigs of fresh rosemary

2 bay leaves

$\frac{1}{2}$ cup Meat Broth (page 83)

1 Preheat the oven to 350°F.

2 In a casserole just large enough to hold the meat, melt the butter with the oil over medium heat. Add the veal. Sprinkle the meat with salt and pepper. Cook, turning occasionally, until browned on all sides. Add the wine, garlic, rosemary, and bay leaves. Cover the casserole with a lid or aluminum foil. Place in the oven and bake for 45 minutes. Turn the meat and add the broth. Cover and bake for 1 hour more, or until the meat is very tender and coming away from the bone. Add a little more broth or water, if necessary, to keep the meat moist. Remove the veal shanks from the casserole and keep them warm.

3 If the juices are too thin, boil them until reduced and slightly syrupy. Strain the juices and skim off the fat.

4 Carve the veal and serve with the pan juices.

To make ahead: Prepare the veal shanks up to 2 hours before serving and reheat if necessary.

I love the look on my friends' faces when I tell them we're having *stinco* for dinner. That's what the shank cut of meat is called in Italian. At Antica Trattoria Suban in Trieste, the specialty of the house is veal stinco, roasted to a rich brown and served with its cooking juices. The owner, Mario Suban, is so proud of the perfectly roasted meat that he has been known to parade it around the room on a silver platter.

In some regions of Italy, veal shanks are cut crosswise into thick slices for osso buco, but in the Veneto and Friuli the shanks usually are cooked whole.

Since butchers in the United States are used to cutting veal shanks into slices, you will have to explain that you want the shank left whole, just trimmed of the excess fat and bony portions above and below the meat. Ask to have the silverskin that covers the meat left intact; it helps the meat keep its shape. As it cooks, the veal shrinks away from the bone, leaving you with a perfect handle for holding the shank while carving. Wrap the end of the bone in a cloth napkin or tea towel for easy handling when slicing.

Antica Trattoria Suban
Via Comici, 2
Trieste (Friuli-Venezia-Giulia)

Use full-flavored but not too salty olives for this stew. Serve it with soft polenta or mashed potatoes to soak up the sauce and follow it with a green salad. A robust red wine such as the Primitivo di Manduria from southern Italy would be a good match.

"They who would know how beautiful the country immediately surrounding Genoa is, should climb (in clear weather) to the top of Monte Faccio, or, at least, ride round the city walls: a feat more easily performed. . . . In not the least picturesque part of this ride, there is a fair specimen of a real Genoese tavern, where the visitor may derive good entertainment from real Genoese dishes, such as Tagliarini; Ravioli; German sausages, strong of garlic, sliced and eaten with fresh green figs; cocks' combs and sheep-kidneys, chopped up with mutton chops and liver; small pieces of some unknown part of a calf, twisted into small shreds, fried, and served up in a great dish like whitebait; and other curiosities of that kind."

Charles Dickens, *Pictures from Italy*

Veal Stew with Tomatoes and Olives

SPEZZATINO DI VITELLO

2 tablespoons olive oil

2 pounds boneless veal shoulder, cut into $1^1/_2$-inch chunks

1 medium onion, finely chopped

Freshly ground pepper, to taste

1 cup chopped fresh or canned Italian tomatoes

3 garlic cloves, finely chopped

1 cup dry white wine

$^1/_2$ cup green olives, pitted and chopped

$^1/_2$ cup imported black olives, such as Gaeta, pitted and chopped

Salt

1 In a large saucepan over medium heat, heat the oil. Add the veal and onion. Cook, stirring occasionally, until the meat is lightly browned on all sides. Season to taste with pepper. (Since the olives will add salt, do not add any at this time.) Add the tomatoes, garlic, and wine. Bring the liquid to a simmer.

2 Cover and cook for $1^1/_4$ hours, or until the veal is tender when pierced with a fork. If there is a lot of liquid, uncover the pot and cook the stew until it is reduced.

3 Stir in the olives and cook for 5 minutes. Taste for salt. Serve hot.

Veal Chops with Sautéed Sweet Peppers

COSTOLETTE DI VITELLO CON PEPERONI

4 tablespoons olive oil

2 medium red bell peppers, cut into ½-inch strips

2 medium yellow bell peppers, cut into ½-inch strips

2 large garlic cloves, finely chopped

2 tablespoons drained capers, chopped

Salt and freshly ground pepper, to taste

4 veal loin chops, about 1 inch thick

½ cup dry white wine

2 tablespoons chopped fresh parsley

1 In a large heavy skillet over medium-low heat, heat 2 tablespoons of the olive oil. Add the peppers and garlic and stir once or twice. Cook, stirring occasionally, until the peppers are tender and lightly browned, about 15 to 20 minutes. Add the capers, salt, and pepper. Cook for 1 minute more. Transfer the peppers to a plate. Wipe out the skillet.

2 Pat the veal chops dry with paper towels.

3 In a heavy skillet large enough to hold the chops in a single layer, heat the remaining oil over medium heat. Add the veal chops and brown them well on both sides, about 6 minutes. Sprinkle the chops with salt and pepper. Spoon off the excess fat. Add the wine to the pan and bring it to a simmer, scraping the bottom of the pan. Cover and cook until the chops are done to taste, about 2 minutes for medium-rare. Transfer the chops to a warm serving platter.

4 Raise the heat under the skillet and boil the liquid until it is reduced and slightly syrupy. Add the peppers to the skillet and reheat for 1 minute. Stir in the parsley. Taste for seasoning.

5 Spoon the peppers over the chops and serve.

The charm of veal for the Italians is the opportunity it gives them to utilize their culinary artistry to the full. Meats with more individualistic flavors refuse to enter with becoming modesty into the harmonious blends which are the triumph of Italian cooking," wrote Waverley Root in *Food*. One very harmonious blend is this combination of veal chops with red and yellow peppers, garlic, and capers.

While a barbecue means grilled steaks, hot dogs, or hamburgers to most people, at my parents' home it meant *spiedini,* which translates as little skewered things. Spiedini can take many forms, but the kind my family liked best were made of thin veal cutlets wrapped around a slice of prosciutto and a piece of mozzarella. Thin slices of beef, pork, or even swordfish (see page 208), each with a different filling, are also prepared this way for grilling or broiling.

Veal Rolls with Prosciutto and Mozzarella

SPIEDINI DI VITELLO

1 pound veal cutlets

Salt and freshly ground pepper, to taste

2 ounces thinly sliced prosciutto

4 ounces mozzarella, cut into $1 \times {}^1/_4 \times {}^1/_4$-inch sticks

2 tablespoons chopped Italian flat-leaf parsley

1 large garlic clove, minced

2 tablespoons olive oil

${}^1/_2$ cup dry bread crumbs

1 Place the veal cutlets between 2 sheets of plastic wrap. With a meat pounder or rubber mallet, pound the veal to an even $^1/_4$-inch thickness. Cut the veal into 3×2-inch pieces.

2 Sprinkle the veal with salt and pepper. Place a slice of prosciutto on each cutlet trimming it to fit. Place a stick of mozzarella in the center. Sprinkle with a pinch of the parsley and garlic. Roll up the cutlets.

3 Hold 2 skewers parallel about 1 inch apart, like the tines of a carving fork. Spear one of the veal rolls on the skewers, pushing the roll down toward the handle or base. If the skewers do not have handles, leave 1 or 2 inches clear at the base for easy handling. Thread as many rolls on the skewers as fit; they should be barely touching. Use additional skewers as needed. Brush the rolls with the oil and dip them in the bread crumbs.

4 Preheat the grill or broiler.

5 Grill or broil the rolls about 4 inches from the source of the heat, just until the meat is browned and the cheese is slightly melted, about 5 minutes on each side.

6 Serve immediately.

To make ahead: The spiedini can be made through Step 3 several hours before cooking. Cover them with plastic wrap and refrigerate until ready to cook.

Lamb Stew with Potatoes and Tomatoes

AGNELLO CON PATATE E POMODORI

2 tablespoons olive oil

1 large onion, chopped

2 pounds leg of lamb, boned and cut into 1-inch chunks

Salt and freshly ground pepper, to taste

¹/₂ cup dry white wine

1¹/₂ pounds tomatoes, peeled, seeded, and chopped (about 3 cups)

1 tablespoon chopped fresh rosemary leaves

1 pound waxy boiling potatoes, cut into 1-inch pieces

2 tablespoons chopped fresh parsley

1 In a large flameproof casserole over medium heat, heat the olive oil. Add the onion. Dry the lamb pieces and add them to the casserole. Cook, stirring frequently, until lightly browned. Sprinkle with salt and pepper. Add the wine and bring it to a simmer.

2 Stir in the tomatoes and rosemary. Reduce the heat to low. Cover and cook for 30 minutes.

3 Add the potatoes, salt, and pepper. Simmer for 30 minutes, or until the lamb and potatoes are tender. Sprinkle with parsley and serve immediately.

SERVES 4 TO 6

Superstitions abound concerning the herb rosemary. At one time or another, it was believed to keep away moths, prevent nightmares and baldness, stave off the evil eye, and foil black magic—though not necessarily in that order.

I find rosemary much more effective for flavoring roasted meats and stews, especially those made with pork or lamb. I use cut-up leg of lamb for this recipe; it is lean and tender and does not require long cooking.

The shank, in my opinion, is one of the tastiest cuts there is. The meat has lots of flavor from being adjacent to the bone, and it becomes tender and gelatinous as it cooks. Besides, most shank recipes reheat well, so even though they require long, slow cooking, they can be made ahead. The only problem with shanks is their appearance—there is nothing dainty about them. The meat shrinks away from the bone so that by the time they are ready, most shanks look like a caveman's dinner. Lamb shanks cut from the shoulder end are meatier and larger than those from the hind legs. If possible, buy the smaller and more tender hind shanks; they are just right for one serving. If all you can find are large ones, have the butcher cut the shanks crosswise into two-inch-thick slices.

Serve these lamb shanks with Baked Beans with Garlic and Sage (page 282).

Braised Lamb Shanks with Carrots, Celery, and Prosciutto

BRASATO DI STINCO DI AGNELLO

4 tablespoons olive oil

6 small lamb shanks

Salt and freshly ground pepper, to taste

1/2 cup dry white wine

2 cups Meat Broth (page 83)

4 large carrots, cut into 2 × 1/2 × 1/2-inch sticks

4 celery ribs, cut into 2 × 1/2 × 1/2-inch sticks

1 tablespoon unsalted butter

2 ounces prosciutto, cut into thin strips

2 tablespoons chopped fresh parsley

1 In a heavy pot just large enough to hold the lamb in a single layer, heat the olive oil over medium-low heat. Pat the lamb shanks dry with paper towels. Brown them on all sides. Sprinkle with salt and pepper. Spoon off the fat. Add the wine and cook, scraping the bottom of the pan. Bring to a simmer and cook for 1 minute. Add the broth and bring it to a simmer. Cover the pot. Cook over low heat, turning the meat occasionally, until the lamb is very tender when pierced with a fork, about 1 1/4 to 1 1/2 hours.

2 While the lamb is cooking, combine the carrots, celery, butter, and 2 tablespoons water in a small saucepan. Cover and cook over medium heat for 5 minutes, or until the vegetables are almost tender.

3 Add the vegetables, prosciutto, and parsley to the lamb. Cook, uncovered, over medium heat for 5 minutes. Remove the meat and vegetables with a slotted spoon and place them on a warm platter. Cover and keep warm. If there is too much liquid left in the pan, raise the heat under the cooking liquid to high and boil until reduced and slightly thickened. Taste for seasoning.

4 Pour the sauce over the meat and vegetables and serve immediately.

To make ahead: The meat can be completely cooked ahead through Step 1 up to 2 days before serving. Reheat the shanks and proceed with the recipe when ready to serve.

Dora's Spring Lamb Casserole

AGNELLO ALLA DORA

2 tablespoons olive oil

2 medium onions, chopped

3 pounds boneless lamb shoulder and leg, trimmed and cut into 2-inch cubes

Salt and freshly ground pepper, to taste

3 tablespoons finely chopped Italian flat-leaf parsley

2 cups fresh or partially thawed frozen peas

3 large eggs

$^1/_2$ cup freshly grated pecorino romano

1 Preheat the oven to 425°F.

2 In a large shallow casserole over medium heat, heat the olive oil. Add the onions and lamb. Cook, stirring occasionally, until the lamb is lightly browned on all sides, about 20 minutes. Sprinkle with salt and pepper.

3 Add 2 tablespoons of the parsley and $1^1/_2$ cups water. Stir well. Cover and bake, stirring occasionally, for 45 minutes, or until the meat is almost tender. Add more water if necessary to prevent the lamb from drying out. Stir in the peas and cook for 10 minutes more.

4 In a bowl, beat the eggs, cheese, remaining parsley, salt, and pepper until well blended. Pour the mixture evenly over the lamb.

5 Bake, uncovered, for 5 minutes, or until the eggs are just set. Serve immediately.

SERVES 6

Several years ago, Tony Di Dio, a friend who is a terrific cook as well as a wine expert, told me about a restaurant in Manhattan that he liked very much. We met there for dinner and, as promised, the food was excellent and the ambience friendly. It reminded me of family-run trattorias in Italy.

Later I learned that the restaurant's owners, who came from near Bari in southern Italy, had had no prior experience running a restaurant, so they cooked and entertained their clients as if they were guests in their home. The mother, Dora Marzovilla, prepared all of the homemade pasta and focaccia while her son Nicola managed the restaurant and staff.

Today Nicola is the host of another comfortable restaurant called I Trulli, for the characteristic dome-shape stone houses in his home region of Puglia. Dora still does much of the cooking, and the restaurant gets rave reviews for its warm atmosphere and fine food.

Dora shared this recipe with me for an article on Italian Easter that I wrote for the *New York Times*. The eggs and peas form a pretty topping on the stew.

I Trulli
122 East 27 Street
New York, New York

Kid or baby goat is as popular as lamb in many parts of Italy. I have seen it on the menu in Puglia in the south and Lucca in Tuscany in central Italy. This recipe is from the Alto Adige, high in the Alps near Switzerland. It is adapted from one given to me by a native of that region, the late Andreas Hellrigl, the founding chef and owner of Palio Restaurant in New York.

Kid and lamb are often interchangeable, and either meat can be prepared this way. Many Greek, Italian, and Caribbean markets carry kid or can order it for you, especially in spring. Fettuccine with Artichokes (page 140) would be good as a first course.

Palio
151 West 51 Street
New York, New York

Roast Leg of Kid or Lamb with Red Wine

ARROSTO DI CAPRA AL VINO ROSSO

1 leg of kid or shank half of leg of lamb, trimmed (2¹/₂ pounds)
Salt and freshly ground pepper, to taste
3 tablespoons olive oil
2 carrots, chopped
2 medium onions, chopped
2 garlic cloves, chopped
1 leek, chopped
1 celery rib, chopped
1 sprig of fresh rosemary
10 peppercorns
1¹/₂ cups dry red wine
2 cups chicken broth

1 Preheat the oven to 400°F.

2 Sprinkle the meat with salt and pepper. In a large heavy skillet over medium heat, heat the olive oil. Add the meat and cook, turning frequently, until lightly browned on all sides. Add the vegetables, rosemary, and peppercorns. Cook for 10 minutes, stirring occasionally. Transfer the meat to a roasting pan just large enough to hold it. Pour the wine into the skillet and bring it to a simmer, scraping the pan to remove any browned pieces stuck to the bottom and sides. Pour the wine and vegetables into the roasting pan.

3 Place the pan in the oven and roast for 30 minutes, or until most of the liquid has evaporated. Add the broth and roast, turning the meat occasionally, for 45 minutes. Remove the meat to a warm serving platter and cover with foil.

4 Place the roasting pan with the vegetables and cooking juices over medium heat on top of the stove. Scrape the browned bits from the

sides and edges of the pan into the juices and simmer until reduced and thickened. Strain the juices and season with salt and pepper.

5 Slice the meat and serve with juices.

Grilled Lamb, Marches Style

AGNELLO ALLA GRIGLIA

1 large onion, chopped

4 garlic cloves, finely chopped

¼ cup chopped fresh parsley

2 tablespoons chopped fresh thyme

2 tablespoons chopped fresh rosemary leaves

2 tablespoons chopped fresh sage

2 tablespoons chopped fresh marjoram

¼ cup olive oil

Freshly ground pepper

1 boned and butterflied leg of lamb (5½ pounds)

Salt

1 Combine the onion, garlic, herbs, olive oil, and pepper. Spread the mixture on both sides of the lamb. Roll up the meat. Cover with foil and let stand at room temperature for 1 hour or overnight in the refrigerator.

2 Place a grill rack or broiler pan 4 inches from the source of the heat. Preheat the grill or broiler.

3 Unroll the meat and place it on the grill rack or broiler pan. Cook about 10 minutes on each side for medium-rare. Remove the meat from the grill and sprinkle it with salt. Cover and let stand for 10 minutes.

4 Cut the meat at an angle against the grain into thin slices. Serve hot or at room temperature.

SERVES 12

My husband's favorite restaurant in Rome is Il Matriciano, and he has a favorite dish there for each season of the year. In summer, it's the deep-fried zucchini flowers stuffed with anchovies and mozzarella. In winter, it's the house signature dish, bucatini all'Amatriciana, thick spaghetti tubes with a spicy tomato sauce flavored with hot pepper and bits of *guanciale*, cured pork cheek, similar to pancetta. In the fall Charles looks forward to the crème brûlée, certainly one of the best I've ever tasted. And spring means roast baby lamb seasoned with white wine and rosemary.

Lamb that young and tender is seldom available in the United States, so back home, I prefer this recipe, typical of the Marches region in central Italy, which makes the most of our more mature lamb. A boneless butterflied leg of lamb cooks evenly and it easily serves a crowd. For fewer servings, the same herb marinade can be used for lamb chops or skewered chunks of lamb.

This lamb goes well with Eggplant, Zucchini, and Potato Stew (page 292) or Beans with Onion Spoons (page 283).

Il Matriciano
Via dei Gracchi, 33
Rome

SERVES 8

Venison is becoming more widely available in the United States. Food specialty shops and even some supermarkets carry it, or you may know a hunter who can supply you with some. If you prefer, lean beef chuck can be substituted. The apple, juniper berries, and spices add a subtle tart-sweet flavor to either meat. This stew, from the Alto Adige region, improves if it is cooked in advance and reheated. Polenta is the perfect accompaniment.

Spiced Venison or Beef Stew

STUFATO DI CERVO

6 tablespoons olive oil

2 pounds boneless venison or beef chuck cut into 2-inch pieces

2 cups dry red wine

2 medium onions, chopped

2 medium carrots, chopped

1/2 cup finely chopped celery

1/4 cup finely chopped fresh parsley

1 garlic clove, finely chopped

5 juniper berries

4 fresh sage leaves or 1 teaspoon dried sage

1/2 teaspoon dried marjoram

1 small tart apple, peeled, cored, and chopped

Coarse salt and freshly ground pepper, to taste

1 In a large skillet over medium heat, heat 3 tablespoons of the olive oil. Dry the meat well. Place a few pieces at a time in the pan without crowding and cook, turning occasionally, until browned on all sides. Transfer the meat to a platter. Brown the remaining meat in the same manner.

2 Drain off the fat in the skillet. Add 1/2 cup of the wine and bring it to a boil over high heat, scraping the browned bits off the pan.

3 In a large casserole over medium heat, heat the remaining oil. Add the onions, carrots, celery, parsley, garlic, juniper berries, sage, marjoram, and apple. Cook, stirring frequently, until lightly browned, about 10 minutes.

4 Add the meat, skillet juices, and remaining wine. Bring to a simmer. Add salt and pepper. Partially cover the pan and reduce the heat to low. Cook, stirring occasionally, until the meat is fork tender, about 3 hours. Serve immediately.

To make ahead: The stew can be completely cooked ahead up to 2 days before serving. Reheat gently.

Delfina's Rabbit with Olives and Pine Nuts

CONIGLIO CON OLIVE E PINOLI

1/4 cup olive oil

1 rabbit, thawed if frozen, cut into 8 pieces (about 2 1/2 pounds)

2 medium onions, finely chopped

2 celery ribs, finely chopped

2 garlic cloves, finely chopped

1 large carrot, finely chopped

2 bay leaves

2 tablespoons chopped fresh parsley

1 sprig of fresh rosemary

1 sprig of fresh sage

Salt and freshly ground pepper, to taste

1/2 cup dry white wine

1 cup chicken broth

4 ounces imported black olives, such as Gaeta, pitted and coarsely chopped (about 3/4 cup)

2 tablespoons pine nuts

1 In a large skillet over medium heat, heat the oil. Rinse and dry the rabbit pieces. Brown them for about 5 minutes on each side. Push the rabbit pieces aside and add the onions, celery, garlic, carrot, bay leaves, parsley, rosemary, and sage. Cook, stirring occasionally, until the onions are tender, about 5 minutes. Sprinkle with salt and pepper. Add the wine and bring to a simmer. Cook for 2 minutes, or until most of the liquid has evaporated. Add the broth. Reduce the heat to low. Cover and cook, turning the rabbit occasionally, until

SERVES 4

The tiny medieval village of Artimino in Tuscany is the location of a jewel of a restaurant called Da Delfina. Delfina, who founded the restaurant more than forty years ago, was once the cook at the nearby royal hunting lodge. Today Carlo Cioni, Delfina's friendly and knowledgeable son, is the host. He inherited his mother's passion for the region's food and wine. Taking note of our interest, he sent out a series of small tastes of dishes typical of the area but little known anywhere else. Though the food is traditional, everything Carlo serves seems up-to-date. This rabbit, for example, was served with mashed potatoes flavored with extra virgin olive oil. With it we drank a bottle of Carmignano Riserva from Contini Bonacossi.

Since the restaurant is a member of the Unione di Ristoranti del Buon Riccordo (see page 275), I have only to glance at the plate from Da Delfina hanging on my kitchen wall to recall several splendid meals we enjoyed there.

Da Delfina
Artimino (Tuscany)

tender when pierced with a fork, about 30 minutes. Remove the rabbit pieces to a plate.

2 Discard the bay leaves. Scrape the remaining contents of the skillet into a blender or food processor and puree until smooth.

3 Place the rabbit and pureed mixture back in the skillet over medium heat. Stir in the olives and pine nuts. Cook, basting the rabbit with sauce, for 5 minutes, or until hot.

4 Serve immediately.

Giorgio Rocca succeeded his father as the chef and owner of Il Giardino di Felicin in Monforte d'Alba. Giorgio's wife Rosina helps out in the kitchen and dining room while their son Nino acts as the wine steward. During the truffle season in the fall, the restaurant and the simple but cozy rooms upstairs are always fully booked. Guests come from all over the world to indulge in the region's "white diamonds," as the truffles are called, shaved over Giorgio's *tajarin,* or egg-rich tagliatelle. But no matter how busy he is, Giorgio always finds time to visit with his guests. Since he speaks five languages, communication is never a problem.

The inn is surrounded by pear and other fruit trees and a rosemary bush that is as high as the roof. The scent of rosemary perfumes the air whenever a breeze blows, and a sprig or two of the herb is always added to the meat and game dishes made in the kitchen.

This is a typical Piedmontese way of cooking rabbit. Serve with soft polenta (see page 191).

Braised Rabbit with Sweet Peppers and Garlic

CONIGLIO IN PEPERONATA

1 rabbit, thawed if frozen, cut into 8 pieces (about 2^1/$_2$ pounds)

4 tablespoons olive oil

4 garlic cloves, finely chopped

1 tablespoon chopped fresh rosemary leaves

1 bay leaf

Salt and freshly ground pepper, to taste

^{1}/$_3$ cup red wine vinegar

1 cup chicken broth

1 medium red bell pepper, cored, seeded, and thinly sliced

1 medium green bell pepper, cored, seeded, and thinly sliced

3 anchovy fillets, chopped

1 Rinse the rabbit pieces and pat them dry. In a large heavy skillet over medium heat, heat 3 tablespoons of the olive oil. Add the rabbit pieces in a single layer and cook, turning occasionally, until lightly browned, about 5 minutes. Add three quarters of the garlic, all the rosemary, and the bay leaf and cook, stirring, for 30 seconds. Sprinkle the rabbit pieces with salt and pepper, pour on the vinegar, and raise the heat to medium high. Stir the rabbit pieces, scraping the bottom of the skillet. Cook until most of the vinegar has evapo-

rated, about 1 minute. Add the broth, reduce the heat to low, cover, and simmer until the rabbit is tender when pierced with a fork, about 30 minutes.

2   In a medium skillet, heat the remaining 1 tablespoon olive oil. Add the peppers, anchovies, and remaining garlic and cook, stirring, over medium heat until the peppers begin to brown, about 5 minutes. Season with salt and pepper.

3   When the rabbit is tender, remove the pieces to a shallow serving dish and keep warm. Stir the peppers into the cooking liquid. Raise the heat and boil rapidly until the liquid is reduced and thickened, about 2 minutes.

4   Spoon the sauce over the rabbit and serve immediately.

Il Giardino di Felicin
Monforte d'Alba (Piedmont)

"Happy Memory" Restaurants

Some of my favorite Italian restaurants are members of a group called the *Unione di Ristoranti del Buon Riccordo.* Roughly translated as the "society of restaurants of the happy memory," the organization is a loosely knit collection of about 120 eateries located throughout Italy, with a handful in other countries. They include all kinds of establishments from simple trattorias to elegant restaurants. Though their styles may differ, all are dedicated to offering classic or creative Italian cooking based on products of their region.

Members of the Unione have the group's logo posted near the door. A diner who orders the designated *specialita della casa,* which is indicated on the menu of all happy memory restaurants, receives as a gift a hand-painted plate with the name and location of the restaurant and a whimsical depiction of its specialty. Some plates even include a local landmark, like the coliseum in Rome, or the duomo in Milan.

Many collectors try to acquire a complete set of all the plates issued throughout the approximately twenty-five years of the Unione's existence. Such a set, which today would comprise about three hundred plates, is not easy to assemble, since many restaurants have changed their specialties and the design of their plates over the years. Some longtime members of the Unione have changed specialties several times and can boast a number of different designs. Other restaurants are no longer members of the Unione or may even be out of business. Rarest of all are plates with errors, such as the one from Ristorante Hotel Milano in Belgirate that depicts a salmon trout leaping below, instead of over, the waters of Lake Maggiore. To an avid collector this plate may be worth thousands of dollars. To me a plate's real value is not monetary—rather it is a lasting souvenir of a memorable meal. My collection hangs on the walls of my kitchen to remind me of my favorite Italian dining experiences.

When I was growing up, holidays and special occasions called for fresh chicken or rabbit. My mother and I would walk to the live poultry market and make our selection, which would be plucked or skinned to order. My grandmother always maintained that white rabbits were tastier and more tender than the others, though I really don't know why.

Rabbit is eaten extensively in Italy and other European countries. The meat is very low in fat and calories and the flavor is mild, much like chicken. In fact, chicken can be substituted in any rabbit recipe, though it will need less cooking.

If you can, buy small fresh rabbits weighing three pounds or less. Larger, frozen rabbits can be tough. We ate this dish in San Remo, a pretty resort town near the Italian/French border, known for its olives.

Rabbit with Herbs and Olives

CONIGLIO ALLA SANREMESE

1 rabbit, thawed if frozen, cut into 2-inch pieces ($2^{1}/_2$ to 3 pounds)

3 tablespoons olive oil

3 large garlic cloves, finely chopped

1 tablespoon chopped fresh rosemary leaves

1 teaspoon chopped fresh thyme

1 bay leaf

Freshly ground pepper, to taste

1 cup chicken broth

$^{1}/_2$ cup dry white wine

$^{1}/_2$ cup Ligurian or niçoise olives (about 6 ounces)

1 Rinse the rabbit pieces and pat dry with paper towels. In a large skillet over medium heat, heat the olive oil. Cook the rabbit, turning occasionally, until browned on all sides, about 15 minutes. Stir in the garlic, rosemary, thyme, bay leaf, and pepper. Add the broth and wine and bring to a simmer. Cover and cook over low heat for 15 minutes, turning the pieces occasionally. Add the olives and cook, covered, for 15 to 20 minutes more, or until the rabbit is tender when pierced with a fork. With a slotted spoon, transfer the rabbit and olives to a serving dish. Cover and keep warm.

2 Increase the heat to high and boil the pan juices until they are reduced and thickened, about 2 minutes. Discard the bay leaf.

3 Pour the juices over the rabbit and serve immediately.

Vegetables ... Verdure

*T*O ITALIANS, VEGETABLES ARE *very important to a meal, giving it shape and character, so they are listed on the menu under the heading* contorni, *meaning contours or shapes.*

As each new vegetable arrives in season, it is welcomed with enthusiasm. When asparagus, fava beans, artichokes, or mushrooms, for instance, come on the market, Italians rush out to buy them—and they don't mind eating them every day while they are at their peak and best in flavor. Restaurants often offer special menus featuring a seasonal vegetable in several courses; asparagus and mushrooms are good examples of this practice. No one considers it too much.

Vegetables that accompany a main course of fish or meat are often very simple. Steamed greens dressed with olive oil and lemon juice and fried potatoes are typical. Stuffed vegetables, salads with ingredients beyond mixed greens and tomatoes, in fact, many complex vegetable dishes, are more likely to be presented as antipasti, though some can work both ways. How to serve them is up to you.

Potatoes, curiously enough, are not served as a substitute for pasta or rice in Italy or even classified as starches the way they sometimes are in America. Instead, potatoes are regarded as just another vegetable, and Italians have no qualms about serving them at the same meal as, or even in the same dish with, pasta, as in Pasta and Potatoes (page 121) and The Flag (page 119).

SERVES 4

Asparagus and Parmigiano-Reggiano are a heaven-blessed match. This all-in-the-skillet method is very quick and easy to do. The asparagus seem to drink in the flavor of the butter, even though you are using only a small amount. You must, however, keep an eye on the skillet. If the water evaporates too quickly, the asparagus may scorch.

You can also make this dish by boiling the asparagus and draining them, then coating them with butter and cheese just before serving. I often do that when I want to prepare the dish ahead.

Skillet Asparagus Parmesan

ASPARAGI IN PADELLA ALLA PARMIGIANA

1 pound medium to thick asparagus
1 tablespoon unsalted butter
Salt and freshly ground pepper, to taste
1/4 cup freshly grated Parmigiano-Reggiano

1 Soak the asparagus in cool water for 10 minutes. Trim off the tough lower ends where the stems turn from green to white. Peel the asparagus with a swivel-blade vegetable peeler.

2 In a large skillet with a tight-fitting lid, combine the butter and 2 tablespoons water. Add the asparagus and sprinkle with salt.

3 Cover and cook over medium-low heat until the asparagus are almost tender, about 5 minutes, depending on the thickness. Watch carefully so that they do not scorch. Turn the asparagus to be sure they are coated with butter. Sprinkle the asparagus with pepper and cheese. Cover and cook for 1 minute more, or until the asparagus are tender and the cheese is melted.

4 Serve hot.

Roman Artichoke Stew

LA VIGNAROLA

2 medium to large artichokes

2 tablespoons olive oil

2 ounces pancetta, cut into small dice ($^1/_4$ cup)

2 green onions, thinly sliced

1 cup shelled and peeled fava beans or frozen baby lima beans

Salt and freshly ground pepper, to taste

5 to 6 leaves romaine lettuce, cut crosswise into thin strips

1 cup fresh or frozen peas

1 To trim the artichokes, remove all the leaves except the pale tender ones that form the central cone. Cut the artichokes lengthwise in half. Scoop out the chokes. Cut each half into 3 or 4 wedges.

2 In a large skillet over medium heat, heat the oil with the pancetta. Cook, stirring frequently, until the pancetta begins to turn golden, about 8 minutes. Stir in the green onions. Add the artichokes, favas, and $^1/_2$ cup water. Season with salt and pepper. Lower the heat. Cover and cook for 10 minutes, or until the artichokes are almost tender when pierced with a knife. Stir in the lettuce and peas. Cover and cook for 3 minutes more, or until the lettuce is wilted and the artichokes are tender.

3 Serve hot or at room temperature.

SERVES 4

One of the first signs of spring in Rome is the heaps of fresh artichokes in the markets, especially the large round ones called *mammole* that are grown on little farms just outside the city. Romans eat artichokes raw in salads, fried, stuffed, steamed, in soup, and over pasta. This dish is the quintessence of spring in its ingredients. At La Campana, a popular Roman trattoria, la vignarola is substantial enough to be served as a main dish.

In the United States, artichokes are available all year round, but their peak season runs from March to May. When shopping, look for artichokes that are compact, firm, and heavy for their size, with the leaves tightly closed. Check around the base to see that there are no holes or bruised areas. A touch of purple on the leaves indicates a better-tasting artichoke.

For stuffing, I prefer medium-size artichokes because very large artichokes, while they look attractive, are difficult to cook through evenly. The centers remain hard even after the leaves and outer portions become tender. This recipe, though, is good for either medium or large artichokes since they are sliced before cooking.

La Campana
Vicolo della Campana, 18
Rome

Waiting for a bus is often boring, but never in Naples. We stood in the Piazza del Gesù Nuovo in the shadow of a giant *guglia,* a baroque steeple-like monument with a statue of the Madonna on top, and watched two men unloading a truck filled to overflowing with crates of fresh artichokes, their long stems and leaves still attached. As the men worked, they would call out to passersby and their cohort who was stacking the crates at the curb outside the *fruttivendolo,* or produce shop. They took frequent breaks to smoke a cigarette, watch a pretty girl go by, or argue good-naturedly about this or that. Little by little, a crowd formed at the bus stop. Attracted by the antics of the three men, few were able to resist stopping at the produce shop and joining in the conversation. When the bus finally arrived, practically everyone who boarded carried a big plastic sack with artichoke leaves poking out.

The simplest stuffing for artichokes is made with bread crumbs flavored with parsley, garlic, and cheese. This version is more complex since it contains porcini mushrooms and prosciutto. Stuffed artichokes should be served as a separate course on their own plate either as an antipasto or after the main course.

Stuffed Artichokes with Porcini and Prosciutto

CARCIOFI RIPIENI DI FUNGHI E PROSCIUTTO

1/2 ounce (1/2 cup) dried porcini mushrooms

1/2 lemon

6 medium artichokes

3/4 cup dry bread crumbs

1 egg, beaten

3 tablespoons extra virgin olive oil

1/3 cup freshly grated Parmigiano-Reggiano

2 ounces finely chopped prosciutto (1/2 cup)

1 garlic clove, finely chopped

1/4 teaspoon dried marjoram

Salt and freshly ground pepper, to taste

1 Place the mushrooms in a bowl with 1 cup warm tap water. Let soak for at least 30 minutes. Drain the mushrooms, reserving the liquid. Strain the liquid through a paper coffee filter or strainer lined with dampened cheesecloth. Rinse the mushrooms under running water examining each piece. Pay special attention to the stem pieces which may have bits of soil clinging to the base. Drain well and chop.

2 Squeeze the juice of the lemon into a large bowl of cold water. Set aside.

3 Trim the stems of the artichokes even with the base so they stand upright. With a large knife, trim off the top 1 inch of each artichoke. Bend back and snap off the small leaves around the base. With scissors, trim the pointed tops off the remaining leaves. Gently spread the leaves open to reveal the choke. With a small knife with a rounded tip, scrape out the fuzzy leaves. As each artichoke is finished, drop it into the lemon water.

4 Soak the bread crumbs in the mushroom liquid, squeeze them until they are just moist, and put them in a medium bowl. Combine

with the egg, oil, cheese, prosciutto, garlic, marjoram, salt, and pepper. Mix well.

5 Stuff the mixture into the center of each artichoke and between the leaves.

6 Place the artichokes in a saucepan just large enough to hold them upright. Pour water around the artichokes to a depth of 1 inch. Cover and simmer for 30 to 45 minutes, or until the artichoke hearts are tender when pierced with a knife. Serve warm or at room temperature.

Asparagus with Egg Sauce

ASPARAGI ALLE UOVE

1 pound asparagus

Salt, to taste

SAUCE

2 eggs

1/4 cup vegetable oil

1 tablespoon white wine vinegar

1 teaspoon Dijon mustard

1 teaspoon fresh lemon juice

Salt and freshly ground pepper, to taste

1 tablespoon snipped fresh chives

1 tablespoon chopped fresh parsley

1 Soak the asparagus in cold water for 10 minutes. Trim off the tough lower portion of each stalk where the color changes from green to white.

2 Bring about 1 inch of water to a boil in a large skillet. Add the asparagus and salt. Simmer for 5 to 10 minutes, or until the asparagus are barely tender.

3 Place the eggs in a small saucepan with water to cover. Bring to a boil. Reduce the heat to low and simmer for 8 minutes. Drain the eggs and cool them under cold water.

4 Peel the eggs and separate the whites and the yolks. Place the yolks

SERVES 4

Velocius quam asparagi coquantur—as quick as cooking asparagus. My high school Latin teacher, Sister Margaret John, used to hurry us along with this famous line of Caesar's. The cooking time for asparagus should be just enough so that a spear curves gently when it is picked up by the stem. Not long. The exact number of minutes depends on the thickness of the asparagus.

Sometimes asparagus can be sandy, so it is a good idea to soak them in cool water for ten minutes or so before cooking. If the spears are very slim, I do not peel them. If they are wider than a pencil, though, I do. A swivel blade vegetable peeler pares away the tough outer skin swiftly and easily.

This pretty combination of green asparagus and yellow and white eggs can be served as a salad course or antipasto. The flavor of the dressing is so delicate, I prefer to use a neutral-flavored vegetable oil rather than olive oil.

in a medium bowl and mash them with a wire whisk. Beat in the oil, vinegar, mustard, lemon juice, salt, and pepper until well blended.

5 Chop the egg whites. Gently stir the egg whites, chives, and parsley into the egg yolk mixture.

6 Place the asparagus on 4 serving dishes and spoon on the sauce.

To make ahead: The asparagus and eggs can be cooked up to 2 hours ahead of serving.

Baked Beans with Garlic and Sage

FAGIOLI AL FORNO

8 ounces (about 1 cup) dried cannellini or Great Northern beans

1 large garlic clove

1 sprig of fresh sage

3 tablespoons extra virgin olive oil

Salt, to taste

1 Rinse the beans and remove any small stones or shriveled beans. Place the beans in a bowl with cold water to cover by 2 inches. Refrigerate for at least 4 hours or overnight.

2 Preheat the oven to 300°F.

3 Drain the beans and place them in a flameproof casserole with a cover. Add fresh water to cover by 1 inch. Add the garlic, sage, and olive oil. Cover and bring just to a simmer over low heat. Place the casserole in the oven and cook until the beans are very tender, about 1 hour and 15 minutes. (Cooking time may vary, depending on the age and size of the beans.) The liquid should just cover the beans. If necessary add a little hot water to the pot. Test several beans by tasting them for doneness since they may not all be ready at the same time.

4 When the beans are tender and creamy, add salt and cook for 10 minutes more. Do not overcook or the beans may begin to break apart.

MAKES ABOUT 3 CUPS

A famous painting by Annibale Carracci (1560–1609), a Bolognese, is called the *Mangiatore di Fagioli,* the bean eater. It depicts a *contadino,* or farmer, sitting down to eat a big bowl of *fagioli dell'occhio,* black-eyed peas, a legume native to the region.

The beans that explorers brought back from the New World did not become known in Italy until the sixteenth century. Pietro Andrea Mattioli, a Sienese botanist, described the strange new food as follows: "When eaten, they bloat the stomach but they generate virile seed and encourage sexual intercourse, and even more so if they are eaten with long pepper, sugar and galingale."

This recipe describes a basic method of cooking beans, and all kinds can be cooked this way. Just adjust the cooking time to the size of the beans. They can be eaten as a side dish with pork, grilled steak, or chicken, or used as an ingredient in pasta, soup, or salad. The recipe can easily be doubled.

To make ahead: The beans can be cooked ahead up to 3 days before serving. Let cool then cover and refrigerate. Reheat gently.

Beans with Onion Spoons

FAGIOLI CON CUCCHIAI DI CIPOLLA

8 ounces (about 1 cup) dried cannellini or Great Northern beans

2 ounces thickly sliced pancetta, coarsely chopped ($^1/_4$ cup)

1 celery rib, finely chopped

1 teaspoon fennel seeds

Extra virgin olive oil

Salt, to taste

1 large red onion

Freshly ground pepper

Layers of sweet red onion make crunchy "spoons" for these creamy, aromatic beans.

I find that soaking beans is essential, no matter what the package says. Beans that have not been soaked for at least several hours cook unevenly; they never turn out as tender as they should be. In my opinion, there is nothing worse than crisp, under-cooked beans.

1 Rinse the beans and remove any small stones or shriveled beans. Soak the beans covered with 2 inches of cold water in the refrigerator for at least 4 hours or overnight. Drain the beans.

2 Place in a large pot. Add cold water to cover by 1 inch. Add the pancetta, celery, fennel seeds, and 2 tablespoons olive oil. Bring the liquid to a simmer and cook over very low heat until the beans are tender and creamy, about 1 hour and 15 minutes. (Cooking time may vary, depending on the size and age of the beans.) Add warm water if necessary to keep the beans just covered. Add salt about 10 minutes before the end of the cooking time. There should be just enough liquid left to keep the beans moist.

3 Cut the onion in quarters through the root. Peel each quarter. Separate the layers to form "spoons."

4 Arrange the onion spoons on a serving plate. Spoon the warm beans into the onion layers. Drizzle with olive oil and grind pepper over all just before serving.

To make ahead: The beans can be cooked up to 3 days before serving. Reheat gently.

Grated beets cook quickly but grating them can be messy. The neatest way to do this is in a food processor with a grating disk, though an inexpensive mandoline-type grater/slicer works well, too. Serve these beets with roast pork or braised quail.

Buttered Beets with Pine Nuts

BIETOLE AL BURRO CON PINOLI

1 bunch of beets, tops and root ends trimmed (4 medium beets, about 1 pound)

2 tablespoons pine nuts

2 tablespoons unsalted butter

Salt, to taste

1 to 2 teaspoons balsamic vinegar

1 Scrub the beets and peel them with a swivel-blade vegetable peeler. If using a food processor, cut the beets into quarters. Grate the beets.

2 Heat a large skillet over medium heat. Toast the pine nuts, stirring often, for 1 minute, or until golden brown. Remove the pine nuts from the pan.

3 Add the butter, beets, 2 tablespoons water, and salt. Cover and cook over low heat, stirring occasionally, for 5 to 10 minutes, or until the beets are tender. Remove the beets from the heat. Stir in the balsamic vinegar.

4 Transfer to a serving dish and sprinkle with the pine nuts. Serve immediately.

Microwaving Beets

When the weather is hot, I try to avoid turning on the oven. Rather than roasting the beets, I cook them in the microwave oven. To do this, place the trimmed beets on a microwavesafe plate and cover with plastic wrap. Don't cook too many at once. Cook on high (100%), turning beets occasionally, until tender. Four medium beets take about 8 minutes. Since microwave ovens vary, consult your oven manufacturer's instructions for best results. Once the beets are tender, cool and peel them.

Minted Beet Salad

BIETOLE ALLA MENTA

2 bunches of beets (8 medium beets, about 2 pounds)

1 small garlic clove, very finely chopped

3 tablespoons extra virgin olive oil

2 tablespoons red wine vinegar

Coarse salt and freshly ground pepper, to taste

2 tablespoons chopped fresh mint leaves

1 Preheat the oven to 425°F. Place a large sheet of aluminum foil in a roasting pan just large enough to contain the beets in a single layer.

2 Scrub the beets and trim off the tops and stems. (If the tops are fresh looking, set them aside to cook as you would spinach or chard.) Place the beets on the foil in the pan and fold up the ends to completely enclose them. Seal the edges by folding them over several times.

3 Bake the beets until tender when pierced with a knife, about 45 minutes to 1 hour, depending on the size. (You can pierce them right through the foil, but be careful of the escaping steam.) Let the beets cool. Slip and peel off the skins with a paring knife. Cut the beets into bite-size pieces.

4 Toss the beets with the garlic, olive oil, vinegar, salt, and pepper. Serve immediately or cover and chill. Sprinkle with mint just before serving.

SERVES 6

Garlic has been the vehicle in the United States of a self-reversing snobbery. Before I left America to live in Europe in 1927, you were looked down upon if you ate garlic, a food fit only for ditchdiggers; when I returned in 1940, you were looked down upon if you didn't eat it. It had become the hallmark of gastronomic sophistication and I was overwhelmed by meals offered by thoughtful friends, who catered to my supposedly acquired dashing Gallic tastes by including garlic in every dish except ice cream; their intentions were good but their premise was faulty," wrote Waverley Root in *Food*.

Beets have a natural affinity for the flavors of garlic and mint as evidenced in this sprightly salad. Although I grow several varieties of mint in my garden, I prefer spearmint or peppermint for most cooking purposes, including this salad. Serve it at room temperature or lightly chilled.

Broccoli rabe goes by several different names in the market, including rapini, broccoli di rape, bitter broccoli, and so on. Whatever they call it, it looks like ordinary broccoli with a number of thin stems instead of a large central stem and larger leaves. The tips should be dark green and tightly closed.

The flavor of broccoli rabe is much stronger than ordinary broccoli, an acquired taste for some. It is the perfect vegetable to accompany roast pork or Italian sausages. Broccoli rabe cooked this way also makes a delicious sauce for pasta, especially orecchiette.

At Vecchia Roma Restaurant in Rome, broccoli flavored with pancetta and garlic is served over a cloud of soft polenta. The dish replaces pasta or risotto as a first course; it can even be a meal in one. I sometimes serve it alone as a side dish with roast pork or chicken.

Vecchia Roma
Via delle Tribuna di Campitelli
Rome

Broccoli Rabe with Garlic and Hot Pepper

CIMA DI RAPE COL PEPERONCINO

1 pound broccoli rabe

Coarse salt, to taste

3 tablespoons olive oil

2 large garlic cloves, thinly sliced

Pinch of crushed red pepper

1 Trim the base of the broccoli rabe stems and discard any bruised or yellowed leaves. Cut the broccoli into 2-inch lengths.

2 Bring about 2 quarts of water to a boil. Add the broccoli rabe and salt. Cook for 5 minutes, or until the broccoli is almost tender. Drain well.

3 Dry the pot and add the oil, garlic, and red pepper. Cook over medium-low heat until the garlic turns golden. Add the broccoli rabe and stir well. Cover and cook for 5 minutes more, or until tender. Taste for salt.

4 Serve hot or at room temperature.

Broccoli, Pancetta, and Garlic

BROCCOLI, PANCETTA, E AGLIO

1 large bunch of broccoli (1¹/₂ pounds)

Salt, to taste

2 tablespoons olive oil

2 thick slices of pancetta (2 ounces), cut into matchstick strips

4 large garlic cloves, thinly sliced

¹/₂ teaspoon crushed red pepper, or to taste

1 Trim the broccoli and cut it into florets. Peel the stems and cut them into 2 × ¹/₂ × ¹/₂-inch wedges.

2 Bring a large saucepan of water to a boil. Add the broccoli and salt. Cook for 3 minutes. The broccoli will be very crisp. Drain the broccoli.

3 In a large skillet over medium heat, cook the oil and pancetta for 5 minutes, or until the pancetta is golden brown. Add the garlic and red pepper and cook for 2 minutes more, or until the garlic is golden. Add the broccoli, 2 tablespoons water, and a sprinkle of salt. Cook, stirring occasionally, until the broccoli is tender and beginning to turn brown, about 5 minutes.

4 Serve hot.

Smothered Cauliflower

CAVOLFIORE STUFATO

1 medium cauliflower (about 1 pound)

3 tablespoons olive oil

2 garlic cloves, thinly sliced

Salt, to taste

¹/₃ cup black olives, such as Gaeta, pitted and sliced

2 tablespoons chopped fresh parsley

1 Wash the cauliflower well and trim off the lower part of the stem. Cut the cauliflower into 1-inch florets.

2 Pour the oil into a large skillet and add the cauliflower. Cook over medium heat. When the cauliflower begins to brown, add the garlic and a pinch of salt. (The olives will add more salt later.) Add ¹/₄ cup water. Cover and cook over low heat until the cauliflower is tender when pierced with a knife and the water has evaporated, about 10 minutes. Add the olives and parsley. Cook, uncovered, for 2 minutes more, stirring 3 or 4 times.

3 Serve hot or at room temperature.

SERVES 4

Cauliflower becomes infused with the flavor of olives and takes on a creamy texture when cooked this way. Naturally, you will need good-tasting olives, such as Italian Gaeta.

In spring, gray-green caper plants spring out from stone walls and rock crevices all over southern Italy. The small flower buds are picked before they turn into brushlike pink flowers. These buds are a very important seasoning in Italian cooking.

Capers must be gathered by hand. During the season, people forage the wild ones, climbing over rocks and stone walls to get at the plants, which seem to prefer the most inaccessible places. A bent wire coat hanger is the usual tool of choice to lift up the stems so that the buds can be removed. In the kitchen, the capers are either used fresh, when they are at their most delicate, in salads or sauces, or packed in salt or preserved in vinegar for longer storage. If you can find them, choose capers packed in salt; they have a much better flavor. Rinse off the salt and pat the capers dry before adding them to a dish. Some cooks consider the tiniest capers to be the best, not because they taste better, but because they make a pretty garnish and do not need to be chopped. Larger capers are fine for most cooking purposes, and they are less expensive.

Capers and cabbage make a simple, light, refreshing salad that goes well with barbecued chicken or grilled fish.

Cabbage and Caper Salad

INSALATA DI CAVOLO E CAPPERI

4 cups finely shredded cabbage (1 pound)
$1/3$ cup drained capers
2 tablespoons chopped fresh parsley
3 tablespoons extra virgin olive oil
2 tablespoons white wine vinegar
Salt and freshly ground pepper, to taste

1 In a large serving bowl, combine the cabbage, capers, and parsley.

2 Whisk together the oil, vinegar, salt, and pepper. Pour the dressing over the salad and toss well.

3 Serve immediately.

Browned Cabbage with Hot Pepper

CAVOLO AL'AGLIO E PEPERONCINO

1 large head of cabbage (about 3 pounds)

¼ cup olive oil

4 large garlic cloves, finely chopped

½ teaspoon crushed red pepper, or to taste

Coarse salt, to taste

1 Cut the cabbage in quarters through the stem. Remove the outer leaves. Cut out and discard the hard core. Cut the cabbage into 1-inch pieces.

2 In a large pot over medium-low heat, heat the oil, garlic, and red pepper for 30 seconds, or until the garlic is fragrant but not brown. Add the cabbage and stir well. Cover and cook, stirring often, for 20 minutes, or until the cabbage is lightly browned and tender. Season with salt.

3 Serve hot.

SERVES 8

Garlic and hot pepper elevate the homey flavor of cabbage to nothing short of fantastic. Serve it with Braised Pork Loin with Grapes and Tiny Onions (page 244), Pork Chops in Red Wine and Juniper (page 253), or grilled sausages.

Eggplants come in many different colors, from cream to purple to chocolate brown, and even purple and white stripes. They can be tiny or large, long, round, or pear shape. The flavor, however, is pretty much the same no matter what the color or shape.

Ask any Italian gardener and he will tell you that there are definitely male and female eggplants. Male eggplants are preferred because they supposedly have fewer seeds to destroy the smooth texture and make them bitter tasting. You can tell the difference by looking at the shape of the scar in the depression at the blossom end. The male eggplant has a round dot that looks like a dimple while the female has a dash. This is not as simple as it sounds, but fortunately it is not as important as it once was now that eggplant varieties have been bred to have a minimum of seeds no matter what the gender.

When buying eggplants, look for firm, shiny ones with no bruises or dents. Brown, rusty-looking spots are a sign that the eggplants are old or have been mishandled. For purple eggplants, the darker the color, the riper and tastier it will be. The green calyx at the stem end should look fresh, not brownish. Medium-size eggplants are best. I find that salting eggplant is necessary to remove the bitter juices that can ruin the eggplant's flavor.

Sweet-and-Sour Eggplant

MELANZANE IN AGRODOLCE

1 medium eggplant (about 1 pound)
Salt
¹/₄ cup olive oil
¹/₄ cup red wine vinegar
2 tablespoons sugar

1 Cut the eggplant into 1-inch pieces. Place them in a colander and sprinkle generously with salt. Invert a plate over the eggplant and weight it with a heavy can. Let drain for 1 hour. Rinse the eggplant and dry the pieces well with paper towels.

2 In a large skillet over medium heat, heat the oil until it is very hot. Add the eggplant and cook, stirring frequently, until browned. Remove the eggplant pieces to paper towels to drain.

3 Wipe out the skillet. Pour in the vinegar and sugar. Return the eggplant to the skillet and cook, stirring, until the liquid is absorbed. Transfer the eggplant to a serving dish and let cool completely. Serve at room temperature.

To make ahead: This can be made 1 or 2 days before serving and refrigerated. Bring back to room temperature before serving.

Grilled Corn on the Cob, Neapolitan Style

PANOCCHE DI MAIS ALLA BRACE

4 very fresh ears of corn
Salt, to taste

1 Trim the corn, discarding the leaves and silk.

2 Bring a large pot of water to a boil and add a generous amount of salt. Drop in the corn and cook for 3 to 4 minutes, or until just tender. Remove the corn and pat it dry.

3 Prepare a barbecue grill. Place the rack about 4 inches from the source of the heat.

4 Place the corn on the grill. Cook it, turning frequently, until lightly browned, about 5 minutes. Serve hot.

To make ahead: The corn can be boiled ahead of time. Just before serving, prepare the grill and grill the corn.

Not so long ago, the poor people of Naples lived in one-room flats, known as *bassi*, because they were located on the ground floor of large apartment houses. Whole families crowded into these tiny windowless spaces, which opened directly onto the narrow streets of the older sections of the city. The *bassi* had no cooking facilities, so it was customary for the inhabitants to buy their meals from street vendors. Though living conditions have much improved, Neapolitans still enjoy eating street food, like grilled corn, especially as a summer treat.

Normally, corn on the cob is considered animal food in Italy. I don't know if the Neapolitans learned to enjoy it because they were so hungry, or if it was a taste acquired abroad by an emigrant son who brought it back home with him from the United States. Either way, the cooking method gives the ears a delightful popcorn flavor, without the butter.

Cianfotta, sometimes spelled *giambotta*, means a mixture or a mess. This version is a delicious mess of vegetables, perfect for summertime when eggplant and zucchini are at their peak. I often serve it with some good bread for a meatless meal. Vary the ingredients according to what you have on hand and don't hesitate to increase or decrease the amount of one or another.

The eggplant here is fried in half an inch of vegetable oil. This method results in crisp, brown eggplant that is less oily than eggplant fried in a small amount of oil. The hot deep oil seals the eggplant cubes and prevents them from soaking up an excessive amount. I prefer corn oil for deep-frying because its mild flavor does not interfere with the flavors of the other ingredients.

Eggplant, Zucchini, and Potato Stew

CIANFOTTA

2 medium eggplants (about 2 pounds)

Salt, to taste

Vegetable oil, for frying

2 tablespoons olive oil

2 medium onions, sliced

2 large potatoes, peeled and cut into bite-size pieces

2 medium-size ripe tomatoes, peeled, seeded, and cut into bite-size pieces

2 medium red bell peppers, seeded and cut into $1/2$-inch strips

2 small zucchini, scrubbed and thickly sliced

1 garlic clove, chopped

Freshly ground pepper, to taste

$1/2$ cup chopped fresh basil or parsley

1 Trim the eggplants and cut them into 1-inch pieces. Make a layer of eggplant in a large colander. Sprinkle generously with salt. Repeat layering the eggplant and salt until all of the pieces have been used. Invert a plate over the eggplant and place a weight such as a heavy can on top. Let stand for 30 minutes to 1 hour to drain. Rinse the eggplant and dry with paper towels.

2 Pour enough of the vegetable oil to reach a $1/2$-inch depth in a large heavy skillet. Heat the oil over medium-high heat. To judge if it is hot enough, carefully place a piece of the eggplant in the oil. If it bubbles, add more eggplant to make a single layer. Do not crowd the pan. Cook, stirring once or twice, until browned and crisp. Remove the eggplant with a slotted spoon and drain on paper towels. Fry the remaining eggplant in the same way.

3 In a large pot over medium heat, heat the olive oil. Add the onions and cook until tender, about 10 minutes. Add the potatoes, tomatoes, peppers, zucchini, garlic, $1/2$ cup water, salt, and pepper. Cover and cook on low heat for 20 minutes, stirring occasionally. Add a little water if the mixture becomes too dry. Add the eggplant and cook for 10 minutes more, or until the vegetables are tender. Remove from the heat and stir in the basil or parsley.

4 Serve warm.

Escarole with Raisins and Garlic

SCAROLA CON L'UVA E AGLIO

1 pound escarole (1 medium head)

2 garlic cloves, finely chopped

2 tablespoons olive oil

$1/4$ cup raisins

Salt, to taste

1 Trim the escarole discarding any bruised outer leaves. Cut off the base. Separate the leaves and wash them well under cool running water paying close attention to the whitish rib in the center of each leaf where soil collects. Stack the leaves and cut them crosswise into 1-inch strips.

2 In a large saucepan over medium heat, cook the garlic in the oil. When the garlic is golden and fragrant, about 1 minute, add the escarole, raisins, and salt. Turn the heat to low. Cover and cook, stirring occasionally, until the escarole is wilted and tender, 10 to 15 minutes.

3 Serve hot, warm, or at room temperature.

SERVES 6

When good greens are scarce in the winter, escarole is at its best. The broad green and white leaves with paler yellow inner leaves are chewy and slightly bitter. Use them raw in salads or cooked with garlic, oil, and hot pepper. Southern Italians stuff the centers of young tender heads with anchovies and cheese and braise them. If you have not yet acquired a taste for escarole, try this recipe. The sweetness of the raisins balances the slightly bitter flavor of the greens. This dish goes very well with Swordfish Rolls (page 208).

Green beans for salads or in sauces such as this one can be boiled ahead of time, but do not refrigerate them—their flavor changes and they lose their freshness and delicacy. After they are boiled, drain the beans and dry them. Wrap them in a towel and leave them at room temperature for up to three hours, or until ready to make the sauce.

When it comes to trimming green beans, I remove only the stem end unless the other end is bruised. Rather than snapping the stems off, line up the beans a few at a time and trim them with a big knife.

Green Beans with Garlic and Anchovies

FAGIOLINI AL AGLIO E ACCIUGHE

1 pound green beans, trimmed

Salt, to taste

2 tablespoons olive oil

1 garlic clove, finely chopped

4 anchovy fillets, drained and finely chopped

¼ cup chopped fresh parsley

Freshly ground pepper, to taste

1 Bring a large saucepan of water to a boil. Add the green beans and salt. Cook until the beans are tender yet still crisp, about 5 minutes. Drain well. Dry the saucepan.

2 In the same pan, combine the oil, garlic, and anchovies. Cook over low heat, stirring, for 1 minute. Add the green beans, parsley, salt, and pepper. Stir well until the beans are heated through and coated with the garlic mixture.

3 Serve hot or at room temperature.

Green Bean, Cucumber, and Tomato Salad

INSALATA DI FAGIOLINI

SERVES 4

Crunchy Kirby cucumbers, the kind used for pickling, sweet tomatoes, and tender green beans make a refreshing summer salad. If only dark green cucumbers with waxed skins are available, peel them before adding them to the other ingredients.

1 pound green beans, trimmed

Salt, to taste

1 medium cucumber, preferably Kirby, scrubbed and thinly sliced

1 medium-size ripe tomato, seeded and diced

1/2 cup thinly sliced red onion

3 tablespoons extra virgin olive oil

1 to 2 tablespoons fresh lemon or lime juice

1 teaspoon chopped fresh oregano or marjoram or 1/4 teaspoon
   dried oregano or marjoram

Freshly ground pepper, to taste

1 Bring a large saucepan of water to a boil. Add the green beans and salt. Cook for 5 minutes, or until the beans are tender but still firm. Drain the beans and cool them under cold running water. Drain and pat dry.

2 In a large bowl, combine the beans, cucumber, tomato, and onion.

3 Whisk the remaining ingredients until well blended and pour over the salad. Toss well.

4 Serve within 1 hour.

Toward the end of July, the markets around Lucca are full of skinny, stringless green beans nearly a foot long that look like the long beans you sometimes see in Chinese markets. These Italian beans are called *fagiolini di Sant'Anna* since they are at their peak on the saint's feast day, July 26. In the Lucca market, I asked a farmer's wife who was selling the beans how she prepared them. This is her recipe, which works nicely with ordinary green beans so long as they are very thin.

Green Beans for the Feast of Saint Anna

FAGIOLINI DI SANT'ANNA

2 medium-size ripe tomatoes

1 pound green beans, trimmed

2 small carrots, peeled and sliced

1 small onion, finely chopped

1 small celery rib, finely chopped

2 tablespoons chopped fresh basil

2 tablespoons olive oil

Salt and freshly ground pepper, to taste

1 Bring a large saucepan of water to a boil. Add the tomatoes and boil for 30 seconds. Remove with a slotted spoon. Peel, seed, and chop the tomatoes.

2 Drop the beans into the water and cook for 4 to 5 minutes, or until almost tender. Drain the beans and set aside.

3 In a large saucepan over medium heat, cook the carrots, onion, celery, and basil in the oil until tender but not browned, about 5 minutes. Add the tomatoes to the vegetable mixture. Cook for 10 minutes, or until most of the juices have evaporated. Add the green beans, $1/4$ cup water, salt, and pepper. Cook for 5 minutes, or until the beans are tender and the liquid is reduced.

4 Serve warm or at room temperature.

Glazed Mushrooms and Onions

STUFATO DI FUNGHI E CIPOLLINE

1 pound small white onions

4 tablespoons (¹/₂ stick) unsalted butter

1 pound small white mushrooms, trimmed

1 tablespoon finely chopped fresh rosemary leaves

Salt and freshly ground pepper, to taste

1 Bring a medium saucepan of water to a boil. Add the onions and cook for 30 seconds. Pour the onions into a colander in the sink and cool them under running water. Drain well. With a small sharp knife, trim off a thin layer from the root end of each onion and slip off the skin.

2 In a large skillet with a tight-fitting cover over medium heat, melt the butter. Add the onions, mushrooms, rosemary, salt, and pepper. Toss gently to coat the vegetables with the butter. Cover and reduce the heat to low. Cook, stirring occasionally, until the juices have evaporated and the vegetables are glazed, 20 to 25 minutes.

3 Serve hot.

Button mushrooms and pearl onions cooked in butter and their own juices take on a handsome brown glaze and rich, woodsy flavor. Take care that the vegetable juices do not dry up too quickly, or the vegetables may begin to scorch. If this threatens to happen, quickly add a little water to the pan and turn the heat down. This mushroom dish is perfect with Chicken Breasts with Gorgonzola (page 225), a juicy rare steak, or hamburger.

Colorful peppers in a savory anchovy and tomato sauce are good with roast pork or grilled spareribs. They also make a fine topping for Polenta Crostini (page 192) or toasted bread as an antipasto.

Sweet Peppers with Capers and Anchovies

PEPERONI CON CAPPERI

2 tablespoons olive oil

4 large red or yellow bell peppers, seeded and cut into $1/2$-inch strips

2 large garlic cloves, sliced

1 large ripe tomato, peeled, seeded, and chopped, or 1 cup chopped canned Italian tomatoes

Salt and freshly ground pepper, to taste

6 anchovy fillets, drained and chopped

2 tablespoons chopped fresh parsley

1 tablespoon chopped capers

1 In a large skillet over medium heat, heat the oil. Add the peppers and garlic. Cook, stirring often, until the peppers are lightly browned, 10 to 15 minutes. Add the tomato, salt, and pepper. Cover and cook over low heat until the peppers are tender, 10 to 15 minutes. Remove the skillet from the heat. Stir in the anchovies, parsley, and capers.

2 Serve at room temperature.

Potato and Tomato Salad

INSALATA DI POMODORI E PATATE

1¹/₂ pounds small waxy potatoes, preferably Yukon Gold

1 medium red onion

1¹/₂ tablespoons chopped fresh oregano leaves or ¹/₂ teaspoon dried oregano

Salt and freshly ground pepper, to taste

3 tablespoons extra virgin olive oil

2 medium-size ripe tomatoes

1 Scrub the potatoes and place them in a saucepan with cold water to cover. Cover the pan and bring the water to a simmer. Cook for 20 to 25 minutes, or until the potatoes are tender when pierced with a knife. Drain and let cool. Peel the potatoes and cut them into 1-inch chunks.

2 Cut the onion lengthwise in half, then cut it crosswise into thin slices. In a large bowl, combine the potatoes, onion, oregano, salt, and pepper. Drizzle with the olive oil and toss well.

3 Core the tomatoes and cut them into bite-size pieces. Arrange the tomatoes on top of the potatoes.

4 Toss the salad just before serving.

To make ahead: This salad can be made up to 1 hour before serving. It is best at room temperature.

SERVES 6

Franca and Lucio Landini are the owners of the Viticcio winery in Tuscany. They grow all their own grapes and make superb Chianti and other excellent wines. From the tower at the center of their hilltop home near Greve, you can see for miles across the rolling Tuscan countryside. Franca maintains an enviable vegetable garden. One day she prepared a simple lunch for us, which included this salad of garden-fresh potatoes and tomatoes drizzled with extra virgin olive oil from their estate.

If fresh oregano is not available, substitute another fresh herb such as marjoram, thyme, or basil, or dried oregano.

Theo Schoennegger, the chef at New York's fashionable San Domenico Restaurant, gave me this recipe for a tangy potato salad from his home region of the Alto Adige. I never imagined that yogurt and olive oil would blend so well.

This salad goes well with cold ham or chicken, poached salmon, or grilled leg of lamb.

San Domenico
240 Central Park South
New York, New York

Spring Potato and Watercress Salad with Horseradish

INSALATA DI PATATE, CRESCIONE, E CREN

1¼ pounds small waxy potatoes, scrubbed

Salt, to taste

½ cup plain yogurt

¼ cup extra virgin olive oil

2 tablespoons peeled and minced fresh horseradish

Freshly ground pepper, to taste

1 large bunch of watercress, tough stems removed (about 4 cups)

1 Place the potatoes in a medium saucepan with cold water to cover and salt. Bring to a simmer and cook until the potatoes are tender when pierced with a knife, about 20 minutes. Drain and slice thin.

2 In a bowl, whisk together the yogurt, olive oil, horseradish, salt, and pepper until smooth and well blended.

3 Pour half the dressing over the potatoes and mix well. Add the watercress and drizzle with the remaining dressing.

4 Toss gently and serve.

Crusty Potatoes with Tomatoes and Onions

PATATE GRATINATE

1 1/2 *pounds baking or boiling potatoes, peeled and sliced* 1/8 *inch thick*

1 *large onion, thinly sliced*

4 *tablespoons olive oil*

Salt and freshly ground pepper, to taste

2 *medium-size ripe tomatoes, peeled, seeded, and chopped, or*
    1 *cup chopped canned Italian tomatoes*

1/2 *teaspoon dried oregano*

1/4 *cup freshly grated pecorino romano*

1/4 *cup dry bread crumbs*

1 Preheat the oven to 400°F. Oil a 12 × 9 × 2-inch roasting pan.

2 Combine the potatoes with the onion, 3 tablespoons of the olive oil, salt, and pepper in the pan. Sprinkle the potatoes with the tomatoes, oregano, and cheese. Toss the bread crumbs with the remaining oil. Scatter the crumbs over the vegetables.

3 Bake for 45 minutes, or until the potatoes are tender and the topping is browned.

4 Serve hot or warm.

Baked with tomatoes and onions, these potatoes have a crusty brown topping of bread crumbs and cheese. Served with a green salad, the dish is substantial enough for a meatless meal, but it is also a perfect accompaniment to most roasts.

I like to bake the potatoes in an enameled cast-iron roasting pan. Because it's so heavy, it holds the heat well and the potatoes brown nicely on the bottom. If you want to make more potatoes, use two pans so that the potato layer is not too thick and the potatoes cook evenly.

SERVES 8

My father used to make this Neapolitan-style mashed potato casserole for all of our holiday meals. I thought about reducing the amount of cheese to make it less rich, but decided against it—it's just too good the way it is.

Potato, Cheese, and Prosciutto Casserole

SFORMATO DI PATATE

2 pounds baking potatoes, scrubbed (about 6 medium)

3 tablespoons fine dry bread crumbs

1 cup whole milk ricotta

1 cup milk

1 cup plus 2 tablespoons freshly grated Parmigiano-Reggiano

2 eggs, beaten

1/4 teaspoon freshly grated nutmeg

Salt and freshly ground pepper, to taste

1 cup diced mozzarella, preferably fresh (8 ounces)

4 ounces thinly sliced prosciutto, cut into narrow strips

1 Place the potatoes in a large saucepan with cold water to cover. Cover and bring to a boil. Cook until the potatoes are tender when pierced with a knife, about 25 minutes. Drain and cool slightly.

2 Preheat the oven to 375°F. Butter a 12 × 9 × 2-inch oval baking dish or 3-quart shallow casserole and sprinkle with 1 tablespoon of the bread crumbs.

3 Peel and mash the potatoes. Stir in the ricotta, milk, 1 cup of the Parmigiano, the eggs, and nutmeg. Season with salt and pepper. Stir in the mozzarella and prosciutto.

4 Spoon the mixture evenly into the baking dish. Sprinkle with the remaining Parmigiano and bread crumbs.

5 Bake until the top is golden and the center is heated through, 40 to 45 minutes.

6 Let stand 10 minutes before serving.

To make ahead: The casserole can be completely assembled through Step 4 and refrigerated for several hours or overnight. Uncover and bake as directed, adding 15 minutes or so to the baking time if the dish has been refrigerated.

Roast Potatoes with Onion and Rosemary

PATATE AL FORNO

2 pounds potatoes, preferably Yukon Gold, scrubbed and cut into
  1-inch pieces
1/4 cup olive oil
1 small onion, finely chopped
2 tablespoons chopped fresh rosemary leaves
Coarse salt and freshly ground pepper, to taste

1 Preheat the oven to 400°F.

2 Pat the potato pieces dry. In a baking pan large enough to hold them in a single layer, combine the potatoes with the remaining ingredients. Roast the potatoes, stirring every 15 minutes, until tender and browned, about 1 hour.

3 Serve hot.

SERVES 6

I've never met a potato dish I didn't like, and these crusty brown potatoes are no exception. I've tried this recipe with many kinds of baking and boiling potatoes, and though the results are different, they all taste good. My first choice is Yukon Gold. You can substitute sage, thyme, or oregano for the rosemary and/or garlic for the onion.

Because they belong to the same family of vegetables that includes nightshade, eggplants, tomatoes, and potatoes were at one time believed to be inedible, even poisonous. An old southern Italian and Sicilian superstition held that if you wanted to get rid of a foe, all you needed to do was write that person's name on a slip of paper, fasten the paper to a potato, and bury it underground. The enemy would soon be joining the potato.

In this spicy recipe from the Basilicata region above the toe of the Italian boot, potato chunks are sautéed with garlic and chilies. Serve them with grilled spareribs or sausages or as an accompaniment to a frittata.

Fried Potatoes with Garlic and Hot Pepper

PATATE FRITTE ALL'AGLIO E PEPERONCINO

2 pounds waxy potatoes, scrubbed

4 large garlic cloves

1/3 cup olive oil

1 small red chili, crushed, or 1/2 teaspoon crushed red pepper, or to taste

Salt, to taste

1 Cut the potatoes into 1-inch pieces. Pat them dry.

2 Place the garlic on a cutting board and crush lightly with the flat side of a heavy knife. Remove the peel and stem ends.

3 In a large skillet over medium heat, heat the oil. Add the potatoes and cook, stirring frequently, until they begin to brown, about 10 minutes. Add the garlic, red pepper, and salt. Cover and cook, stirring the potatoes occasionally, for 15 to 20 minutes, or until the potatoes are golden and tender when pierced with a fork. Remove the potatoes with a slotted spoon.

4 Serve immediately.

Fennel Mashed Potatoes

PURÈ DI PATATE E FINOCCHIO

1 pound baking potatoes, peeled and cut into 1-inch chunks

Salt, to taste

1 medium fennel bulb, trimmed and cut into 4 to 6 wedges

2 tablespoons extra virgin olive oil

Freshly ground pepper, to taste

1 Place the potatoes in a saucepan with cold water to cover by 1 inch. Add salt to taste. Cover and cook until the potatoes are tender when pierced with a fork, about 20 minutes.

2 In another saucepan, combine the fennel with cold water to cover by 1 inch. Add salt to taste. Cover and cook until the fennel is tender when pierced with a fork, about 15 minutes. Drain the fennel and pass it through a food mill or puree it in a food processor.

3 Drain the potatoes and mash them with a potato masher, ricer, or food mill into a large bowl. (Do not be tempted to use a food processor, or the potatoes will be gluey.) Combine the potatoes with the fennel, olive oil, salt, and pepper.

4 Serve hot.

To make ahead: Spoon the potatoes into an oiled casserole dish. Cover and refrigerate until ready to serve. Uncover and bake in a 350°F. oven for 30 minutes or until heated through.

SERVES 4

When I was growing up, fennel at our house was always eaten raw, cut into wedges and served as a *digestivo,* usually at the end of a holiday meal. But Italians are much more creative than that implies. They use wild and cultivated fennel both raw and cooked. This pale green, fluffy puree, for example, is very subtle, with the fennel adding lightness and character to the potatoes without a lot of fat. The puree can be made ahead then reheated. Its taste goes well with pork and game birds.

SERVES 4

Lumpy mashed potatoes streaked with red pepper and garlic and spotted with a brown crust are terrific with roasts or grilled meats. Peeling the potatoes is optional. I rarely do.

Use a flavorful variety of potato here, such as Yukon Gold or Finnish Yellow. You may have to shop around to find them.

Mashed Potatoes, Devil's Style

PATATE SCHIACCIATE AL DIAVOLO

1 pound small boiling potatoes, such as Yukon Gold, scrubbed

Salt, to taste

¹/₄ cup olive oil

2 garlic cloves, minced

¹/₂ teaspoon crushed red pepper, or to taste

1 Place the potatoes in a pot with cold water to cover. Bring to a boil and cook until the potatoes are very tender when pierced with a knife, about 20 minutes. Drain well. Coarsely mash the potatoes. Season with salt.

2 In a medium nonstick skillet over medium heat, heat the oil with the garlic and red pepper for 30 seconds, or until the garlic is fragrant. Add the potatoes. Cook, stirring frequently, for 10 minutes, or until the potatoes are lightly browned in spots.

3 Serve immediately.

To make ahead: The potatoes can be boiled ahead of time. Just before serving, mash them and proceed with the recipe.

Potato-stuffed Vegetables, Ligurian Style

VERDURE RIPIENE DI PATATE

1 pound boiling potatoes, scrubbed

$^1/_3$ cup plus 2 tablespoons freshly grated Parmigiano-Reggiano

$^1/_3$ cup chopped fresh basil

1 garlic clove, minced

Pinch of dried marjoram

3 tablespoons olive oil

Salt and freshly ground pepper, to taste

4 plum tomatoes

2 medium red or yellow bell peppers

1 Place the potatoes in a large saucepan with cold water to cover. Cover the pan and bring the water to a simmer. Cook until the potatoes are tender when pierced with a knife, about 20 minutes. Drain the potatoes and let them cool slightly. Peel off the skins. Mash the potatoes with a ricer, food mill, or masher. Stir in $^1/_3$ cup of the cheese, the basil, garlic, marjoram, oil, salt, and pepper.

2 Preheat the oven to 450°F. Oil a large roasting pan.

3 Cut the tomatoes lengthwise in half and scoop out the seeds. Cut the peppers into 4 or 6 wedges and remove the stems, seeds, and membranes. Fill the tomato halves and pepper wedges with the potato mixture, mounding it slightly. Place the vegetables in the pan. Sprinkle with the remaining cheese. Bake for 30 minutes, or until the peppers and tomatoes are tender when pierced with a fork.

4 Serve hot or at room temperature.

SERVES 8

Vincenzo Corrado, a cook and a monk of the Celestine order during the late eighteenth century, was the first Italian to record a recipe for tomatoes. Until his time, tomatoes were grown mostly as ornamental plants. He called his recipe *Pomodori alla Certosina,* or Tomatoes in the Style of the Monks, but it was hardly austere, consisting as it did of tomatoes stuffed with truffles, anchovies, cooked fish, and fried leafy greens and served with a tomato sauce.

In this dish, derived from one I tasted at the restaurant Manuelina in Liguria in northwestern Italy, tomatoes and peppers are stuffed with a much simpler filling of mashed potatoes seasoned with herbs and cheese. Serve the vegetables hot or at room temperature as a side dish or antipasto.

Manuelina
Recco (Liguria)

SERVES 4

In the Veneto, little fish like sardines are often prepared *in saor*, meaning with vinegar and onions. I like the slightly bittersweet flavor of radicchio prepared this way, too. Serve this as a cooked salad or as an antipasto.

Radicchio in White Wine

RADICCHIO IN SAOR

1 large head of radicchio (about 8 ounces)

3 tablespoons olive oil

Salt, to taste

1 medium onion, chopped

1/2 cup dry white wine

2 tablespoons white wine vinegar

Freshly ground pepper, to taste

1 Trim the radicchio, discarding any bruised leaves. Cut the head into 8 wedges. Heat the oil in a large skillet over medium heat. Add the radicchio wedges, cut sides down, and sprinkle with salt. Cook, turning once, until the radicchio is browned on both sides, about 10 minutes. Remove the wedges to a serving platter with a slotted spoon.

2 Add the onion, wine, and vinegar to the skillet. Bring to a simmer and cook for 10 minutes, or until most of the liquid has evaporated but the onions are not completely dry. Pour the contents of the skillet over the radicchio. Sprinkle with pepper.

3 Serve at room temperature.

Butternut Squash with Parmigiano-Reggiano

ZUCCA AL PARMIGIANO

1 small butternut squash (about 1¹/₂ pounds)

Salt and freshly ground pepper, to taste

2 tablespoons unsalted butter

¹/₃ cup freshly grated Parmigiano-Reggiano

1 Peel the squash and cut it lengthwise in half. Remove the seeds and fibers. Cut the squash into ¹/₄-inch-thick slices.

2 Preheat the oven to 375°F. Butter a roasting pan large enough to hold the squash in a shallow layer.

3 Arrange the squash slices overlapping slightly in the pan. Sprinkle with salt and pepper and dot with butter. Bake the squash for 30 minutes, or until tender. Sprinkle with the cheese. Bake for 5 minutes more.

4 Serve hot.

Among the simplest ways to prepare vegetables is to bake them with butter or olive oil and parmesan cheese. Most vegetables, fennel or zucchini for example, need to be partially cooked first in salted water. Butternut squash does not.

When buying zucchini, always look for small to medium-size firm ones with a glossy and unbruised surface. Large zucchini are watery, have too many seeds, and lack flavor. Sometimes zucchini have grit or sand imbedded in their skins, so it is important to scrub them with a soft vegetable brush. If you feel any rough spots, scrape them off with a paring knife or vegetable peeler.

Zucchini with Onion and Parsley

ZUCCHINI IN PADELLA

1 pound zucchini, scrubbed (2 to 3 medium)

2 tablespoons unsalted butter

1 small onion, very finely chopped

Salt and freshly ground pepper, to taste

3 tablespoons chopped Italian flat-leaf parsley

1 Trim the ends of the zucchini and cut into $1/8$-inch slices.

2 In a medium skillet over medium-low heat, melt the butter. Add the onion and cook until softened, 3 to 5 minutes.

3 Add the zucchini and toss to coat with the butter. Cover and cook for 5 minutes, or until the zucchini is just tender when pierced with a fork. Add the salt, pepper, and parsley and toss well.

4 Serve immediately.

Zucchini with Garlic and Herbs

ZUCCHINI AL'AGLIO

4 medium zucchini, scrubbed (about 1¹/₂ pounds)

4 tablespoons olive oil

1 garlic clove, very finely chopped

1 tablespoon chopped fresh parsley

1 tablespoon chopped fresh basil

¹/₂ teaspoon dried oregano

Salt and freshly ground pepper, to taste

1 Trim the ends from the zucchini and cut into 2 × ¹/₄ × ¹/₄-inch sticks, like french fries.

2 In a large skillet over medium heat, heat the oil. Add the zucchini and cook, stirring occasionally, until lightly browned, about 10 minutes.

3 Stir in the garlic, herbs, salt, and pepper. Cook for 2 minutes more.

4 Serve hot or at room temperature.

SERVES 6

Tender zucchini sticks browned with garlic and herbs are a good accompaniment to almost any grilled main dish. Yellow summer squash can also be prepared this way. Or use a combination of the two for color contrast.

In this version of *cianfotta,* the mess of vegetables is roasted rather than stewed as on page 292. The oven heat concentrates the flavors and browns the vegetables, bringing out their sweetness. The eggplant becomes soft and creamy and the other vegetables turn a rich brown color. A sprinkle of fresh basil on the hot vegetables is an aromatic final touch.

Though it seems like a lot of vegetables to start with, they become considerably reduced as they cook. But do not be tempted to increase the quantity of vegetables in the pan. If it becomes too crowded, the vegetables will steam without turning brown and turn out bland and watery. If you want to increase the quantity, use a larger roasting pan or use two pans. There should not be more than one layer of vegetables in the pan.

Roasted Summer Vegetables

CIANFOTTA AL FORNO

1 medium eggplant (about 12 ounces)

Salt, to taste

1 large red, yellow, or green bell pepper

1 large onion

2 medium potatoes, scrubbed

3 ripe plum tomatoes

4 garlic cloves, peeled

1/3 cup olive oil

Freshly ground pepper, to taste

1/4 cup chopped fresh basil

1   Cut the eggplant into 1-inch cubes. Place them in a colander and sprinkle generously with salt. Invert a plate over the eggplant and weight it with a heavy can. Let stand for 60 minutes to drain. Rinse the eggplant and dry the pieces well with paper towels.

2   Preheat the oven to 400°F.

3   Cut the pepper, onion, and potatoes into 1-inch cubes. Cut the tomatoes into quarters.

4   Combine the cut-up vegetables and garlic cloves in a 12 × 9 × 2-inch roasting pan. The vegetables should be only 1 layer deep. Toss the vegetables with oil, salt, and pepper. Roast the vegetables for about 1 hour, turning them every 15 minutes or so, until they are tender and browned. Remove the vegetables to a serving dish, scraping up the browned bits. Sprinkle with basil.

5   Serve warm or at room temperature.

Roasted Winter Vegetables

VERDURE AL FORNO

1 small fennel bulb, trimmed and cut into 6 wedges

2 medium turnips, peeled and quartered

2 medium carrots, peeled and cut into 1-inch lengths

2 medium parsnips, peeled and cut into 1-inch lengths

2 medium potatoes, scrubbed and cut into quarters

2 medium onions, peeled and cut into quarters

4 garlic cloves, peeled

1/3 cup olive oil

Salt and freshly ground pepper, to taste

1 Preheat the oven to 425°F.

2 Combine the cut-up vegetables and garlic cloves in a 12 × 9 × 2-inch roasting pan. The vegetables should be only 1 layer deep. Toss the vegetables with oil, salt, and pepper. Roast the vegetables for about 1 hour and 10 minutes, turning them every 15 minutes, until they are tender and browned. Remove the vegetables to a serving dish, scraping up the browned bits.

3 Serve hot.

SERVES 4

The colors of roasted fall or winter vegetables are soft, pale, and golden as opposed to the vibrant shades of summer vegetables. The firmer texture of root vegetables makes it necessary to cook them at a higher temperature than you would soft summer vegetables.

Fairer Than Turnip

*Oh, your face is much
    sweeter than mustard,
Fairer than turnip. A snail
    has pushed its vehicle
On it, and made it as it
    is—so lusted.
Your teeth are parsnip white,
    and your sweet giggle
Would doubtless turn the
    Pope's heart into custard.
Your eyes are just as
    colorful as treacle,
Your hair is blond and
    white like bulbs of leeks:
Oh make me alive!
That's all my spirit seeks.*

Michelangelo

SERVES 8

After the frenetic traffic on the Via Roma in Naples, the Piazza Dante seems almost quiet and the restaurant Dante e Beatrice a tranquil haven. We were delighted with this simple salad we had there. It was made with tiny spring vegetables dressed at the last minute with oil, salt, and a bit of vinegar. You can cook the vegetables in advance but don't combine them or add the dressing until the last minute. That way, each vegetable retains its individual flavor.

Trattoria Dante e Beatrice
Piazza Dante, 44/45
Naples (Campania)

Fiorentin mangia fagioli
Lecca piatti e ramaioli
The Florentine eats the beans,
then licks the plates and
ladles clean.

Old Tuscan proverb

Spring Vegetable Salad

INSALATA PRIMAVERA

2 small zucchini, scrubbed and trimmed (12 ounces)

8 ounces tender thin green beans

1 pound small potatoes, preferably Yukon Gold or Finnish Yellow, scrubbed

1 cup cherry tomatoes, halved

4 green onions, thinly sliced

1/4 cup extra virgin olive oil

1 to 2 tablespoons red or white wine vinegar

Salt, to taste

1/4 cup torn fresh basil leaves

1 Bring a large pot of water to a boil. Add the zucchini and cook until barely tender, about 10 minutes. Remove the zucchini with tongs and rinse under cold water to stop the cooking.

2 Add the green beans to the water and cook for 5 to 7 minutes, or until crisp yet tender. Remove with a slotted spoon. Cool under running water. Drain and pat dry. Cut into 1-inch pieces.

3 Add the potatoes to the water and cook until tender when pierced with a knife, about 20 minutes. Drain and let cool slightly. Peel and cut the potatoes into bite-size pieces.

4 Just before serving, cut the zucchini 1/2 inch thick. Combine the zucchini, green beans, potatoes, cherry tomatoes, and green onions in a serving bowl.

5 Whisk the olive oil and vinegar together with the salt. Toss the vegetables with the dressing. Scatter the basil over the top.

6 Serve immediately.

To make ahead: Cook the zucchini, green beans, and potatoes up to 3 hours before serving. Keep them at room temperature.

Bread ... Pane

I F I WAS BLINDFOLDED *and dropped off somewhere in Italy, I probably could tell where I was just by tasting the local bread. Every region has its local varieties and specialties that aren't made exactly the same way anywhere else. Typical examples are the crunchy* michette *or* rosette *rolls of Lombardy; the crusty, unsalted* pane toscano *of Tuscany; the cottony, refined* coppietta, *or couple bread, of Emilia-Romagna; the chewy, golden, full-flavored loaves of Campania; and the nutty, sesame-coated semolina breads of Sicily. Breads may vary even from town to town within the same region.*

In Italy, bread appears on every table and at every meal. With the exception of focaccia and a few specialty breads, it is always served at room temperature, especially in restaurants. At one time, a housewife would make up big batches of dough, enough for bread to last a week, and bake it in a wood-burning oven. This was usually done on Sunday so that a roast or a pot of beans for Sunday dinner could be placed in the embers to cook slowly after the bread had been baked.

Now that many Italian women work outside the home and with quality bread widely available at neighborhood and village bakeries, few Italian cooks make it at home anymore. Most buy loaves of fresh bread daily and only occasionally make specialty breads like focaccia or pizza at home.

Every time I go to Naples I can't stop eating the local bread with its thick golden crust and chewy cream-colored crumb. One day after a morning spent in one of the city's great museums, I wandered over to a table near the exit where a big guest book had been set up for visitors to sign. I peeked at the comments, including several from some American teenagers who had just passed through. To my amazement one had written "I love Italy! I love Naples! But why is the bread so hard?" How sad! The poor child must have been brought up on packaged white bread and did not recognize good bread when she finally tasted it.

Crisp, chewy, flavorful bread is essential to an Italian meal. Seek out bakeries in your area that make good-tasting loaves. Fortunately, there has been a resurgence of interest in bread baking in recent years, and better breads are available just about everywhere.

If you would like to make your own, this chapter includes a recipe for a simple Italian-style bread that you can make at home plus recipes for focaccias, a stuffed pizza, and *taralli* that can be served with antipasto.

Home-style Country Bread

PANE CASALINGA

STARTER

1 package (2¹/₂ teaspoons) active dry yeast or instant yeast

1 cup warm water (105° to 110°F.)

1 cup unbleached all-purpose flour or bread flour

DOUGH

3¹/₂ to 4 cups unbleached all-purpose or bread flour

¹/₂ cup whole wheat flour

2 teaspoons salt

1 To make the starter, sprinkle the yeast over the warm water and whisk until creamy. Stir in the flour. Cover with plastic wrap and leave at room temperature for at least 1 hour or overnight. The mixture will be thick and bubbly. The longer the starter sits, the better the flavor will be. After 24 hours, store the starter in the refrigerator for up to 3 days.

2 In a heavy-duty mixer bowl fitted with a dough hook or in a food processor fitted with the metal blade, combine 3¹/₂ cups all-purpose flour, the whole wheat flour, and salt. Scrape the starter into the bowl and add 1 cup warm water. Stir on low speed or process until the dough is smooth and elastic, about 5 minutes. Add more flour as necessary for the dough to hold a soft shape yet remain sticky.

3 Lightly oil a 4- to 6-quart bowl. Scrape the dough into the bowl. Cover with plastic wrap and let rise in a warm draftfree place for 2 to 3 hours, or until tripled in volume.

4 Turn the dough out onto a lightly floured surface. Dust the top with flour. Flatten the dough with your hands to eliminate the air bubbles.

5 Cut the dough into 2 pieces. Shape each piece into a ball or, if you prefer, a long loaf. Sprinkle a work surface or baking sheet generously with flour. Place the loaves several inches apart. Cover with a towel and let rise for 45 minutes, or until doubled.

MAKES 2 LOAVES

This bread recipe produces a chewy, crusty, professional-looking loaf. It begins with a starter, a mixture of a small amount of flour, water, and yeast that is left to ferment before adding it to the remaining flour and water. The purpose of a starter is to reduce the amount of yeast required and impart a fuller flavor to the bread. Bread made with a starter keeps better, too.

The dough for this bread is moist and sticky. Use a heavy-duty mixer with a dough hook, if you have one, or use a food processor with the steel blade. It is very difficult to knead by hand unless you add a lot of flour, and that will make the bread denser.

Baking the bread in a steamy environment makes the crust chewy and crisp. Professional ovens have steam vents built in, but this effect can be duplicated by pouring water into a hot pan placed in the bottom of the oven. Be sure to protect your hands and forearms when you do this since the water evaporates quickly and the rising steam can scald.

Baking the bread on a pizza stone or quarry tiles helps achieve a firm crunchy crust. A good alternative is a heavy baking sheet placed in the oven to preheat while the dough completes its second rise.

6 About 45 minutes before baking the bread, preheat the oven to 450°F. Place an empty roasting pan on the lowest rack of the oven. Place a pizza stone or quarry tiles or a heavy metal baking sheet in the oven on the rack set at the next higher level.

7 When the dough is risen, sprinkle a pizza peel or baking sheet with cornmeal. Gently slip 1 loaf onto the pizza peel or baking sheet. Slash the top with a serrated knife, making several cuts about $^1/_2$ inch deep. Slide the loaf into the oven. Repeat with the second loaf.

8 Protecting your hand and forearm with a long oven mitt, immediately pour about 2 cups of hot water into the pan. Quickly shut the oven door to retain the steam.

9 Bake the loaves until they are browned and the loaves sound hollow when tapped on the bottom, about 40 minutes. (Check the internal temperature by inserting an instant-read thermometer, if you like. The temperature should be 200° to 210°F.)

10 Transfer the loaves to a wire rack. Cool completely before slicing.

How to Tell When a Loaf of Bread Is Done

Most bread recipes suggest thumping the bottom of a loaf of bread to tell if it is done. They say it should sound hollow. For all the bread I have baked, I am still not quite sure what that sound is. A much more reliable method is to take the bread's temperature with an instant-read thermometer. When you think the bread is ready, turn the loaf over and insert the thermometer in the center or thickest part. Most breads are ready when the temperature registers between 190° and 210°F. The higher temperature is better for breads made with wet, sticky doughs.

Tomato Focaccia

FOCACCIA DI POMODORI

1 package (2¹/₂ teaspoons) active dry yeast

1¹/₂ cups warm water (105° to 110° F.)

6 tablespoons olive oil

3¹/₂ to 4 cups unbleached all-purpose flour or bread flour

Coarse salt

4 to 5 plum or Roma tomatoes

¹/₂ teaspoon dried oregano

1 In a large bowl, sprinkle the yeast over the water. Whisk until the yeast is creamy and dissolved.

2 Stir in 3 tablespoons of the oil. Add 3¹/₂ cups flour and 1 teaspoon salt. Stir until a soft dough forms.

3 Turn the dough out onto a lightly floured surface and knead until smooth and elastic, about 10 minutes, adding more flour if necessary to make a moist but nonsticky dough.

4 Place the dough in a large oiled bowl. Turn the dough to grease the top. Cover loosely with a towel and let rise in a warm draftfree place until doubled in bulk, about 1¹/₂ hours.

5 Oil a 15 × 10 × 1-inch jelly-roll pan. Flatten the dough gently to eliminate air bubbles, handling it as little as possible. Stretch and pat the dough out to fit the pan. Cover with a towel and let rise for 1 hour.

6 Cut the tomatoes in quarters lengthwise and scoop out the seeds and juice. Cut the quarters crosswise into ¹/₄-inch-thick slices.

7 Dimple the dough by making deep indentations with your fingertips at 1-inch intervals all over the surface. Press a piece of tomato in each indentation.

8 Drizzle the surface with the remaining 3 tablespoons olive oil. Sprinkle with the oregano and salt. Bake for 25 to 30 minutes, or until golden.

The sleepy Sicilian town of Salemi comes to life every March in anticipation of the Feast of San Giuseppe, or Saint Joseph, the patron saint of Sicily. All year long, the women of the town sculpt miniature ornaments made from an inedible bread dough in the shape of roses, birds, flower baskets, fruits, pea pods, fish, animals, angels, and other figures. The bread ornaments are attached to garlands of boxwood and laurel that are strung across the streets and fastened to the gates of the city to decorate the streets, shops, churches, and homes. The purpose is to celebrate the coming of Spring, which coincides with Saint Joseph's day, and the rebirth of nature after the long dark winter.

Sicilians make all manner of excellent breads, including this simple focaccia topped with pieces of tomato, which is great with cheese, cold meats, or a salad. The dough can be made by hand, in a heavy-duty mixer, or in a food processor.

9 Serve warm, cut into squares.

To make ahead: The focaccia can be made completely ahead. Cool it on a wire rack then cut it into 2 or 4 pieces, whatever is convenient. Wrap the pieces individually in aluminum foil and freeze them for up to 1 month. To reheat, unwrap the frozen focaccia and place it in a hot oven until lightly toasted, about 15 minutes.

SERVES 8

Focaccia is a simple flat bread found throughout Italy and its name is derived from the Latin word *focus,* meaning hearth. There are many regional variations, but focaccia usually is made from a simple white bread dough flattened to one-inch thickness and baked in a pan. Olive oil, herbs, or vegetables may be sprinkled or pressed into the top. This version, made crunchy and colorful with golden cornmeal and olives, is my interpretation of one I purchased at a bakery in Venice.

Polenta and Olive Focaccia

FOCACCIA DI GRANOTURCO

1 package (2$^{1}/_{2}$ teaspoons) active dry yeast

$^{1}/_{4}$ cup warm water (105° to 110° F.)

1$^{1}/_{4}$ cups warm milk (105° to 110° F.)

2 tablespoons olive oil

3 to 3$^{1}/_{2}$ cups unbleached all-purpose flour or bread flour

1 cup fine yellow cornmeal

1 teaspoon salt

1 cup black olives, pitted and coarsely chopped

1 In a large bowl, sprinkle the yeast over the warm water. Let stand for 5 minutes to soften.

2 Stir in the milk and olive oil. Add 3 cups of the flour, the cornmeal, and salt. Stir well until a dough forms.

3 Turn the dough out onto a lightly floured surface. Knead the dough until smooth and elastic, adding flour as needed to prevent the dough from sticking.

4 Oil a large bowl. Place the dough in the bowl, turning it over to oil the top. Cover with a towel and let rise in a warm draftfree place until doubled in bulk, about 1 hour.

5 Flatten the dough to eliminate air bubbles. Knead in the olives.

6 Oil a 15 × 10 × 1-inch jelly-roll pan. Add the dough, patting it with your hands to fit the pan evenly. Cover with a towel and let rise until puffy, about 45 minutes.

7 Preheat the oven to 450°F.

8 Bake the dough until browned and crusty, about 30 minutes. Slide the bread onto a rack to cool slightly.

9 Cut into 3 × 2-inch rectangles and serve warm.

To make ahead: The focaccia can be made completely ahead. Cool it on a wire rack then cut it into 2 or 4 pieces, whatever is convenient. Wrap the pieces individually in aluminum foil and freeze them for up to 1 month. To reheat, unwrap the frozen focaccia and place it in a hot oven until lightly toasted, about 15 minutes.

Green Onion Pizza

PIZZA DI CIPOLLINE

DOUGH

1 package (2¹/2 teaspoons) active dry yeast

1 cup warm water (105° to 110°F.)

2 tablespoons olive oil

3 cups unbleached all-purpose flour

2 teaspoons salt

FILLING

4 bunches of green onion (about 1 pound)

3 tablespoons olive oil

1 cup large green olives, pitted and coarsely chopped

1 To make the dough, in a large bowl, sprinkle the yeast over the water. Let stand for 5 minutes until the yeast is creamy.

2 Stir the mixture until the yeast is dissolved. Add the olive oil, flour, and salt. Stir the mixture until a soft dough forms.

SERVES 8

Pizza is a term used loosely in Italy to describe many kinds of stuffed and unstuffed sweet or savory pies. Stuffed savory pizzas can be made with all kinds of fillings. One that my family traditionally ate on Christmas Eve was *pizza di scarola,* two layers of savory pastry filled with sautéed escarole, garlic, anchovies, and olives.

Stuffed pizzas are great for picnics and all kinds of moveable feasts. In fact, when I spotted this pie in a bakery in Monopoli, in southern Italy, I bought several slices to take with me on the plane ride back to the States the next day. The pie held up well, and I was the envy of my fellow travelers who had nothing to eat but airline food.

"Love bread

   Heart of the home

   Perfume of the mind

   Joy of the hearth

Respect bread

   Sweat of the brow

   Pride of labor

   Poem of sacrifice

Honor bread

   Glory of the fields

   Fragrance of the earth

   Feast of life

Do not waste bread

   Richness of the homeland

   The most exquisite gift of God

   The holiest prize of human

   effort"

From a bag of bread from the Gran Forno Fasciana e Zuzzè in Vallelunga, Sicily

3 Turn the dough out onto a lightly floured surface. Knead until smooth and elastic, about 10 minutes, adding more flour if the dough feels sticky.

4 Oil a large bowl and place the dough in it, turning it once to oil the top. Cover with a towel and let rise in a warm draftfree place until doubled in bulk, about 2 hours.

5 To make the filling, trim the green onions by removing the root end and any bruised outer leaves. Trim about 1 inch from the tops. Cut the onions lengthwise in half, then crosswise into $1/2$-inch pieces. You should have about 3 cups.

6 In a large skillet, heat the oil over medium-low heat. Add the onions and cover the pan. Cook, stirring occasionally, until the onions are tender but not browned, about 5 minutes. Remove from the heat. Stir in the olives and let cool.

7 Preheat the oven to 450°F.

8 Punch down the dough and cut it into 2 pieces. With a rolling pin, roll out 1 piece of dough to a 12-inch circle on a lightly floured surface. Transfer the dough to a large baking sheet reshaping it as needed. Spread the filling evenly over the dough, leaving a $1/2$-inch border. Roll out the remaining dough to a 12-inch circle. Place the circle over the filling, stretching it gently to meet the edge of the bottom circle. Press the edges tightly together to seal. With a small, sharp knife, cut several slits in the top of the dough.

9 Bake for 25 minutes, or until browned and crisp.

10 To serve hot, transfer the pizza to a cutting board and cut into wedges. To serve at room temperature, slide the pizza onto a rack to cool.

Cook's note: To make the dough in a food processor, place the flour and salt in the processor fitted with the steel blade. Turn on the machine and add the yeast mixture. Process until the dough forms a ball and is smooth and elastic. Knead briefly to form a ball. Continue with Step 4.

Parmesan Focaccia

FOCACCIA DI PARMIGIANO-REGGIANO

1 package (2^1/$_2$ teaspoons) active dry yeast

1 cup warm water (105° to 110° F.)

^{1}/$_4$ cup olive oil

1 cup freshly grated Parmigiano-Reggiano

2 tablespoons finely chopped fresh sage or 1 tablespoon dried sage

^{1}/$_4$ cup finely chopped onion

About 3^1/$_2$ cups unbleached all-purpose flour or bread flour

1 teaspoon salt

1   In a large bowl, sprinkle the yeast over the water. Let stand for 5 minutes until the yeast is creamy.

2   Stir the mixture until the yeast is dissolved. Add the oil, cheese, sage, and onion and stir well. Add 3 cups of flour and the salt. Stir the mixture until a soft dough forms.

3   Turn the dough out onto a lightly floured surface. Knead until smooth and elastic, about 10 minutes, adding more flour if the dough feels sticky.

4   Oil a large bowl and place the dough in it, turning it once to oil the top. Cover with a towel and let rise in a warm draftfree place until doubled in bulk, about 1^1/$_2$ hours.

5   Oil a 12 × 9-inch baking pan. Flatten the dough to eliminate air bubbles. Stretch and pat out the dough to fit the prepared pan. Cover loosely with a towel and let rise in a warm draftfree place for 30 minutes, or until puffed.

6   Preheat the oven to 450°F.

7   Bake the focaccia until golden brown and crisp, about 20 minutes.

8   Cut into 3 × 2-inch rectangles. Serve warm.

At the weekly outdoor market in Parma, where everything from clothing and kitchen gadgets to fresh fish and produce is for sale, I bought what has become one of my favorite gadgets, a *dosacaffè*. It stores and measures just the right amount of ground coffee for an espresso maker. One of my other purchases was this focaccia flavored with Parmigiano-Reggiano, fresh sage, and onions. The cheese and onions give it a moist texture and rich flavor. Like most focaccias, it freezes and reheats well.

To make ahead: The focaccia can be made completely ahead. Cool it on a wire rack then cut it into 2 or 4 pieces, whatever is convenient. Wrap the pieces individually in aluminum foil and freeze them for up to 1 month. To reheat, unwrap the frozen focaccia and place it in a hot oven until lightly toasted, about 15 minutes.

The Duke's Rustic Brioche

BRIOCHE RUSTICA

1/2 cup warm milk (105° to 110°F.)

1 package (2 1/2 teaspoons) active dry yeast

4 tablespoons (1/2 stick) unsalted butter, softened

1 tablespoon sugar

1/2 teaspoon salt

1/2 cup grated Parmigiano-Reggiano

2 large eggs, at room temperature

2 1/2 cups unbleached all-purpose flour or bread flour

2 ounces sharp provolone, rind removed, cut into small dice (1/2 cup)

1 ounce sliced boiled ham, chopped (1/4 cup)

1 ounce sliced Genoa salami, chopped (1/4 cup)

1 Butter and flour a 10-inch tube pan.

2 Pour the milk into a small bowl. Stir in the yeast. Let stand for 5 minutes until creamy.

3 In a large mixer bowl, beat the butter, sugar, and salt until blended. Beat in the Parmigiano, then add the eggs, one at a time. Stir in the milk. The mixture will look curdled. Add the flour and beat until smooth.

SERVES 8 TO 10

This antipasto bread speckled with meats and cheeses has a light golden color. Because it is made with a rich dough containing eggs and butter, similar to French brioche, the texture is tender, more like cake than bread.

Probably the earliest written recipe for this bread was published in *La Cucina teorico pratica*, a book by Ippolito Cavalcanti, Duke of Buonvicino, who was born in Afragola near Naples in 1787. Much of his book is concerned with derivations of French cuisine fashionable at that time and appealing to his aristocratic readers, but Cavalcanti was also the first writer to record original Neapolitan recipes, which he wrote in the local vernacular to distinguish them from the more patrician selections. This recipe seems to be a hybrid of French and Neapolitan cooking techniques and ingredients.

Some contemporary recipes for this bread suggest serving it with the center filled with a ragù of peas, green beans, or mushrooms in a cream sauce. That seems exceedingly rich to me, perhaps a throwback to its aristocratic ori-

4 Turn the dough out onto a lightly floured surface and shape it into a ball. With a rolling pin, roll out the dough to a 22 × 8-inch rectangle. Sprinkle the provolone, ham, and salami over the dough, leaving a 1-inch border on the long sides. Roll up the dough from 1 long side into a cylinder. Pinch the seam to seal. Place the cylinder, seam side down, in the prepared pan. Pinch the 2 ends together to seal. Cover the pan with plastic wrap. Put the pan in a warm draftfree place to rise for 1½ hours, or until the dough is level with the rim.

5 Preheat the oven to 350°F.

6 Bake for 35 minutes, or until golden brown. Turn the ring out onto a rack to cool to room temperature before slicing.

Cook's note: The bread tastes best the day it is made. Wrap leftovers in foil and store them in the refrigerator. To reheat, cut the bread into slices and bake in a 350°F. oven until lightly toasted.

Crisp Almond and Black Pepper Rings

TARALLI CON LE MANDORLE

1 package (2½ teaspoons) active dry yeast

1 cup warm water (105° to 110°F.)

½ cup olive oil

3½ cups unbleached all-purpose flour or bread flour

2 teaspoons salt

2 teaspoons finely ground black pepper

1 cup almonds, coarsely chopped

1 In a large mixing bowl, sprinkle the yeast over the water. Stir well until the yeast is creamy and dissolved.

gins. I serve it in slices accompanied by olives and roasted peppers for an antipasto or with a green salad or a bowl of vegetable soup for a meal. Leftover slices are good lightly toasted with drinks or a glass of wine.

Life imitates theater in Naples. The whole city, with its magical setting, is like a stage and someone is always singing, shouting, or creating some spectacle that you have to stop and watch. A perfect place for people-watching is the Via Caracciolo, the broad boulevard that curves around the bay. Vendors sell *taralli,* crunchy almond and black pepper rings, just as pretzel vendors do in New York City. One hot afternoon, we bought some taralli and strolled along the broad esplanade busy among the families, pensioners, and teenagers out for a breath of sea air.

Suddenly we saw a vision in white. A bride had come to have her photo taken against the dramatic backdrop of the Castel del'Ovo with Vesuvius in the distance. We smiled and watched as the bride and groom and their very formally dressed entourage climbed on the sea wall and clambered over the rocks, posing for photos while scantily clad swimmers frolicked in the water behind them.

Charming, we thought, but soon realized that our bride was not alone. There was another just a short distance away. Then another, and another, appeared. At one point, I counted eight couples, each with their photographers, assistants, wedding parties, and families. Brides of every description seemed to be headed in every direction, dragging the heavy trains of their elaborate gowns over the pavement. And the grooms were not to be outdone. One wore a red silk tuxedo. Wedding parties came and went all afternoon and even into the night.

These taralli will keep a long time in a tightly sealed container, though in our house they tend to disappear quickly. Serve them with a glass of wine and a piece of sharp provolone cheese or as an accompaniment to salads or soups. Neapolitan taralli are made with *sugno,* or lard, but this version, made with olive oil, is equally delicious and a lot more digestible.

2 Add the olive oil to the yeast and stir well. Combine the flour, salt, and pepper and stir into the yeast mixture.

3 Turn the dough out onto a lightly floured surface. Knead until smooth and elastic, about 10 minutes. Knead in the almonds.

4 Oil a large bowl and place the dough in it, turning to oil the top. Cover the bowl with a kitchen towel and let rise in a warm draft-free place until doubled, about $1^{1}/_{2}$ hours.

5 Preheat the oven to 350°F.

6 Punch down the dough. Cut it into 8 pieces. Keeping the remainder covered with an overturned bowl or plastic wrap, divide 1 piece into 4 smaller pieces. Shape each piece into a 6-inch rope. Twist each rope 3 times and shape it into a ring, pinching the ends together to seal. Place the rings about 1 inch apart on ungreased baking sheets.

7 Bake the rings for 1 hour or until browned and crisp. Turn off the oven and let the rings cool in the oven for 1 hour so that they will be thoroughly dry. Remove from the oven and cool completely on a wire rack.

8 Store in airtight containers at room temperature.

Fruit Desserts …
Frutta

FRUIT COMPLETES THE MEAL *for most Italians, either as an ingredient in a dessert or as dessert itself. In restaurants and at home, a bowl of fruits is placed on the table after lunch and dinner, and young and old gladly choose a piece or two. No one needs to be persuaded to eat fruit. Apples, pears, oranges, tangerines, bananas, and grapes are usual in winter, and berries, cherries, peaches, apricots, nectarines, and plums, depending on the region and the growing season, are the highlights of spring and summer. Italians do not expect to eat fruits out of season, and, in fact, they prefer not to. They wisely*

wait until each fruit is available locally, knowing that it will taste better and cost less.

In the warmer months, a bowl of ice water is sometimes set out with the fruit bowl for dipping and refreshing the fruit. Firmer fruits, like pears and apples, are peeled and eaten somewhat ceremoniously with a knife and fork, a skill I doubt I will ever master. I find the ritual of sharing, choosing, rinsing, peeling, and eating fruit relaxing and satisfying. What is more, it gives my brain's appetite control center time to receive that very slow-moving message from my stomach announcing that it has had enough before I confront the decision of whether and how much dessert to eat.

This is not to say that Italians do not eat cakes, cookies, and other sweets. They do, but usually only on special occasions and not until they have eaten some fruit. At home, we generally have fresh fruit in season for dessert. When company comes, we still have fruit, though I usually offer some biscotti or a cake to follow.

This chapter includes desserts made with fresh fruit for every season, including *macedonia*, the ubiquitous Italian fruit salad; pears baked with biscotti crumbs; and several kinds of *granita*, or Italian ice. You must try Figs with Honey and Mascarpone when you can get good ripe figs.

The Fruit Bowl

We never had a floral centerpiece on the holiday table when I was growing up. No candles, either. My father's attitude was that if you couldn't eat or drink it, it didn't belong on the table. One of his favorite tasks was to arrange the fruit bowl centerpiece. He started by taking out my mother's antique cut-crystal footed bowl and polishing it until it sparkled. Then he would arrange a base of firm fruits like apples and oranges on the bottom. Next came slightly softer fruits like pears or peaches, depending on the season. A spray of bananas emerged from the top and a cascade of different colored grapes tumbled down the sides. If fresh fennel or fava beans were available, they would be interspersed among the fruits. Persimmons, cherries, and strawberries were seasonal additions. Melons always taste better slightly chilled, so they were cut up and served later on a separate platter.

Since the fruit bowl was on the table before the meal began, everyone had a chance to admire it and sniff its sweet aromas. It was only natural to take a piece or two after the main course was taken away and before the cakes and pastries were brought in.

A Fresh Taste of Italy

Apples in White Wine with Rum Cream

Mele al Vino con Crema

4 Golden Delicious apples

2 cups dry white wine

¹/₂ cup sugar

1 strip (3 inches) of lemon zest

SAUCE

1 cup milk

1 cup heavy cream

3 large egg yolks

¹/₄ cup sugar

1 tablespoon rum

1 teaspoon pure vanilla extract

Ground cinnamon

1 Peel the apples and cut them into quarters. Remove the cores and stems.

2 In a large saucepan over medium heat, heat the wine and sugar. Cook, stirring, until the sugar dissolves. Add the apples and lemon zest. Reduce the heat to low. Cover and cook until the apples are just tender when pierced, 5 to 8 minutes. With a slotted spoon, remove the apples to a bowl.

3 Boil the liquid until it becomes thick and syrupy. Spoon the syrup over the apples and refrigerate until chilled.

4 To make the sauce, in a medium saucepan over medium-low heat, heat the milk and cream until little bubbles form around the edges.

5 In a medium bowl, whisk the egg yolks with the sugar until blended. Gradually whisk the hot milk into the egg yolks, stirring constantly. Transfer the mixture to the saucepan and cook over low

In the Trentino-Alto Adige region in northeastern Italy, apple orchards blanket the valleys while vineyards cover the hillsides. It was inevitable that someone would devise a way to combine the two fruits in one dessert. Golden Delicious apples are poached in a crisp, dry white wine and served chilled with a rum-scented custard sauce.

heat, stirring until the custard thickens, wisps of steam appear on the surface, and the mixture lightly coats the back of a spoon. Immediately strain the custard into a bowl. Stir in the rum and vanilla. Let cool, then cover and refrigerate until serving time.

6 Divide the apples and syrup among 6 serving bowls. Top with the sauce. Sprinkle very lightly with ground cinnamon.

Figs with Honey and Mascarpone

FICHI AL MIELE E MASCARPONE

8 ripe green or black figs
About 1 cup mascarpone cheese, at room temperature
About $1/4$ cup honey

1 Cut the figs into halves or quarters if large.

2 Place $1/4$ cup of mascarpone on each of 4 plates. Surround the mascarpone with the figs. Drizzle with honey. Serve immediately.

SERVES 4

One of the pleasures of being in Italy in September is plucking ripe figs from the tree and eating them while they are still warm from the sun. Fig trees grow wild, so there's always plenty for everyone. Figs taste best when they are fully ripe. Both green and black figs should be be soft and yielding to the touch. If they are really at their peak, you will see what the Italians call a tear in the eye, a drop of fig nectar that is beginning to seep out of the blossom end. Since figs bruise easily, handle them gently and eat them as soon as possible after picking or buying them.

Fresh figs are often peeled before eating. Take a sharp paring knife and make a small cut at the stem end of the fig. Grasping the peel between the knife blade and your thumb, pull it down toward the base and remove it. Continue to peel off the skin in strips around the rest of the fig.

Strawberries in Red Wine

FRAGOLE AL VINO ROSSO

SERVES 4

2 pints strawberries, rinsed and hulled

1/4 cup sugar, or to taste

1 tablespoon fresh lemon juice

1 cup fruity red wine, such as barbera

1 cup mascarpone cheese, at room temperature

1 Halve or quarter the berries if they are large. Place them in a large bowl with the sugar, lemon juice, and wine. Let stand at room temperature, stirring occasionally, for 1 hour.

2 Spoon the berries into bowls and serve with the mascarpone.

The inviting perfume of strawberries steeping in red wine greeted us as we arrived for a picnic lunch at the Citro Dairy in Battipaglia south of Naples. First, we toured the dairy and watched the cheesemakers as they cooked vats of water buffalo milk and turned it into mozzarella. Afterward, we sat in the grass under a shade tree and ate big bowls of berries with freshly made mascarpone and thick slices of coarse country bread to soak up the juices.

When local strawberries are at their peak, there is no need to do anything to them to improve their flavor, but a red wine and sugar soak often can give a boost to berries that are less than perfect.

Roasted Chestnuts

CASTAGNE AL FORNO

SERVES 8

Roasted chestnuts are an essential part of the dessert assortment at Italian holiday meals. Serve them with a sweet dessert wine or a bowl of fresh fruit.

1 pound chestnuts

1 Preheat the oven to 425°F.

2 Place the chestnuts flat side down on a cutting board. Cut an X in each with the tip of a small sharp knife.

3 Place the chestnuts on a large piece of aluminum foil and add 2 tablespoons water. Fold up the ends of the foil to form a sealed pouch. Place the pouch in a metal baking pan. Roast the chestnuts until tender when pierced with a small knife, about 45 to 60 minutes.

4 Place the chestnuts in a basket and serve hot.

Cook's note: Chestnuts can also be roasted this way to use in desserts such as the Chocolate-Chestnut Truffles (page 373) and the Chestnut Tart (page 362), though boiling them makes peeling easier (see page 363). Let the chestnuts cool slightly, then remove the shell and the inner skin.

SERVES 6

A friend was buying pears in a Manhattan supermarket when a man came up to her and asked her to help him select some for himself. "Pears are always under-ripe or overripe," he complained. "I never seem to know when they are ready." She chose a few that looked promising, then advised him to keep them for a few days at room temperature. He thanked her and walked away, but returned a few moments later and handed her his business card, saying, "Please call me and let me know when your pears are ripe, so that I'll know it's time to eat mine."

Pears are picked when they are mature but not ripened. Their flavor and texture actually develop better after picking than they would on the tree. Buy pears when they are still firm and store them at room temperature. When the flesh near the stem end yields to gentle pressure, the pears are ready.

Serve ripe pears with a wedge of cheese such as gorgonzola or Parmigiano-Reggiano for a simple dessert. When pears are less than perfect, their flavor can be improved by cooking them, as in this dessert of baked pears with a cookie crumb stuffing.

Biscotti-stuffed Baked Pears

PERE RIPIENE AL FORNO

1 cup dry white wine

¹/₂ cup plus 2 tablespoons sugar

1 strip (2 inches) of lemon zest

¹/₂ cup savoiardi or other biscotti or cookie crumbs, such as vanilla wafers

2 tablespoons melted butter

¹/₂ cup golden raisins

4 firm ripe pears, such as Bartlett

1 Preheat the oven to 350°F. Butter a baking dish just large enough to hold the pears in a single layer when cut in half.

2 Stir the wine and ¹/₂ cup sugar together. Pour the mixture into the dish and add the lemon zest.

3 Combine the cookie crumbs, butter, and remaining 2 tablespoons sugar. Stir in the raisins.

4 Cut the pears lengthwise in half. Scoop out the cores and stems using the tip of a swivel-blade vegetable peeler or a melon baller. Stuff the pears with the crumb mixture. Place the pears cut side up in the baking dish. Bake for 45 minutes, or until the pears are tender when pierced with a knife.

5 Serve warm with the pan juices.

The Count's Strawberries and Ice Cream

FRAGOLE CON GELATO

2 pints strawberries

Sugar, to taste

2 pints vanilla ice cream, softened

1 Rinse the strawberries and drain them well. Pat dry on paper towels. Set aside a few berries for garnish. Remove the stems from the remainder. If the strawberries are large, cut them into halves or quarters.

2 Place the berries in a deep glass bowl with a 6- to 8-cup capacity. Add sugar to taste, if desired. Top with the ice cream. Smooth the ice cream with a spatula. Place the remaining strawberries on top and serve immediately.

SERVES 6

Count Zecca and his family produce fine wines in Puglia. When I was attending a food writers' conference in Lecce, he invited a group of us to dinner at his home. The Zeccas live in a splendid seventeenth-century villa furnished with antiques fit for a museum. In the dining room, the table was set with red roses, ornate porcelain, and massive silverware. The Count told us that most of the food the cook had prepared for our dinner was made from organic products from his farm. We ate tender ravioli filled with sheep's milk ricotta, fresh whole grain bread, and cold poached bass served with olive oil mayonnaise and ripe tomatoes. The cook returned again bearing the simplest yet most exquisite dessert. She had topped juicy strawberries with a layer of vanilla ice cream in a cut-crystal bowl. The melting ice cream blended with the red berry juices to form a light, velvety pink sauce. If you want to serve a special dessert but don't have a lot of time, this is it.

Strawberries are really the best fruit to use, especially when small local berries are in the market, but this dessert works almost as well with sliced peaches and raspberries or blueberries. Don't bother to use a superpremium brand of ice cream: A quality brick ice cream, or even frozen vanilla yogurt, is closer to the light texture of Italian gelato.

SERVES 4

At the Hotel Laurin on Lake Garda, you can dine in the romantic, Liberty-style dining room or on the elegant shady terrace. The specialty is fresh fish from the lake. These berry-filled melon halves are served there as an appetizer, though I prefer to serve them for dessert.

Hotel Laurin
Salo (Lombardy)

Berry Bowls with Sparkling Wine

MELONE E FRUTTI DI BOSCO ALLO SPUMANTE

2 small cantaloupes, chilled
2 cups assorted berries, such as strawberries, blueberries,
raspberries, and blackberries
Sugar, to taste
1 half bottle (375 ml) chilled sparkling wine

1 Cut the cantaloupes in half crosswise and scoop out the seeds. Place the melon halves in shallow bowls.

2 Rinse the berries and pat them dry. Remove the stems. Cut large strawberries into bite-size pieces. Toss the berries with sugar, if desired. Spoon the berries into the melon halves.

3 Just before serving, gently pour on the wine. Serve immediately.

Fresh Fall or Winter Fruit Salad

MACEDONIA DI FRUTTA FRESCA

6 cups cut-up seasonal fruits, including apples, plums, pears, kiwi,
bananas, grapes, tangerines, oranges
½ cup orange marmalade or apricot jam
2 tablespoons maraschino liqueur, kirsch, wine, or orange juice

1 Combine the fruits in a large bowl.

2 Stir together the marmalade and liqueur and pour the mixture over the fruits. Stir gently.

3 Cover and chill for 1 hour before serving.

One of the lushest fruit displays anywhere can be found at the Roman trattoria Otello alla Concordia. In the center of the pretty garden room is a stone lion head fountain that spouts water into a large marble tub. Surrounding the tub and hanging from the wall above it is an assortment of most of the fruits, and quite a few vegetables, too, known to man. I counted three kinds of grapes, four types of apples, two pear varieties, pineapples, figs, watermelons, kiwi, and lemons, plus peppers and tomatoes the last time I was there. Most of the fruit is eaten plain, and the rest finds its way into fruit salad, which in Italy is always called *macedonia*. The name comes from the Balkan country of the same name, which was assembled from a group of small states, like the bits of fruit in the salad.

Maraschino is a clear liqueur made from sour cherries, which is used primarily in fruit salads and to flavor cakes. Do not confuse it with the bright red maraschino cherries sold in jars. If you can't find maraschino liqueur, substitute kirsch, white wine, or even orange juice.

Otello alla Concordia
Via della Croce, 81
Rome

Granita Tips

For quick granita any time, try these tips.

- Keep a batch of chilled sugar syrup in a covered jar in the refrigerator. Equal parts of sugar and water are the most useful proportions. You can always dilute the syrup with water if necessary.
- Keep a pan and metal spoon in the freezer, especially in warm weather. If you start with chilled utensils, the granita will freeze that much sooner.
- Keep a metal spoon in the pan between stirrings to avoid reducing the temperature any more than necessary.
- Make granita from any kind of fruit juice, fruit puree, tea, or coffee. Add chilled sugar syrup to taste and balance the flavor with a splash of fresh lemon or lime juice. Remember that freezing will make the mixture taste less sweet, so always start with a very sweet mixture. Freeze as indicated in the recipes.
- Remember that alcohol and liqueurs will inhibit freezing. Do not add more than a tablespoon or two, if at all, to the granita mixture. If you like, spoon a liqueur over the ice just before serving.
- Make granita in an ice cream maker if you like; the texture will be smooth instead of grainy. Follow the manufacturer's instructions.
- Make granita ahead by allowing the liquid mixture to freeze solid for up to three days before serving. Remove the pan from the freezer and let it soften briefly before serving. Either scrape it with a spoon into grains or flakes or break the solid block of ice into chunks and puree them in a food processor or heavy-duty mixer. The food processor or mixer will produce an ice with a smoother texture.

White Grape Granita

GRANITA DI UVA

¹/₂ cup sugar

3 cups seedless green grapes, stems removed (about 1¹/₂ pounds)

1¹/₂ cups chilled white grape juice

1 In a small saucepan, combine the sugar and 1 cup water. Bring to a simmer and stir occasionally until the sugar is dissolved, about 3 minutes. Remove from the heat and let cool completely. Place in the refrigerator to chill.

2 Place a 12 × 9 × 2-inch metal pan and metal spoon in the freezer.

3 In a blender or food processor, puree the grapes until smooth. Strain the puree into a large bowl. Add the grape juice and sugar syrup to taste. Stir until well blended. Pour the mixture into the chilled pan.

4 Place the pan in the freezer for 30 minutes, or until ice crystals form around the edges. Stir the ice crystals into the center of the mixture. Return the pan to the freezer and continue freezing, stirring every 30 minutes, until all of the liquid is frozen, about 2 to 2¹/₂ hours.

5 To serve, scoop the granita into serving dishes.

To make ahead: The sugar syrup may be made ahead and refrigerated, covered, up to 1 week in advance. The granita may be made up to 24 hours before serving. If it gets too hard to scoop, scrape up the ice crystals with the side of a spoon.

MAKES 5 CUPS

During the warm summer months, I keep a jar of sugar syrup in the refrigerator, so that I can make granita any time I want. Practically any fruit or fruit juice can be used. White grape juice in jars is always on the supermarket shelf, and seedless green grapes seem to be available year round, making this granita particularly convenient—as well as refreshing.

MAKES ABOUT 6 CUPS

Just looking at the cool green color of this granita will make the temperature seem lower on a sweltering day.

Letter of advice to Francesco di Marco Datini from his doctor, written in May 1404:

"As to the fruit to which you bear so sweet a love, I grant you almonds, both fresh and dried, as many as you like; and nuts, both fresh and dry and well cleaned . . . and fresh and dried figs before a meal, and also grapes; but after a meal, beware of them. Take melons, in season, before a meal, and cast not away what is in them, for that is the best and most medicinal part. And I will grant you many cherries, well ripe, before a meal; but by God, after a meal let them be. And I beseech you, since I am so generous in conceding fruit to you according to your mind, be so courteous to me as to cast aside the others which are so harmful, such as baccelli (young fava beans), apples, chestnuts, and pears."

Iris Origo, The Merchant of Prato

Honeydew Granita

GRANITA DI MELONE

1/2 cup sugar
1 very ripe honeydew melon (about 3 pounds)
3 tablespoons fresh lemon juice

1 In a small saucepan, combine the sugar and 1 cup water. Bring to a simmer and stir occasionally until the sugar is dissolved, about 3 minutes. Remove from the heat and let cool completely. Place in the refrigerator to chill.

2 Place a 12 × 9 × 2-inch metal pan and metal spoon in the freezer.

3 Peel and seed the melon and cut it into chunks. You should have about 6 cups.

4 In a blender or food processor, combine the melon and sugar syrup. Blend or process until smooth. Add the lemon juice. Pour the mixture into the chilled pan.

5 Place the pan in the freezer for 30 minutes, or until ice crystals form around the edges. Stir well. Continue freezing and stirring the mixture every 20 to 30 minutes, or as ice crystals form. When all of the liquid is frozen, about 3 hours, transfer the granita to a plastic container and seal tightly. Keep in the freezer.

6 Remove from the freezer to soften about 15 minutes before serving, if necessary.

To make ahead: The sugar syrup may be made ahead and refrigerated, covered, up to 1 week in advance. The granita may be made up to 24 hours ahead of time. If it gets too hard to scoop, scrape up the ice crystals with the side of a spoon.

Lime Granita

GRANITA DI LIMONE VERDE

³/₄ cup sugar

1 teaspoon grated lime zest

¹/₂ cup fresh lime juice (about 4 limes)

1   In a small saucepan, combine the sugar and 3 cups water. Bring to a simmer and stir occasionally until the sugar is dissolved, about 3 minutes. Remove from the heat and let cool completely. Place in the refrigerator to chill.

2   Place a 12 × 9 × 2-inch metal pan and metal spoon in the freezer.

3   Combine the lime zest, lime juice, and sugar syrup and pour the mixture into the chilled pan. Place the pan in the freezer for 30 minutes, or until ice crystals form around the edges. Stir well. Continue freezing and stirring the mixture every 20 to 30 minutes, or as ice crystals form. When all of the liquid is frozen, about 3 hours, transfer the granita to a plastic container and seal tightly. Keep in the freezer.

4   Remove from the freezer to soften about 15 minutes before serving, if necessary.

To make ahead: The sugar syrup may be made ahead and refrigerated, covered, up to 1 week in advance. The granita may be made up to 24 hours ahead of time. If it gets too hard to scoop, scrape up the ice crystals with the side of a spoon.

MAKES 6 CUPS

Granita made with fresh lemon juice is a summer staple throughout southern Italy. Lime juice is an interesting alternative. Try it with a tablespoon or two of grappa on each portion.

Peaches simply marinated in red wine are one of summer's most looked-forward-to desserts. Even more extraordinary is this granita, which takes the combination to new heights. The technique here is slightly different from the other granita recipes. Cooking the peaches makes even less-than-perfect fruit taste great.

". . . in every piazza, on bancarelle [stalls] and trays, roasted chestnuts, oranges, delicious wild strawberries, biscuits and aqua-vita were displayed . . . and in summer the melonaro, melon vender, who claimed that his melons refreshed you and washed your face at one and the same time."

Peter Gunn, *Naples: A Palimpsest*
(London, 1961)

Peach and Red Wine Granita

GRANITA DI PESCHE E VINO ROSSO

2¹/₂ cups peeled, pitted, and sliced peaches (about 5 large peaches)
³/₄ cup sugar
¹/₃ cup dry red wine
1 tablespoon fresh lemon juice

1   In a medium saucepan, combine the peaches, sugar, and 2 cups water. Bring to a simmer and stir occasionally until the peaches are very tender when pierced with a fork, about 5 minutes. Remove from the heat and let cool completely.

2   Place a $12 \times 9 \times 2$-inch metal pan and metal spoon in the freezer.

3   In a blender or food processor, combine the peaches and their cooking liquid, the wine, and lemon juice. Blend or process until smooth. Pour the mixture into the chilled pan.

4   Place the pan in the freezer for 30 minutes, or until ice crystals form around the edges. Stir well. Continue freezing and stirring the mixture every 20 to 30 minutes, or as ice crystals form. When all of the liquid is frozen, about 3 hours, transfer the granita to a plastic container and seal tightly. Keep in the freezer.

5   Remove from the freezer to soften about 15 minutes before serving, if necessary.

To make ahead: The peach puree may be made ahead and refrigerated, covered, up to 2 days in advance. The granita may be made up to 24 hours ahead of time. If it gets too hard to scoop, scrape up the ice crystals with the side of a spoon.

Biscotti, Tarts, Cakes, and Other Desserts ... Biscotti, Crostate, Torte, e Dolci

ITALIAN HOMEMADE DESSERTS ARE *so good that I wrote an entire book about them called* La Dolce Vita *with almost two hundred recipes. When I completed it, I thought I would never be able to write another word on the subject, but once I started to assemble dessert recipes for this book, I realized how much more there was to be done.*

In this chapter you will find cooked or baked desserts for all occasions, including biscotti, tarts, cakes, and puddings. Some, like the Chocolate-Cheese Tart, are quite rich while others, like the Lemon–Pine Nut Meringues, are light and low in calories. Hard, crunchy cookies, like Hazelnut Anise Biscotti,

Chocolate-Cherry Biscotti, and Little Devil Cookies, are particularly good to have on hand to serve with a glass of wine or a cup of tea when friends drop by or when you are looking for a little something sweet. Since they are good keepers, I make up a batch every couple of weeks and store them in a big glass jar on my kitchen counter so they are always available for munching.

For festive occasions, the desserts to try are the sophisticated Chestnut Tart, the Chocolate-Almond Truffle Cake, and the Little Golden Hearts cookies. Classic desserts include Chocolate Pudding with Pine Nuts and Citron, fried Gossips from Naples, and Sweet Ricotta Puffs. Many traditional Italian desserts are fried rather than baked, since until recent years many homes did not have ovens. For Christmas, Panforte and the Chocolate-Chestnut Truffles are an essential part of my holiday baking. I start my day with cappuccino, and I always enjoy a cup of espresso after a meal. In between, one of my favorite treats is a Caffè Shakerato, a coffee concoction you can easily make at home without elaborate equipment.

Tips for Making Perfect Biscotti

- Some biscotti batters can be very sticky. To shape them neatly into logs, first scoop up gobs of batter with two rubber spatulas. Arrange the gobs on the baking sheets in rows according to the length and width indicated in the recipe. Moisten your hands with cool water. Pat the dough to smooth it into a neat log.
- When making biscotti, use baking sheets that do not have raised sides all around. This will make it easier to slide the partially baked logs off the baking sheet and onto the cutting board for slicing.
- If you have only pans with raised sides (jelly-roll pans or sheet pans as opposed to baking sheets), turn them over and bake on the reverse side or bottom.
- To remove biscotti logs from the pan, first slide a metal spatula under the logs their entire length to loosen them. Use a long metal spatula or two shorter spatulas held side by side to slide the logs onto the cutting board.
- To cut biscotti, use a large heavy chef's knife. Holding the knife at a slight angle to the end of a log, place the tip of the knife on the cutting board and press down, slicing firmly and neatly through the log. Do not use a sawing motion; it may tear the still soft dough.
- Stand the biscotti on the baking sheet about $1/2$ inch apart. If any refuse to stand, just bake them on the cut side and turn them over halfway through the baking time.

Hazelnut Anise Biscotti

ANICINI

1 cup hazelnuts (about 5 ounces)

2¹/₄ cups all-purpose flour

1 teaspoon baking powder

¹/₂ teaspoon salt

4 teaspoons anise seeds

3 large eggs

1 cup sugar

1 teaspoon pure vanilla extract

1 Preheat the oven to 325°F.

2 Place the hazelnuts in a small pan. Bake for 8 to 12 minutes, or until lightly toasted. Place the nuts in a kitchen towel and rub them to remove the skins. Let cool.

3 Raise the oven temperature to 350°F. Butter a large baking sheet.

4 In a medium bowl, combine the flour, baking powder, salt, and anise seeds.

5 In a large bowl, using an electric mixer, beat the eggs, sugar, and vanilla until very pale and thick, about 3 minutes. Stir in the dry ingredients, then the hazelnuts. The dough will be very soft.

6 With 2 rubber spatulas, scoop the dough onto the cookie sheet forming three 10-inch logs about 2 inches apart. Smooth the logs with a spatula or with moistened hands. Bake for 30 minutes, or until lightly browned and the loaves spring back when touched in the center.

7 Carefully transfer the logs to a cutting board. Using a heavy chef's knife, slice the logs crosswise ¹/₂ inch thick. Stand the slices on a baking sheet ¹/₂ inch apart. Bake for 10 to 15 minutes, or until crisp.

8 Transfer to a wire rack to cool.

To make ahead: These cookies keep well in a tightly sealed container at room temperature for up to 1 month.

Traditional biscotti are baked into logs, then sliced and baked a second time until toasted and dry. Most recipes for this type of biscotti call for laying the sliced cookies flat to bake and turning them halfway through the baking time to brown the other side. I prefer to place the cookie slices in a standing position on the baking sheet with a half- to one-inch space between them, eliminating the need to turn the cookies. Since these cookies are made without butter, they have a light, crisp texture.

Italian biscotti are very simply flavored, usually with just a bit of vanilla or lemon or orange zest. This is an Americanized version of Italian biscotti that I developed for an article that first appeared in *Food & Wine* magazine. These cookies pack a lot of flavor for relatively few calories and are very low in fat.

Chocolate-Cherry Biscotti

BISCOTTI DI CIOCCOLATO E CILIEGE

1¹/₃ cups all-purpose flour

¹/₂ cup unsweetened cocoa powder, sifted

1 teaspoon baking powder

¹/₂ teaspoon salt

2 large eggs

1 cup sugar

1 teaspoon pure vanilla extract

1 cup dried sweet cherries

1 Preheat the oven to 350°F. Line a baking sheet with aluminum foil.

2 In a medium bowl, combine the flour, cocoa, baking powder, and salt.

3 In a large mixer bowl, using an electric mixer, beat the eggs, sugar, and vanilla until very pale and thick, about 3 minutes. Stir in the dry ingredients. Add the cherries.

4 Divide the dough in half. Dampen hands and shape each half into a 12-inch log 2 inches apart on the baking sheet. Bake for 30 minutes, or until the loaves spring back when touched lightly in the center.

5 Carefully slide the logs onto a cutting board. With a sharp heavy chef's knife, cut each log into ¹/₂-inch slices. Stand the pieces on the baking sheet ¹/₂ inch apart. Bake for 10 minutes, or until crisp.

6 Cool on wire racks.

To make ahead: These cookies keep well in a tightly sealed container at room temperature for up to 1 month.

Little Golden Hearts

Cuoricini di Mais

1²/₃ cups all-purpose flour

1 cup finely ground yellow cornmeal

²/₃ cup sugar

1¹/₂ teaspoons baking powder

¹/₂ teaspoon salt

1 large egg

2 large egg yolks

12 tablespoons (1¹/₂ sticks) unsalted butter, melted and cooled

1 teaspoon grated lemon zest

CHOCOLATE GLAZE

4 ounces semisweet or bittersweet chocolate

2 to 3 tablespoons unsalted butter

1 In a large bowl, combine the flour, cornmeal, sugar, baking powder, and salt.

2 In a small bowl, beat the egg and egg yolks together. Stir in the melted butter and lemon zest. With a wooden spoon, stir the egg mixture into the dry ingredients until well blended. The mixture will look crumbly.

3 Place a large sheet of plastic wrap on a flat surface. Pour half the dough onto the plastic wrap and shape it into a disk. Use the plastic wrap to press the dough together. Wrap tightly and chill at least 1 hour or overnight. Place a second piece of plastic wrap on a flat surface and repeat with the remaining dough.

4 Preheat the oven to 375°F. Butter and flour 2 large baking sheets.

5 Remove the dough from the refrigerator and let it warm up briefly at room temperature, until it is soft enough to roll out. Roll out 1 piece of the dough between 2 sheets of plastic wrap ¹/₄ inch thick. With a 2-inch heart-shape cookie cutter, cut out pieces of dough. Place the pieces 1 inch apart on the baking sheets.

Yellow cornmeal makes these buttery little cookies extra crunchy. You can serve them plain though they are very pretty drizzled with stripes of chocolate. Use a bar chocolate for this recipe, which has a high percentage of cocoa butter so it melts easily. Chocolate chips are formulated to keep their shape and not melt.

6 Bake the cookies for 12 to 15 minutes, or until lightly browned around the edges. Let cool on the sheets for 1 minute, then transfer to wire racks set over wax paper to cool completely.

7 Place the chocolate and butter in a bowl set over but not touching simmering water. Let soften. Stir until smooth. Dip a fork into the chocolate and drizzle it in diagonal stripes over the cookies. Let set for 1 hour in a cool place.

To make ahead: Store, layers separated by wax paper, in airtight containers in a cool place or in the refrigerator. These keep for 1 week.

Lemon—Pine Nut Meringues

MERINGHE DI LIMONE

3 large egg whites, at room temperature

Pinch of salt

1/2 cup sugar

1 teaspoon grated lemon zest

1/2 cup pine nuts

1 Preheat the oven to 250°F. Line 2 baking sheets with parchment paper.

2 In a large mixing bowl, beat the whites on medium speed until foamy. Add the salt and continue beating, gradually adding the sugar, until stiff peaks form and the mixture is shiny. Stir in the lemon zest and pine nuts.

3 Drop the batter by the heaping tablespoonful onto the baking sheets, placing the mounds about 1 inch apart. Bake for 40 minutes. Turn off the oven and leave the cookies to dry for 3 hours in the closed oven.

4 Peel the cookies off the parchment paper.

To make ahead: Store the cookies in a tightly sealed container at room temperature for up to 1 week.

MAKES 3 DOZEN

Make these lemony low-fat cookies on a dry day so that they will turn out crisp. Orange zest can be substituted for the lemon.

Anna's Almond Cookies

AMARETTI DI ANNA

MAKES ABOUT
3 DOZEN

Vegetable oil

2¹/₂ cups blanched almonds (13 ounces)

²/₃ cup sugar

Grated zest of 1 lemon

2 large egg whites

Pinch of salt

¹/₂ teaspoon pure vanilla extract

¹/₂ teaspoon almond extract

40 whole unblanched almonds or pine nuts or candied cherries

At Regaleali, Anna Tasca Lanza makes these chewy cookies with a combination of sweet and bitter almonds. Bitter almonds have an intense, concentrated almond flavor, but they are not sold in the United States since they can be toxic if eaten in quantity. Almond extract is substituted for the bitter almonds.

Parchment paper prevents the cookies from sticking to the pan. Anna showed me a good trick to keep the stiff parchment paper in place. She oils the pan first with a little vegetable oil.

1 Preheat the oven to 350°F. Brush 1 or 2 large baking sheets with oil. Line the sheets with parchment paper.

2 In a food processor or blender, process the almonds in small batches with a tablespoon of the sugar until finely ground. In a large bowl, combine the almonds, remaining sugar, and lemon zest.

3 In a large mixer bowl, beat the egg whites with a pinch of salt until stiff but not dry. Beat in the vanilla and almond extract. Stir the egg white mixture into the almond mixture until well blended.

4 Roll the nut mixture into 1-inch balls. Flatten slightly and place about 1 inch apart on the baking sheet. Insert an almond or pine nut pointed end up in the center of each one or top with a candied cherry. Bake for 25 to 30 minutes, or until the cookies are lightly browned.

5 Let cool briefly, then transfer to wire racks to cool completely.

To make ahead: Amaretti are best the day they are baked. They can be baked ahead and frozen in tightly sealed plastic bags for up to 1 month.

In the old section of Monopoli in Puglia, the Santa Caterina bakery sells wonderful cookies, cakes, bread, and savory pies. I was especially taken with these dry crunchy cookies, called little devils because they are spicy. These are the kind of cookies that no Italian home ever seems to be without, ready to serve when friends drop by. Serve them with a glass of sweet dessert wine for dipping.

Santa Caterina
Monopoli (Puglia)

Little Devil Cookies

DIAVOLACCI

3¹/2 *cups all-purpose flour*

1¹/2 *cups almonds, toasted and finely ground (8 ounces)*

2 *teaspoons baking powder*

1 *teaspoon ground cinnamon*

¹/2 *teaspoon ground cloves*

¹/4 *teaspoon finely ground black pepper*

4 *large eggs*

¹/4 *cup olive oil*

1 *cup sugar*

1   Preheat the oven to 350°F. Line 2 baking sheets with aluminum foil or parchment paper.

2   In a large bowl combine the flour, almonds, baking powder, cinnamon, cloves, and pepper.

3   In a large mixer bowl, beat the eggs, olive oil, and sugar on high speed until well blended. On low speed, stir in the dry ingredients. The dough will be thick and sticky.

4   Divide the dough into 8 portions. With floured hands, roll out 1 portion of the dough on a lightly floured surface into a rope about 1 inch thick. With a small knife, cut the rope on the diagonal into 1-inch pieces. Place the pieces 1 inch apart on the baking sheets. Repeat with the remaining dough. Bake for 40 minutes, or until lightly browned and firm.

5   Transfer to wire racks to cool.

To make ahead: These cookies keep very well for 2 weeks in a tightly sealed container in a cool dry place.

Spiced Chocolate Cookies

BISCOTTI CON LE SPEZIE

10 tablespoons (1¼ sticks) unsalted butter

½ cup milk

2 large eggs, beaten

1 teaspoon pure vanilla extract

3 cups all-purpose flour

1 cup sugar

½ cup unsweetened cocoa powder, sifted

1 teaspoon ground cinnamon

1 teaspoon freshly grated nutmeg

1 teaspoon ground cloves

1 teaspoon salt

1 teaspoon finely ground black pepper

2½ teaspoons baking powder

1 cup finely chopped walnuts

FROSTING

1½ cups confectioners' sugar

1 teaspoon unsalted butter, softened

1 teaspoon pure vanilla extract

2 to 3 tablespoons hot milk

MAKES ABOUT
7 DOZEN

I adapted this recipe from one given to me by Carol Tabone, a cooking teacher and the owner of a cooking school in Cincinatti, Ohio. The cookies, spicy and chocolatey, make excellent Christmas cookies. Of course they go well with coffee or tea, but I also like them with red wine.

1 Preheat the oven to 375°F. Butter and flour 3 baking sheets or line them with aluminum foil.

2 In a small saucepan, heat the butter and milk until the butter is just melted. Let cool. Stir in the beaten eggs and vanilla.

3 In a large bowl, combine all of the dry ingredients and the nuts. Add the egg mixture and mix well.

4 Pinch off small pieces of dough and roll them between the palms of your hands into 1-inch balls. Place the balls 1 inch apart on the baking sheets. Bake for 18 to 20 minutes, or until the cookies are puffed and lightly cracked.

5 Let cool for 10 minutes on the baking sheets then transfer to racks to cool completely.

6 To make the frosting, combine the confectioners' sugar, butter, vanilla, and enough milk to make the consistency of heavy cream. Stir until smooth. Dip the top of each cookie into the frosting.

7 Place the cookies on a rack, frosted side up, until hardened.

To make ahead: When the frosting is firm, store in an airtight container in a cool dry place for up to 2 weeks.

The Dating Game

Every year on August 14, the Genoese celebrate the anniversary of the marriage between Opizzo Fieschi and Bianca de' Bianchi of Siena, a couple of nobles who were married in the year 1240. Local bakers prepare a special cake called the Torta dei Fieschi, which is made with sponge cake, pastry cream, and hazelnuts. Everyone who would like a slice is given a card with a single word written on it. The object is to find your mate, the person of the opposite sex who has a card with the same word written on it. People go around shouting their word and those who find a mate are invited to enjoy a slice of torta.

isola d'elba

secchetto

Chocolate-Cheese Tart

CROSTATA DI RICOTTA E CIOCCOLATO

CRUST

1½ cups all-purpose flour

⅓ cup sugar

½ teaspoon salt

8 tablespoons (1 stick) cold unsalted butter, cut into bits

1 large egg, lightly beaten

FILLING

4 ounces semisweet or bittersweet chocolate

1 container (15 ounces) ricotta cheese

¼ cup sugar

1 large egg

1 teaspoon pure vanilla extract

½ teaspoon almond extract

SERVES 8

This thin tart is like a three-layer cake with almost equal parts of buttery crust, dark chocolate filling, and creamy cheese topping. The simple crust does not need to be rolled out. It was inspired by a similar tart I tasted at La Mora, a restaurant outside of Lucca.

La Mora
Ponte a Moriano (Tuscany)

1 To make the crust, in a large bowl, combine the flour, sugar, and salt. With a pastry blender or 2 knives, cut in the butter until the mixture resembles coarse meal. Stir in the egg until a soft dough forms. If the mixture seems dry, add a few drops of cold water. Pat into the bottom and up the sides of a 9-inch fluted tart pan with a removable bottom. Refrigerate for 30 minutes.

2 Preheat the oven to 350°F. Place the oven rack in the lower third of the oven.

3 To make the filling, chop the chocolate into ¼-inch pieces. Scatter the pieces evenly in the tart shell. In a large bowl, beat together the ricotta, sugar, egg, vanilla, and almond extract. Spread the mixture in the prepared tart shell over the chocolate layer. Bake for 45 minutes or until the top is puffed and the crust is golden brown.

4 Cool for 10 minutes on a rack. Place the pan on a coffee can or similar tall object and slide the rim down. Let the tart cool completely.

5 Serve at room temperature or lightly chilled. Store in the refrigerator, wrapped in foil or plastic wrap, for up to 3 days.

Tips on Tart Making

The doughs used to make pasta and bread require long kneading to make them chewy and firm. But the pastry for a crostata or tart should be tender and melt in your mouth. To accomplish this, the dough must be handled as little as possible and be kept cool. Follow these simple tips:

- To make the dough, start with cold unsalted butter and cut it into small bits for easy blending.
- Use a pastry blender or two knives to blend the butter into the flour just until it resembles coarse meal.
- Use as little liquid as possible in the dough. Too much moisture will make it tough.
- The pastry dough recipes in this book rely mostly on eggs for liquid. Use only large eggs. If the eggs are not terribly fresh or if the flour is very dry, a little additional liquid may be needed. Use cold water and blend in just a few dropfuls until the dough sticks to itself and begins to form a ball.
- If you use a food processor to combine the ingredients, blend them with short pulses. A food processor goes so fast that it can easily overwork the dough, and the heat of the motor can begin to melt the butter. For best results, add the liquid ingredients to the butter and flour mixture by hand.
- The dough is moist enough when it begins to clump together. Dump the dough out onto a piece of plastic wrap and, handling it as little as possible, shape it into a flat disk using the plastic wrap to help. Wrap the disk of dough completely in the plastic.
- Refrigerate the dough until it is firm, at least one hour or overnight. This gives the gluten, the protein in the flour, a chance to relax and the butter to become firm again so that the dough won't be sticky when it is rolled out. The dough can be made as much as three days in advance of baking.
- To roll out the dough, flour the countertop and rolling pin as lightly as possible. Rolling the dough out between two sheets of plastic wrap helps to prevent it from sticking to the counter and rolling pin, and you will not need to add extra flour.
- If the dough is very cold, let it rest briefly at room temperature until it can be rolled without the edges cracking.
- Don't roll out the dough near a hot oven or radiator. If it becomes sticky or soft while you are rolling it out, just put it back in the refrigerator until it is firmed up again.
- Always begin rolling from the center of the dough out to the edge. Never roll back and forth with this type of tender dough or it will toughen. Rotate the disk of dough a quarter turn each time you roll it to keep it round. Turn the dough over several times.
- If the dough tears, pinch it together to seal it or patch it with a piece of dough taken from the edge.
- Refrigerate the tart shell for twenty to thirty minutes to firm it before filling and baking.
- Cool the tart on a wire rack for ten minutes before removing the rim.
- To remove the tart pan rim, place the pan on a coffee can or similar tall object and slide the rim down. Let the tart cool completely before serving.

The Elephant's Crostata

LA CROSTATA DEL'ELEFANTE

2¹/₂ cups all-purpose flour

1 cup ground toasted almonds (6 ounces)

1 teaspoon baking powder

1 teaspoon ground cinnamon

¹/₂ teaspoon ground cloves

¹/₂ teaspoon salt

8 tablespoons (1 stick) cold unsalted butter, cut into bits

1 cup sugar

2 large eggs

1 teaspoon grated fresh lemon zest

1 cup red currant or raspberry jam

Confectioners' sugar, in a shaker

1 On a piece of wax paper, combine the flour, almonds, baking powder, cinnamon, cloves, and salt.

2 In a large bowl, beat the butter until softened. Beat in the sugar until light and fluffy. Add the eggs, one at a time, beating well after each one. Beat in the lemon zest. Add the dry ingredients and stir just until blended. Divide the dough into 2 disks, one slightly larger than the other. Wrap each disk in plastic wrap and refrigerate for 1 hour or overnight.

3 Preheat the oven to 375°F.

4 On a lightly floured surface, roll out the larger piece of dough into a 12-inch circle. Gently press the dough into a 10-inch tart pan with a removable bottom. Trim off all but a ¹/₂-inch border of dough. Fold the border of dough in against the inside of the rim and press it into place. Chill the tart shell at least 30 minutes.

5 Spread the jam evenly in the tart shell. Roll out the remaining dough to an 11-inch circle. Cut the dough into ¹/₂-inch-wide strips. Arrange half the strips 1 inch apart across the filling. Press the ends against the sides of the tart shell to seal. Rotate the tart pan halfway.

Since it is so far north, only about forty-three kilometers from Austria and the Brenner Pass, the Italian town of Bressanone has a Tyrolean atmosphere. Street signs are posted in German and Italian and most residents seem more comfortable speaking the former.

The Hotel Elefante, a complex of buildings some of which date back several centuries, is a landmark. According to legend, the hotel was named for the elephant that was sent by Suleiman the Great, ruler of the Ottoman Empire, as a gift to the Archduke Maximilian in Vienna. The animal was able to travel as far as Venice by boat but had to walk the rest of the way. The elephant and its entourage stopped to rest at several inns, including the one in Bressanone. The innkeepers, who were surely astonished at the sight of the huge beast, renamed their hotel in its honor.

The food in this ruggedly beautiful area has a definite Tyrolean influence. Unlike the rest of Italy, where breakfast normally consists at most of fruit, rolls, and coffee, the morning meal at the Elefante is much more substantial. We were offered a variety of breads made with rye, cornmeal, buckwheat, and other whole grains; sunflower, sesame, and poppy seed rolls; local cheeses; hams and other cured meats; cups of thick, rich, homemade yogurt topped with fresh cherries or strawberries in syrup; and pastries. Among the offerings was this nut, spice, and fruit tart that reminded me of the classic Austrian Linzertorte. The filling was a thick jam made with the local *mirtilli rossi,* red blueberries. Currant or raspberry jam makes a good substitute.

The dough is very tender and buttery so keep it cool as you work. If you prefer, roll the dough out between two sheets of plastic wrap or wax paper.

Hotel Elefante
Bressanone (Trentino-Alto Adige)

Place the remaining strips of dough 1 inch apart across the tart to form a lattice pattern. Press the ends against the sides of the tart shell to seal. Trim off the excess dough. Bake the tart for 40 minutes, or until the crust is browned.

6   Cool on a rack for 10 minutes. Place the pan on a coffee can or similar tall object and slide the rim down. Let the tart cool completely.

7   Just before serving, sprinkle with confectioners' sugar. Store wrapped in plastic or foil wrap at room temperature for up to 3 days.

Capri Lemon Tart

CROSTATA DI LIMONE

PASTRY

1¹/₃ cups all-purpose flour

3 tablespoons sugar

¹/₂ teaspoon salt

6 tablespoons (³/₄ stick) cold unsalted butter, cut into bits

1 large egg, lightly beaten

1 teaspoon pure vanilla extract

FILLING

¹/₃ cup sugar

1 tablespoon cornstarch

³/₄ cup milk

SERVES 8

Lemons grow everywhere on Capri and find their way into all kinds of desserts. We had lemon profiteroles with lemon icing, lemon ice cream, and, of course, lemon granita. My favorite was this airy lemon tart.

One day we ate at Da Paolino, a charming trattoria tucked away in a lemon grove. The tablecloths and seat cushions were covered in a lemon motif print, and we sat in the garden under, what else, a lemon tree. Charles decided the "lemon thing" had gone too far when a big fat lemon fell off the tree and plopped into his water glass. If it had been his wine glass, he would have been really mad!

I could not resist buying a bot-

354

2 large eggs, separated

2 tablespoons fresh lemon juice

2 teaspoons freshly grated lemon zest

1/2 teaspoon salt

Confectioners' sugar, in a shaker

1 To make the pastry, in a large bowl, combine the flour, sugar, and salt. With a pastry blender or 2 knives, blend in the butter until the mixture resembles coarse meal. Add the egg and vanilla and toss the mixture with a fork until the egg is incorporated. If the mixture seems dry, add a few drops of cold water. Gather the dough together and shape it into a disk. Wrap it in plastic wrap. Refrigerate for at least 1 hour or overnight.

2 On a lightly floured surface, roll out the dough to a 12-inch circle. Fit the dough into a 9- or 10-inch fluted tart pan with a removable bottom. Trim off all but a 1/2-inch border of dough. Fold the border of dough in against the inside of the rim and press it into place. Chill the tart shell for at least 30 minutes.

3 Preheat the oven to 350°F. Place the oven rack in the center of the oven.

4 Butter a sheet of aluminum foil just large enough to fit in the tart shell. Line the tart shell with the foil, buttered side down. Bake the shell for 15 minutes. Carefully remove the foil. Prick the bottom of the shell at 1-inch intervals. Bake the shell for 10 minutes more, or until lightly browned.

5 To make the filling, in a medium bowl, stir together the sugar and cornstarch. Add the milk and egg yolks and beat well. Stir in the lemon juice and lemon zest.

6 In a separate bowl with an electric mixer, beat the egg whites with the salt on low speed until foamy. Increase the speed to high and beat until soft peaks form. Gently fold the whites into the yolk mixture. Place the tart shell in the oven. Pour the filling into the shell. Bake for 25 minutes, or until the center is puffed and golden.

7 Cool the tart for 10 minutes on a rack. Place the pan on a coffee can or similar tall object and slide the rim down. Transfer the tart to a serving plate. Let cool completely.

8 Sprinkle generously with confectioners' sugar before serving. Cover with foil or plastic wrap and store in the refrigerator for up to 3 days.

tle of Da Paolino's homemade and intensely flavored limoncello, a lemon liqueur, to take home with us. Limoncello is available in some liquor stores in the United States. Keep the bottle in the refrigerator and serve it in frosted glasses at the end of a summer meal.

Da Paolino
Capri (Campania)

SERVES 8

January in Milan can be cold and bleak, but it's a great time for shopping. All the expensive shops on the Via Montenapoleone are open, and their splendid goods are on sale. Exhausted by the effort of shopping, we fell into the elegant Caffè Sant'Ambroeus and restored ourselves with a wedge of this tart. The tender apple and raisin filling in a buttery pastry shell was crowned with a golden almond paste lattice. With a cup of cappuccino to warm us, we were soon out again.

Making this tart at home is not difficult, but piping the lattice topping can be a bit tricky if you've never worked with a pastry bag before. Practice by piping a series of parallel lines on a flat plate. Then give the plate a 180° turn and pipe out another series of parallel lines perpendicular to the first set. When you feel comfortable with the procedure, scrape the practice lattice lines back into the bag and repeat it on top of the filled tart.

Caffè Sant'Ambroeus
Corso Matteotti 7
Milan (Lombardy)

Apple Lattice Tart

CROSTATA DI MELE AL MARZAPANE

CRUST

1¹/₃ cups all-purpose flour

3 tablespoons sugar

¹/₂ teaspoon salt

8 tablespoons (1 stick) cold unsalted butter, cut into bits

1 large egg, lightly beaten

1 teaspoon pure vanilla extract

FILLING

1¹/₂ pounds Golden Delicious apples, peeled and cut into thin slices (3 large apples)

1 cup sugar

¹/₂ cup golden raisins

3 tablespoons fine dry bread crumbs

1 teaspoon ground cinnamon

2 tablespoons fresh lemon juice

TOPPING

1 package (7 to 8 ounces) almond paste

1 tablespoon unsalted butter, softened

1 large egg

1 teaspoon pure vanilla extract

1 teaspoon grated lemon zest

¹/₄ cup all-purpose flour

1 large egg yolk plus 2 teaspoons water

Confectioners' sugar, in a shaker

1 To make the crust, in a large bowl, combine the flour, sugar, and salt. With a pastry blender or 2 knives, cut in the butter until the mixture resembles a coarse meal. In a small bowl, beat the egg and

vanilla until blended. Stir the liquid into the flour mixture just until a dough forms. Add a few drops of cold water if it seems dry. On a piece of plastic wrap, shape the dough into a flat disk. Wrap the plastic around the dough and refrigerate for at least 1 hour or overnight.

2 On a lightly floured surface, roll out the dough to an 11-inch circle. Transfer the dough to a 9-inch tart pan with a removable bottom. Trim off all but a 1/2-inch border of dough. Fold the border against the inside of the pan and press it into place, building it up slightly above the rim. Refrigerate the shell while you prepare the filling, about 30 minutes.

3 Preheat the oven to 350°F. Place the oven rack in the center of the oven.

4 To make the filling, combine all of the filling ingredients in a large bowl. Pile the apple mixture into the prepared tart shell, pressing it lightly to fit.

5 To make the topping, crumble the almond paste into a food processor fitted with a steel blade or an electric mixer bowl. Add the butter, egg, vanilla, and lemon zest and blend or beat until smooth. Add the flour and stir just until blended. Spoon the mixture into a pastry bag fitted with a 1/2-inch tip. Pipe the mixture around the border of the dough being careful not to let it touch the pan or it will stick when it bakes. Pipe the remainder in a lattice pattern over the filling. Beat the egg yolk and water. Brush the glaze over the lattice topping. Place the tart in the oven. Place a baking sheet on the rack beneath it to catch any drips. Bake for 1 hour and 15 minutes, or until the topping is browned and the apple juices are bubbling. If the topping browns too rapidly, fold a sheet of aluminum foil into a tent and loosely cover the tart.

6 Cool the tart on a rack for 10 minutes. The apple juices will settle and thicken as the tart cools. Place the pan on a coffee can or similar tall object and slide the rim down. Let the tart cool completely.

7 Sprinkle with confectioners' sugar before serving. Use a serrated knife to cut the tart. Cover with foil or plastic wrap and store in the refrigerator for up to 3 days.

This apple pie from the Alto Adige is called a torte, but it's more like a double crust tart than a cake. Precooking the apples concentrates the juices and keeps the crust from getting soggy.

Apple Torte

TORTA RIPIENE DI MELE

CRUST

2¹/₂ cups all-purpose flour

²/₃ cup sugar

2 teaspoons baking powder

1 teaspoon salt

10 tablespoons (1¹/₄ sticks) cold unsalted butter, cut into small bits

1 large egg, at room temperature

3 to 4 tablespoons cold milk

2 teaspoons pure vanilla extract

FILLING

2 tablespoons unsalted butter

5 large Granny Smith apples, peeled, cored, and cut into 1-inch
     chunks (about 2¹/₂ pounds)

¹/₂ cup sugar

1 teaspoon freshly grated lemon zest

1 large egg yolk beaten with 1 teaspoon water

Confectioners' sugar, in a shaker

1 To make the dough, in a large bowl, combine the flour, sugar, baking powder, and salt. With a pastry blender or 2 knives, cut in the butter until the mixture resembles coarse meal. In a small bowl, beat the egg, 3 tablespoons of the milk, and the vanilla until blended. Stir the liquid into the flour mixture just until a dough forms. Add the remaining tablespoon of milk if needed. Gather the dough into a ball. Divide the dough into 2 pieces, one twice as large as the other. Shape each piece into a flat disk. Wrap each in plastic wrap and chill for at least 1 hour or overnight.

2 To make the filling, in a large saucepan over low heat, melt the butter. Add the apples and sugar. Cover and cook for 5 minutes, or

until the apples release their juices. Uncover and cook, stirring occasionally, until the apples are tender, about 10 minutes. Stir in the lemon zest. Set aside and let cool completely.

3 Preheat the oven to 350°F.

4 On a lightly floured surface, roll out the larger piece of dough to an 11-inch circle. Press the dough into a 9-inch tart pan with a removable bottom. Trim off all but a $^{1}/_{2}$-inch border of the dough. Fold the border against the inside of the pan and press it into place, building it up slightly above the rim. Spread the apple filling in the pan.

5 Roll out the remaining piece of dough to a 10-inch circle. Place it over the filling. Pinch the top and bottom layers of dough together to seal around the edge of the pan. Trim off the excess dough. Brush the top of the torte with the egg yolk mixture. Cut 6 to 8 small slits in the surface to allow steam to escape. Bake for 45 to 50 minutes, or until golden brown.

6 Cool the torte on a rack for 10 minutes. Remove the rim by placing the pan on a coffee can or similar tall object and sliding the rim down. Place the torte on the rack to cool completely.

7 Sprinkle with confectioners' sugar and serve. Cover with foil or plastic wrap and store in the refrigerator for up to 3 days.

Using a Pastry Bag

If you do not have a pastry bag, substitute a quart-size heavy-duty plastic food storage bag. Open the bag and stand it in a tall container folding the collar around the rim to hold it open wide. Spoon the mixture you are piping into the bag, pushing it to the bottom. Close the bag and twist it just above the level of the mixture. With scissors, snip off a corner of the bag and pipe the mixture out.

Saluti dal
RISTORANTE
"ALBERTO" al Portico d'Ottavia

Little two-crust tartlets filled with custard, chocolate, or almond paste are typical of Puglia. These are a bit fussy to make, but not difficult.

You will need about eighteen tartlet pans. The exact yield depends on the size and capacity of the pans you use. If possible, choose pans about 2^1/$_2$ inches in diameter by about ^{1}/$_2$ inch deep. Avoid pans that have an intricate shape, which will make it difficult to remove the tartlets. Miniature muffin tins can be used, but it is difficult to make the edges of the top crust even.

Cherry-Almond Tartlets

BOCCONOTI

DOUGH

2 cups all-purpose flour

^{1}/$_4$ cup sugar

2 teaspoons baking powder

^{1}/$_2$ teaspoon salt

8 tablespoons (1 stick) cold unsalted butter, cut into small bits

1 large egg, at room temperature

1 teaspoon pure vanilla extract

About ^{1}/$_4$ cup sour cherry preserves

FILLING

1 large egg

2 tablespoons sugar

4 ounces almond paste (about ^{1}/$_2$ cup)

2 tablespoons all-purpose flour

1 large egg yolk beaten with 1 teaspoon water

1 To make the dough, in a large bowl, combine the flour, sugar, baking powder, and salt. With a pastry blender or 2 knives, cut in the butter until the mixture resembles coarse meal. In a small bowl, beat the egg and vanilla. Stir the egg mixture into the dry ingredients until a soft dough forms. Gather the dough into a ball. Divide the dough into 2 disks. Wrap each disk in plastic wrap. Refrigerate for at least 1 hour or overnight.

2 Remove the dough from the refrigerator and let it stand at room temperature until it softens slightly.

3 Preheat the oven to 350°F. Place the oven rack in the center of the oven.

4 On a lightly floured surface, roll out 1 piece of dough ^{1}/$_8$ inch thick. For 2^1/$_2$-inch tartlets, cut out the dough into 3-inch circles with a biscuit or cookie cutter. Gently press each circle into a tartlet pan. If the dough tears, press the torn edges together to seal. Reroll the scraps, if necessary, to make 18 tartlets. Spread ¹/₂ teaspoon of the preserves in the bottom of each tartlet.

5 To make the filling, in a medium bowl, beat the egg and sugar until foamy. Crumble the almond paste into the egg mixture and beat until smooth. Gently fold in the flour. Spoon the almond paste mixture into the tartlet pans, filling them to about ¹/₄ inch from the top.

6 Roll out the remaining piece of dough. Cut out eighteen 2¹/₂-inch circles. Place a circle of dough on top of each tartlet. Press the edges together to seal. Trim off any overhanging dough with your fingers or a small knife. Brush the tops of the tartlets with the egg wash. Cut 3 or 4 small slits in the top of each. Place the tart pans 1 inch apart on a baking sheet. Bake for 35 to 40 minutes, or until the tops are browned and puffed.

7 Place the tart pans on a rack to cool for 10 minutes. Insert the tip of a small knife between the tarts and the pans to loosen them. Remove the tarts and cool completely on the rack. Place the tartlets in an airtight container and store in the refrigerator for up to 5 days.

To make ahead: These tartlets freeze well. Wrap each individually in foil. Place the wrapped tartlets in a plastic bag and seal tightly. Freeze for up to 1 month. To defrost, unwrap the tartlets and leave at room temperature for 30 minutes.

SERVES 8

Chestnuts are an autumn and winter treat all over Italy. The shiny, mahogany brown nuts are roasted until they are tender and creamy and served hot after dinner. Their slightly sweet flavor goes well with wine. In Piedmont and the Val d'Aosta, freshly roasted chestnuts are sometimes tossed in sugar and grappa, the fiery grape brandy distilled from the skins and stems of grapes that have been pressed to make wine. Pastry shops sell chestnuts glazed or preserved in syrup, to be eaten as a confection or spooned over ice cream with a dash of rum. Chestnuts are also pureed and mixed into cakes, which are then decorated on top with chocolate or buttercream chestnuts. When I was growing up and even today, no Thanksgiving or Christmas dinner was complete without a basket of hot roasted chestnuts at the end of the meal.

Rum-flavored chestnut puree is the filling for this unusual tart from Piedmont. The cooked chestnuts packed in jars can be used in this recipe, but do not substitute sweetened chestnut puree—it would be too sweet. Serve the tart with whipped cream or a scoop of vanilla ice cream.

Chestnut Tart

CROSTATA DI CASTAGNA

1/3 cup golden raisins

3 tablespoons rum

CRUST

2 1/3 cups all-purpose flour

1/3 cup sugar

1 teaspoon salt

12 tablespoons (1 1/2 sticks) cold unsalted butter, cut into bits

1 large egg

1 large egg yolk

1 teaspoon pure vanilla extract

FILLING

8 ounces chestnuts, boiled and peeled (see next page)

3 tablespoons sugar

1 teaspoon pure vanilla extract

1 cup heavy cream

2 large eggs

Confectioners' sugar, in a shaker

1 Combine the raisins and rum. Let stand for 1 hour or overnight.

2 To make the crust, in a large bowl, combine the flour, sugar, and salt. With a pastry blender or 2 knives, blend in the butter until the mixture resembles coarse meal. Add the egg, egg yolk, and vanilla and toss with a fork until the liquid is incorporated. If the mixture seems dry, add a few drops of cold water as needed.

3 Gather the dough together and shape it into 2 disks, one slightly larger than the other. Wrap each disk in plastic wrap. Chill for at least 1 hour or overnight.

4 On a lightly floured surface, roll out the larger piece of dough to

362

a 12-inch circle about $^1/_8$ inch thick. Fit the dough into a 10-inch fluted tart pan with a removable bottom. Trim off all but a $^1/_2$-inch border of dough. Fold the excess dough in against the inside of the pan and press it into place. Chill the tart shell for 30 minutes.

5 Preheat the oven to 350°F. Place the oven rack on the lowest setting.

6 To make the filling, in a food processor fitted with the steel blade or a blender, combine the chestnuts, sugar, and vanilla. With the machine running, gradually add the cream. Process until smooth, stopping the machine once or twice to scrape down the sides of the container. Add the eggs, one at a time, beating after each one until smooth. Remove the processor bowl from the base of the machine. Lightly stir in the raisins and rum. Pour the mixture into the crust and smooth the surface.

7 Roll out the remaining dough to an 11-inch circle about $^1/_8$ inch thick and, with a fluted pastry wheel, cut it into $^1/_2$-inch-wide strips. Arrange the strips over the filling about 1 inch apart, going first from top to bottom, then from left to right, to form a lattice pattern. Press the ends of the strips against the sides of the tart shell to seal. Bake the tart for 60 minutes, or until the filling is puffed and the crust is golden.

8 Let cool on a rack for 10 minutes. Remove the pan rim by placing the tart on a coffee can or similar tall object and sliding the rim down. Cool completely on a rack.

9 Just before serving, sprinkle with confectioners' sugar. Cover with foil or plastic wrap and store in the refrigerator for up to 3 days.

Peeling and Cooking Chestnuts

Place the chestnuts, still in their shells, flat side down, on a cutting board. With the point of a small knife, make a deep X in each one, cutting through the skin and into the flesh. Bring a medium saucepan of water to a boil over medium heat. Add the chestnuts and cook for ten to fifteen minutes. Remove the chestnuts, two at a time, with a slotted spoon and peel off the shells and skin.

Place the peeled chestnuts in a clean saucepan with cold water to cover. Bring the water to a simmer and cook until the chestnuts are tender when pierced with a knife, about twenty minutes. Drain and pat dry before using. Eight ounces of chestnuts will make a little more than $1^1/_4$ cups cooked chestnuts.

The original recipe for this cake was given to me by a chef in the Veneto who recommended it so highly, I could hardly wait to try it. But when I put the ingredients together, the batter was dry as dust—something must have gotten lost in the translation. I hated to give up on it, though, since the mixture contained so many expensive ingredients. Besides, I was in a chocolate mood. I decided to experiment by adding some milk and another egg, but with little hope of salvaging the mess. When the batter looked moist enough, I poured it into a pan and baked it. The result was amazingly good. Since then, I have done some fine-tuning, and now the cake is a perfect dessert for chocolate-lovers, though I am not sure if that chef would recognize it.

The cake is made without flour. It is quite rich but not too sweet—more like a chocolate truffle than a cake. It tastes best at room temperature. Try it with a scoop of vanilla ice cream or a dollop of whipped cream.

Chocolate-Almond Truffle Cake

TORTA AL CIOCCOLATO E MANDORLE

1 cup blanched almonds, toasted and cooled (5 ounces)
1¼ cups sugar
¾ cup unsweetened cocoa powder
8 tablespoons (1 stick) unsalted butter, softened
4 large eggs
¾ cup milk
2 tablespoons amaretto or rum
Confectioners' sugar, in a shaker

1 Preheat the oven to 325°F. Butter and flour a 9-inch springform pan.

2 In a food processor or blender, grind the almonds with 2 tablespoons of the sugar until fine. Add the cocoa and pulse just until blended.

3 In a large mixer bowl, beat the butter with the remaining sugar until light and fluffy, 3 minutes. Beat in the eggs, one at a time. Stir in half of the cocoa mixture. Stir in half of the milk. Stir in the remaining cocoa mixture, the remaining milk, and the amaretto. Pour the batter into the prepared pan. Bake for 50 minutes, or until the top is slightly puffed and the center is just set.

4 Cool for 10 minutes on a rack. Remove the pan rim. Cool completely.

5 Just before serving, sprinkle with confectioners' sugar. Cover with foil or plastic wrap and store in the refrigerator for up to 3 days.

Apple Cake

TORTA DI MELE

SERVES 8

This is a simple cake that goes well with afternoon tea or coffee. Substitute a firm ripe pear for the apple if you like. The cake is best eaten the day it is made.

1²/₃ cups all-purpose flour

1¹/₂ teaspoons baking powder

8 tablespoons (1 stick) unsalted butter, softened

³/₄ cup sugar

3 large eggs

1 teaspoon pure vanilla extract

1 teaspoon freshly grated lemon zest

¹/₂ cup milk

1 large or 2 medium Golden Delicious apples, peeled, cored, and thinly sliced

¹/₃ cup apricot jam

1 Preheat the oven to 325°F. Place the oven rack in the center of the oven. Butter and flour a 9-inch springform pan.

2 In a medium bowl, combine the flour and baking powder.

3 In a large bowl, beat the butter and sugar until light and fluffy. Add the eggs, one at a time, beating after each one until smooth. Beat in the vanilla and lemon zest. Stir in half of the flour mixture, then stir in the milk. Stir in the remaining flour just until blended. Spread the batter evenly in the pan. Arrange the apple slices, overlapping slightly in a pinwheel pattern. Bake for 55 to 60 minutes, or until a cake tester inserted in the center comes out clean.

4 Let cool on a rack 10 minutes. Remove the sides of the pan.

5 Heat the jam until melted and push it through a sieve. Brush the jam over the apples.

6 Let the cake cool completely before cutting.

Cake for breakfast is not at all unusual in Italy, and this one made with yellow cornmeal is typical. It's good at other times of the day, too. For dessert, I split it into layers, fill it with orange or strawberry preserves, and serve it with whipped cream.

Sweet Polenta Cake

POLENTA DOLCE

³/₄ cup all-purpose flour

¹/₄ cup finely ground yellow cornmeal

4 large eggs, at room temperature

³/₄ cup sugar

1 teaspoon freshly grated lemon zest

1 teaspoon freshly grated orange zest

1 teaspoon pure vanilla extract

³/₄ cup jam or preserves, such as apricot or blueberry jam or orange marmalade

Confectioners' sugar, in a shaker

Whipped cream, for garnish

1 Preheat the oven to 350°F. Butter an 8-inch springform pan and dust it with flour. Tap out the excess.

2 In a medium bowl, stir together the flour and cornmeal.

3 In a large bowl, beat the egg yolks with an electric mixer just until blended. Gradually beat in ¹/₂ cup of the sugar until the mixture is light and pale yellow, about 3 minutes. Beat in the lemon and orange zests and the vanilla extract.

4 In a large bowl with clean beaters, beat the egg whites just until foamy. Gradually add the remaining ¹/₄ cup sugar and beat until soft peaks form. With a rubber spatula, fold the egg whites into the egg yolk mixture. Gently fold in the dry ingredients. Scrape the mixture into the baking pan. Bake for 30 minutes, or until the center is puffed and springs back when touched in the center.

5 Unmold the cake onto a rack and let cool completely.

6 With a long serrated knife, cut the cake into 2 layers. Spread the bottom layer with the jam. Replace the top of the cake.

7 Sprinkle with confectioners' sugar and serve with dollops of whipped cream.

To make ahead: The cake can be made through Step 5 up to 24 hours before serving. Let it cool completely, then wrap it tightly in plastic wrap. Store at room temperature. Fill the cake before serving.

Fisherman's Bread

PANE DEL PESCATORE

2 cups all-purpose flour

2 teaspoons baking powder

1/3 cup sugar

1 tablespoon fennel or anise seeds

1 cup golden raisins

2 tablespoons pine nuts

1/4 cup diced candied orange peel

1/4 cup diced candied citron

1 large egg

1/4 cup milk

1/4 cup dry Marsala

2 tablespoons unsalted butter, melted

SERVES 12

Sailors took long-lasting breads of this type on sea voyages, hence the name. This one, from Genoa and the surrounding region, is flavored with fennel or anise seeds, pine nuts, raisins, and candied fruit. Unlike most Italian sweet breads, it is made without yeast. It makes a terrific tea bread or light dessert, and it is especially good for breakfast, sliced thin and lightly toasted.

1 Preheat the oven to 375°F. Butter a baking sheet.

2 In a large bowl, combine the flour, baking powder, sugar, and fennel seeds and stir to blend. Add the raisins, pine nuts, candied orange peel, and citron.

3 In a small bowl, lightly beat the egg. Add the milk, Marsala, and melted butter. Stir the egg mixture into the dry ingredients with a wooden spoon until thoroughly blended. Turn the dough out onto a lightly floured surface and knead until smooth, about 2 minutes. The dough will be slightly sticky. Divide the dough into 2 pieces. Shape each piece into a flat 6 × 4-inch oval and place the ovals sev-

eral inches apart on the baking sheet. Bake for 40 minutes, or until the top is golden brown.

4 Cool on racks.

5 Cover with foil or plastic wrap and store at room temperature for up to 3 days or freeze for up to 1 month.

SERVES 12

Panforte, literally "strong bread," is more like a chewy candy than a cake. Most versions use lots of candied fruits in the mixture, but I have substituted dried figs since they are readily available and better tasting.

At Christmastime in Tuscany people play a game with panforte that is something like shuffleboard. A player tosses the paper-wrapped panforte onto a long bare table, and it slides to the other end. The one who tosses the panforte farthest without having it fall off the table wins and gets to keep the panforte.

Panforte

PANFORTE

¹/₂ cup all-purpose flour

2 tablespoons unsweetened cocoa powder

1 teaspoon ground cinnamon

¹/₄ teaspoon ground coriander

¹/₄ teaspoon freshly grated nutmeg

¹/₄ teaspoon ground cloves

Pinch of ground white pepper

1¹/₂ cups coarsely chopped toasted walnuts (8 ounces)

1¹/₂ cups coarsely chopped dried figs (10 ounces)

¹/₂ cup coarsely chopped candied orange peel

¹/₂ cup coarsely chopped candied citron

²/₃ cup sugar

²/₃ cup honey

Confectioners' sugar, in a shaker

1 Preheat the oven to 300°F. Generously butter the sides and bottom of a 9-inch springform pan. Place a circle of parchment paper in the bottom of the pan and butter the paper.

2 In a medium bowl, combine the flour, cocoa, and spices.

3 In large bowl, combine the walnuts, figs, candied orange peel, and citron. Add the flour mixture and stir well to break up any lumps.

4 In a small saucepan, combine the sugar and honey. Cook over low heat, stirring occasionally, until the mixture forms a firm ball when dropped into cold water, 245°F. on a candy thermometer. Immediately pour the syrup into the fruit and nut mixture. Stir rapidly with a wooden spoon until the flour no longer looks dry. Scrape the mixture into the pan. Flatten the top with a wet rubber spatula. Bake for 45 minutes. The cake will look soft, but it will firm as it cools.

5 Place the pan on a rack to cool completely. Remove the rim of the pan and invert the cake onto a piece of wax paper. Peel off the parchment paper. Turn the cake right side up and place it on a serving plate.

6 Sprinkle generously with confectioners' sugar. Cut into thin wedges to serve. Cover with foil or plastic wrap and store at room temperature for up to 1 week.

An Unexpected Gift

Gioacchino Rossini once received a surprise from the Spanish Marquise Aguado, an old friend. The marquise had Rossini nominated as a member of an ancient order of knights. He sent Rossini an iron cross, the symbol of the order.

Rossini, however, was expecting a box of Spanish sweets, which he had requested the marquise to send him. Disappointed, he sent the cross back to the marquise with a note that said, "The sweet that you sent me is too hard to digest, and I have many crosses to bear already."

It is amazing how perfectly delicious the simplest things can be. You need only five ingredients to make these elegant little puddings—they look like crème caramel but are even more delicate, with a slight cheesecake flavor from the ricotta. Serve them plain or with a few raspberries or a sliced strawberry.

Caramel Ricotta Pudding

BUDINO DI RICOTTA

1 cup plus 3 tablespoons sugar

1 container (15 ounces) whole milk ricotta

2 large eggs

1/4 cup milk

1 1/2 teaspoons pure vanilla extract

1 Preheat the oven to 325°F.

2 In a small saucepan, combine 1 cup sugar and 1/4 cup water. Cook over medium heat, stirring occasionally until the sugar dissolves. When the mixture begins to boil, stop stirring and cook until the syrup starts to brown around the edges. Then gently swirl the pan over the heat until the syrup is an even golden brown. Immediately pour the caramel into six 6-ounce custard cups. Protect your hand with an oven mitt and swirl the cups to coat the bottom with the caramel. Let cool briefly.

3 In a food processor or blender or using an electric mixer, beat the ricotta for 5 minutes, or until very smooth. Blend in the eggs, milk, remaining sugar, and vanilla. Pour into the cups. Place the cups in a roasting pan and place the pan in the oven. Pour hot tap water into the pan around the cups to reach about halfway up the side. Bake for 50 to 55 minutes, or until the tops are set but the centers are still very soft and jiggly when the cups are tapped.

4 Place the cups on a rack to cool slightly. Cover the cups and refrigerate for several hours or overnight.

5 To serve, run a small knife around the pudding and invert onto serving plates.

To make ahead: The custards can be baked and refrigerated for up to 3 days before serving.

Little Rice Puddings

BUDINI DI RISO

4$\frac{1}{2}$ cups milk

$\frac{2}{3}$ cup Arborio, Vialone Nano, or other medium-grain rice

$\frac{3}{4}$ cup sugar

2 large eggs

1 tablespoon rum or brandy

1 teaspoon pure vanilla extract

1 teaspoon freshly grated orange zest

$\frac{1}{2}$ cup golden raisins

1 In a large saucepan over low heat, bring the milk to a simmer. Add the rice and sugar. Cook, stirring occasionally, for 40 minutes, or until the rice is very tender. Transfer to a bowl and let cool, stirring occasionally.

2 Preheat the oven to 325°F. Butter eight 6-ounce custard cups.

3 Beat the eggs with the rum, vanilla, and orange zest. Stir the mixture into the cooled rice. Add the raisins. Spoon the rice mixture into the prepared cups. Bake for 25 to 30 minutes, or until the filling is just set.

4 Cool for 10 minutes on a rack.

5 Run a small knife around the inside of the cups and invert onto serving dishes. Serve warm.

SERVES 8

These little baked rice puddings come from Parma. I first tasted them one frosty morning when I stopped into a likely looking caffè for a cup of coffee. The shop was filled with office workers and shoppers taking a mid-morning break, and they all seemed to be having a pudding with their cappuccino.

Sometimes these are baked in *pasta frolla*, tender pastry dough, to make tartlets, but they are lighter and more puddinglike this way. Once baked, the puddings are firm enough to be unmolded.

I don't think I ever quite believed my mother when she told me that the chocolate pudding we bought at the pastry shop around Eastertime was made with pig's blood. I loved its deep, dark, spicy flavor and dismissed the blood story as some kind of mysterious grown-up's joke. But Mom was right. Pig's blood is the traditional thickening ingredient, hence the name *Sanguinaccio*. These days, cooks usually substitute corn or potato starch, as in this recipe. Somewhere between a thick sauce and a thin pudding, this is normally served at Eastertime with Gossips (page 375) for dipping. If you prefer a smooth pudding, leave out the candied fruits and pine nuts.

Chocolate Pudding with Pine Nuts and Citron

SANGUINACCIO

2 tablespoons cornstarch

1/4 cup sifted unsweetened cocoa powder

1/4 cup sugar

1/4 teaspoon ground cinnamon

2 cups cold milk

3 ounces bittersweet chocolate, broken up

1 teaspoon pure vanilla extract

1 tablespoon chopped candied citron or raisins

1 tablespoon pine nuts

1 In a medium saucepan, combine the cornstarch, cocoa, sugar, and cinnamon. Gradually whisk in the milk. Place over medium heat and cook, stirring constantly, until the mixture comes to a boil. Cook for 1 minute more, until thick. Remove the pudding from the heat. Add the chocolate and let stand until softened. Whisk until smooth. Pour into a bowl. Stir in the vanilla, citron, and pine nuts.

2 Place plastic wrap directly on the surface and let cool. Refrigerate for several hours until serving time.

3 Spoon the pudding into parfait glasses and serve.

To make ahead: The pudding can be made up to 24 hours before serving.

Chocolate-Chestnut Truffles

TARTUFI DI CASTAGNE

4 ounces semisweet chocolate

1 cup cooked peeled chestnuts (about 8 ounces unpeeled)

About 1/3 cup heavy cream

1 tablespoon dark rum

1/4 cup unsweetened cocoa powder, sifted

1 Break up the chocolate and place it in the top half of a double boiler. Set over a saucepan partly filled with simmering water. Heat, stirring occasionally, until smooth and melted. Remove the bowl and let cool.

2 In a food processor or blender, puree the chestnuts with 2 tablespoons of the cream and the rum until very smooth. Stir in the chocolate and just enough cream to make a soft consistency that barely holds a shape.

3 Spread the cocoa on a plate. Drop a tablespoonful of the chestnut mixture into the cocoa. With a fork, turn it until coated. If the mixture gets too soft to handle, refrigerate it briefly. Transfer the truffle to a paper candy cup or place it on a sheet of wax paper on a cookie sheet. Repeat with the remaining chestnut mixture.

4 When all of the truffles have been shaped, refrigerate them until firm, at least 1 hour. Transfer the truffles to an airtight container. Refrigerate until ready to serve.

To make ahead: Truffles keep well for up to 2 weeks in the refrigerator. They can also be frozen for up to 1 month. If frozen, defrost in the refrigerator for 1 hour. Let stand at room temperature for 15 minutes before serving.

Chestnuts make these chocolate truffles smooth and mellow. Since the fresh chestnut season is short, I buy one or two jars of cooked chestnuts when I see them, usually around the holiday season. Though they are expensive, they are convenient —and the flavor is very good. To prepare fresh chestnuts, see page 363.

Ubiquitous at Italian street fairs in New York City is the zeppole stand where a burly man—I think the same one goes to every street fair—can be found flinging gobs of soft dough into a huge vat of boiling oil. When the dough bobs up to the surface and turns brown, it is done. Dusted with confectioners' sugar, these little fritters are hard to resist. You have to eat them right away, though, or their charm is lost.

Zeppole are sometimes known as *sfince* and there are many different versions. Special ones are made in Sicily to celebrate Saint Joseph's Day on March 19. Some have a cakelike batter shaped into a ring before frying and are stuffed with ricotta or pastry cream.

The version that follows is very simple and makes a fine last-minute dessert or snack. If you have the ingredients on hand, you can easily make up a batch to serve with coffee when friends drop by. My mom used to make them for us on Sunday nights. Since Sunday lunch was always substantial, we did not need an evening meal, just something to tide us over.

Sweet Ricotta Puffs

ZEPPOLE

2 large eggs

2 tablespoons sugar

1 teaspoon pure vanilla extract

1 cup (8 ounces) ricotta cheese

1/2 teaspoon freshly grated orange or lemon zest

1/2 cup all-purpose flour

2 teaspoons baking powder

Pinch of salt

Vegetable oil, for deep-frying

Confectioners' sugar, in a shaker

1 In a large bowl, whisk the eggs, sugar, and vanilla until frothy. Beat in the ricotta and citrus zest.

2 In a medium bowl, combine the flour, baking powder, and salt. Stir the dry ingredients into the ricotta mixture.

3 Pour enough oil to reach a depth of 1 inch into a deep-fryer, wide saucepan, or deep skillet. Heat the oil over medium heat until it reaches 375°F. on a deep-frying thermometer. Test the temperature of the oil by dropping in a small amount of the batter. The oil should bubble up and the batter quickly rise to the surface.

4 Drop the mixture by the tablespoonful into the hot oil. Do not crowd the pan or the fritters will stick together. Cook until golden on both sides. Drain on paper towels.

5 Sprinkle with confectioners' sugar and serve immediately.

Cook's note: Instead of confectioners' sugar, roll the puffs in granulated sugar mixed with a little ground cinnamon and/or nutmeg.

Gossips

CHIACCHIERE

2 cups all-purpose flour

1 teaspoon salt

2 large eggs

2 tablespoons olive oil

2 tablespoons grappa or brandy

Vegetable oil, for frying

Confectioners' sugar, for dusting

1 In a large bowl, combine the flour and salt.

2 In a medium bowl, beat the eggs, oil, and grappa together. Stir the mixture into the flour until a dough forms. On a lightly floured surface, knead the dough until smooth and not sticky. Wrap in plastic wrap and let rest for 30 minutes.

3 Roll out the dough to an 8-inch circle about ¹⁄₈ inch thick. With a fluted pastry wheel, cut the dough into 2 × 1-inch ribbons.

4 Fill a deep-fryer with vegetable oil according to the manufacturer's directions or pour enough oil to reach a depth of 2 inches into a large heavy saucepan. Heat the oil to 375°F. on a deep-frying thermometer and/or test the oil by dropping in a small piece of dough. If it bubbles up rapidly, the oil is ready.

5 Add a few strips of dough to the pan without crowding the pieces. Fry until golden brown and crisp, 1 to 2 minutes. Remove with a slotted spoon. Drain the strips on paper towels. Fry the remainder in the same way.

6 When all of the strips are done, place them in a large roasting pan. Place the confectioners' sugar in a sieve and shake it generously over the cookies. Toss the cookies until well coated.

To make ahead: Store in a tightly sealed container at room temperature for up to 1 week.

MAKES ABOUT
5 DOZEN

The crunchy sound these cookies make when you chew them and the telltale trail of confectioners' sugar give them their name. At Eastertime, Neapolitans serve these cookies with Sanguinaccio (page 372) for dipping. If you are feeling creative, cut the dough into fanciful shapes like butterflies or twists.

Once when preparing to teach a cooking class at a New Jersey restaurant owned by Antonia Froio, a chef who is a native of Modena in Italy, I spotted a pot of cold coffee and asked Toni if I might have some on ice. She looked horrified and whisked away the stale coffee, only to return moments later with a goblet of foamy, fresh, iced espresso. As Toni described how she had made it, I was reminded of the *caffè shakerato* I had had one day at a café on Lake Maggiore.

You can make all kinds of shakeratos—plain or with milk or liqueurs. Here, at last, is a use for that martini shaker you received as a wedding gift! Or you can blend the ingredients in an electric blender.

Caffè Shakerato

2 demitasse cups freshly brewed, hot strong espresso (about $1/4$ cup)
Sugar (optional)
4 ice cubes

Combine the coffee and sugar, if using, and stir until dissolved. Place the coffee in a shaker or blender jar with the ice. Cover and shake or blend until the ice cubes are practically dissolved and a foamy top appears on the surface. Carefully pour the mixture into two goblets. (If you are using a shaker with a strainer top, remove the top so that it does not deflate the foam.)

Cook's notes: For Iced Cappuccino Shakerato, make the coffee and shake or blend it. Add milk to taste and shake again. Pour into a goblet and top with a sprinkling of ground cinnamon or cocoa powder. For Caffè Shakerato with Liqueur or Bitters, add an ounce of a sweet liqueur or bitter *digestivo,* such as Averna, to the coffee and ice.

Wine ... Vino

LIKE BREAD, WINE IS *always present on the Italian table and is an essential component of most meals, not just special occasions or holidays. Wine is made in every region of Italy so it's plentiful and inexpensive. In a trattoria, a carafe of* vino locale *may cost less than a bottle of mineral water.*

Wine is considered a healthful beverage and a splash is even poured into a child's glass of aranciata, *or orange soda, or cola. Most of the wine that is consumed is simple vino locale, regional wine that has a natural affinity for the local cooking.*

In many trattorias, the waiter will often ask if you prefer vino bianco *or vino rosso.* If you ask for a wine list and there is none, he may bring you several bottles to examine. Some places, though not all, charge you only for the amount of wine you drink. If you leave half of the wine, you are charged only for half.

Deciding which wine to drink with an Italian meal in the United States is a little more complicated. Some varieties of wine and some producers' wines are not imported, and those that are are often quite expensive. Even so, there are many excellent wines to choose from.

Though it is difficult to generalize because wine styles differ according to where and how they are made, the age, the producer, the particular vintage, and many other factors, the following are some of the Italian wines that Charles and I enjoy and the names of the producers who make them.

The food suggestions are intentionally broad. Many combinations work well. Find a wine shop in your area with a good selection and ask a knowledgeable salesperson to recommend wines. Try several kinds and keep a list of those you like. In no time at all you will become familiar with a number of wines and the foods they complement.

Dry Table Wines

Light to Medium Whites Serve these wines with seafood or vegetable salads, lobster, poached white fish, goat cheese, sliced prosciutto, antipasto.

WINE VARIETY	REGION	PRODUCER
Arneis	Piedmont	Vietti, Bruno Giacosa, Ceretto
Breganze di Breganze	Veneto	Maculan
Frascati	Latium	Fontana Candida
Galestro	Tuscany	Antinori, Castello di Gabbiano
Orvieto	Umbria	Castello della Sala, Bigi
Pinot Grigio	Friuli-Venezia-Giulia	Livio Felluga, Franco Furlan
Soave	Veneto	Roberto Anselmi, Pieropan, Guerreri-Rizzardi
Trebbiano	Abruzzi	Edoardo Valentini, Dino Illuminati, Casal Thaulero
Verdicchio	Marches	Fazi-Battaglia
Vernaccia	Tuscany	Teruzzi & Puthod, Falchini

Full-Flavored Whites Drink these with fish or vegetable *fritto misto,* grilled or poached salmon or other dark-fleshed fish, seafood soups and stews, pasta with cream sauces, risotto with vegetables or cheese, chicken.

WINE VARIETY	REGION	PRODUCER
Chardonnay	Friuli-Venezia-Giulia	Eno Friulia, Jermann
Fiano di Avellino	Campania	Mastroberardino
Gavi	Piedmont	Villa Banfi, La Chiara
Greco di Tufo	Campania	Mastroberardino
Tocai	Friuli-Venezia-Giulia	Livio Felluga, Abbazia di Rosazo
Torre di Giano	Umbria	Lungarotti

Light Red Wines These wines go well with grilled salmon and other fatty fish, pasta with light tomato and fish sauces, pasta or risotto with vegetables, roast chicken, and chicken salad.

WINE VARIETY	REGION	PRODUCER
Bardolino	Veneto	Bolla, Guerreri-Rizzardi
Dolcetto	Piedmont	Pio Cesare, Prunotto, Ratti, Vietti
Valpolicella	Veneto	Giuseppe Quintarelli, Masi, Tommasi, Anselmi, Allegrini

Medium Red Wines Serve with mushroom risotto; roast or grilled chicken, pork, lamb, or veal chops or roasts; steak; hearty soups; grilled mushrooms; and pasta with rich tomato and meat ragù.

WINE VARIETY	REGION	PRODUCER
Barbera	Piedmont	Vietti, Bruno Giacosa
Chianti	Tuscany	Ruffino, Vitticio, Brolio, Castello di Gabbiano Monsanto
Merlot	Friuli-Venezia-Giulia	Livio Felluga
Montepulciano d'Abruzzo	Abruzzi	Casal Thaulero, Edoardo Valentini, Pepe, Dino Illuminati
Rubesco	Umbria	Lungarotti
Taurasi	Campania	Mastroberardino

Full-Flavored Red Wines Serve these big reds with game dishes, stewed meats, grilled lamb or beef, and sharp cheeses.

WINE VARIETY	REGION	PRODUCER
Aglianico del Vulture	Basilicata	Fratelli D'Angelo, Sasso
Amarone	Veneto	Quintarelli, Allegrini, Anselm, Bertani, Masi
Barbaresco	Piedmont	Ceretto, Gaja, Bruno Giacosa, Pio Cesare, Vietti, Fontanafredda
Barolo	Piedmont	Conterno, Contratto, Vietti, Borgogno, Fontanafredda, Ratti, Pio Cesare
Colle Picchioni	Latium	Paola Di Mauro
Salice Salentino	Puglia	Leone De Castris, Cosimo Taurino, Zecca
Primitivo di Manduria	Puglia	Savese

Dessert Wines

Sweet Sparkling Wines These light, sparkling, low-alcohol wines go best with fresh fruit, cookies, and cakes.

WINE VARIETY	REGION	PRODUCER
Asti Spumante	Piedmont	Cinzano, Gancia Fontanafredda, Martini & Rossi
Moscato d'Asti	Piedmont	Vietti, Santo Stefano

Dry to Sweet Wines These rich, intensely flavored dessert wines range from dry to sweet. Serve them with cheese, nuts, biscotti, plain cakes, and crostata.

WINE VARIETY	REGION	PRODUCER
Marsala	Sicily	Florio, De Bartoli, Rallo
Picolit	Veneto	Livio Felluga, Franco Furlan
Vin Santo	Tuscany and Umbria	Brolio, Antinori, Lungarotti

Bibliography

Adami, Italia, *Cucina genovese e ligure* (Florence: Edizione del Riccio, 1977).

Alberini, Massimo, *Storia del pranzo all'italiana* (Milan: Rizzoli, 1966).

Anderson, Burton, *Treasures of the Italian Table* (New York: William Morrow and Company, 1994).

————, *The Wine Atlas of Italy* (New York: Simon and Schuster, 1990).

Antonini, Giuseppina Perusini, *Mangiare e ber friulano* (Milan: Franco Angeli, 1988).

Artusi, Pellegrino, *La scienza in cucina e l'arte di mangiar bene* (Rome: Newton Compton, 1988).

Checchini, Paola, *In Cucina con Rossini* (Ancona, 1995).

Da Mosto, Ranieri, *Il Veneto in cucinia* (Florence: Giunti Martello, 1974).

Dickens, Charles, *Pictures from Italy* (New York: Ecco Press, 1988).

Di Corato, Riccardo, *838 Frutti e verdure d'Italia* (Milan: Sonzogno, 1984).

Doglio, Sandro, *La Tradizione gastronomica italiana: Piemonte* (Milan: Edizione Sipiel, 1991).

Francesconi, Jeanne Carola, *La Cucina napoletana* (Rome: Newton Compton, 1992).

Giobbi, Edward, *Italian Family Cooking* (New York: Random House, 1971).

Gleijeses, Vittorio, *A Napoli si mangia cosi* (Naples: La Botteguccia, 1990).

Goria, Giovanni, *La Cucina del Piemonte* (Padua: Franco Muzzio Editore, 1990).

Italian Food Lovers Book of Days, The (Berkeley: Ten Speed Press, 1995).

James, Henry, *Italian Hours* (New York: Ecco Press, 1987).

Lantermo, Alberta, *Piemonte in bocca* (Palermo: Edikronos, 1981).

Milioni, Stefano, Columbus Menu. (New York: Italian Trade Commission, 1992.)

Minarelli, Maria Luisa, "Polenta e Champagne."

————, "Il Futurismo e gli spaghetti."

Moretti, Anita, *Cucina milanese e lombarda* (Florence: Edizione del Riccio, 1980).

Origo, Iris, *The Merchant of Prato* (Harmondsworth, England: Penguin Books, Ltd., 1986).

Parenti, Giovanni Righi, *La Grande cucina toscana,* Vols. I & II (Milan: SugarCo Edizioni, 1986).

Pepe, Antonietta, *Cucina pugliese* (Florence: Edizione del Riccio, 1981).

Rivieccio, Maria Zaniboni, *Polenta, piatto da re* (Milan: IdeaLibri, 1986).

Romano, Franca Colonna, *Into the Soul of Sicily* (Palermo, 1977).

————, *Il Sole ai fornelli* (Milan: Rizzoli, 1982).

Root, Waverley, *Food* (New York: Simon and Schuster, 1980).

Sada, Luigi, *La Cucina pugliese* (Rome: Newton Compton, 1994).

Serra, Anna e Piero, *La Cucina della Campania* (Naples: Franco De Mauro Editore, 1983).

Simeti, Mary Taylor, *Pomp and Sustenance: Twenty Five Centuries of Sicilian Food* (New York: Knopf, 1989).

Trillin, Calvin. *Travels with Alice* (New York: Vintage Books, 1979).

Valli, Emilia, *La Cucina friulana* (Padua: Franco Muzzio, 1992).

Yagley, Robert, *Poems from the Table: The Fruits of the Earth in Verse* (New York: Barnes & Noble, 1995).

Zanini de Vita, Oretta, "Truffles and Glorious Melodies," *Italy Italy* (November 1988).

Mail-Order Sources

Equipment

The Baker's Catalogue
King Arthur Flour
RR2, Box 56
Norwich, VT 05055
800-827-6836
Baking and pasta making equipment.

Beer and Wine Crafts
450 Fletcher Parkway
Suite 112
El Cajon, CA 92020
619-447-9191
Vinegar-making supplies.

Milan Laboratories
57 Spring Street
New York, NY 10012
800-BEER-KEG
Vinegar-making supplies.

Sweet Celebrations
7009 Washington Avenue South
Edina, MN 55439
800-328-6722
Bakeware.

Williams-Sonoma
P.O. Box 7456
San Francisco, CA 94120-7456
800-541-2233
Instant-read thermometers, baking stones,
baking pans, pasta equipment.

Ingredients

The Baker's Catalogue
(See above) Flour.

Balducci's
424 Avenue of the Americas
New York, NY 10011
800-225-3822
Pancetta, prosciutto di Parma, pasta, olive oil,
vinegars, medium-grain rice, grains, quail,
sausages, cheeses, fresh and jarred chestnuts,
and many other products.

Dean and DeLuca
121 Prince Street
New York, NY 10012
212-254-8776
Olive oil, vinegars, dried beans, cheeses,
dried porcini mushrooms, dried beans, and
many other Italian products.

The Mozzarella Company
2944 Elm Street
Dallas, TX 75226
214-741-4072
800-798-2954
Fresh mozzarella and ricotta, sheep's milk
cheeses.

Sweet Celebrations
(See above) Chocolate.

Williams-Sonoma
(See above) Parmigiano-Reggiano, olive
oil, vinegar.

Zingerman's Delicatessen
422 Detroit Street
Ann Arbor, MI 48104
313-663-3400
Oils, vinegars, rice, pasta, olives, capers,
and many other Italian products.

Index